PHP Solutions

Dynamic Web Design Made Easy
Second Edition

David Powers

friendsof

DESIGNER TO DESIGNER™

an Apress® company

PHP Solutions: Dynamic Web Design Made Easy, Second Edition

Copyright © 2010 by DAVID POWERS

The source code for this book is freely available to readers at www.friendsofed.com in the Downloads section.

Credits

Lead Editor:
Ben Renow-Clarke

Technical Reviewers:
Kristian Besley and Jason Nadon

Editorial Board:
Steve Anglin, Mark Beckner, Ewan Buckingham, Tony Campbell, Gary Cornell, Jonathan Gennick, Michelle Lowman, Matthew Moodie, Jeffrey Pepper, Frank Pohlmann, Ben Renow-Clarke, Dominic Shakeshaft, Matt Wade, Tom Welsh

Project Manager:
Anita Castro

Copy Editor:
Heather Lang

Compositor:
Bronkella Publishing, LLC

Indexer:
Toma Mulligan

Artist:
April Milne

Cover Designer:
Anna Ishchenko

Cover Artist:
Corné van Doreen

Contents at a Glance

Contents

CONTENTS

About the Author

David Powers is the author of a series of highly successful books on PHP and web development. He began developing websites in 1994 when—as Editor, BBC Japanese TV—he needed a way to promote his fledgling TV channel but didn't have an advertising budget. He persuaded the IT department to let him have some space on the BBC's server and hand-coded a bilingual website from scratch. That experience ignited a passion for web development that burns just as brightly as ever.

After leaving the BBC in 1999, David developed an online system with PHP and MySQL to deliver daily economic and political analysis in Japanese for the clients of a leading international consultancy. Since 2004, he has devoted most of his time to writing books and teaching web development.

David is an Adobe Community Professional and Adobe Certified Instructor for Dreamweaver. In 2010, he became one of the first people to qualify as a PHP 5.3 Zend Certified Engineer.

About the Technical Reviewers

Kristian Besley is the lead developer at Beetroot Design (www.beetrootdesign.co.uk) where he develops web applications, websites, educational interactions and games written mainly in various combinations of PHP, Flash and Javascript.

He has been working with computers and the web for far too long. He also spends far too much time hacking and developing for open-source applications - including Moodle - so that they work just so. Health warning: he has an unhealthy obsession with making his applications super-RSS compatible and overly configurable.

His past and current clients include the BBC, Pearson Education, Welsh Assembly Government and loads of clients with acronyms such as JISC, BECTA, MAWWFIRE and - possibly his favourite of all (well, just try saying it out loud) - SWWETN.

When he isn't working, he's working elsewhere lecturing in Interactive Media (at Gower College Swansea) or providing geeky technical assistance to a whole gamut of institutions or individuals in an effort to save them time and money (at his own expense!!!).

He has authored and co-authored a large number of books for friends of ED and Apress including the Foundation Flash series, Flash MX Video, Foundation ActionScript for Flash (with the wonderful David Powers) and Flash MX Creativity. His words have also graced the pages of Computer Arts a few times too.

Kristian currently resides with his family in Swansea, Wales and is a proud fluent Welsh speaker with a passion for pushing the language on the web and in bilingual web applications where humanly possible.

Jason Nadon has ten years experience building and supporting complex web applications. He is an active member of the web developer community and teaches several classes in his hometown in Michigan. He has been in the Information Technology field for more than twelve years and holds several industry certifications. He is currently working as an Infrastructure Manager for a global information company.

Acknowledgments

My thanks go to everyone who was involved in the production of this book. The original idea to write *PHP Solutions* came from Chris Mills, my editor for many years at Apress/friends of ED, who's now Developer Relations Manager at Opera and a passionate advocate of web standards. It was a great idea, Chris. Thanks to your help, the first edition of this book became my biggest seller. The invitation to write this second edition came from Chris's successor, Ben Renow-Clarke. Like Chris, Ben has given me free rein to shape this book according to my own ideas but has always put himself in the position of the reader, nudging me in the right direction when an explanation wasn't clear enough or a chapter was badly organized.

I'm grateful to Kris Besley and Jason Nadon, who scoured my text and code for errors. Much though I hate to admit it, they did find some. Kris, in particular, made some really good suggestions for improving the code. *Diolch yn fawr iawn.* Any mistakes that remain are my responsibility alone.

Most of all, thanks to you for reading. I hope you enjoy the book as much as I have enjoyed writing it.

Introduction

When the first edition of *PHP Solutions* was published, I was concerned that the subtitle, *Dynamic Web Design Made Easy*, sounded overambitious. PHP is not difficult, but nor is it like an instant cake mix: just add water and stir. Every website is different, so it's impossible to grab a script, paste it into a web page, and expect it to work. My aim was to help web designers with little or no knowledge of programming gain the confidence to dive into the code and adjust it to their own requirements.

The enduring popularity of the first edition suggests that many readers took up the challenge. Part of the book's success stemmed from the use of clear, straightforward language, highlighting points where you might make mistakes, with advice on how to solve problems. Another factor was its emphasis on forward and backward compatibility. The solutions were based on PHP 5, but alternatives were provided for readers still stuck on PHP 4.

Time has moved on. PHP 5 is now a mature and stable platform. This new edition of *PHP Solutions* requires PHP 5.2 and MySQL 4.1 or later. Some code will work with earlier versions, but most of it won't. The emphasis on future compatibility remains unchanged. All the code in this book avoids features destined for removal when work resumes on PHP 6 (at the time of this writing, it's not known when that will be).

The decision to drop support for older versions of PHP and MySQL has been liberating. When friends of ED asked me to prepare a new edition of this book, I initially thought it would involve just brushing away a few cobwebs. As soon as I started reviewing the code, I realized just how much the need to cater for PHP 4 had constrained me. It's also fair to say that my coding style and knowledge of PHP had expanded greatly in the intervening years.

As a result, this new edition is a major rewrite. The basic structure of the book remains the same, but every chapter has been thoroughly revised, and an extra two have been added. In some cases, little remains of the original chapter other than the title. For example, the file upload and thumbnail creation scripts in Chapters 6 and 8 have been completely refactored as PHP 5 custom classes, and the mail processing script in Chapter 5 has been rewritten to make it easier to redeploy in different websites. Other big changes include a class to check password strength in Chapter 9 and detailed coverage of the date and time classes introduced in PHP 5.2 and 5.3. Want to display the date of events on the second Tuesday of each month? Chapter 14 shows how to do it in half a dozen lines of code. Chapter 16 adds coverage of foreign key constraints in InnoDB, the default storage engine in MySQL 5.5.

I hesitated before devoting so much attention to using PHP classes. Many regard them as an advanced subject, not suitable for readers who don't have a programming background. But the advantages far outweighed my reservations. In simple terms, a class is a collection of predefined functions designed to perform related tasks. The beauty of using classes is that they're project-neutral. Admittedly, the file upload class in Chapter 6 is longer than the equivalent script in the first edition of *PHP Solutions*, but you can reuse it in multiple projects with just a few lines of code. If you're in hurry or are daunted by the prospect of building class definitions, you can simply use the finished files. However, I encourage you to explore the class definitions. The code will teach you a lot of PHP that you'll find useful in other situations.

Each chapter takes you through a series of stages in a single project, with each stage building on the previous one. By working through each chapter, you get the full picture of how everything fits together. You can later refer to the individual stages to refresh your memory about a particular technique. Although this isn't a reference book, Chapter 3 is a primer on PHP syntax, and some chapters contain short reference sections—notably Chapter 7 (reading from and writing to files), Chapter 9 (sessions), Chapter 10 (MySQL data types), Chapter 11 (MySQL prepared statements), Chapter 13 (the four essential SQL commands), and Chapter 14 (working with dates and times).

So, how easy is easy? I have done my best to ease your path, but there is no magic potion. It requires some effort on your part. Don't attempt to do everything at once. Add dynamic features to your site a few at a time. Get to understand how they work, and your efforts will be amply rewarded. Adding PHP and MySQL to your skills will enable you to build websites that offer much richer content and an interactive user experience.

Using the example files

All the files necessary for working through this book can be downloaded from the friends of ED website at `http://www.friendsofed.com/downloads.html`. Make sure you select the download link for *PHP Solutions: Dynamic Web Design Made Easy, Second Edition*. The code is very different from the first edition.

Set up a PHP development environment, as described in Chapter 2. Unzip the files, and copy the `phpsols` folder and all its contents into your web server's document root. The code for each chapter is in a folder named after the chapter: `ch01`, `ch02`, and so on. Follow the instructions in each PHP solution, and copy the relevant files to the site root or the work folder indicated.

Where a page undergoes several changes during a chapter, I have numbered the different versions like this: `index_01.php`, `index_02.php`, and so on. When copying a file that has a number, remove the underscore and number from the filename, so `index_01.php` becomes `index.php`. If you are using a program like Dreamweaver that prompts you to update links when moving files from one folder to another, do *not* update them. The links in the files are designed to pick up the right images and style sheets when located in the target folder. I have done this so you can use a file comparison utility to check your files against mine.

If you don't have a file comparison utility, I strongly urge you to install one. It will save you hours of head scratching when trying to spot the difference between your version and mine. A missing semicolon or mistyped variable can be hard to spot in dozens of lines of code. Windows users can download WinMerge for free from `http://winmerge.org/`. I use Beyond Compare (`www.scootersoftware.com`). It's not free but is excellent and reasonably priced. BBEdit on a Mac includes a file comparison utility. Alternatively, use the file comparison feature in TextWrangler, which can be downloaded free from `www.barebones.com/products/textwrangler/`.

The HTML code in the example files and text uses HTML5 syntax, but I have avoided using elements that are not supported by older browsers. Even Internet Explorer 6 understands the HTML5 DOCTYPE declaration, and new form elements that older browsers don't recognize are rendered as text input fields.

Layout conventions

To keep this book as clear and easy to follow as possible, the following text conventions are used throughout.

Important words or concepts are normally highlighted on the first appearance in **bold type**.

Code is presented in `fixed-width font`.

New or changed code is normally presented in `bold fixed-width font`.

Pseudo-code and variable input are written in `italic fixed-width font`.

Menu commands are written in the form **Menu ➤ Submenu ➤ Submenu**.

Where I want to draw your attention to something, I've highlighted it like this:

Ahem, don't say I didn't warn you.

Sometimes code won't fit on a single line in a book. Where this happens, I use an arrow like this: ➡.

```
This is a very, very long section of code that should be written all on the same ➡
line without a break.
```

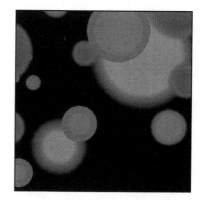

Chapter 1

What Is PHP—And Why Should I Care?

One of the first things most people want to know about PHP is what the initials stand for. Then they wish they had never asked. Officially, PHP stands for **PHP: Hypertext Preprocessor**. It's an ugly name that gives the impression that it's strictly for nerds or propellerheads. Nothing could be further from the truth.

PHP is a scripting language that brings websites to life in the following ways:

- Sending feedback from your website directly to your mailbox
- Uploading files through a web page
- Generating thumbnails from larger images
- Reading and writing to files
- Displaying and updating information dynamically
- Using a database to display and store information
- Making websites searchable
- And much more . . .

By reading this book, you'll be able to do all that. PHP is easy to learn; it's platform-neutral, so the same code runs on Windows, Mac OS X, and Linux; and all the software you need to develop with PHP is open source and therefore free. Several years ago, there was a lighthearted debate on the PHP General mailing list (http://news.php.net/php.general) about changing what PHP stands for. Among the suggestions were Positively Happy People and Pretty Happy Programmers. The aim of this book is to help you put PHP to practical use—and in the process understand what makes PHP programmers so happy.

In this chapter, you'll learn about the following:

- How PHP has grown into the most widely used technology for dynamic websites
- How PHP makes web pages dynamic
- How difficult—or easy—PHP is to learn
- Whether PHP is safe
- What software you need to write PHP

How PHP has grown

Although PHP is now the most widely used technology for creating dynamic websites, it started out with rather modest ambitions—and a different name—in 1995. Originally called Personal Home Page Tools (PHP Tools), one of its goals was to create a guestbook by gathering information from an online form and displaying it on a web page. Shortly afterward, the ability to communicate with a database was added. When version 3 was released in 1998, it was decided to drop Personal Home Page from the name, because it sounded like something for hobbyists and didn't do justice to the range of sophisticated features that had been added. PHP 3 was described as "a very programmer-friendly scripting language suitable for people with little or no programming experience as well as the seasoned web developer who needs to get things done quickly."

Since then, PHP has developed even further, adding extensive support for object-oriented programming (OOP) in PHP 5. One of the language's great attractions, though, is that it remains true to its roots. You can start writing useful scripts without the need to learn lots of theory, yet be confident in the knowledge that you're using a technology with the capability to develop industrial-strength applications. PHP is the language that drives the highly popular content management systems (CMSs), Drupal (http://drupal.org/), Joomla! (www.joomla.org), and WordPress (http://wordpress.org/). It also runs some of the most heavily used websites, including Facebook (www.facebook.com) and Wikipedia (www.wikipedia.org).

PHP can now be regarded as a mature technology in the sense that it has a large user base, is widely supported, and has many advanced features. New features are being continually added, although these are mainly of interest to advanced users.

> At the time of this writing, the current version is PHP 5.3. Development of PHP 6 was suspended indefinitely in early 2010, when it was realized the original plans had been too ambitious.
>
> The emphasis in this book is on code that works now, not on what might work at some unspecified time in the future. Care has also been taken to avoid using features that have been deprecated—in other words, marked for removal from the next major version of PHP.

How PHP makes pages dynamic

PHP was originally designed to be embedded in the HTML of a web page, and that's the way it's often still used. For example, if you want to display the current year in a copyright notice, you could put this in your footer:

```
<p>&copy; <?php echo date('Y'); ?> PHP Solutions</p>
```

On a PHP—enabled web server, the code between the `<?php` and `?>` tags is automatically processed and displays the year like this:

© 2010 PHP Solutions

This is only a trivial example, but it illustrates some of the advantages of using PHP:

- You can enjoy your New Year's party without worrying about updating your copyright notice. Anyone accessing your site after the stroke of midnight sees the correct year.
- Unlike using JavaScript to display the date, the processing is done on the web server, so it doesn't rely on JavaScript being enabled in the user's browser.
- The date is calculated by the web server, so it's not affected if the clock in the user's computer is set incorrectly.

Although it's convenient to embed PHP code in HTML like this, it often results in typing the same code repeatedly, which is boring and leads to mistakes. It can also make your web pages difficult to maintain, particularly once you start using more complex PHP code. Consequently, it's common practice to store a lot of dynamic code in separate files and use PHP to build your pages from the different components. The separate files—or *include files*, as they're usually called—can contain either only PHP, only HTML, or a mixture of both.

At first, it can be difficult to get used to this way of working, but it's much more efficient. As a simple example, you can put your website's navigation menu in an include file and use PHP to include it in each page. Whenever you need to make any changes to the menu, you edit just one file—the include file—and the changes are automatically reflected in every page that includes the menu. Just imagine how much time that saves on a website with dozens of pages.

With an ordinary HTML page, the content is fixed by the web developer at design time and uploaded to the web server. When somebody visits the page, the web server simply sends the HTML and other assets, such as images and style sheet. It's a simple transaction—the request comes from the browser, and the fixed content is sent back by the server. When you build web pages with PHP, much more goes on. Figure 1-1 shows what happens.

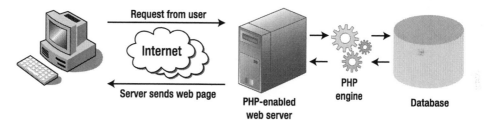

Figure 1-1. The web server builds each PHP page dynamically in response to a request.

When a PHP–driven website is visited, it sets in train the following sequence of events:

1. The browser sends a request to the web server.
2. The web server hands the request to the PHP engine, which is embedded in the server.
3. The PHP engine processes the code. In many cases, it might also query a database before building the page.
4. The server sends the completed page back to the browser.

This process usually takes only a fraction of a second, so the visitor to a PHP website is unlikely to notice any delay. Because each page is built individually, PHP pages can respond to user input, displaying different content when a user logs in or showing the results of a database search.

Creating pages that think for themselves

PHP is a **server-side language**. The PHP code remains on the web server. After it has been processed, the server sends only the output of the script. Normally, this is HTML, but PHP can also be used to generate other web languages, such as Extensible Markup Language (XML).

PHP enables you to introduce logic into your web pages. This logic is based on alternatives. Some decisions are based on information that PHP gleans from the server: the date, the time, the day of the week, information in the page's URL, and so on. If it's Wednesday, show Wednesday's TV schedules. At other times, decisions are based on user input, which PHP extracts from online forms. If you have registered with a site, display your personalized information . . . that sort of thing.

As a result, you can create an infinite variety of output from a single script. For example, if you visit my blog at `http://foundationphp.com/blog/` (see Figure 1-2), and click various internal links, what you see is always the same page but with different content. Admittedly, I tend to write always about the same kinds of subjects, but that's my fault, not PHP's.

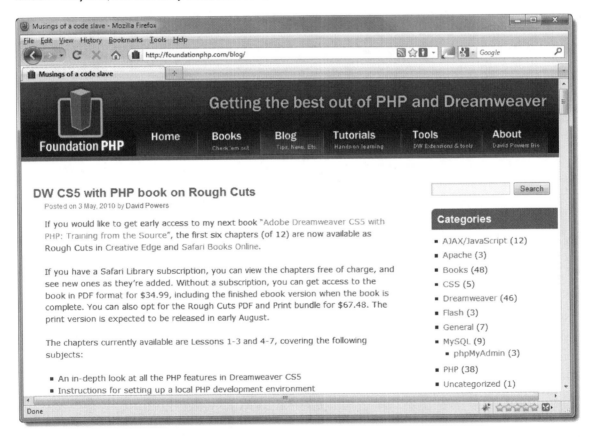

Figure 1-2. Blogs are a good example of sites ideally suited to PHP.

How hard is PHP to use and learn?

PHP isn't rocket science, but at the same time, don't expect to become an expert in five minutes. Perhaps the biggest shock to newcomers is that PHP is far less tolerant of mistakes than browsers are with HTML. If you omit a closing tag in HTML, most browsers will still render the page. If you omit a closing quote, semicolon, or brace in PHP, you'll get an uncompromising error message like the one shown in Figure 1-3. This isn't just a feature of PHP but of all server-side technologies, including ASP, ASP.NET, and ColdFusion.

A missing parenthesis turns this...

into this.

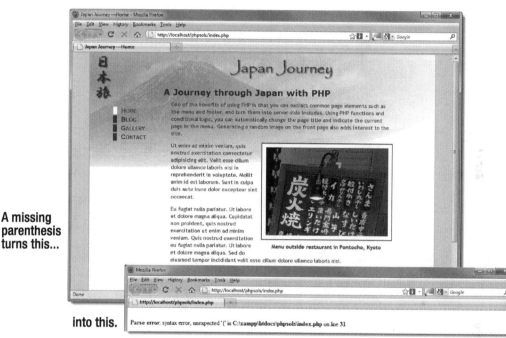

Figure 1-3. Server-side languages like PHP are intolerant of most coding errors.

If you're the sort of web designer or developer who uses a visual design tool, such as Adobe Dreamweaver or Microsoft Expression Web, and never looks at the underlying code, it's time to rethink your approach. Mixing PHP with poorly structured HTML is likely to lead to problems. PHP uses loops to perform repetitive tasks, such as displaying the results of a database search. A **loop** repeats the same section of code—usually a mixture of PHP and HTML—until all results have been displayed. If you put the loop in the wrong place, or if your HTML is badly structured, your page is likely to collapse like a house of cards. If you're not already in the habit of doing so, it's a good idea to check your pages using the World Wide Web Consortium's (W3C) Markup Validation Service (http://validator.w3.org/unicorn).

> *The W3C is the international body that develops standards—such as HTML and CSS—and guidelines to ensure the long-term growth of the Web. It's led by the inventor of the World Wide Web, Tim Berners-Lee. To learn about the W3C's mission, see www.w3.org/Consortium/mission.*

Can I just copy and paste the code?

There's nothing wrong with copying the code in this book. That's what it's there for. Copying is the way we all learn as children, but most of us progress from the copycat stage by asking questions and beginning to experiment on our own. Rather than attempt to teach you PHP by going through a series of boring exercises that have no immediate value to your web pages, I've structured this book so that you jump straight into applying your newfound knowledge to practical projects. At the same time, I explain what the code is for and why it's there. Even if you don't understand exactly how it all works, this should give you sufficient knowledge to know which parts of the code to adapt to your own needs and which parts are best left alone.

PHP is a toolbox full of powerful features. It has thousands of built-in functions that perform all sorts of tasks, such as converting text to uppercase, generating thumbnail images from full-sized ones, or connecting to a database. The real power comes from combining these functions in different ways and adding your own conditional logic. To get the best out of this book, you need to start experimenting with the tools you learn about in these pages and come up with your own solutions.

How safe is PHP?

PHP is like the electricity or kitchen knives in your home: handled properly, it's very safe; handled irresponsibly, it can do a lot of damage. One of the inspirations for the first edition of this book was a spate of malicious attacks that erupted in late 2005. The attacks exploited a vulnerability in email scripts, turning websites into spam relays. Few people were immune. I certainly wasn't, but once I was alerted to the problem, I plugged the hole and stopped the attacks in their tracks. However, day after day, people were sending frantic pleas for help to online forums. Even when they were told how to deal with the problem, their response became even more frantic. Many admitted they didn't know the first thing about any of the code they were using in their websites. For someone building websites as a hobby, this might be understandable, but many of these people were "professionals" who had built sites on behalf of clients. The clients were naturally unhappy when their mailboxes started filling with spam. They were no doubt even unhappier when their domains were suspended by hosting companies fed up with insecure scripts on their servers.

The moral of this story is not that PHP is unsafe; nor does everyone need to become a security expert to use PHP. What is important is to understand the basic principle of PHP safety: *always check user input before processing it*. You'll find that to be a constant theme throughout this book. Most security risks can be eliminated with very little effort.

Perhaps the most worrying aspect is that, more than five years after this exploit was first revealed, I still see people using insecure email scripts. The best way to protect yourself is to understand the code you're using. Even if you can't solve a problem yourself, you can implement any remedies suggested to you by the author of the script or another expert.

What software do I need to write PHP?

Strictly speaking, you don't need any special software to write PHP scripts. PHP code is plain text and can be created in any text editor, such as Notepad on Windows or TextEdit on Mac OS X. Having said that, you would need to be a masochist to use a plain text editor. Your current web development program might already support PHP. If it doesn't there's a wide choice of programs—both paid-for and free—that have features designed to speed up the development process.

What to look for when choosing a PHP editor

If there's a mistake in your code, your page will probably never make it as far as the browser, and all you'll see is an error message. You should choose a script editor that has the following features:

- **PHP syntax checking**: This used to be found only in expensive, dedicated programs, but it's now a feature in several free programs. Syntax checkers monitor the code as you type and highlight errors, saving a great deal of time and frustration.
- **PHP syntax coloring**: Code is highlighted in different colors according to the role it plays. If your code is in an unexpected color, it's a sure sign you've made a mistake.
- **PHP code hints**: PHP has so many built-in functions, it can be difficult to remember how to use them—even for an experienced user. Many script editors automatically display tooltips with reminders of how a particular piece of code works.
- **Line numbering**: Finding a specific line quickly makes troubleshooting a lot simpler.
- **A "balance braces" feature**: Parentheses (( )), square brackets ([ ]), and curly braces ({ }) must always be in matching pairs. It's easy to forget to close a pair. All good script editors help find the matching parenthesis, bracket, or brace.

The following sections describe some of the script editors you might like to consider. It's by no means an exhaustive list but is based on personal experience.

General purpose web development tools with PHP support

Two of the most widely used integrated development environments (IDEs) for building websites, Adobe Dreamweaver (www.adobe.com/products/dreamweaver/) and Microsoft Expression Web (www.microsoft.com/expression/products/web_overview.aspx), have built-in support for PHP.

- **Dreamweaver CS5**: Dreamweaver is a good, standards-compliant visual editor. PHP support was taken to a completely new level in Dreamweaver CS5 with the addition of syntax checking, embedded documentation (complete with examples), and autocompletion of variables. Particularly useful is the ability to work in PHP includes, while keeping the main page visible in the workspace (see Figure 1-4).

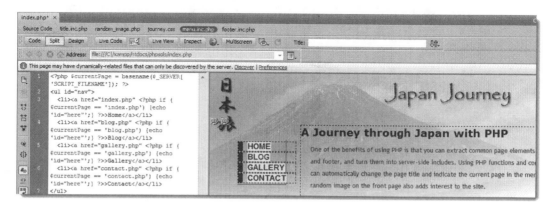

Figure 1-4. Dreamweaver CS5 lets you edit PHP include files and view the results in Live View.

- **Expression Web**: The level of PHP support in versions 2, 3, and 4 of Expression Web is similar to that offered in older versions of Dreamweaver—in other words, syntax coloring, code hints for PHP core functions, and line numbers. The big drawback at the time of this writing is there's no support for syntax checking.

Dedicated script editors

Even if you don't plan to do a lot of PHP development, you should consider using a dedicated script editor if your web development IDE doesn't support syntax checking. The following dedicated script editors have all the essential features, such as syntax checking and code hints. They also support HTML and CSS but lack the visual display offered by Dreamweaver or Expression Web.

- **Zend Studio** (www.zend.com/en/products/studio/): If you're really serious about PHP development, Zend Studio is the most fully featured IDE for PHP. It's created by Zend, the company run by leading contributors to the development of PHP. Zend Studio runs on Windows, Mac OS X, and Linux. Its main drawback is cost, although the price includes 12 months of free upgrades and support.
- **PhpED** (www.nusphere.com/products/phped.htm): This is available in three different versions. The least expensive version has all the features you need as a beginner. If you need the more advanced features later, you can upgrade to one of the other versions. Windows only.
- **PHP Development Tools** (www.eclipse.org/pdt/): PDT is actually a cut-down version of Zend Studio and has the advantage of being free. The disadvantage is that at the time of this writing, the documentation for PDT is almost nonexistent. It runs on Eclipse, the open source IDE that supports multiple computer languages. If you have used Eclipse for other languages, you should find it relatively easy to use. PDT runs on Windows, Mac OS X, and Linux and is available either as an Eclipse plug-in or as an all-in-one package that automatically installs Eclipse and the PDT plug-in.
- **Komodo Edit** (www.activestate.com/komodo-edit): This is a free, open source IDE for PHP and a number of other popular computer languages. It's available for Windows, Mac OS X, and Linux. It's a cut-down version of Komodo IDE, which is a paid-for program with more advanced features. There are separate download links for a free trial of Komodo IDE, which is time-limited, and for Komodo Edit, which doesn't expire.

So, let's get on with it . . .

This chapter has provided only a brief overview of what PHP can do to add dynamic features to your websites and what software you need. The first stage in working with PHP is to set up a testing environment. The next chapter covers the process for both Windows and Mac OS X.

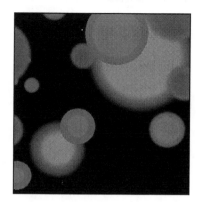

Chapter 2

Getting Ready to Work with PHP

Now that you've decided to use PHP to enrich your web pages, you need to make sure that you have everything you need to get on with the rest of this book. Although you can test everything on your remote server, it's usually more convenient to test PHP pages on your local computer. Everything you need to install is free. In this chapter, I'll explain the various options and give instructions for both Windows and Mac OS X.

What this chapter covers:

- Determining what you need
- Deciding whether to create a local testing setup
- Using a ready-made package
- Making sure PHP has the right settings

Checking whether your website supports PHP

The easiest way to find out whether your website supports PHP is to ask your hosting company. The other way to find out is to upload a PHP page to your website and see if it works. Even if you know that your site supports PHP, do the following test to confirm which version is running:

1. Open a text editor, such as Notepad or TextEdit, and type the following code into a blank page:

   ```
   <?php echo phpversion(); ?>
   ```

2. Save the file as phpversion.php. It's important to make sure that your operating system doesn't add a .txt filename extension after the .php. Mac users should also make sure that TextEdit doesn't save the file in Rich Text Format (RTF). If you're at all unsure, use phpversion.php from the ch02 folder in the files accompanying this book.

3. Upload `phpversion.php` to your website in the same way you would an HTML page, and then type the URL into a browser. Assuming you upload the file to the top level of your site, the URL will be something like `http://www.example.com/phpversion.php`.

    If you see a three-part number like **5.3.3** displayed onscreen, you're in business: PHP is enabled. The number tells you which version of PHP is running on your server. *You need a minimum of 5.2.0 to use the code in this book.*

    If you get a message that says something like **Parse error**, it means PHP is supported but that you have made a mistake in typing the file. Use the version in the `ch02` folder instead.

    If you just see the original code, it means PHP is not supported.

Official support for PHP 4 was terminated in August 2008. Although PHP 4 was excellent, the time to lay it to rest has long since passed. PHP 5 has been around since 2004. It's faster and has more features, and most important of all, it's actively maintained, making it more secure.

At the time of this writing, two series are being currently maintained: PHP 5.2 and PHP 5.3. All the code in this book has been designed to run on both versions, and it avoids using features that are scheduled to be removed from future versions. If your server is running a version earlier than PHP 5.2, contact your host and tell them you want the most recent stable version of PHP. If your host refuses, it's time to change your hosting company.

Deciding where to test your pages

Unlike ordinary web pages, you can't just double-click PHP pages in Windows Explorer or Finder on a Mac and view them in your browser. They need to be **parsed**—processed—through a web server that supports PHP. If your hosting company supports PHP, you can upload your files to your website and test them there. However, you need to upload the file every time you make a change. In the early days, you'll probably find you have to do this often because of some minor mistake in your code. As you become more experienced, you'll still need to upload files frequently because you'll want to experiment with different ideas.

If you want to get working with PHP straight away, by all means use your own website as a test bed. However, you'll soon discover the need for a local PHP test environment. The rest of this chapter is devoted to showing you how to do it, with instructions for Windows and Mac OS X.

What you need for a local test environment

To test PHP pages on your local computer, you need to install the following:

- A web server (Apache or IIS)
- PHP

To work with a database, you'll also need MySQL and a web-based front end for MySQL called phpMyAdmin. All the software you need is free. The only cost to you is the time it takes to download the necessary files, plus, of course, the time to make sure everything is set up correctly. In most cases, you should be up and running in less than an hour, probably considerably less.

You don't need any special equipment. A web server is a piece of software that displays web pages, not a separate computer. As long as you have at least 1GB of free disk space, you should be able to install all the software on your computer—even one with modest specifications.

> *If you already have a PHP test environment on your local computer, there's no need to reinstall. Just check the section at the end of the chapter titled "Checking your PHP (Windows and Mac)."*

Individual programs or an all-in-one package?

For many years, I advocated installing each component of a PHP testing environment separately, rather than using a package that installs Apache, PHP, MySQL, and phpMyAdmin automatically in a single operation. My advice was based on the dubious quality of some early all-in-one packages, which installed easily but were next to impossible to uninstall or upgrade. The all-in-one packages currently available are excellent, and I have no hesitation in recommending them. On my computers, I use XAMPP for Windows (`www.apachefriends.org/en/xampp-windows.html`) and MAMP for Mac OS X (`www.mamp.info/en/mamp/index.html`).

> *Setting up a PHP testing environment with an all-in-one package is normally trouble free. The main cause of difficulty is a conflict with another program using port 80, which Apache and IIS use to listen for page requests. If Skype is installed, go to the **Advanced** section of **Skype Preferences**, and make sure it's not using port 80. Try 42815 as the incoming port instead.*

Setting up on Windows

These instructions have been tested on Windows 7, Windows Vista, and Windows XP. Make sure that you're logged on as an Administrator before proceeding.

Getting Windows to display filename extensions

By default, most Windows computers hide the three- or four-letter filename extension, such as .doc or .html, so all you see in dialog boxes and Windows Explorer is thisfile instead of thisfile.doc or thisfile.html. The ability to see these filename extensions is essential for working with PHP.

Use these instructions to enable the display of filename extensions in Windows 7 and Windows Vista:

1. Open **Start ➤ Computer**.

2. Select **Organize ➤ Folder and Search Options**.

3. In the dialog box that opens, select the **View** tab.

4. In the **Advanced settings** section, uncheck the box marked **Hide extensions for known file types**.

5. Click **OK**.

Use these instructions in Windows XP:

1. Open **Start ➤ My Computer**.

2. Select **Tools ➤ Folder Options**.

3. In the dialog box that opens, select the **View** tab.

4. Uncheck the box marked **Hide extensions for known file types**.

5. Click **OK**.

I recommend that you leave your computer at this setting because it is more secure—you can tell if a virus writer has attached an .exe or .scr executable file to an innocent-looking document.

Choosing a web server

Most PHP installations run on the Apache web server. Both are open source and work well together. However, Windows has its own web server, Internet Information Services (IIS), which also supports PHP. In fact, Microsoft has worked closely with the PHP development team to improve the performance of PHP on IIS to roughly the same level as Apache. So, which should you choose?

The answer depends on whether you develop web pages using ASP or ASP.NET, or intend to do so. ASP and ASP.NET require IIS. You can install Apache on the same computer as IIS, but they both listen for requests on port 80. You can't run both servers simultaneously on the same port.

Unless you need IIS for ASP or ASP.NET, I recommend that you install Apache, using XAMPP or one of the other popular all-in-one packages, as described in the next section. For instructions on how to install PHP in IIS, skip ahead to "Installing PHP with the Microsoft Web Platform Installer."

Installing XAMPP on Windows

XAMPP installs Apache, PHP, MySQL, phpMyAdmin, and several other tools on your computer in a single operation. Apart from the time it takes to download, the installation process normally takes less than five minutes. Once it has been installed, you need to change a few settings, but most changes can be made through a web interface.

XAMPP isn't the only all-in-one package. Two others are WampServer (www.wampserver.com/en/) and EasyPHP (www.easyphp.org). They all install the software you need to develop PHP. The main difference lies in the interface they provide to control the web server and database.

The following instructions describe how to install XAMPP:

1. In a browser, go to www.apachefriends.org/en/xampp-windows.html#641, and download XAMPP for Windows. Choose the Basic package self-extracting RAR archive.

2. Close all applications on your computer, and double-click the .exe file you downloaded. A dialog box asks you where you want to install XAMPP. The default is C:\. If you select the default, all the necessary files are extracted to a new folder called C:\xampp.

3. At the end of the extraction process, the installer opens a Windows Command Prompt window with a series of questions about installation options. Type **y** or **n**, depending on your preference, and press Enter.

4. After you have set the options, you should see a message telling you that XAMPP is ready. Type **1**, and press Enter to start the XAMPP Control Panel (see Figure 2-1).

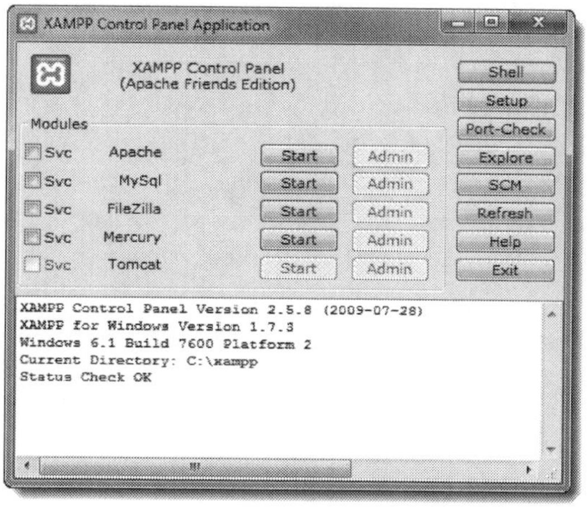

Figure 2-1. The XAMPP Control Panel

5. Type **x**, and press Enter to close the Command Prompt window.

6. Start Apache and MySQL by clicking the top two **Start** buttons in the XAMPP Control Panel. FileZilla, Mercury, and Tomcat are not required for a PHP testing environment and are not covered in this book. If the servers start up without error, the control panel should display **Running** alongside Apache and MySQL, and the labels on the **Start** buttons should change to **Stop**, as shown in Figure 2-2.

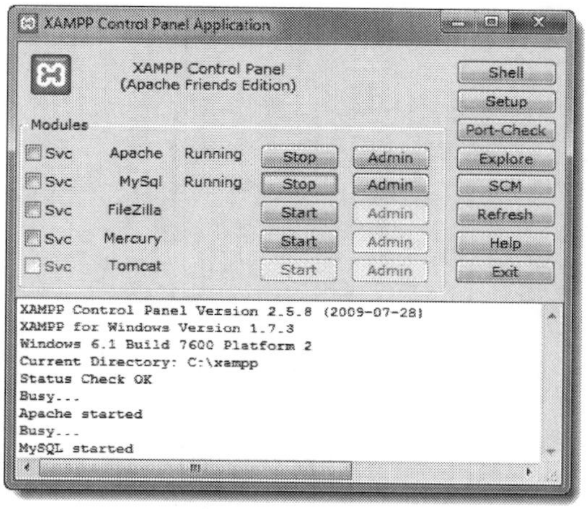

Figure 2-2. The XAMPP Control Panel confirms the servers are running.

Troubleshooting

If Apache or MySQL fail to start, check the following:

- If Apache reports an error on startup, double-click `C:\xampp\apache\logs\error.log` in Windows Explorer, and scroll to the bottom of the file to read any error messages.
- Check that another program isn't using port 80. Your security software should indicate any program that has initiated communication on port 80. This port is used for HTTP (Hypertext Transfer Protocol), so the program is usually web-related.
- The error log for MySQL is located in the `C:\xampp\mysql\data` folder. It's in a file that uses the same name as your computer followed by an `.err` filename extension. Double-click its icon, and select Notepad when prompted to select a program to use.
- If the error logs don't reveal the cause, try disabling any security software temporarily. If that solves problem, adjust the settings in the security software before re-enabling it.

> The **Explore** button in the XAMPP Control Panel is a quick way to open the xampp folder. The **Port-Check** button will let you know what's running on each port, so you can see if you have a conflict on port 80.

Configuring XAMPP

After installing XAMPP, you need to create a password for the main administrative account in the MySQL database. This is how you do it:

1. Make sure that Apache and MySQL are running. Launch a browser, type `http://localhost/` into the address bar, and press Enter.

2. You should see a web page offering a choice of languages. Select the language you want to use. This launches the XAMPP welcome screen, as shown in Figure 2-3.

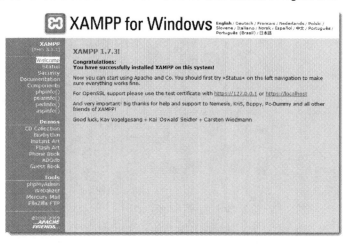

Figure 2-3. The XAMPP Welcome screen

3. Click **Security** in the menu on the left of the screen. This opens a new browser window or tab with a report on your installation's security status. Scroll down below the status report, and click the following link: `http://localhost/security/xamppsecurity.php`.

This displays the screen shown in Figure 2-4, which prompts you to create a password for the MySQL superuser, root. Even if you are the only person using the computer, it's good practice to password protect the MySQL database.

4. Enter your chosen password in both fields. It can contain special characters but should not have any spaces.

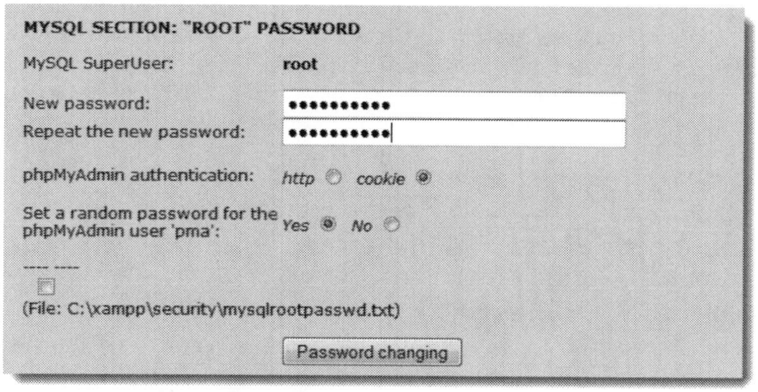

MYSQL SECTION: "ROOT" PASSWORD

MySQL SuperUser:	**root**
New password:	••••••••••
Repeat the new password:	••••••••••
phpMyAdmin authentication:	*http* ○ *cookie* ◉
Set a random password for the phpMyAdmin user 'pma':	*Yes* ◉ *No* ○

☐

(File: C:\xampp\security\mysqlrootpasswd.txt)

[Password changing]

Figure 2-4. Setting the MySQL root password in XAMPP.

5. Immediately below the password fields is a pair of radio buttons that determine how phpMyAdmin connects to MySQL as the root superuser. The default is to store it in a cookie. This is fine for a local development environment.

6. You are also asked whether to set a random password for the phpMyAdmin pma user. phpMyAdmin uses this for advanced features beyond the scope of this book, but the default **Yes** is fine.

7. If you're worried about forgetting the root superuser password, select the check box to store it in a plain text file at `C:\xampp\security\mysqlrootpassword.txt`. How much of a security risk this represents depends on who else has access to your computer.

8. After making your choices, click the **Password changing** button.

Starting Apache and MySQL automatically with XAMPP

The Apache web server needs to be running whenever you test your PHP scripts. MySQL also needs to be running if your script accesses a database. Forgetting to switch them on is a common mistake. Apache and MySQL consume few computer resources, so many developers leave them running all the time. To launch them automatically as Windows services each time your computer starts, select the **Svc** check boxes alongside Apache and MySQL in the XAMPP Control Panel. On the other hand, the XAMPP Control Panel makes it easy to run the servers whenever you need them. The servers take only a few seconds to start and stop, so it's up to you if you want to leave them running or only start them when required.

Congratulations. You now have a working PHP development environment on your computer. Skip to "Checking you PHP settings (Windows and Mac)" later in this chapter.

> *If you run into problems with installing or running XAMPP, the best place to start looking for answers is in the XAMPP forum at www.apachefriends.org/f/viewforum.php?f=34.*

Installing PHP with the Microsoft Web Platform Installer

If you need to use IIS instead of Apache, the easiest way to install PHP is with the Microsoft Web Platform Installer (Web PI). The Web PI automatically downloads the correct version of PHP and integrates it into your IIS server. At the time of this writing, the Web PI doesn't support MySQL or phpMyAdmin, so you need to install them separately afterward. If you haven't yet installed IIS or the .NET framework, the Web PI can install them at the same time as PHP.

1. Download the Web PI from www.microsoft.com/web/downloads/platform.aspx. If you are using Internet Explorer, click Run to install it. Otherwise, save the .exe file to your local computer, and double-click it to install the Web PI.

   You need to remain online, because the Web PI connects to Microsoft to find the most up-to-date components and then asks which ones you want to install (see Figure 2-5).

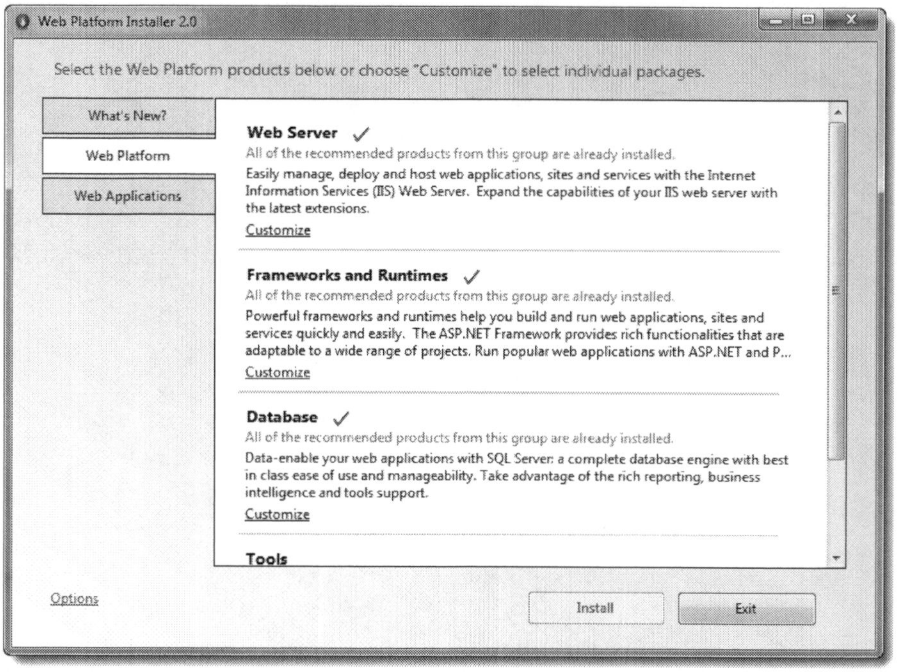

Figure 2-5. The Microsoft Web Platform Installer makes it easy to integrate PHP in IIS.

2. Select **Web Platform** from the menu on the left. To select the components you want to install, click the **Customize** link in the relevant section. IIS and ASP are located in the **Web Server** section. PHP and ASP.NET are in the **Frameworks and Runtimes** section.

3. At the time of this writing, the **Database** section supports only Microsoft SQL Server. If you want to use this database instead of MySQL, you also need to select the Microsoft SQL Server Driver for PHP.

> *Using PHP with Microsoft SQL Server is beyond the scope of this book. However, the chapters on database connection show how to use PHP Data Objects (PDO), which work with all major databases, including Microsoft SQL Server and MySQL.*

4. After you have made your selections, click Install. The Web PI downloads the necessary components and installs them on your computer.

5. When the installation is complete, launch your browser, type `http://localhost/` in the address bar, and press Enter. In Windows 7, Windows Vista, and other recent versions of Windows, you should see the IIS welcome page.

6. If this is the first time you have installed IIS, you need to change the permissions on the folder where IIS stores websites:

   - In Windows Explorer, locate `C:\inetpub\wwwroot`, right-click, and select **Properties**.

   - Select the **Security** tab, and click **Edit**.

   - In the **Group Or User Names** section at the top of the panel, select **IIS_IUSRS**, and select the **Allow** check box for the **Write** permission in the lower half of the panel.

   - Click **OK** twice to close the **Permissions** and **Properties** panels.

Installing MySQL separately (for IIS only)

The Web PI doesn't install MySQL, so you need to download and install it independently. During the configuration process, you're prompted to create a password for the root superuser. This is the main administrative user account in MySQL. Make a note of the password, because you won't be able to access MySQL without it.

1. Go to the MySQL downloads page at `http://dev.mysql.com/downloads/mysql/`. Select Microsoft Windows from the Select Platform menu, and download the MSI Installer Essentials for your operating system (there are different versions for 32-bit and 64-bit Windows).

2. Double-click the installer file, and follow the onscreen instructions. Choose **Typical Install**.

3. At the end of the installation process, select the option to configure the MySQL server, and click Finish.

4. In the MySQL Server Instance Configuration Wizard, select the following options:

- **Configuration type**: **Detailed Configuration**
- **Server type**: **Developer Machine**
- **Database usage**: **Multifunctional Database**
- **Number of concurrent connections**: **Decision Support (DSS)/OLAP**
- **Networking options**: Accept the default settings.
- **Default character set**: Accept the default setting.
- **Windows options**: Select **Install As Windows Service** and **Include Bin Directory in Windows Path.**
- **Security**: Enter and confirm a password for the root superuser.

5. Click **Execute** to configure MySQL.

Installing phpMyAdmin separately (for IIS only)

phpMyAdmin is a web-based front end for MySQL. Use the following instructions to install it in IIS:

1. Go to www.phpmyadmin.net/home_page/, and download the latest version of phpMyAdmin.

2. Unzip the downloaded file. It extracts the contents to a folder called phpMyAdmin-x.x.x, where x represents the version number.

3. Rename the folder phpMyAdmin, and move it to C:\inetpub\wwwroot\phpmyadmin.

4. Create a new subfolder called config in C:\inetpub\wwwroot\phpmyadmin.

5. Open a browser, type http://localhost/phpmyadmin/setup/index.php in the address bar, and press Enter. Ignore any warning about the connection not being secure. It applies only if you are installing phpMyAdmin on a live server on the Internet.

6. Click the **New Server** button in the **Servers** section. This loads a form with most of the necessary information already filled in. Verify the following settings:

- **Server hostname**: **localhost**
- **Server port**: Leave blank
- **Server socket**: Leave blank
- **Connection type**: **tcp**
- **Authentication type**: **config**
- **User for config auth**: **root**
- **Password for config auth**: Enter your MySQL root password.

7. Click **Save**. The next screen will probably warn you that using the `config` authentication type is not desirable for live hosts. This is not important in a local testing environment. However, if you share the computer with others and want to force users to log into phpMyAdmin, click the **Edit** link in the **Servers** section to return to the setup, and select **http** as the authentication type.

   You might also see a warning that you didn't set up a phpMyAdmin database. You can set one up later if you decide to use the advanced features of phpMyAdmin.

8. Scroll down to the **Configuration file** section near the bottom of the page, and click **Save**.

9. Open the `config` folder in Windows Explorer. You should see a new file called `config.inc.php`. Move it the main `phpmyadmin` folder.

10. Delete the `config` folder.

11. Type `http://localhost/phpmyadmin/` in your browser address bar, and press Enter to load phpMyAdmin to verify you have installed it correctly.

Congratulations. You now have a working PHP development environment on your computer. Skip to "Checking you PHP settings (Windows and Mac)" later in this chapter.

Setting up on Mac OS X

The Apache web server and PHP are preinstalled on Mac OS X, but they are not enabled by default. Rather than using the preinstalled versions, I recommend that you use MAMP, which installs Apache, PHP, MySQL, and phpMyAdmin in a single operation.

To avoid conflicts with the preinstalled versions of Apache and PHP, MAMP locates all the applications in a dedicated folder on your hard disk. This makes it easier to uninstall everything by simply dragging the MAMP folder to the Trash if you decide you no longer want MAMP on your computer.

Installing MAMP

Before you begin, check that the preinstalled versions of Apache and PHP are not running. You should also be logged into your computer with administrative privileges.

1. Open **System Preferences**, and select **Sharing** in **Internet & Network**.

2. Make sure that **Web Sharing** is *not* selected. If MySQL is installed on your computer (it's not installed by default), make sure it's turned off, and deselect the option to launch it when you start your computer.

3. Go to `www.mamp.info/en/downloads/index.html`, and select the link for **MAMP & MAMP PRO**. This downloads a disk image that contains both the free and commercial versions of MAMP.

4. When the download completes, you will be presented with a license agreement. You must click **Agree** to continue with mounting the disk image.

5. Drag the **MAMP** folder onto the shortcut icon for the **Applications** folder.

6. Verify that MAMP has been copied to your Applications folder, and eject the disk image.

Testing and configuring MAMP

By default, MAMP uses nonstandard ports for Apache and MySQL. Unless you're using multiple installations of Apache and MySQL, you should change the port settings.

1. Double-click the **MAMP** icon in Applications/MAMP. Your default browser should launch and present you with the MAMP welcome page. Note that the URL in the browser address bar begins with http://localhost:8888. The :8888 indicates that Apache is listening for requests on the nonstandard port 8888.

2. Minimize the browser, and locate the MAMP control panel (see Figure 2-6), which should be running on your desktop. The green lights alongside Apache Server and MySQL Server indicate that both servers are running.

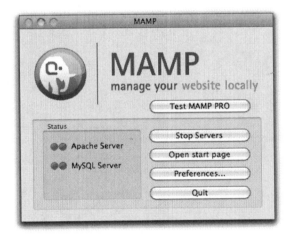

Figure 2-6. The MAMP control panel

3. Click the **Preferences** button, and select **Ports** at the top of the panel that opens. It shows Apache and MySQL are running on ports 8888 and 8889 (see Figure 2-7).

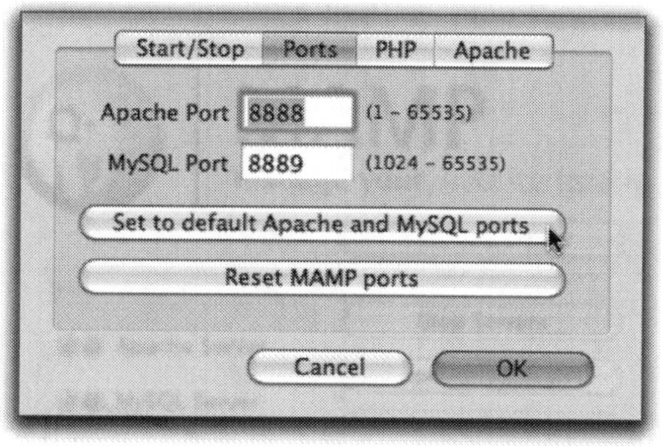

Figure 2-7. Changing the Apache and MySQL ports

4. Click **Set to default Apache and MySQL ports**, as shown in Figure 2-7. The numbers change to the standard ports: 80 for Apache and 3306 for MySQL.

5. Click **OK**, and enter your Mac password when prompted. MAMP restarts both servers.

> *If any other program is using port 80, Apache won't restart. If you can't find what's preventing Apache from using port 80, open the MAMP preference panel, and click **Reset MAMP ports**.*

6. When both lights are green again, click **Open start page** in the MAMP Control Panel. This reloads the MAMP welcome page into your browser. This time, the URL is likely to have :80 after localhost. Because port 80 is the default, the addition of :80 is unnecessary, so it doesn't matter if it's missing. The only time you need the colon followed by a number is if you use nonstandard ports.

If you were expecting to have to do more, that's all there is to it. The Windows section was longer because of the different options for XAMPP and IIS. If you run into difficulties, the best place to look for help is in the MAMP forum (http://forum.mamp.info/index.php?c=1).

Checking your PHP settings (Windows and Mac)

After installing PHP, it's a good idea to inspect how it has been configured. In addition to the core features, PHP has a large number of optional extensions. Which ones have been installed depends on the package you chose. XAMPP, MAMP, and the Microsoft Web PI install all the extensions that you need for this book. However, some of the basic configuration settings might be slightly different. To avoid unexpected problems, adjust your PHP configuration to match the settings recommended in the following pages.

1. Make sure that Apache or IIS is running on your local computer.

2. If you installed XAMPP or MAMP, click the **phpinfo** link in the XAMPP or MAMP welcome page. In XAMPP, it's in the menu on the left of the screen. In MAMP, it's in the menu at the top of the browser window. Skip to step 6.

    If you installed PHP in IIS, continue with step 3.

3. Open Notepad or a script editor, and type the following script:

    `<?php phpinfo(); ?>`

    There should be nothing else in the file.

4. Save the file as `phpinfo.php` in `C:\inetpub\wwwroot`.

5. Type `http://localhost/phpinfo.php` in your browser address bar, and press Enter.

    You should see a page similar to Figure 2-8 displaying the version of PHP running in your local testing environment followed by extensive details of your PHP configuration.

PHP Version 5.3.1	php
System	Windows NT DAVID7 6.1 build 7600 ((null)) i586
Build Date	Nov 20 2009 17:20:57
Compiler	MSVC6 (Visual C++ 6.0)
Architecture	x86
Configure Command	cscript /nologo configure.js "--enable-snapshot-build"
Server API	Apache 2.0 Handler
Virtual Directory Support	enabled
Configuration File (php.ini) Path	no value
Loaded Configuration File	C:\xampp\php\php.ini
Scan this dir for additional .ini files	(none)
Additional .ini files parsed	(none)
PHP API	20090626
	20090626

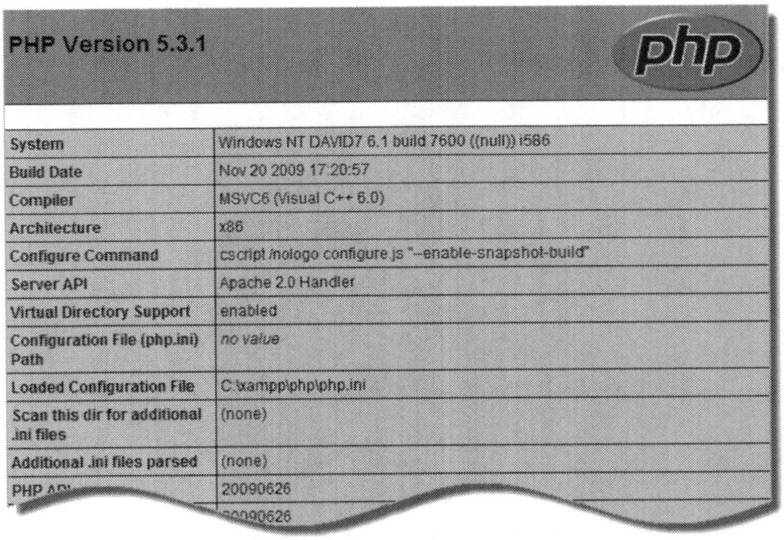

Figure 2-8. Running the `phpinfo()` command displays full details of your PHP configuration.

6. Make a note of the value of **Loaded Configuration File**. This tells you where to find `php.ini`, the text file that you need to edit to change most settings in PHP.

7. Scroll down to the section labeled **Core** (in PHP 5.2, it's called **PHP Core**), and compare the settings with those recommended in Table 2-1. Make a note of any differences, so you can change them as described later in this chapter.

Table 2-1. Recommended PHP configuration settings

Directive	Local value	Remarks
display_errors	**On**	Essential for debugging mistakes in your scripts. If set to **Off**, some errors result in a completely blank screen, leaving you clueless as to the possible cause.
error_reporting	**32767**	This sets error reporting to the highest level. In PHP 5.2, the value should be 6143.
file_uploads	**On**	Allows you to use PHP to upload files to a website.
log_errors	**Off**	With display_errors set on, you don't need to fill your hard disk with an error log.
magic_quotes_gpc	**Off**	See "Eliminating magic quotes."

8. The rest of the configuration page shows you which PHP extensions are enabled. Although the page seems to go on forever, they're all listed in alphabetical order after **Core** (or **PHP Core**). To work with this book, make sure the following extensions are enabled:

    *   **gd**: Enables PHP to generate and modify images and fonts.
    *   **mbstring**: Provides multilingual support.
    *   **mysqli**: Connects to MySQL (note the "i," which stands for "improved" and distinguishes this extension from the older mysql one, which should no longer be used).
    *   **PDO**: Provides software-neutral support for databases (optional).
    *   **pdo_mysql**: Alternative method of connecting to MySQL (optional).
    *   **session**: Sessions maintain information associated with a user and are used, among other things, for user authentication.
    *   **SPL**: This is the Standard PHP Library, which improves performance with loops and file manipulation.

If you installed XAMPP, MAMP, or used the Microsoft Web PI to install PHP, all the extensions listed here should be enabled. If you used a different method to install PHP, and any of the extensions are missing from your setup, you need to upgrade your PHP testing environment.

You should also run phpinfo() on your remote server to check which features are enabled. If the listed extensions aren't supported, some of the code in this book won't work when you upload your files to your website. PDO and pdo_mysql aren't always enabled on shared hosting, but you can use mysqli instead. The advantage of PDO is that it's software-neutral, so you can adapt scripts to work with a database other than MySQL by changing only one or two lines of code. Using mysqli ties you to MySQL.

If any of the Core settings in your setup are different from the recommendations in Table 2-1, you need to edit the PHP configuration file, php.ini, as described in "Editing php.ini." Before doing so, read the next section about magic quotes, because it might influence which setting you use for magic_quotes_gpc.

Eliminating magic quotes

Quotation marks need special handling when querying a database, so the developers of PHP had what they thought was the brilliant idea to insert a backslash automatically in front of single and double quotes in text submitted from an online form. They called this idea **magic quotes**. For a while, most people were happy. It was good magic; it made life easier for beginners and went a long way toward solving security problems. Then, people realized magic quotes didn't really do the job properly. Worse, they littered dynamically generated text with unsightly backslashes.

Eventually, it was decided that magic quotes should have no future in PHP; but by then, the damage had already been done. Countless scripts that rely on magic quotes had already been deployed on websites. Simply removing the feature would cause mayhem. So, magic quotes are being phased out gradually. In PHP 5.3, magic quotes are disabled by default, but system administrators can still turn them back on. However, that won't be possible in the next major version of PHP. The feature will no longer exist.

Because magic quotes are destined for the chop, all the scripts in this book are written on the assumption that `magic_quotes_gpc` in your PHP configuration is set to **Off**. However, that presents a problem if the setting on your remote server is **On**.

To find out whether your remote server has magic quotes on or off, upload `phpinfo.php` from the `ch02` folder to your website. This contains a single-line script `<?php phpinfo(); ?>` that displays your PHP configuration. Load the page into a browser, and find the line indicated in Figure 2-9. It's in the section labeled **Core** close to the top of the page.

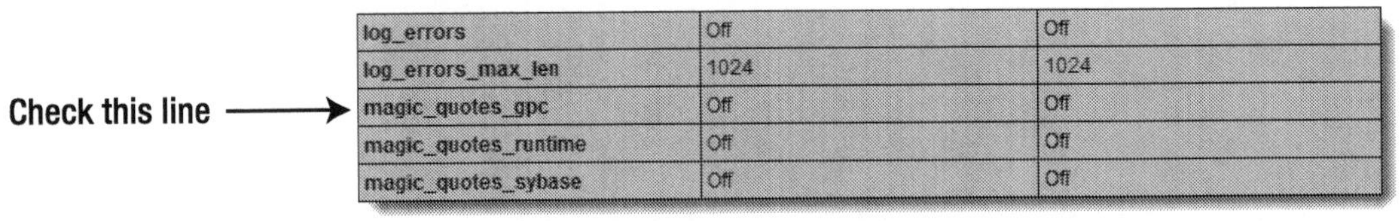

log_errors	Off	Off
log_errors_max_len	1024	1024
magic_quotes_gpc	Off	Off
magic_quotes_runtime	Off	Off
magic_quotes_sybase	Off	Off

Check this line ──────────▶

Figure 2-9. Checking whether magic quotes are enabled

Delete phpinfo.php, or move it to a password-protected folder after checking your remote server's settings. Leaving it publicly accessible exposes details that malicious users might try to exploit.

If the value of `magic_quotes_gpc` is **Off**, you're in luck. Just check that it's also turned off in your testing environment.

If the value of `magic_quotes_gpc` is **On**, you need to turn off magic quotes. There are three ways to do so, as follows:

- If your hosting company allows you to edit `php.ini`, the PHP configuration file, this is the best option. Change the value of `magic_quotes_gpc` from `On` to `Off`, and restart the web server. Some companies allow you to make changes through a web interface, but you might need to edit the configuration file manually in a text editor.

- If you don't have control over the settings in php.ini, but your hosting company uses Apache and allows you to control your configuration with an .htaccess file, add the following line to the .htaccess file in the top-level folder of your website:
  php_flag magic_quotes_gpc Off
- If neither option is available, you need to include nuke_magic_quotes.php at the beginning of all scripts that process the input of online forms. The file contains a script that strips the backslashes from form input. Chapter 4 describes how to include external scripts in PHP.

> *Using nuke_magic_quotes.php is inefficient. If you can't edit php.ini or use an .htaccess file, ask your hosting company if you can transfer to a server where magic quotes are disabled.*

If you can't turn off magic quotes on your remote server, make sure magic_quotes_gpc is set to **On** in your local testing environment.

Editing php.ini

The PHP configuration file, php.ini, is a very long file, which tends to unnerve newcomers to programming, but there's nothing to worry about. It's written in plain text, and one reason for its length is that it contains copious comments explaining the various options. That said, it's a good idea to make a backup copy before editing php.ini in case you make a mistake.

How you open php.ini for editing depends on your operating system and how you installed PHP:

- If you used an all-in-one package, such as XAMPP, on Windows, double-click php.ini in Windows Explorer. The file opens automatically in Notepad.
- If you installed PHP using the Microsoft Web PI, php.ini is normally located in a subfolder of Program Files. Although you can open php.ini by double-clicking it, you won't be able to save any changes you make. Instead, select **Start ➤ All Programs ➤ Accessories**, right-click **Notepad**, and select **Run as Administrator** from the context menu. Inside Notepad, select **File ➤ Open**, and set the option to display **All Files (*.*)**. Navigate to the folder where php.ini is located, select the file, and click **Open**.
- On Mac OS X, php.ini is displayed in Finder as an executable file. Use a text editor, such as BBEdit or TextWrangler (both available from www.barebones.com), to open php.ini.

Lines that begin with a semicolon (;) are comments. The lines you need to edit do not begin with a semicolon.

Use your text editor's Find functionality to locate the directives you need to change to match the recommended settings in Table 2-1. Most directives are preceded by one or more examples of how they should be set. Make sure you don't edit one of the commented examples by mistake.

For directives that use On or Off, just change the value to the recommended one. For example, if you need to turn on the display of error messages, edit this line:

display_errors = Off

Change it to this:

```
display_errors = On
```

To set the level of error reporting, you need to use PHP constants, which are written in uppercase and are case-sensitive.

For PHP 5.3, the directive should look like this:

```
error_reporting = E_ALL | E_STRICT
```

The character between E_ALL and E_STRICT is a vertical pipe. On most keyboards, you insert it by holding down the Shift key and typing a backslash.

To set the level of error reporting on PHP 5.2, use this:

```
error_reporting = E_ALL
```

After editing php.ini, save the file, and restart Apache or IIS for the changes to take effect.

If the web server won't start, check the log files, as described earlier in this chapter, and be thankful you followed the advice to make a backup of php.ini before editing it. Start again with a fresh copy of php.ini, and check your edits carefully.

Where to locate your PHP files

You need to create your files in a location where the web server can process them. Normally, this means that the files should be in the server's document root or a subfolder of the document root. The default location of the document root for the most common setups is as follows:

- **XAMPP**: C:\xampp\htdocs
- **WampServer**: C:\wamp\www
- **EasyPHP**: C:\EasyPHP\www
- **IIS**: C:\inetpub\wwwroot
- **MAMP**: Macintosh HD:Applications:MAMP:htdocs

To view a PHP page, you need to load it in a browser using a URL. The URL for the web server's document root in your local testing environment is http://localhost/.

If you store the files for this book in a subfolder of the document root called phpsols, the URL is http://localhost/phpsols/ followed by the name of the folder (if any) and file.

If your web server uses a nonstandard port, add the port number preceded by a colon after localhost. For example, if you installed MAMP and decided against using the default Apache and MySQL ports, use http://localhost:8888/ instead of http://localhost/.

In some rare cases, you might need to use `http://127.0.0.1/` instead of `http://localhost/`. `127.0.0.1` is the loopback IP address all computers use to refer to the local machine.

The alternative to storing your PHP files in the web server's document root is to use virtual hosts. A **virtual host** creates a unique address for each site and is how hosting companies manage shared hosting. Setting up virtual hosts involves editing one of your computer's system files to register the host name on your local machine. You also need to tell the web server in your local testing environment where the files are located. The process isn't difficult, but it needs to be done each time you set up a new virtual host.

The advantage of setting up each site in a virtual host is that it matches more accurately the structure of a live website. However, when learning PHP, it's probably more convenient to use a subfolder of your testing server's document root. Once you have gained experience with PHP, you can advance to using virtual hosts. Instructions for setting up virtual hosts in Apache are on my website at the following addresses:

- **Windows**: `http://foundationphp.com/tutorials/apache22_vhosts.php`
- **MAMP**: `http://foundationphp.com/tutorials/vhosts_mamp.php`

Creating a new website in IIS on Windows 7 and Windows Vista is the equivalent of creating a virtual host. The first stage involves editing the `hosts` file in `C:\Windows\System32\drivers\etc` in the same way as described on my website for setting up a virtual host on Apache. Then register the new site in Internet Information Services (IIS) Manager by selecting **Sites** in the **Connections** panel. Right-click and select **Add Web Site**.

IIS on Windows XP does not support more than one website. You can store files in a virtual directory, but the URL remains `http://localhost/foldername/`.

Remember to start the web server in your testing environment to view PHP pages.

What's next?

Now that you've got a working test bed for PHP, you're no doubt raring to go. The last thing I want to do is dampen any enthusiasm, but before using any PHP in a live website, it's important to have a basic understanding of the basic rules of the language. So before jumping into the really cool stuff, the next chapter explains how to write PHP. Don't skip it—it's really important stuff. You may also be pleasantly surprised at how few rules there are.

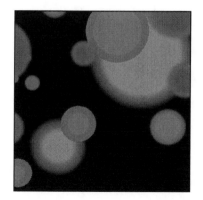

Chapter 3

How to Write PHP Scripts

If you're the sort of person who runs screaming at the sight of code, this is probably going to be the chapter you enjoy least, but it's an important one—and I've tried to make it as user friendly as possible. I've divided this chapter into two parts: the first section offers a quick overview of how PHP works and gives you the basic rules; the second section goes into more detail.

Depending on your style of working, you can read just the first section and come back to the more detailed parts later, or you can read the chapter straight through. However, don't attempt to memorize everything at one sitting. The best way to learn anything is by doing it. Coming back to the second part of the chapter for a little information at a time is likely to be much more effective.

If you're already familiar with PHP, you may want to skim through the main headings to see what this chapter contains and brush up your knowledge on any aspects that you're a bit hazy about.

This chapter covers:

- Understanding how PHP is structured
- Embedding PHP in a web page
- Storing data in variables and arrays
- Getting PHP to make decisions
- Looping through repetitive tasks
- Using functions for preset tasks
- Understanding PHP objects and classes
- Displaying PHP output
- Understanding PHP error messages

PHP: The big picture

At first glance, PHP code can look quite intimidating, but once you understand the basics, you'll discover that the structure is remarkably simple. If you have worked with any other computer language, such as JavaScript or ActionScript, you'll find they have a lot in common.

Every PHP page *must* have the following:

- The correct filename extension, usually .php
- Opening and closing PHP tags surrounding each block of PHP code (although the closing PHP tag can be omitted in certain circumstances)

A typical PHP page will use some or all of the following elements:

- Variables to act as placeholders for unknown or changing values
- Arrays to hold multiple values
- Conditional statements to make decisions
- Loops to perform repetitive tasks
- Functions or objects to perform preset tasks

Let's take a quick look at each of these in turn, starting with the filename and the opening and closing tags.

Telling the server to process PHP

PHP is a **server-side language**. This means that the web server processes your PHP code and sends only the results—usually as HTML—to the browser. Because all the action is on the server, you need to tell it that your pages contain PHP code. This involves two simple steps, namely:

- Give every page a PHP filename extension—the default is .php. Do not use anything other than .php unless you are told to specifically by your hosting company.
- Enclose all PHP code within PHP tags.

The opening tag is <?php and the closing tag is ?>. If you put the tags on the same line as surrounding code, there doesn't need to be a space before the opening tag or after the closing one, but there must be a space after the php in the opening tag like this:

```
<p>This is HTML with embedded PHP<?php //some PHP code ?>.</p>
```

When inserting more than one line of PHP, it's a good idea to put the opening and closing tags on separate lines for the sake of clarity.

```
<?php
// some PHP code
// more PHP code
?>
```

You may come across <? as an alternative short version of the opening tag. However, <? doesn't work on all servers. Stick with <?php, which is guaranteed to work.

To save space, most examples in this book omit the PHP tags. You must always use them when writing your own scripts or embedding PHP into a web page.

Embedding PHP in a web page

PHP is an **embedded** language. This means that you can insert blocks of PHP code inside ordinary web pages. When somebody visits your site and requests a PHP page, the server sends it to the PHP engine, which reads the page from top to bottom looking for PHP tags. HTML passes through untouched, but whenever the PHP engine encounters a `<?php` tag, it starts processing your code and continues until it reaches the closing `?>` tag. If the PHP code produces any output, it's inserted at that point.

You can have multiple PHP code blocks on a page, but they cannot be nested inside each other.

Figure 3-1 shows a block of PHP code embedded in an ordinary web page and what it looks like in a browser and in a page source view after it has been passed through the PHP engine. The code calculates the current year, checks whether it's different from a fixed year (represented by `$startYear` in line 26 of the code on the left of the figure), and displays the appropriate year range in a copyright statement. As you can see from the page source view at the bottom right of the figure, there's no trace of PHP in what's sent to the browser.

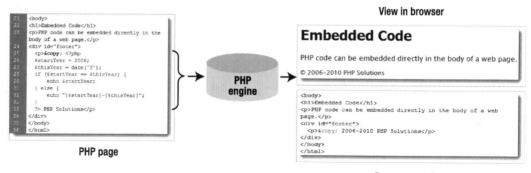

Figure 3-1. The PHP code remains on the server; only the output is sent to the browser.

PHP doesn't always produce direct output for the browser. It may, for instance, check the contents of form input before sending an email message or inserting information into a database. So some code blocks are placed above or below the main HTML code, or in external files. Code that produces direct output, however, always goes where you want the output to be displayed.

Storing PHP in an external file

As well as embedding PHP in HTML, it's common practice to store frequently used code in separate files. When a file contains only PHP code, the opening `<?php` tag is mandatory, but the closing `?>` tag is optional. In fact, the recommended practice is to leave out the closing PHP tag. However, you *must* use the closing ?> tag if the external file contains HTML after the PHP code.

Using variables to represent changing values

The code in Figure 3-1 probably looks like an awfully long-winded way to display a range of years. Surely it's much simpler to just type out the actual dates? Yes, it is, but the PHP solution saves you time in the long run. Instead of you needing to update the copyright statement every year, the PHP code does it automatically. You write the code once and forget it. What's more, as you'll see in the next chapter, if you store the code in an external file, any changes to the external file are reflected on every page of your site.

This ability to display the year automatically relies on two key aspects of PHP: **variables** and **functions**. As the name suggests, functions do things; they perform preset tasks, such as getting the current date and converting it into human readable form. I'll cover functions a little later, so let's take variables first. The script in Figure 3-1 contains two variables: $startYear and $thisYear.

> A **variable** is simply a name that you give to something that may change or that you don't know in advance. Variables in PHP always begin with $ (a dollar sign).

Although the concept of variables sounds abstract, we use variables all the time in everyday life. When you meet somebody for the first time, one of the first things you ask is "What's your name?" It doesn't matter whether the person you've just met is Tom, Dick, or Harry, the word "name" remains constant. Similarly, with your bank account, money goes in and out all of the time (mostly out, it seems), but as Figure 3-2 shows, it doesn't matter whether you're scraping the bottom of the barrel or as rich as Croesus, the amount available is always referred to as the balance.

Figure 3-2. The balance on your bank statement is an everyday example of a variable—the name stays the same, even though the value may change from day to day.

So, "name" and "balance" are everyday variables. Just put a dollar sign in front of them, and you have two ready-made PHP variables, like this:

```
$name
$balance
```

Simple.

Naming variables

You can choose just about anything you like as the name for a variable, as long as you keep the following rules in mind:

- Variables always begin with a dollar sign ($).
- The first character after the dollar sign cannot be a number.
- No spaces or punctuation marks are allowed, except for the underscore (_).
- Variable names are case-sensitive: $startYear and $startyear are not the same.

When choosing names for variables, it makes sense to choose something that tells you what it's for. The variables you've seen so far—$startYear, $thisYear, $name, and $balance—are good examples. Because you can't use spaces in variable names, it's a good idea to capitalize the first letter of the second or subsequent words when combining them (sometimes called **camel case**). Alternatively, you can use an underscore ($start_year, $this_year, etc.). Technically speaking, you can use an underscore as the first character after the dollar sign, but starting a variable name with an underscore is normally reserved for special situations, such as creating protected properties in a class (you'll learn about protected properties in Chapter 6). PHP predefined variables (e.g., the superglobal arrays described a little later in this chapter) also begin with an underscore.

Don't try to save time by using really short variables. Using $sy, $ty, $n, and $b instead of the more descriptive ones makes code harder to understand—and that makes it hard to write. More important, it makes errors more difficult to spot. As always, there are exceptions to a rule. By convention, $i, $j, and $k are frequently used to keep count of the number of times a loop has run; and $e is used in error checking. You'll see examples of these later in this chapter.

> Although you have considerable freedom in the choice of variable names, you can't use $this, because it has a special meaning in PHP object-oriented programming. It's also advisable to avoid using any of the keywords listed at http://docs.php.net/manual/en/reserved.php.

Assigning values to variables

Variables get their values from a variety of sources, including the following:

- User input through online forms
- A database
- An external source, such as a news feed or XML file
- The result of a calculation
- Direct inclusion in the PHP code

Wherever the value comes from, it's always assigned with an equal sign (=), like this:

```
$variable = value;
```

The variable goes on the left of the equal sign, and the value goes on the right. Because it assigns a value, the equal sign is called the **assignment operator**.

Familiarity with the equal sign from childhood makes it difficult to get out of the habit of thinking that it means "is equal to." However, PHP uses two equal signs (==) to signify equality. This is one of the biggest causes of beginner mistakes—and it often catches more experienced developers, too. The difference between = and == is covered in more detail later in this chapter.

Ending commands with a semicolon

PHP is written as a series of commands or statements. Each **statement** normally tells the PHP engine to perform a particular action, and it must always be followed by a semicolon, like this:

```
<?php
do this;
now do something else;
?>
```

As with all rules, there is an exception: you can omit the semicolon if there's only one statement in the code block. However, *don't do it*. Unlike JavaScript or ActionScript, PHP won't automatically assume there should be a semicolon at the end of a line if you miss it out. This has a nice side-effect: you can spread long statements over several lines and lay out your code for ease of reading. PHP, like HTML, ignores whitespace in code. Instead, it relies on semicolons to indicate where one command ends and the next one begins.

> *Using a semicolon at the end of a PHP statement (or command) is always right. A missing semicolon will bring your script to a grinding halt.*

Commenting scripts

PHP treats everything between the opening and closing PHP tags as statements to be executed, unless you tell it not to do so by marking a section of code as a comment. The following three reasons explain why you may want to do this:

- To insert a reminder of what the script does
- To insert a placeholder for code to be added later
- To disable a section of code temporarily

When a script is fresh in your mind, it may seem unnecessary to insert anything that isn't going to be processed. However, if you need to revise the script several months later, you'll find comments much easier to read than trying to follow the code on its own. Comments are also vital when you're working in a team. They help your colleagues understand what the code is intended to do.

During testing, it's often useful to prevent a line of code, or even a whole section, from running. PHP ignores anything marked as a comment, so this is a useful way of turning on and off code.

There are three ways of adding comments: two for single-line comments and one for comments that stretch over several lines.

Single-line comments

The most common method of adding a single-line comment is to precede it with two forward slashes, like this:

```
// this is a comment and will be ignored by the PHP engine
```

PHP ignores everything from the double slashes to the end of the line, so you can also place comments alongside code (but only to the right):

```
$startYear = 2006; // this is a valid comment
```

Comments aren't PHP statements, so they don't end with a semicolon. But don't forget the semicolon at the end of a PHP statement that's on the same line as a comment.

An alternative style uses the hash or pound sign (#) like this:

```
# this is another type of comment that will be ignored by the PHP engine
$startYear = 2006; # this also works as a comment
```

Because # stands out prominently when several are used together, this style of commenting often indicates sections of a longer script, like this:

```
##################
## Menu section ##
##################
```

Multiline comments

For a comment to stretch over several lines, use the same style of comments as in Cascading Style Sheets (CSS), JavaScript, and ActionScript. Anything between /* and */ is treated as a comment, like this:

```
/* This is a comment that stretches
   over several lines. It uses the same
   beginning and end markers as in CSS. */
```

Multiline comments are particularly useful when testing or troubleshooting, as they can be used to disable long sections of script without the need to delete them.

> *A combination of good comments and well-chosen variable names makes code easier to understand and maintain.*

Using arrays to store multiple values

In common with other computing languages, PHP lets you store multiple values in a special type of variable called an **array**. The simple way of thinking about arrays is that they're like a shopping list. Although each item might be different, you can refer to them collectively by a single name. Figure 3-3 demonstrates this concept: the variable $shoppingList refers collectively to all five items—wine, fish, bread, grapes, and cheese.

Figure 3-3. Arrays are variables that store multiple items, just like a shopping list.

Individual items—or **array elements**—are identified by means of a number in square brackets immediately following the variable name. PHP assigns the number automatically, but it's important to note that the numbering always begins at 0. So the first item in the array, wine in our example, is referred to as $shoppingList[0], not $shoppingList[1]. And although there are five items, the last one (cheese) is $shoppingList[4]. The number is referred to as the array **key** or **index**, and this type of array is called an **indexed array**.

PHP uses another type of array, in which the key is a word (or any combination of letters and numbers). For instance, an array containing details of this book might look like this:

```
$book['title'] = 'PHP Solutions: Dynamic Web Design Made Easy, Second Edition';
$book['author'] = 'David Powers';
$book['publisher'] = 'friends of ED';
$book['ISBN'] = '978-1-4302-3249-0';
```

This type of array is called an **associative array**. Note that the array key is enclosed in quotes (single or double, it doesn't matter). It mustn't contain any spaces or punctuation, except for the underscore.

Arrays are an important—and useful—part of PHP. You'll use them a lot, starting with the next chapter, when you'll store details of images in an array to display a random image on a web page. Arrays are also used extensively with a database, as you fetch the results of a search in a series of arrays. You can learn the various ways of creating arrays in the second half of this chapter.

PHP's built-in superglobal arrays

PHP has several built-in arrays that are automatically populated with really useful information. They are called **superglobal arrays**, and all begin with a dollar sign followed by an underscore. Two that you will meet frequently are $_POST and $_GET. They contain information passed from forms through the Hypertext Transfer Protocol (HTTP) post and get methods, respectively. The superglobals are all associative arrays, and the keys of $_POST and $_GET are automatically derived from the names of form elements.

Let's say you have a text input field called address in a form; PHP automatically creates an array element called $_POST['address'] when the form is submitted by the post method or $_GET['address'] if you use the get method. As Figure 3-4 shows, $_POST['address'] contains whatever value a visitor enters in the text field, enabling you to display it onscreen, insert it in a database, send it to your email inbox, or do whatever you want with it.

Figure 3-4. You can retrieve the values of user input through the $_POST array, which is created automatically when a form is submitted using the post method.

You'll work with the $_POST array in Chapter 5, when you send the content of an online feedback form by email to your inbox. Other superglobal arrays that you'll use in this book are $_SERVER, to get information from the web server in Chapters 4, 12, and 13, $_FILES to upload files to your website in Chapter 6, and $_SESSION, to create a simple login system in Chapters 9 and 17.

> *Don't forget that PHP is case-sensitive. All superglobal array names are written in uppercase. $_Post or $_Get, for example, won't work.*

Understanding when to use quotes

If you look closely at the PHP code block in Figure 3-1, you'll notice that the value assigned to the first variable isn't enclosed in quotes. It looks like this:

```
$startYear = 2006;
```

Yet all the examples in "Using arrays to store multiple values" *did* use quotes, like this:

```
$book['title'] = 'PHP Solutions: Dynamic Web Design Made Easy, Second Edition';
```

The simple rules are as follows:

- **Numbers**: No quotes
- **Text**: Requires quotes

As a general principle, it doesn't matter whether you use single or double quotes around text—or a **string**, as text is called in PHP and other computer languages. The situation is actually a bit more complex than that, as explained in the second half of this chapter, because there's a subtle difference in the way single and double quotes are treated by the PHP engine.

> *The word "string" is borrowed from computer and mathematical science, where it means a sequence of simple objects—in this case, the characters in text.*

The important thing to remember for now is that *quotes must always be in matching pairs*. This means you need to be careful about including apostrophes in a single-quoted string or double quotes in a double-quoted string. Take a look at the following line of code:

```
$book['description'] = 'This is David's latest book on PHP.';
```

At first glance, there seems nothing wrong with it. However, the PHP engine sees things differently from the human eye, as Figure 3-5 demonstrates.

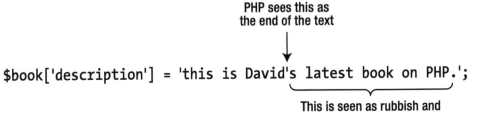

Figure 3-5. An apostrophe inside a single-quoted string confuses the PHP engine.

There are two ways around this problem:

- Use double quotes if the text includes any apostrophes.
- Precede apostrophes with a backslash (this is known as **escaping**).

So, either of the following is acceptable:

```
$book['description'] = "This is David's latest book on PHP.";
$book['description'] = 'This is David\'s latest book on PHP.';
```

The same applies with double quotes in a double-quoted string (although with the rules reversed). The following code causes a problem:

```
$play = "Shakespeare's "Macbeth"";
```

In this case, the apostrophe is fine, because it doesn't conflict with the double quotes, but the opening quotes in front of *Macbeth* bring the string to a premature end. To solve the problem, either of the following is acceptable:

```
$play = 'Shakespeare\'s "Macbeth"';
$play = "Shakespeare's \"Macbeth\"";
```

In the first example, the entire string has been enclosed in single quotes. This gets around the problem of the double quotes surrounding *Macbeth* but introduces the need to escape the apostrophe in *Shakespeare's*. The apostrophe presents no problem in a double-quoted string, but the double quotes around *Macbeth* both need to be escaped. So, to summarize:

- Single quotes and apostrophes are fine inside a double-quoted string.
- Double quotes are fine inside a single-quoted string.
- Anything else must be escaped with a backslash.

The key is to remember that the outermost quotes must match. My preference is to use single quotes and to reserve double quotes for situations where they have a special meaning, as described in the second half of this chapter.

Special cases: true, false, and null

Although text should be enclosed in quotes, three special cases—true, false, and null—should never be enclosed in quotes unless you want to treat them as genuine text (or strings). The first two mean what you would expect; the last one, null, means "nothing" or "no value."

> Technically speaking, *true* and *false* are **Boolean values**. The name comes from a nineteenth-century mathematician, George Boole, who devised a system of logical operations that subsequently became the basis of much modern-day computing. It's a complicated subject, but you can find out more at *http://en.wikipedia.org/wiki/Boolean_logic*. For most people, it's sufficient to know that Boolean means *true* or *false*.

As the next section explains, PHP makes decisions on the basis of whether something equates to true or false. Putting quotes around false has surprising consequences. The following code

```
$OK = false;
```

does exactly what you expect: it makes $OK false. Now, take a look at this:

```
$OK = 'false';
```

This does exactly the opposite of what you might expect: it makes $OK true! Why? Because the quotes around false turn it into a string, and PHP treats strings as true. (There's a more detailed explanation in "The truth according to PHP" in the second half of this chapter.)

The other thing to note about true, false, and null is that they are *case-insensitive*. The following examples are all valid:

```
$OK = TRUE;
$OK = tRuE;
$OK = true;
```

So, to recap: PHP treats true, false, and null as special cases.

- Don't enclose them in quotes.
- They are case-insensitive.

Making decisions

Decisions, decisions, decisions . . . Life is full of decisions. So is PHP. They give it the ability to display different output according to circumstances. Decision-making in PHP uses **conditional statements**. The most common of these uses if and closely follows the structure of normal language. In real life, you may be faced with the following decision (admittedly not very often if you live in Britain): if the weather's hot, I'll go to the beach.

In PHP pseudo-code, the same decision looks like this:

```
if (the weather's hot) {
  I'll go to the beach;
}
```

The condition being tested goes inside parentheses, and the resulting action goes between curly braces. This is the basic decision-making pattern:

```
if (condition is true) {
  // code to be executed if condition is true
}
```

Confusion alert: I mentioned earlier that statements must always be followed by a semicolon. This applies only to the statements (or commands) inside the curly braces. Although called a conditional statement, this decision-making pattern is one of PHP's control structures, and it shouldn't be followed by a semicolon. Think of the semicolon as a command that means "do it." The curly braces surround the command statements and keep them together as a group.

The code inside the curly braces is executed *only* if the condition is `true`. If it's `false`, PHP ignores everything between the braces and moves on to the next section of code. How PHP determines whether a condition is `true` or `false` is described in the following section.

Sometimes, the `if` statement is all you need, but you often want a default action to be invoked if the condition isn't met. To do this, use `else`, like this:

```
if (condition is true) {
  // code to be executed if condition is true
} else {
  // default code to run if condition is false
}
```

What if you want more alternatives? One way is to add more conditional statements like this:

```
if (condition is true) {
  // code to be executed if condition is true
} else {
  // default code to run if condition is false
}
if (second condition is true) {
  // code to be executed if second condition is true
} else {
  // default code to run if second condition is false
}
```

However, it's important to realize that *both* conditional statements will be run. If you want only one code block to be executed, use `elseif` like this:

```
if (condition is true) {
  // code to be executed if first condition is true
```

```
} elseif (second condition is true) {
  // code to be executed if first condition fails
  // but second condition is true
} else {
  // default code if both conditions are false
}
```

You can use as many `elseif` clauses in a conditional statement as you like. It's important to note that *only the first one* that equates to `true` will be executed; all others will be ignored, even if they're also true. This means you need to build conditional statements in the order of priority that you want them to be evaluated. It's strictly a first-come, first-served hierarchy.

> Although `elseif` is normally written as one word, you can use `else if` as separate words.

An alternative decision-making structure, the `switch` statement, is described in the second half of this chapter.

Making comparisons

Conditional statements are interested in only one thing: whether the condition being tested equates to `true`. If it's not `true`, it must be `false`. There's no room for half-measures or maybes. Conditions often depend on the comparison of two values. Is this bigger than that? Are they both the same? And so on.

To test for equality, PHP uses two equal signs (==) like this:

```
if ($status == 'administrator') {
  // send to admin page
} else {
  // refuse entry to admin area
}
```

> Don't use a single equal sign in the first line (`$status = 'administrator'`). Doing so will open the admin area of your website to everyone. Why? Because this automatically sets the value of `$status` to administrator; it doesn't compare the two values. To compare values, you must use two equal signs. It's an easy mistake to make, but one with potentially disastrous consequences.

Size comparisons are performed using the mathematical symbols for less than (<) and greater than (>). Let's say you're checking the size of a file before allowing it to be uploaded to your server. You could set a maximum size of 50kB like this (1 kilobyte = 1024 bytes):

```
if ($bytes > 51200) {
  // display error message and abandon upload
} else {
  // continue upload
}
```

You can test for multiple conditions simultaneously. Details are in the second half of this chapter.

Using indenting and whitespace for clarity

Indenting code helps to keep statements in logical groups, making it easier to understand the flow of the script. There are no fixed rules; PHP ignores any whitespace inside code, so you can adopt any style you like. The important thing is to be consistent so that you can spot anything that looks out of place.

The limited width of the printed page means that I normally use just two spaces to indent code in this book, but most people find that tabbing four or five spaces makes for the most readable code. Perhaps the biggest difference in styles lies in the way individual developers arrange curly braces. I put the opening curly brace of a code block on the same line as the preceding code, and put the closing brace on a new line after the code block, like this:

```
if ($bytes > 51200) {
    // display error message and abandon upload
} else {
    // continue upload
}
```

However, others prefer this style:

```
if ($bytes > 51200)
    {
        // display error message and abandon upload
    }
else
    {
        // continue upload
    }
```

The style isn't important. What matters is that your code is consistent and easy to read.

Using loops for repetitive tasks

Loops are huge time-savers because they perform the same task over and over again, yet involve very little code. They're frequently used with arrays and database results. You can step through each item one at a time looking for matches or performing a specific task. Loops are particularly powerful in combination with conditional statements, allowing you to perform operations selectively on a large amount of data in a single sweep. Loops are best understood by working with them in a real situation, but details of all looping structures, together with examples, are in the second half of this chapter.

Using functions for preset tasks

As I mentioned earlier, **functions** do things . . . lots of things, mind-bogglingly so in PHP. A typical PHP setup gives you access to several thousand built-in functions. Don't worry: you'll only ever need to use a handful, but it's reassuring to know that PHP is a full-featured language capable of industrial-strength applications.

The functions you'll be using in this book do really useful things, such as get the height and width of an image, create thumbnails from existing images, query a database, send email, and much, much more. You can identify functions in PHP code because they're always followed by a pair of parentheses. Sometimes, the parentheses are empty, as in the case of phpversion(), which you used in phptest.php in the previous chapter. Often, though, the parentheses contain variables, numbers, or strings, like this line of code from the script in Figure 3-1:

```
$thisYear = date('Y');
```

This calculates the current year and stores it in the variable $thisYear. It works by feeding the string 'Y' to the built-in PHP function date(). Placing a value between the parentheses like this is known as **passing an argument** to a function. The function takes the value in the argument and processes it to produce (or **return**) the result. For instance, if you pass the string 'M' as an argument to date() instead of 'Y', it will return the current month as a three-letter abbreviation (e.g., Mar, Apr, May). As the following example shows, you capture the result of a function by assigning it to a suitably named variable:

```
$thisMonth = date('M');
```

The date() function is covered in depth in Chapter 14.

Some functions take more than one argument. When this happens, separate the arguments with commas inside the parentheses, like this:

```
$mailSent = mail($to, $subject, $message);
```

It doesn't take a genius to work out that this sends an email to the address stored in the first argument, with the subject line stored in the second argument, and the message stored in the third one. You'll see how this function works in Chapter 5.

> You'll often come across the term "parameter" in place of "argument." There is a technical difference between the two words, but for all practical purposes, they are interchangeable.

As if all the built-in functions weren't enough, PHP lets you build your own custom functions. Even if you don't relish the idea of creating your own, throughout this book you'll use some that I have made. You use them in exactly the same way.

Understanding PHP classes and objects

Functions and variables give PHP tremendous power and flexibility, but classes and objects take the language to an even higher level. Classes are the fundamental building blocks of **object-oriented programming** (OOP), an approach to programming that's designed to make code reusable and easier to maintain. PHP isn't an object-oriented language, but it has supported OOP since version 3. Unfortunately, PHP's original implementation of OOP had severe shortcomings. The problems were rectified in PHP 5, but in a way that was incompatible with PHP 4, slowing down widespread adoption of OOP in PHP. Now that PHP 4 is no longer supported, use of classes and objects is likely to increase significantly. In fact, you'll start building classes in Chapter 6.

An **object** is a sophisticated data type that can store and manipulate values. A **class** is the code that defines an object's features and can be regarded as a blueprint for making objects. Among PHP's many built-in classes, two of particular interest are the DateTime and DateTimeZone classes, which deal with dates and time zones. Two other classes that you'll use in this book are MySQLi and PDO, which are used for communicating with databases.

To create an object, you use the new keyword with the class name like this:

```
$now = new DateTime();
```

This creates an **instance** of the DateTime class and stores it in a DateTime object called $now. What distinguishes this from the date() function in the preceding section is that a DateTime object is aware not only of the date and time it was created but also of the time zone used by the web server. The date() function, on the other hand, simply generates a number or string containing the date formatted according to the arguments passed to it.

In the preceding example, no arguments were passed to the class, but classes can take arguments in the same way as functions, as you'll see in the next example.

Most classes also have properties and methods, which are similar to variables and functions, except that they're related to a particular instance of a class. For example, you can use the DateTime class's methods to change certain values, such as the month, year, or time zone. A DateTime object is also capable of performing date calculations, which are much more complicated using ordinary functions.

You access an object's properties and methods using the -> operator. To reset the time zone of a DateTime object, pass a DateTimeZone object as an argument to the setTimezone() method like this:

```
$westcoast = new DateTimeZone('America/Los_Angeles');
$now->setTimezone($westcoast);
```

This resets the date and time stored in $now to the current date and time in Los Angeles, regardless of where the web server is located, automatically making any adjustments for daylight saving time.

The DateTime and DateTimeZone classes don't have properties, but you access an object's properties using the -> operator in the same way like this:

```
$someObject->propertyName
```

Don't worry if you find the concepts of objects, properties, and methods difficult to grasp. All you need to know is how to instantiate objects with the new keyword and how to access properties and methods with the -> operator.

> For an in-depth discussion of OOP in PHP with extensive hands-on examples, see my book PHP Object-Oriented Solutions *(friends of ED, 2008, ISBN: 978-1-4302-1011-5).*

Displaying PHP output

There's not much point in all this wizardry going on behind the scenes unless you can display the results in your web page. There are two ways of doing this in PHP: using echo or print. There are some subtle differences between the two, but they are so subtle, you can regard echo or print as identical. I prefer echo for the simple reason that it's one fewer letter to type.

You can use echo with variables, numbers, and strings. Simply put it in front of whatever you want to display, like this:

```
$name = 'David';
echo $name;    // displays David
echo 5;        // displays 5
```

```
echo 'David'; // displays David
```

The important thing to remember about echo and print, when using them with a variable, is that they work only with variables that contain a single value. You cannot use them to display the contents of an array or of a database result. This is where loops are so useful: you use echo or print inside the loop to display each element individually. You will see plenty of examples of this in action throughout the rest of the book.

You may see scripts that use parentheses with echo and print, like this:

```
echo('David'); // displays David
```

The parentheses make no difference. Unless you enjoy typing for the sake of it, leave them out.

Joining strings together

PHP has a rather unusual way of joining strings (text). Although many other computer languages use the plus sign (+), PHP uses a period, dot, or full stop (.) like this:

```
$firstName = 'David';
$lastName = 'Powers';
echo $firstName.$lastName; // displays DavidPowers
```

As the comment in the final line of code indicates, when two strings are joined like this, PHP leaves no gap between them. Don't be fooled into thinking that adding a space after the period will do the trick. It won't. You can put as much space on either side of the period as you like; the result will always be the same, because PHP ignores whitespace in code. In fact, it's recommended to leave a space on either side of the period for readability.

To display a space in the final output, you must either include a space in one of the strings or insert the space as a string in its own right, like this:

```
echo $firstName . ' ' . $lastName; // displays David Powers
```

> The period—or **concatenation operator**, to give it its correct name—can be difficult to spot among a lot of other code. Make sure the font size in your script editor is large enough to read without straining to see the difference between periods and commas.

Working with numbers

PHP can do a lot with numbers—from simple addition to complex math. The second half of this chapter contains details of the arithmetic operators you can use with PHP. All you need to remember at the moment is that numbers mustn't contain any punctuation other than a decimal point. PHP will choke if you feed it numbers that contain commas (or anything else) as the thousands separator.

Understanding PHP error messages

Error messages are an unfortunate fact of life, so you need to understand what they're trying to tell you. The following illustration shows a typical error message.

Severity of error   **What went wrong**   **Where it went wrong**

↓   ↓   ↓

Parse error: syntax error, unexpected T_ECHO in C:**\htdocs\phpsolutions\downloads\ch03\functions4.php** on line **15**

The first thing to realize about PHP error messages is that they report the line where PHP discovered a problem. Most newcomers—quite naturally—assume that's where they've got to look for their mistake. Wrong . . .

What PHP is telling you most of the time is that something unexpected has happened. In other words, the mistake lies *before* that point. The preceding error message means that PHP discovered an echo command where there shouldn't have been one. (Error messages always prefix PHP elements with **T_**, which stands for token. Just ignore it.)

Instead of worrying what might be wrong with the echo command (probably nothing), start working backward, looking for anything missing, probably a semicolon or closing quote on a previous line.

Sometimes, the message reports the error on the last line of the script. That always means you have omitted a closing curly brace somewhere further up the page.

There are seven main categories of error, presented here in descending order of importance:

- **Fatal error**: Any HTML output preceding the error will be displayed, but once the error is encountered—as the name suggests—everything else is killed stone dead. A fatal error is normally caused by referring to a nonexistent file or function.

- **Recoverable error**: This type of error occurs only when a particular type of error known as an **exception** is thrown. The error message contains much detail, explaining the cause and location of the problem, but it can be difficult for beginners to understand. To avoid recoverable errors, use try and catch blocks as described in "Handling exceptions."

- **Parse error**: This means there's a mistake in your code syntax, such as mismatched quotes or a missing semicolon or closing brace. It stops the script in its tracks, and it doesn't even allow any HTML output to be displayed.

- **Warning**: This alerts you to a serious problem, such as a missing include file. (Include files are the subject of Chapter 4.) However, the error is not serious enough to prevent the rest of the script from being executed.

- **Deprecated**: Introduced in PHP 5.3.0, this warns you about features that are scheduled to be removed from the next major version of PHP. If you see this type of error message, you should seriously consider updating your script, as it could suddenly stop working if your server is upgraded.

- **Strict**: This type of error message warns you about using techniques that are not considered good practice.

- **Notice**: This advises you about relatively minor issues, such as the use of a nondeclared variable. Although this type of error won't stop your page from displaying (and you can turn off the display of notices), you should always try to eliminate them. Any error is a threat to your output.

Handling exceptions

PHP 5 introduced a new way of handling errors—common to many other programming languages—known as exceptions. When a problem arises, many built-in classes automatically **throw an exception**—or generate a special type of object that contains details of what caused the error and where it arose. You can also throw custom exceptions, using the keyword throw like this:

```
if (error occurs) {
  throw new Exception('Houston, we have a problem');
}
```

The string inside the parentheses is used as the error message. Obviously, in a real script, you need to make the message more explicit.

When an exception is thrown, you should deal with it in a separate code block called—appropriately enough—catch.

When using objects, wrap your main script in a block called try, and put the error handling code in a catch block. If an exception is thrown, the PHP engine abandons the code in the try block, and executes only the code in the catch block. The advantage is that you can use the catch block to redirect the user to an error page, rather than displaying an ugly error message onscreen—or a blank screen if the display of error messages is turned off, as it should be in a live website.

During the development stage, you should use the catch block to display the error message generated by the exception like this:

```
try {
  // main script goes here
} catch (Exception $e) {
  echo $e->getMessage();
}
```

This produces an error message that's usually much easier to understand than the lengthy message generated by a recoverable error. In the case of the previous example, it would output "Houston, we have a problem." Although I advised you earlier to use descriptive variable names, using $e for an exception is a common convention.

PHP: A quick reference

The first half of this chapter gave you a high-level overview of PHP and should be sufficient to get you started. The rest of this chapter goes into greater detail about individual aspects of writing PHP scripts. Rather than plowing straight on, I suggest you take a short break and then move on to the next chapter. Come back to this reference section when you've gained some practical experience of working with PHP, as it will make much more sense then.

The following sections don't attempt to cover every aspect of PHP syntax. For that, you should refer to the PHP documentation at http://docs.php.net/manual/en/ or a more detailed reference book, such as *Beginning PHP and MySQL: From Novice to Professional, Fourth Edition* by W. Jason Gilmore (Apress, 2010, ISBN: 978-1-4302-3114-1).

Using PHP in an existing website

There is no problem mixing .html and .php pages in the same website. However, PHP code will be processed only in files that have the .php filename extension, so it's a good idea to give the same extension to all your pages, even if they don't all contain dynamic features. That way, you have the flexibility to add PHP to pages without breaking existing links or losing search engine rankings.

Data types in PHP

PHP is what's known as a **weakly typed** language. In practice, this means that, unlike some other computer languages (e.g., Java or C#), PHP doesn't care what type of data you store in a variable.

Most of the time, this is very convenient, although you need to be careful with user input. You may expect a user to enter a number in a form, but PHP won't object if it encounters a word instead. Checking user input carefully is one of the major themes of later chapters.

Even though PHP is weakly typed, it uses the following eight data types:

- **Integer**: This is a whole number, such as 1, 25, 42, or 2006. Integers must not contain any commas or other punctuation as thousand separators. You can also use hexadecimal numbers, which should be preceded by 0x (e.g., 0xFFFFFF, 0x000000).
- **Floating-point number**: This is a number that contains a decimal point, such as 9.99, 98.6, or 2.1. PHP does not support the use of the comma as the decimal point, as is common in many European countries. You must use a period. Like integers, floating-point numbers must not contain thousand-separators. (This type is also referred to as **float** or **double**.)
- **String**: A string is text of any length. It can be as short as zero characters (an empty string), and it has no upper limit.
- **Boolean**: This type has only two values: true or false. However, PHP treats other values as implicitly true or false. See "The truth according to PHP" later in this chapter.
- **Array**: An array is a variable capable of storing multiple values, although it may contain none at all (an empty array). Arrays can hold any data type, including other arrays. An array of arrays is called a **multidimensional array**. See "Creating arrays" later in this chapter for details of how to populate an array with values.
- **Object**: An object is a sophisticated data type capable of storing and manipulating values. You'll learn more about objects in Chapter 6.
- **Resource**: When PHP connects to an external data source, such as a file or database, it stores a reference to it as a resource.
- **NULL:** This is a special data type that indicates that a variable has no value.

An important side-effect of PHP's weak typing is that, if you enclose an integer or floating-point number in quotes, PHP automatically converts it from a string to a number, allowing you to perform calculations without the need for any special handling. This is different from JavaScript and ActionScript, and it can have unexpected consequences. When PHP sees the plus sign (+), it assumes you want to perform addition, and it tries to convert strings to integers or floating-point numbers, as in the following example (the code is in data_conversion1.php in the ch03 folder):

```
$fruit = '2 apples';
```

```
$veg = ' 2 carrots';
echo $fruit + $veg;  // displays 4
```

PHP sees that both $fruit and $veg begin with a number, so it extracts the number and ignores the rest. However, if the string doesn't begin with a number, PHP converts it to 0, as shown in this example (the code is in data_conversion2.php):

```
$fruit = '2 apples';
$veg = ' and 2 carrots';
echo $fruit + $veg;  // displays 2
```

Weak typing is a mixed blessing. It makes PHP very easy for beginners, but it means you often need to check that a variable contains the correct data type before using it.

Doing calculations with PHP

PHP is highly adept at working with numbers and can perform a wide variety of calculations, from simple arithmetic to complex math. This reference section covers only the standard arithmetic operators. See http://docs.php.net/manual/en/book.math.php for details of the mathematical functions and constants supported by PHP.

> A **constant** is similar to a variable in that it uses a name to represent a value. However, the value of a constant, once defined, cannot be changed. All PHP predefined constants are in uppercase. Unlike variables, they do not begin with a dollar sign. For example, the constant for π (pi) is M_PI.

Arithmetic operators

The standard arithmetic operators all work the way you would expect, although some of them look slightly different from those you learned at school. For instance, an asterisk (*) is used as the multiplication sign, and a forward slash (/) is used to indicate division. Table 3-1 shows examples of how the standard arithmetic operators work. To demonstrate their effect, the following variables have been set:

```
$x = 20;
$y = 10;
$z = 3;
```

Table 3-1. Arithmetic operators in PHP

Operation	Operator	Example	Result
Addition	+	$x + $y	30
Subtraction	-	$x - $y	10
Multiplication	*	$x * $y	200
Division	/	$x / $y	2

Operation	Operator	Example	Result
Modulo division	%	$x % $z	2
Increment (add 1)	++	$x++	21
Decrement (subtract 1)	--	$y--	9

The modulo operator returns the remainder of a division, as follows:

```
26 % 5     // result is 1
26 % 27    // result is 26
10 % 2     // result is 0
```

A practical use of modulo division is to work out whether a number is odd or even. $number % 2 always produces 0 or 1. If the result is 0, there is no remainder, so the number must be even.

The increment (++) and decrement (--) operators can come either before or after the variable. When they come before the variable, 1 is added to or subtracted from the value before any further calculation is carried out. When they come after the variable, the main calculation is carried out first, and then 1 is either added or subtracted. Since the dollar sign is an integral part of the variable name, the increment and decrement operators go before the dollar sign when used in front:

```
++$x
--$y
```

Determining the order of calculations

Calculations in PHP follow exactly the same rules as standard arithmetic. Table 3-2 summarizes the precedence of arithmetic operators.

Table 3-2. Precedence of arithmetic operators

Precedence	Group	Operators	Rule
Highest	Parentheses	( )	Operations contained within parentheses are evaluated first. If these expressions are nested, the innermost is evaluated foremost.
Next	Multiplication and division	* / %	These operators are evaluated next. If an expression contains two or more operators, they are evaluated from left to right.
Lowest	Addition and subtraction	+ -	These are the final operators to be evaluated in an expression. If an expression contains two or more operators, they are evaluated from left to right.

Combining calculations and assignment

PHP offers a shorthand way of performing a calculation on a variable and reassigning the result to the variable through **combined assignment operators**. The main ones are listed in Table 3-3.

Table 3-3. Combined arithmetic assignment operators used in PHP

Operator	Example	Equivalent to
+=	$a += $b	$a = $a + $b
-=	$a -= $b	$a = $a - $b
*=	$a *= $b	$a = $a * $b
/=	$a /= $b	$a = $a / $b
%=	$a %= $b	$a = $a % $b

Adding to an existing string

The same convenient shorthand allows you to add new material to the end of an existing string by combining a period and an equal sign, like this:

```
$hamlet = 'To be';
$hamlet .= ' or not to be';
```

Note that you need to create a space at the beginning of the additional text unless you want both strings to run on without a break. This shorthand, known as the **combined concatenation operator**, is extremely useful when combining many strings, such as you need to do when building the content of an email message or looping through the results of a database search.

> *The period in front of the equal sign is easily overlooked when copying code. When you see the same variable repeated at the beginning of a series of statements, it's often a sure sign that you need to use .= instead of = on its own.*

All you ever wanted to know about quotes—and more

Handling quotes within any computer language—not just PHP—can be fraught with difficulties because computers always take the first matching quote as marking the end of a string. Structured Query Language (SQL)—the language used to communicate with databases—also uses strings. Since your strings may include apostrophes, the combination of single and double quotes isn't enough. Moreover, PHP gives variables and escape sequences (certain characters preceded by a backslash) special treatment inside double quotes.

Over the next few pages, I'll unravel this maze and make sense of it all for you.

How PHP treats variables inside strings

Choosing whether to use double quotes or single quotes might just seem like a question of personal preference, but there's an important difference in the way that PHP handles them.

- Anything between single quotes is treated literally as text.
- Double quotes act as a signal to process variables and special characters known as **escape sequences**.

Take a look at the following examples to see what this means. In the first example (the code is in `quotes1.php`), $name is assigned a value and then used in a single-quoted string. As you can see from the screenshot alongside the code, $name is treated like normal text.

```
$name = 'Dolly';
// Single quotes: $name is treated as literal text
echo 'Hello, $name';
```

Hello, $name

If you replace the single quotes in the final line with double ones (see `quotes2.php`), $name is processed and its value is displayed onscreen.

```
$name = 'Dolly';
// Double quotes: $name is processed
echo "Hello, $name";
```

Hello, Dolly

In both examples, the string in the first line is in single quotes. What causes the variable to be processed is the fact that it's in a double-quoted string, not how it originally got its value.

Because double quotes are so useful in this way, many people use them all the time. Technically speaking, using double quotes when you don't need to process any variables is inefficient. My preference is to use single quotes unless the string contains variables.

Using escape sequences inside double quotes

Double quotes have another important effect: they treat escape sequences in a special way. All escape sequences are formed by placing a backslash in front of a character. Most of them are designed to avoid conflicts with characters that are used with variables, but three of them have special meanings: \n inserts a new line character, \r inserts a carriage return, and \t inserts a tab. Table 3-4 lists the main escape sequences supported by PHP.

Table 3-4. The main PHP escape sequences

Escape sequence	Character represented in double-quoted string
\"	Double quote
\n	New line
\r	Carriage return
\t	Tab
\\	Backslash
\$	Dollar sign
\{	Opening curly brace
\}	Closing curly brace
\[	Opening square bracket
\]	Closing square bracket

With the exception of \\, the escape sequences listed in Table 3-4, work only in double-quoted strings. If you use them in a single-quoted string, they will be treated as a literal backslash followed by the second character. A backslash at the end of the string always needs to be escaped. Otherwise, it's interpreted as escaping the following quotation mark. In a single-quoted string, escape single quotes and apostrophes with a backslash as described in the first half of this chapter.

Avoiding the need to escape quotes with heredoc syntax

Using a backslash to escape one or two quotation marks isn't a great burden, but I frequently see examples of code where backslashes seem to have run riot. It must be difficult to type, and it's certainly difficult to read. Moreover, it's totally unnecessary. The PHP **heredoc syntax** offers a relatively simple method of assigning text to a variable without any special handling of quotes.

The name "heredoc" is derived from here-document, a technique used in Unix and Perl programming to pass large amounts of text to a command.

Assigning a string to a variable using heredoc involves the following steps:

1. Type the assignment operator, followed by <<< and an identifier. The identifier can be any combination of letters, numbers, and the underscore, as long as it doesn't begin with a number. The same combination is used later to identify the end of the heredoc.

2. Begin the string on a new line. It can include both single and double quotes. Any variables will be processed in the same way as in a double-quoted string.

3. Place the identifier on a new line after the end of the string. Nothing else should be on the same line, except for a final semicolon. Moreover, the identifier *must* be at the beginning of the line; it *cannot* be indented.

It's a lot easier when you see it in practice. The following simple example can be found in `heredoc.php` in the files for this chapter:

```
$fish = 'whiting';
$mockTurtle = <<< Gryphon
"Will you walk a little faster?" said a $fish to a snail.
"There's a porpoise close behind us, and he's treading on my tail."
Gryphon;
echo $mockTurtle;
```

In this example, Gryphon is the identifier. The string begins on the next line, and *the double quotes are treated as part of the string*. Everything is included until you reach the identifier at the beginning of a new line. As you can see from the following screenshot, the heredoc displays the double quotes and processes the $fish variable.

To achieve the same effect without using the heredoc syntax, you need to add the double quotes and escape them like this:

```
$fish = 'whiting';
$mockTurtle = "\"Will you walk a little faster?\" said a $fish to a snail.
\"There's a porpoise close behind us, and he's treading on my tail.\""
echo $mockTurtle;
```

The heredoc syntax is mainly of value when you have a long string and/or lots of quotes. It's also useful if you want to assign an XML document or a lengthy section of HTML to a variable.

> PHP 5.3 introduced a related technique called **nowdoc syntax**, which treats variables in the same way as single quotes—in other words, as literal text. To create a string using nowdoc syntax, enclose the identifier in single quotes like this: <<< 'Gryphon'. The closing identifier does not use quotes. For more details, see http://docs.php.net/manual/en/language.types.string.php.

Creating arrays

As explained earlier, there are two types of arrays: indexed arrays, which use numbers to identify each element, and associative arrays, which use strings. You can build both types by assigning a value directly to each element. Let's take another look at the $book associative array:

```
$book['title'] = 'PHP Solutions: Dynamic Web Design Made Easy, Second Edition';
$book['author'] = 'David Powers';
$book['publisher'] = 'friends of ED';
$book['ISBN'] = '978-1-4302-3249-0';
```

To build an indexed array the direct way, use numbers instead of strings as the array keys. Indexed arrays are numbered from 0, so to build the $shoppingList array depicted in Figure 3-3, you declare it like this:

```
$shoppingList[0] = 'wine';
$shoppingList[1] = 'fish';
$shoppingList[2] = 'bread';
$shoppingList[3] = 'grapes';
$shoppingList[4] = 'cheese';
```

Although both are perfectly valid ways of creating arrays, it's a nuisance to have to type out the variable name each time, so there's a much shorter way of doing it. The method is slightly different for each type of array.

Using array() to build an indexed array

Instead of declaring each array element individually, you declare the variable name once and assign all the elements by passing them as a comma-separated list to array(), like this:

```
$shoppingList = array('wine', 'fish', 'bread', 'grapes', 'cheese');
```

> The comma must go outside the quotes, unlike American typographic practice. For ease of reading, I have inserted a space following each comma, but it's not necessary to do so.

PHP numbers each array element automatically, beginning from 0, so this creates exactly the same array as if you had numbered them individually. To add a new element to the end of the array, use a pair of empty square brackets like this:

```
$shoppingList[] = 'coffee';
```

PHP uses the next number available, so this becomes $shoppingList[5].

Using array() to build an associative array

The shorthand way of creating an associative array uses the => operator (an equal sign followed by a greater-than sign) to assign a value to each array key. The basic structure looks like this:

```
$arrayName = array('key1' => 'element1', 'key2' => 'element2');
```

So, this is the shorthand way to build the $book array:

```
$book = array(
  'title'     => 'PHP Solutions: Dynamic Web Design Made Easy, Second Edition',
  'author'    => 'David Powers',
  'publisher' => 'friends of ED',
  'ISBN'      => '978-1-4302-3249-0');
```

It's not essential to align the => operators like this, but it makes code easier to read and maintain.

Using array() to create an empty array

There are two reasons you might want to create an empty array, as follows:

- To create (or **initialize**) an array so that it's ready to have elements added to it inside a loop
- To clear all elements from an existing array

To create an empty array, simply use array() with nothing between the parentheses, like this:

```
$shoppingList = array();
```

The $shoppingList array now contains no elements. If you add a new one using $shoppingList[], it will automatically start numbering again at 0.

Multidimensional arrays

Array elements can store any data type, including other arrays. For instance, the $book array holds details of only one book. It might be more convenient to create an array of arrays—in other words, a multidimensional array—containing details of several books, like this:

```
$books = array(
  array(
    'title'     => 'PHP Solutions: Dynamic Web Design Made Easy, Second Edition',
    'author'    => 'David Powers',
    'publisher' => 'friends of ED',
    'ISBN'      => '978-1-4302-3249-0'),
  array(
    'title'     => 'Beginning PHP and MySQL: From Beginner to Professional, ➥
      Fourth Edition',
    'author'    => 'W. Jason Gilmore',
    'publisher' => 'Apress',
    'ISBN'      => 978-1-4302-3114-1')
  );
```

This example shows associative arrays nested inside an indexed array, but multidimensional arrays can nest either type. To refer to a specific element, use the key of both arrays, for example:

```
$books[1]['author']  // value is 'W. Jason Gilmore'
```

Working with multidimensional arrays isn't as difficult as it first looks. The secret is to use a loop to get to the nested array. Then, you can work with it in the same way as an ordinary array. This is how you handle the results of a database search, which is normally contained in a multidimensional array.

Using print_r() to inspect an array

To inspect the content of an array during testing, pass the array to `print_r()` like this (see `inspect_array1.php`):

```
print_r($books);
```

Load `inspect_array1.php` into a browser to see how `print_r()` outputs the contents of an ordinary array. The following screenshot shows how PHP displays a multidimensional array. Often, it helps to switch to Source view to inspect the details, as browsers ignore indenting in the underlying output. Alternatively, add HTML `<pre>` tags outside the PHP code block to preserve the indenting.

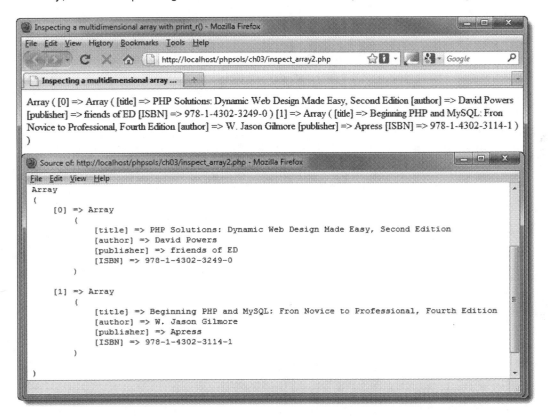

> Always use `print_r()` to inspect arrays; echo and print don't work. To display the contents of an array in a web page, use a `foreach` loop, as described later in this chapter.

The truth according to PHP

Decision-making in PHP conditional statements is based on the mutually exclusive Boolean values, `true` and `false`. If the condition equates to `true`, the code within the conditional block is executed. If `false`, it's ignored. Whether a condition is `true` or `false` is determined in one of these ways:

- A variable set explicitly to one of the Boolean values
- A value PHP interprets implicitly as `true` or `false`
- The comparison of two non-Boolean values

Explicit Boolean values

If a variable is assigned the value `true` or `false` and used in a conditional statement, the decision is based on that value. The keywords `true` and `false` are case-insensitive and must not be enclosed in quotes, for example:

```
$OK = false;
if ($OK) {
  // do something
}
```

The code inside the conditional statement won't be executed, because `$OK` is `false`.

Implicit Boolean values

Using implicit Boolean values provides a convenient shorthand, although it has the disadvantage—at least to beginners—of being less clear. Implicit Boolean values rely on PHP's relatively narrow definition of what it regards as `false`, namely:

- The case-insensitive keywords `false` and `null`
- Zero as an integer (`0`), a floating-point number (`0.0`), or a string (`'0'` or `"0"`)
- An empty string (single or double quotes with no space between them)
- An empty array
- SimpleXML objects created from empty tags

Everything else is `true`.

This definition explains why `"false"` (in quotes) is interpreted by PHP as `true`.

Making decisions by comparing two values

Most `true`/`false` decisions are based on a comparison of two values using **comparison operators**. Table 3-5 lists the comparison operators used in PHP.

Table 3-5. PHP comparison operators used for decision-making

Symbol	Name	Example	Result
`==`	Equality	`$a == $b`	Returns true if $a and $b are equal; otherwise, returns `false`.
`!=`	Inequality	`$a != $b`	Returns true if $a and $b are different; otherwise, returns `false`.

Symbol	Name	Example	Result
===	Identical	$a === $b	Determines whether $a and $b are identical. They must not only have the same value but also be of the same data type (e.g., both integers).
!==	Not identical	$a !== $b	Determines whether $a and $b are not identical (according to the same criteria as the previous operator).
>	Greater than	$a > $b	Returns true if $a is greater than $b.
>=	Greater than or equal to	$a >= $b	Returns true if $a is greater than or equal to $b.
<	Less than	$a < $b	Returns true if $a is less than $b.
<=	Less than or equal to	$a <= $b	Returns true if $a is less than or equal to $b.

When comparing two values, you must always use the equality operator (==), the identical operator (===), or their negative equivalents (!= and !==). A single equal sign assigns a value; it doesn't perform comparisons.

Testing more than one condition

Frequently, comparing two values is not enough. PHP allows you to set a series of conditions using **logical operators** to specify whether all, or just some, need to be fulfilled.

The most important logical operators in PHP are listed in Table 3-6. The logical Not operator applies to individual conditions rather than a series.

Table 3-6. The main logical operators used for decision-making in PHP

Symbol	Name	Example	Result
&&	And	$a && $b	Equates to true if both $a and $b are true.
||	Or	$a || $b	Equates to true if either $a or $b is true; otherwise, false.
!	Not	!$a	Equates to true if $a is *not* true.

Technically speaking, there is no limit to the number of conditions that can be tested. Each condition is considered in turn from left to right, and as soon as a defining point is reached, no further testing is carried out. When using &&, every condition must be fulfilled, so testing stops as soon as one turns out to be `false`. Similarly, when using `||`, only one condition needs to be fulfilled, so testing stops as soon as one turns out to be `true`.

```
$a = 10;
$b = 25;
if ($a > 5 && $b > 20) // returns true
if ($a > 5 || $b > 30) // returns true, $b never tested
```

You should always design your tests to provide the speediest result. If all conditions must be met, evaluate the one most likely to fail first. If only one condition needs to be met, evaluate the one most likely to succeed first. If a set of conditions needs to be considered as a group, enclose them in parentheses.

```
if (($a > 5 && $a < 8) || ($b > 20 && $b < 40))
```

PHP also uses *AND* in place of *&&* and *OR* in place of *||*. However, they aren't exact equivalents. To avoid problems, it's advisable to stick with *&&* and *||*.

Using the switch statement for decision chains

The `switch` statement offers an alternative to `if . . . else` for decision making. The basic structure looks like this:

```
switch(variable being tested) {
  case value1:
    statements to be executed
    break;
  case value2:
    statements to be executed
    break;
  default:
    statements to be executed
}
```

The `case` keyword indicates possible matching values for the variable passed to `switch()`. Each alternative value must be preceded by `case` and followed by a colon. When a match is made, every subsequent line of code is executed until the `break` keyword is encountered, at which point the `switch` statement comes to an end. A simple example follows:

```
switch($myVar) {
  case 1:
    echo '$myVar is 1';
    break;
  case 'apple':
  case 'banana':
  case 'orange':
    echo '$myVar is a fruit';
    break;
  default:
    echo '$myVar is neither 1 nor a fruit';
}
```

The main points to note about `switch` are as follows:

- The expression following the `case` keyword must be a number or a string.
- You can't use comparison operators with `case`. So `case > 100:` isn't allowed.
- Each block of statements should normally end with `break`, unless you specifically want to continue executing code within the `switch` statement.
- You can group several instances of the `case` keyword together to apply the same block of code to them.
- If no match is made, any statements following the `default` keyword are executed. If no default has been set, the `switch` statement exits silently and continues with the next block of code.

Using the ternary operator

The **ternary operator** (`?:`) is a shorthand method of representing a simple conditional statement. Its name comes from the fact that it normally uses three operands. The basic syntax looks like this:

```
condition ? value if true : value if false;
```

Here is an example of it in use:

```
$age = 17;
$fareType = $age > 16 ? 'adult' : 'child';
```

The second line tests the value of $age. If it's greater than 16, $fareType is set to `adult`, otherwise $fareType is set to `child`. The equivalent code using `if . . . else` looks like this:

```
if ($age > 16) {
  $fareType = 'adult';
} else {
  $fareType = 'child';
}
```

The `if . . . else` version is easier to read, but the conditional operator is more compact. Most beginners hate this shorthand, but once you get to know it, you'll realize how convenient it can be.

In PHP 5.3 and later, you can leave out the value between the question mark and the colon. This has the effect of assigning the value of the condition to the variable if the condition is true. In the preceding example, leaving out the value between the question mark and the colon results in $fareType being `true`:

```
$age = 17;
$fareType = $age > 16 ?: 'child'; // $fareType is true
```

In this case, the result is almost certainly not what you want. This shorthand is useful when the condition is a value that PHP treats as implicitly `true`, such as an array with at least one element.

> *Omitting the value between the question mark and the colon is a specialized use of the ternary operator and is not used in the scripts in this book. It is mentioned here only to alert you to its meaning if you come across it elsewhere.*

Creating loops

A **loop** is a section of code that is repeated over and over again until a certain condition is met. Loops are often controlled by setting a variable to count the number of iterations. By increasing the variable by one each time, the loop comes to a halt when the variable gets to a preset number. The other way loops are controlled is by running through each item of an array. When there are no more items to process, the loop stops.

Loops frequently contain conditional statements, so although they're very simple in structure, they can be used to create code that processes data in often sophisticated ways.

Loops using while and do . . . while

The simplest type of loop is called a while loop. Its basic structure looks like this:

```
while (condition is true) {
  do something
}
```

The following code displays every number from 1 through 100 in a browser (you can test it in while.php in the files for this chapter). It begins by setting a variable ($i) to 1 and then using the variable as a counter to control the loop, as well as display the current number onscreen.

```
$i = 1;  // set counter
while ($i <= 100) {
  echo "$i<br>";
  $i++; // increase counter by 1
}
```

> In the first half of this chapter, I warned against using variables with cryptic names. However, using $i as a counter is widely accepted convention. If $i is already in use, the normal practice is to use $j or $k as counters.

A variation of the while loop uses the keyword do and follows this basic pattern:

```
do {
  code to be executed
} while (condition to be tested);
```

The difference between a do . . . while loop and a while loop is that the code within the do block is executed at least once, even if the condition is never true. The following code (in dowhile.php) displays the value of $i once, even though it's greater than the maximum expected.

```
$i = 1000;
do {
  echo "$i<br>";
  $i++; // increase counter by 1
} while ($i <= 100);
```

The danger with while and do . . . while loops is forgetting to set a condition that brings the loop to an end or setting an impossible condition. When this happens, you create an infinite loop that either freezes your computer or causes the browser to crash.

The versatile for loop

The for loop is less prone to generating an infinite loop because you are required to declare all the conditions of the loop in the first line. The for loop uses the following basic pattern:

```
for (initialize loop; condition; code to run after each iteration) {
  code to be executed
}
```

The following code does exactly the same as the previous while loop, displaying every number from 1 to 100 (see forloop.php):

```
for ($i = 1; $i <= 100; $i++) {
  echo "$i<br>";
}
```

The three expressions inside the parentheses control the action of the loop (note that they are separated by semicolons, not commas):

- The first expression is executed before the loop starts. In this case, it sets the initial value of the counter variable $i to 1.
- The second expression sets the condition that determines how long the loop should continue to run. This can be a fixed number, a variable, or an expression that calculates a value.
- The third expression is executed at the end of each iteration of the loop. In this case, it increases $i by 1, but there is nothing stopping you from using bigger steps. For instance, replacing $i++ with $i+=10 in this example would display 1, 11, 21, 31, and so on.

Looping through arrays with foreach

The final type of loop in PHP is used exclusively with arrays. It takes two forms, both of which use temporary variables to handle each array element. If you only need to do something with the value of each array element, the foreach loop takes the following form:

```
foreach (array_name as temporary_variable) {
  do something with temporary_variable
}
```

The following example loops through the $shoppingList array and displays the name of each item (the code is in shopping_list.php):

```
$shoppingList = array('wine', 'fish', 'bread', 'grapes', 'cheese');
foreach ($shoppingList as $item) {
  echo $item . '<br>';
}
```

Although the preceding example uses an indexed array, you can also use the simple form of the foreach loop with an associative array. However, the alternative form of the foreach loop is of more use with associative arrays, because it gives access to both the key and value of each array element. It takes this slightly different form:

```
foreach (array_name as key_variable => value_variable) {
  do something with key_variable and value_variable
}
```

This next example uses the $book associative array from the "Creating arrays" section earlier in the chapter and incorporates the key and value of each element into a simple string, as shown in the screenshot (see book.php):

```
foreach ($book as $key => $value) {
  echo "The value of $key is $value<br>";
}
```

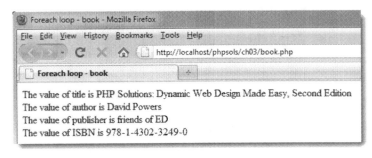

The foreach keyword is one word. Inserting a space between for and each doesn't work.

Breaking out of a loop

To bring a loop prematurely to an end when a certain condition is met, insert the break keyword inside a conditional statement. As soon as the script encounters break, it exits the loop.

To skip an iteration of the loop when a certain condition is met, use the continue keyword. Instead of exiting, it returns to the top of the loop and executes the next iteration. For example, the following loop skips the current element if $photo has no value:

```
foreach ($photos as $photo) {
  if (empty($photo)) continue;
  // code to display a photo
}
```

Modularizing code with functions

Functions offer a convenient way of running frequently performed operations. In addition to the large number of built-in functions, PHP lets you create your own. The advantages are that you write the code only once, rather than needing to retype it everywhere you need it. This not only speeds up your development time but also makes your code easier to read and maintain. If there's a problem with the code in your function, you update it in just one place rather than hunting through your entire site. Moreover, functions usually speed up the processing of your pages.

Building your own functions in PHP is very easy. You simply wrap a block of code in a pair of curly braces and use the `function` keyword to name your new function. The function name is always followed by a pair of parentheses. The following—admittedly trivial—example demonstrates the basic structure of a custom-built function (see `functions1.php` in the files for this chapter):

```
function sayHi() {
  echo 'Hi!';
}
```

Simply putting `sayHi();` in a PHP code block results in **Hi!** being displayed onscreen. This type of function is like a drone: it always performs exactly the same operation. For functions to be responsive to circumstances, you need to pass values to them as arguments (or parameters).

Passing values to functions

Let's say you want to adapt the `sayHi()` function so that it displays someone's name. You do this by inserting a variable between the parentheses in the function declaration. The same variable is then used inside the function to display whatever value is passed to the function. To pass more than one argument to a function, separate the variables with commas inside the opening parentheses. This is how the revised function looks (see `functions2.php`):

```
function sayHi($name) {
  echo "Hi, $name!";
}
```

You can now use this function inside a page to display the value of any variable passed to `sayHi()`. For instance, if you have an online form that saves someone's name in a variable called $visitor, and Ben visits your site, you give him the sort of personal greeting shown alongside by putting `sayHi($visitor);` in your page.

A downside of PHP's weak typing is that if Ben is being particularly uncooperative, he might type **5** into the form instead of his name, giving you not quite the type of high five you might have been expecting.

This illustrates why it's so important to check user input before using it in any critical situation.

It's also important to understand that variables inside a function remain exclusive to the function. This example should illustrate the point (see `functions3.php`):

```
function doubleIt($number) {
  $number *= 2;
  echo "$number<br>";
}
$number = 4;
doubleIt($number);
echo $number;
```

If you view the output of this code in a browser, you may get a very different result from what you expect. The function takes a number, doubles it, and displays it onscreen. Line 5 of the script assigns the value 4 to $number. The next line calls the function and passes it $number as an argument. The function processes $number and displays 8. After the function comes to an end, $number is displayed onscreen by echo. This time, it will be 4 and not 8.

This example demonstrates that the variable $number that has been declared inside the function is limited in **scope** to the function itself. The variable called $number in the main script is totally unrelated to the one inside the function. To avoid confusion, it's a good idea to use variable names in the rest of your script that are different from those used inside functions. This isn't always possible, so it's useful to know that functions work like little black boxes and don't normally have any direct impact on the values of variables in the rest of the script.

Returning values from functions

There's more than one way to get a function to change the value of a variable passed to it as an argument, but the most important method is to use the return keyword and to assign the result either to the same variable or to another one. This can be demonstrated by amending the doubleIt() function like this:

```
function doubleIt($number) {
  return $number *= 2;
}
$num = 4;
$doubled = doubleIt($num);
echo "\$num is: $num<br>";
echo "\$doubled is: $doubled";
```

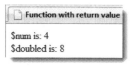

You can test this code in functions4.php. The result is shown in the screenshot following the code. This time, I have used different names for the variables to avoid confusing them. I have also assigned the result of doubleIt($num) to a new variable. The benefit of doing this is that I now have available both the original value and the result of the calculation. You won't always want to keep the original value, but it can be very useful at times.

Where to locate custom-built functions

If your custom-built function is in the same page as it's being used, it doesn't matter where you declare the function; it can be either before or after it's used. It's a good idea, however, to store functions together, either at the top or the bottom of a page. This makes them easier to find and maintain.

Functions that are used in more than one page are best stored in an external file and included in each page. Including external files with include() and require() is covered in detail in Chapter 4. When functions are stored in external files, you must include the external file *before* calling any of its functions.

PHP quick checklist

This chapter contains a lot of information that is impossible to absorb in one sitting, but hopefully the first half has given you a broad overview of how PHP works. Here's a reminder of some of the main points:

- Always give PHP pages the correct filename extension, normally .php.
- Enclose all PHP code between the correct tags: <?php and ?>.
- Avoid the short form of the opening tag: <?. Using <?php is more reliable.
- It's recommended to omit the closing PHP tag in files that contain only PHP code.
- PHP variables begin with $ followed by a letter or the underscore character.
- Choose meaningful variable names, and remember they're case-sensitive.
- Use comments to remind you what your script does.
- Remember that numbers don't require quotes, but strings (text) do.
- You can use single or double quotes, but the outer pair must match.
- Use a backslash to escape quotes of the same type inside a string.
- To store related items together, use an array.
- Use conditional statements, such as if and if . . . else, for decision-making.
- Simplify repetitive tasks with loops.
- Use functions to perform preset tasks.
- Display PHP output with echo or print.
- Inspect the content of arrays with print_r().
- With most error messages, work *backward* from the position indicated.
- Keep smiling—and remember that PHP is *not* difficult.

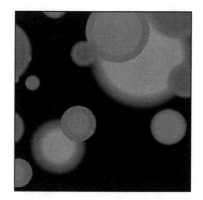

Chapter 4

Lightening Your Workload with Includes

The ability to include the contents of one file inside another is one of the most powerful features of PHP. It's also one of the easiest to implement.

Most pages in a website share common elements, such as a header, footer, and navigation menu. You can alter the look of those elements throughout the site by changing the style rules in an external style sheet. But CSS has only limited ability to change the content of page elements. If you want to add a new item to your menu, you need to edit the HTML in every page that displays it. Web authoring tools, such as Dreamweaver and Expression Web, have templating systems that automatically update all pages connected to a master file, but you still need to upload all the files to your remote server.

That's not necessary with PHP, which supports server-side includes (SSI). A **server-side include** is an external file, which contains dynamic code or HTML (or both) that you want to incorporate into multiple pages. PHP merges the content into each web page on the server. Because each page uses the same external file, you can update a menu or other common element by editing and uploading a single file—a great timesaver.

As you work through this chapter, you'll learn how PHP includes work, where PHP looks for include files, and how to prevent error messages when an include file can't be found. In addition, you'll learn to do some cool tricks with PHP, such as creating a random image generator.

This chapter covers the following topics:

- Understanding the different include commands
- Telling PHP where to find your include files
- Using PHP includes for common page elements
- Protecting sensitive information in include files
- Automating a "you are here" menu link
- Generating a page's title from its filename
- Automatically updating a copyright notice
- Displaying random images complete with captions

- Handling errors with include files
- Changing your web server's `include_path`

Figure 4-1 shows how four elements of a page benefit from a little PHP magic with include files.

Page title is generated automatically

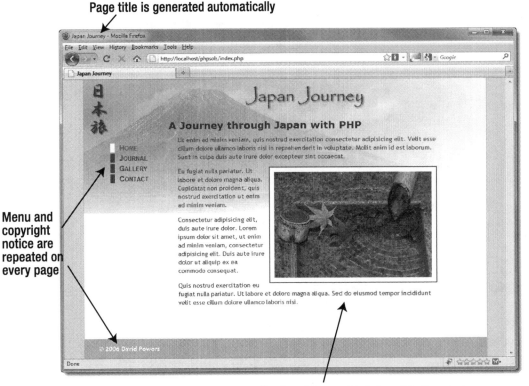

Menu and copyright notice are repeated on every page

Random image adds interest to the page

Figure 4-1. Identifying elements of a static web page that could be improved with PHP

The menu and copyright notice appear on each page. By turning them into include files, you can make changes to just one page and see them propagate throughout the site. With PHP conditional logic, you can also get the menu to display the correct style to indicate which page the visitor is on. Similar PHP wizardry automatically changes the date on the copyright notice and the text in the page title. PHP can also add variety by displaying a random image. JavaScript solutions fail if JavaScript is disabled, but with PHP, your script is guaranteed to work all the time. The images don't need to be the same size; a PHP function inserts the correct width and height attributes in the `<img>` tag. And with a little extra scripting, you can add a caption to each image.

Including code from external files

The ability to include code from other files is a core part of PHP. All that's necessary is to use one of PHP's include commands and tell the server where to find the file.

Introducing the PHP include commands

PHP has four commands that can be used to include code from an external file, namely:

- `include()`
- `include_once()`
- `require()`
- `require_once()`

They all do basically the same thing, so why have four?

The fundamental difference is that `include()` attempts to continue processing a script, even if the external file is missing, whereas `require()` is used in the sense of mandatory: if the file is missing, the PHP engine stops processing and throws a fatal error. In practical terms, this means you should use `include()` if your page would remain usable even without the contents of the external file. Use `require()` if the page depends on the external file.

The other two commands, `include_once()` and `require_once()`, work the same way, but they prevent the same file from being included more than once in a page. This is particularly important when including files that define functions or classes. Attempting to define a function or class more than once in a script triggers a fatal error. So, using `include_once()` or `require_once()` ensures that functions and classes are defined only once, even if the script tries to include the external file more than once, as might happen if the commands are in conditional statements.

So, which should you use? I recommend using `include()` for external files that aren't mission critical, and `require_once()` for files that define functions and classes.

Where PHP looks for include files

To include an external file, you pass the file path to one of the four include commands as a string—in other words, the file path must be in quotes (single or double, it doesn't matter). The file path can be either absolute or relative to the current document. For example, any of the following will work (as long as the target file exists):

```
include('includes/menu.inc.php');
include('C:/xampp/htdocs/phpsols/includes/menu.inc.php');
include('/Applications/MAMP/htdocs/phpsols/includes/menu.inc.php');
```

> PHP accepts forward slashes in Windows file paths.

Using parentheses with the include commands is optional, so the following would also work:

```
include 'includes/menu.inc.php';
include 'C:/xampp/htdocs/phpsols/includes/menu.inc.php';
include '/Applications/MAMP/htdocs/phpsols/includes/menu.inc.php';
```

When using a relative file path, it's recommended to use `./` to indicate that the path begins in the current folder. So, it's more efficient to rewrite the first example like this:

```
include('./includes/menu.inc.php'); // path begins in current folder
```

71

What *doesn't* work is using a file path relative to the site root like this:

```
include('/includes/menu.inc.php'); // THIS WILL NOT WORK
```

If PHP can't find the file, it also looks in the include_path, as defined in your PHP configuration. I'll return to this subject later in this chapter. Before that, let's put PHP includes to practical use. For the time being, I recommend you use file paths relative to the current document.

PHP Solution 4-1: Moving the menu and footer to include files

Let's convert the page shown in Figure 4-1 to use include files. Because the menu and footer appear on every page of the Japan Journey site, they're prime candidates for include files. Here's the code for the body of the page with the menu and footer highlighted in bold.

Listing 4-1. The static version of index.php

```
<body>
<div id="header">
  <h1>Japan Journey</h1>
</div>
<div id="wrapper">
  <ul id="nav">
    <li><a href="index.php" id="here">Home</a></li>
    <li><a href="blog.php">Journal</a></li>
    <li><a href="gallery.php">Gallery</a></li>
    <li><a href="contact.php">Contact</a></li>
  </ul>
  <div id="maincontent">
    <h2>A journey through Japan with PHP</h2>
    <p>One of the benefits of using PHP . . .</p>
    <div id="pictureWrapper">
      <img src="images/water_basin.jpg" alt="Water basin at Ryoanji temple" ➥
        width="350" height="237" class="picBorder">
    </div>
    <p>Ut enim ad minim veniam, quis nostrud . . .</p>
    <p>Eu fugiat nulla pariatur. Ut labore et dolore . . .</p>
    <p>Sed do eiusmod tempor incididunt ullamco . . .</p>
    <p>Quis nostrud exercitation eu fugiat nulla . . .</p>
  </div>
  <div id="footer">
    <p>&copy; 2006&8211;2010 David Powers</p>
  </div>
</div>
</body>
```

1. Copy index_01.php from the ch04 folder to the phpsols site root, and rename it index.php. If you are using a program like Dreamweaver that offers to update the page links, don't update them. The relative links in the download file are correct. Check that the CSS and images are displaying properly by loading index.php into a browser. It should look the same as Figure 4-1.

2. Copy blog.php, gallery.php, and contact.php from the ch04 folder to your site root folder. These pages won't display correctly in a browser yet because the necessary include files still haven't been created. That'll soon change.

3. In index.php, highlight the nav unordered list as shown in bold in Listing 4-1, and cut (Ctrl+X/Cmd+X) it to your computer clipboard.

4. Create a new file called menu.inc.php in the includes folder. Remove any code inserted by your editing program; the file must be completely blank.

5. Paste (Ctrl+V/Cmd+V) the code from your clipboard into menu.inc.php and save the file. The contents of menu.inc.php should look like this:

```
<ul id="nav">
  <li><a href="index.php" id="here">Home</a></li>
  <li><a href="blog.php">Journal</a></li>
  <li><a href="gallery.php">Gallery</a></li>
  <li><a href="contact.php">Contact</a></li>
</ul>
```

6. Don't worry that your new file doesn't have a DOCTYPE declaration or any <html>, <head>, or <body> tags. The other pages that include the contents of this file will supply those elements.

7. Open index.php, and insert the following in the space left by the nav unordered list:

    <?php include('./includes/menu.inc.php'); ?>

    This uses a document-relative path to menu.inc.php. The ./ at the beginning of the path indicates explicitly that the path starts in the current folder and is more efficient.

8. Save index.php, and load the page into a browser. It should look exactly the same as before. Although the menu and the rest of the page are coming from different files, PHP merges them before sending any output to the browser.

Don't forget that PHP code needs to be processed by a web server. If you have stored your files in a subfolder of your server's document root called phpsols, you should access index.php using the URL http://localhost/phpsols/index.php. See "Where to locate your PHP files" in Chapter 2 if you need help finding the server's document root.

9. Do the same with the footer <div>. Cut the lines highlighted in bold in Listing 4-1, and paste them into a blank file called footer.inc.php in the includes folder. Then insert the command to include the new file in the gap left by the footer <div>:

    <?php include('./includes/footer.inc.php'); ?>

10. Save all pages, and reload index.php in your browser. Again, it should look identical to the original page. If you navigate to other pages in the site, the menu and footer should appear on every page. The code in the include files is now serving all pages.

11. To prove that the menu is being drawn from a single file, change the text in the **Journal** link in
    menu.inc.php like this:

    ```
    <li><a href="blog.php">Blog</a></li>
    ```

12. Save menu.inc.php and reload the site. The change is reflected on all pages. You can check
    your code against index_02.php, menu.inc_01.php, and footer.inc_01.php in the ch04
    folder.

As Figure 4-2 shows, there's a problem with the code at the moment. Even when you navigate away from
the home page, the style that indicates which page you're on doesn't change (it's controlled by the here
ID in the <a> tag).

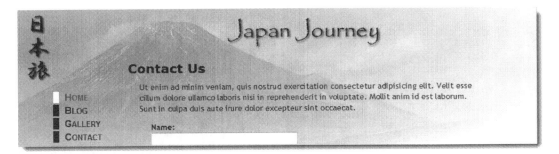

Figure 4-2. The current page indicator still points to the Home page.

Fortunately, that's easily fixed with a little PHP conditional logic. Before doing so, let's take a look at how
the web server and the PHP engine handle include files.

Choosing the right filename extension for includes

As you have just seen, an include file can contain raw HTML. When the PHP engine encounters an include
command, it stops processing PHP at the beginning of the external file and resumes again at the end. If
you want the external file to use PHP code, the code must be enclosed in PHP tags. As a consequence of
this behavior, an include file can have any filename extension.

A common convention is to use .inc as the filename extension to make it clear that the file is intended to
be included in another file. However, most servers treat .inc files as plain text. This poses a security risk
if the file contains sensitive information, such as the username and password to your database. If the file
is stored within your website's root folder, anyone who discovers the name of the file can simply type the
URL in a browser address bar, and the browser will obligingly display all your secret details!

On the other hand, any file with a .php extension is automatically sent to the PHP engine for parsing
before it's sent to the browser. So, as long as your secret information is inside a PHP code block and in a
file with a .php extension, it won't be exposed. That's why many developers use .inc.php as a double
extension for PHP includes. The .inc part reminds you that it's an include file, but servers are only
interested in the .php on the end, which ensures that all PHP code is correctly parsed.

Since it's common practice to store include files in a separate folder—often called includes—you could
argue that .inc.php is superfluous. Which naming convention you choose is up to you, but using .inc on
its own is the least secure.

PHP Solution 4-2: Testing the security of includes

This solution demonstrates the difference between using .inc and .inc.php as the filename extension for an include file. Use index.php and menu.inc.php from the previous section. Alternatively, use index_02.php and menu.inc_01.php from the ch04 folder. If you use the download files, remove the _02 and _01 from the filenames before using them.

1. Rename menu.inc.php to menu.inc, and edit index.php accordingly to include it:

    ```php
    <?php include('./includes/menu.inc'); ?>
    ```

2. Load index.php into a browser. You should see no difference.

3. Amend the code inside menu.inc to store a password inside a PHP variable like this:

    ```
    <ul id="nav">
      <li><a href="index.php" id="here">Home</a></li>
      <?php $password = 'topSecret'; ?>
      <li><a href="blog.php">Blog</a></li>
      <li><a href="gallery.php">Gallery</a></li>
      <li><a href="contact.php">Contact</a></li>
    </ul>
    ```

4. Reload the page. As Figure 4-3 shows, the password remains hidden in the source code. Although the include file doesn't have a .php filename extension, its contents have been merged with index.php, so the PHP code is processed.

Figure 4-3. There's no output from the PHP code, so only the HTML is sent to the browser.

5. Now load menu.inc directly in the browser. Figure 4-4 shows what happens.

Figure 4-4. Loading menu.inc directly in a browser exposes the PHP code.

Neither the server nor the browser knows how to deal with an .inc file, so the entire contents are displayed onscreen: raw HTML, your secret password, everything . . .

6. Change the name of the include file back to menu.inc.php, and load it directly into your browser by adding .php to the end of the URL you used in the previous step. This time, you should see an unordered list of links. Inspect the browser's source view. The PHP isn't exposed.

7. Remove the password PHP code you added to menu.inc.php in step 3, and change the include command inside index.php back to its original setting like this:

    ```php
    <?php include('./includes/menu.inc.php'); ?>
    ```

PHP Solution 4-3: Automatically indicating the current page

Now that you have seen the difference between using .inc and .php as filename extensions, let's fix the problem with the menu not indicating the current page. The solution involves using PHP to find out the filename of the current page and then using conditional statements to insert an ID in the corresponding <a> tag.

Continue working with the same files. Alternatively, use index_02.php, contact.php, gallery.php, blog.php, menu.inc_01.php, and footer.inc_01.php from the ch04 folder, and remove the _01 and _02 from any filenames.

1. Open menu.inc.php. The code currently looks like this:

    ```html
    <ul id="nav">
        <li><a href="index.php" id="here">Home</a></li>
        <li><a href="blog.php">Blog</a></li>
        <li><a href="gallery.php">Gallery</a></li>
        <li><a href="contact.php">Contact</a></li>
    </ul>
    ```

    The style that indicates the current page is controlled by the id="here" highlighted in line 2. You need PHP to insert id="here" into the blog.php <a> tag if the current page is blog.php, into the gallery.php <a> tag if the page is gallery.php, and into the contact.php <a> tag if the page is contact.php.

Hopefully, you have got the hint by now—you need an if statement (see "Making decisions," in Chapter 3) in each `<a>` tag. Line 2 needs to look like this:

```
<li><a href="index.php" <?php if ($currentPage == 'index.php') { ↪
echo 'id="here"'; } ?>>Home</a></li>
```

The other links should be amended in a similar way. But how does $currentPage get its value? You need to find out the filename of the current page.

2.   Leave menu.inc.php to one side for the moment, and create a new PHP page called get_filename.php. Insert the following code between a pair of PHP tags (alternatively, use get_filename.php in the ch04 folder):

```
echo $_SERVER['SCRIPT_FILENAME'];
```

3.   Save get_filename.php, and view it in a browser. On a Windows system, you should see something like the following screenshot. (The version in the ch04 folder contains the code for this step and the next, together with text indicating which is which.)

On Mac OS X, you should see something similar to this:

$_SERVER['SCRIPT_FILENAME'] comes from one of PHP's built-in superglobal arrays, and it always gives you the absolute file path for the current page. What you need now is a way of extracting just the filename.

4.   Amend the code in the previous step like this:

```
echo basename($_SERVER['SCRIPT_FILENAME']);
```

5.   Save get_filename.php, and click the Reload button in your browser. You should now see just the filename: get_filename.php.

The built-in PHP function basename() takes a file path as an argument and extracts the filename. So, there you have it—a way of finding the filename of the current page.

6. Amend the code in `menu.inc.php` like this (the changes are highlighted in bold):

```php
<?php $currentPage = basename($_SERVER['SCRIPT_FILENAME']); ?>
<ul id="nav">
  <li><a href="index.php" <?php if ($currentPage == 'index.php') { ↵
    echo 'id="here"';} ?>>Home</a></li>
  <li><a href="blog.php" <?php if ($currentPage == 'blog.php') { ↵
    echo 'id="here"';} ?>>Blog</a></li>
  <li><a href="gallery.php" <?php if ($currentPage == 'gallery.php') { ↵
    echo 'id="here"';} ?>>Gallery</a></li>
  <li><a href="contact.php" <?php if ($currentPage == 'contact.php') { ↵
    echo 'id="here"';} ?>>Contact</a></li>
</ul>
```

> *Make sure you get the combination of single and double quotes correct. Although enclosing the value of attributes, such as id, in quotes is optional in HTML, it's considered best practice to use them. Since I used double quotes around here, I wrapped the string `'id="here"'` in single quotes. I could have written `"id=\"here\""`, but a mixture of single and double quotes is easier to read.*

7. Save `menu.inc.php`, and load `index.php` into a browser. The menu should look no different from before. Use the menu to navigate to other pages. This time, as shown in Figure 4-5, the border alongside the current page should be white, indicating your location within the site. If you inspect the page's source view in the browser, you'll see that the `here` ID has been automatically inserted into the correct link.

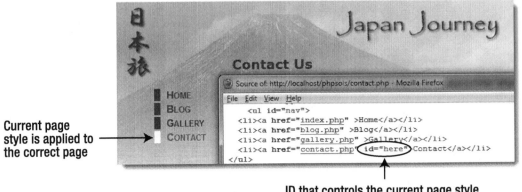

Current page style is applied to the correct page

ID that controls the current page style has been inserted in the correct link

Figure 4-5. Conditional code in the include file produces different output for each page.

If necessary, compare your code with `menu.inc_02.php` in the `ch04` folder.

PHP Solution 4-4: Generating a page's title from its filename

Now that you know how to find the filename of the current page, you might also find it useful to automate the `<title>` tag of each page. This solution uses `basename()` to extract the filename and then uses PHP string functions to format the name ready for insertion in the `<title>` tag.

This works only with filenames that tell you something about the page's contents, but since that's a good practice anyway, it's not really a restriction. Although the following steps use the Japan Journey website, you can try this out with any page.

1. Create a new PHP file called `title.inc.php`, and save it in the `includes` folder.

2. Strip out any code inserted by your script editor, and type in the following code:

```php
<?php
$title = basename($_SERVER['SCRIPT_FILENAME'], '.php');
```

> *Because this file contains only PHP code, do not add a closing PHP tag at the end. The closing PHP tag is optional when nothing follows the PHP code in the same file. Omitting the tag helps avoid a common error with include files known as "headers already sent." You'll learn more about this error in PHP Solution 4-8.*

The `basename()` function used in PHP Solution 4-3 takes an optional second argument: a string containing the filename extension preceded by a leading period. Adding the second argument extracts the filename and strips the filename extension from it. So, this code finds the filename of the current page, strips the `.php` filename extension, and assigns the result to a variable called `$title`.

3. Open `contact.php` and include `title.inc.php` by typing this above the DOCTYPE:

```php
<?php include('./includes/title.inc.php'); ?>
```

4. Amend the `<title>` tag like this:

```php
<title>Japan Journey<?php echo "&#8212;{$title}"; ?></title>
```

This uses echo to display `&#8212;` (the numerical entity for an em dash) followed by the value of `$title`. Because the string is enclosed in double quotes, PHP displays the value of `$title`. The variable `$title` has been enclosed in curly braces because there is no space between the em dash and `$title`. Although not always necessary, it's a good idea to enclose variables in braces when using them without any whitespace in a double-quoted string, as it makes the variable clear to you and the PHP engine. The first few lines of your page should look like this:

```
1  <?php include('./includes/title.inc.php'); ?>
2  <!DOCTYPE HTML>
3  <html>
4  <head>
5  <meta charset=utf-8">
6  <title>Japan Journey<?php echo "&#8212;{$title}"; ?></title>
```

Normally, nothing should precede the DOCTYPE declaration in a web page. However, this doesn't apply to PHP code, as long as it doesn't send any output to the browser. The code in title.inc.php only assigns a value to $title, so the DOCTYPE declaration remains the first output the browser sees.

5. Save both pages, and load contact.php into a browser. The filename without the .php extension has been added to the browser title bar and tab, as shown in Figure 4-6.

Figure 4-6. Once you extract the filename, you can generate the page title dynamically.

6. Not bad, but what if you prefer an initial capital letter for the part of the title derived from the filename? Nothing could be simpler. PHP has a neat little function called ucfirst(), which does exactly that (the name is easy to remember once you realize that uc stands for "uppercase"). Add another line to the code in step 2 like this:

```php
<?php
$title = basename($_SERVER['SCRIPT_FILENAME'], '.php');
$title = ucfirst($title);
```

If you're new to programming, this might look confusing, but it's actually quite simple once you analyze it: the first line of code after the PHP tag gets the filename, strips the .php off the end, and stores it as $title. The next line takes the value of $title, passes it to ucfirst() to capitalize the first letter, and stores the result back in $title. So, if the filename is contact.php, $title starts out as contact, but by the end of the following line, it has become Contact.

You can shorten the code by combining both lines into one like this:

$title = ucfirst(basename($_SERVER['SCRIPT_FILENAME'], '.php'));

When you nest functions like this, PHP processes the innermost one first and passes the result to the outer function. It makes your code shorter, but it's not so easy to read.

7. A drawback with this technique is that filenames consist of only one word—at least they should. If you've picked up bad habits from Windows and Mac OS X permitting spaces in

filenames, get out of them immediately. Spaces are not allowed in URLs, which is why most web design software replaces spaces with %20. You can get around this problem, though, by using an underscore.

Change the filename of contact.php to contact_us.php.

8. Amend the code in title.inc.php like this:

```php
<?php
$title = basename($_SERVER['SCRIPT_FILENAME'], '.php');
$title = str_replace('_', ' ', $title);
$title = ucwords($title);
```

The middle line uses a function called str_replace() to look for every underscore and replace it with a space. The function takes three arguments: the character(s) you want to replace, the replacement character(s), and the string you to change.

> You can also use str_replace() to remove character(s) by using an empty string (a pair of quotes with nothing between them) as the second argument. This replaces the string in the first argument with nothing, effectively removing it.

Instead of ucfirst(), the final line of code uses the related function ucwords(), which gives each word an initial cap.

9. Save title.inc.php, and load the renamed contact_us.php into a browser. Figure 4-7 shows the result.

Figure 4-7. The underscore has been removed, and both words have been given initial caps.

10. Change the name of the file back to contact.php, and reload the file into a browser. The script in title.inc.php still works. There are no underscores to replace, so str_replace() leaves the value of $title untouched, and ucwords() converts the first letter to uppercase, even though there's only one word.

11. The home page of the Japan Journey site is called index.php. As Figure 4-8 shows, applying the current solution to this page doesn't seem quite right.

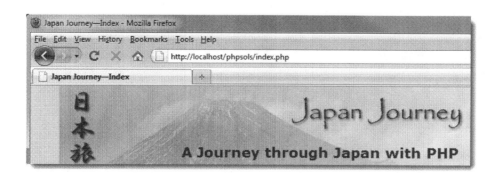

Figure 4-8. Generating the page title from index.php produces an unsatisfactory result.

There are two solutions: either don't apply this technique to such pages or use a conditional statement (an if statement) to handle special cases. For instance, to display **Home** instead of **Index**, amend the code in title.inc.php like this:

```php
<?php
$title = basename($_SERVER['SCRIPT_FILENAME'], '.php');
$title = str_replace('_', ' ', $title);
if ($title == 'index') {
  $title = 'home';
}
$title = ucwords($title);
```

The first line of the conditional statement uses two equal signs to check the value of $title. The following line uses a single equal sign to assign the new value to $title. If the page is called anything other than index.php, the line inside the curly braces is ignored, and $title keeps its original value.

PHP is case-sensitive, so this solution works only if "index" is all lowercase. To do a case-insensitive comparison, change the fourth line of the preceding code like this:

```php
if (strtolower($title) == 'index') {
```

The function strtolower() converts a **string to lower**case—hence its name—and is frequently used to make case-insensitive comparisons. The conversion to lowercase is not permanent, because strtolower($title) isn't assigned to a variable; it's only used to make the comparison. To make a change permanent, you need to assign the result back to a variable as in the final line, when ucwords($title) is assigned back to $title.

To convert a string to uppercase, use strtoupper().

---

12. Save title.inc.php, and reload index.php into a browser. The page title now looks more natural, as shown in Figure 4-9.

Figure 4-9. The conditional statement changes the title on index.php to **Home**.

13. Navigate back to contact.php, and you'll see that the page title is still derived correctly from the page name.

14. There's one final refinement you should make. The PHP code inside the <title> tag relies on the existence of the variable $title, which won't be set if there's a problem with the include file. Before attempting to display the contents of a variable that comes from an external source, it's always a good idea to check that it exists, using a function called isset(). Wrap the echo command inside a conditional statement, and test for the variable's existence like this:

```
<title>Japan Journey<?php if (isset($title)) {echo "&#8212;{$title}";} ➥
?></title>
```

If $title doesn't exist, the rest of the code is ignored, leaving the default site title, **Japan Journey**.

You can check your code against title.inc.php and an updated version of index.php in index_03.php in the ch04 folder.

Creating pages with changing content

So far, you've used PHP to generate different output depending on the page's filename. The next two solutions generate content that changes independently of the filename: a copyright notice that updates the year automatically on January 1 and a random image generator.

PHP Solution 4-5: Automatically updating a copyright notice

At the moment, the copyright notice in footer.inc.php contains only static HTML. This PHP solution shows how to use the date() function to generate the current year automatically. The code also specifies the first year of copyright and uses a conditional statement to determine whether the current year is different. If it is, both years are displayed.

Continue working with the files from PHP Solution 4-4. Alternatively, use index_03.php and footer.inc_01.php from the ch04 folder, and remove the numbers from the filenames. If using the files from the ch04 folder, make sure you have copies of title.inc.php and menu.inc.php in the includes folder.

1. Open `footer.inc.php`. It contains the following HTML:

```
<div id="footer">
  <p>&copy; 2006&#8211;2010 David Powers</p>
</div>
```

   The `&#8211;` between the dates is the numeric entity for an en dash.

2. The advantage of using an include file is that you can update the copyright notice throughout the site by changing this one file. However, it would be much more efficient to increment the year automatically, doing away with the need for updates altogether.

   The PHP `date()` function takes care of that very neatly. Change the code in the paragraph like this:

```
<p>&copy; 2006&#8211;<?php echo date('Y'); ?> David Powers</p>
```

   This replaces the second date and displays the current year using four digits. Make sure you pass an uppercase *Y* as the argument to `date()`.

3. Save `footer.inc.php` and load `index.php` into a browser. The copyright notice at the foot of the page should look the same as before—unless, of course, you're reading this in 2011 or later, in which case the current year will be displayed.

   Like most copyright notices, this covers a range of years, indicating when a site was first launched. Since the first date is in the past, it can be hard-coded. But what if you're creating a new website? You don't want to have to break away from the New Year revelries just to update the copyright notice. There needs to be a better way. Thanks to PHP, you can party to your heart's content on New Year's Eve.

4. To display a range of years, you need to know the start year and the current year. If both years are the same, display only the current year; if they're different, display both with an en dash between them. It's a simple `if. . .else` situation. Change the code in the paragraph in `footer.inc.php` like this:

```
<p>&copy;
<?php
$startYear = 2006;
$thisYear = date('Y');
if ($startYear == $thisYear) {
  echo $startYear;
} else {
  echo "{$startYear}&#8211;{$thisYear}";
}
?>
David Powers</p>
```

   As in PHP Solution 4-4, I've used curly braces around the variables in the `else` clause because they're in a double-quoted string that contains no whitespace.

5. Save `footer.inc.php`, and reload `index.php` in a browser. The copyright notice should look the same as before.

6. Change the argument passed to the date() function to a lowercase *y* like this:

    ```
    $thisYear = date('y');
    ```

7. Save footer.inc.php, and click the Reload button in your browser. The second year is displayed using only the last two digits, as shown in the following screenshot:

This should serve as a reminder that PHP is case-sensitive. Uppercase Y and lowercase y produce different results with the date() function. Forgetting about case sensitivity is one of the most common causes of errors in PHP.

8. Change the argument passed to date() back to an uppercase *Y*. Set the value of $startYear to the current year, and reload the page. This time, you should see only the current year displayed.

    You now have a fully automated copyright notice. The finished code is in footer.inc_02.php in the ch04 folder.

PHP Solution 4-6: Displaying a random image

Displaying a random image is very easy. All you need is a list of available images, which you store in an indexed array (see "Creating arrays" in Chapter 3). Since indexed arrays are numbered from 0, you can select one of the images by generating a random number between 0 and one less than the length of the array. All accomplished in a few lines of code . . .

Continue using the same files. Alternatively, use index_03.php from the ch04 folder and rename it index.php. Since index_03.php uses title.inc.php, menu.inc.php, and footer.inc.php, make sure all three files are in your includes folder. The images are already in the images folder.

1. Create a blank PHP page in the includes folder, and name it random_image.php. Insert the following code (it's also in random_image_01.php in the ch04 folder):

    ```php
    <?php
    $images = array('kinkakuji', 'maiko', 'maiko_phone', 'monk', 'fountains', ➥
      'ryoanji', 'menu', 'basin');
    $i = rand(0, count($images)-1);
    $selectedImage = "images/{$images[$i]}.jpg";
    ```

    This is the complete script: an array of image names minus the .jpg filename extension (there's no need to repeat shared information—they're all JPEG), a random number generator, and a string that builds the correct pathname for the selected file.

    To generate a random number within a range, you pass the minimum and maximum numbers as arguments to the function rand(). Since there are eight images in the array, you need a number between 0 and 7. The simple way to do this would be to use rand(0, 7) — simple, but inefficient. Every time you change the $images array, you need to count how many elements it contains and change the maximum number passed to rand().

It's much easier to get PHP to count them for you, and that's exactly what the count() function does: it counts the number of elements in an array. You need a number one less than the number of elements in the array, so the second argument passed to rand() becomes count($images)-1, and the result is stored in $i.

The random number is used in the final line to build the correct pathname for the selected file. The variable $images[$i] is embedded in a double-quoted string with no whitespace separating it from surrounding characters, so it's enclosed in curly braces. Arrays start at 0, so if the random number is 1, $selectedImage is images/maiko.jpg.

If you're new to PHP, you may find it difficult to understand code like this:

```php
$i = rand(0, count($images)-1);
```

All that's happening is that the second argument passed to rand() is an expression rather than a number. If it makes it easier for you to follow, rewrite the code like this:

```php
$numImages = count($images); // $numImages is 8
$max = $numImages - 1;       // $max is 7
$i = rand(0, $max);          // $i = rand(0, 7)
```

2. Open index.php, and include random_image.php by inserting the command in the same code block as title.inc.php like this:

```php
<?php include('./includes/title.inc.php');
include('./includes/random_image.php'); ?>
```

Since random_image.php doesn't send any direct output to the browser, it's safe to put it above the DOCTYPE.

3. Scroll down inside index.php, and locate the code that displays the image in the maincontent <div>. It looks like this:

```html
<div id="pictureWrapper">
  <img src="images/basin.jpg" alt="Water basin at Ryoanji temple" ➥
    width="350" height="237" class="picBorder">
</div>
```

Instead of using images/basin.jpg as a fixed image, replace it with $selectedImage. All the images have different dimensions, so delete the width and height attributes, and use a generic alt attribute. The code in step 3 should now look like this:

```html
<div id="pictureWrapper">
  <img src="<?php echo $selectedImage; ?>" alt="Random image" ➥
    class="picBorder">
</div>
```

4. Save both random_image.php and index.php, and load index.php into a browser. The image should now be chosen at random. Click the Reload button in your browser, and you should see a variety of images, as shown in Figure 4-10.

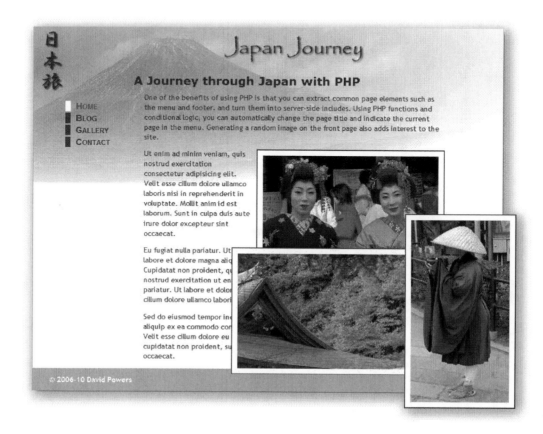

Figure 4-10. Storing image filenames in an indexed array makes it easy to display a random image.

You can check your code against index_04.php and random_image_01.php in the ch04 folder.

This is a simple and effective way of displaying a random image, but it would be much better if you could add a caption and set the width and height for different sized images dynamically.

PHP Solution 4-7: Adding a caption to the random image

This solution uses a multidimensional array—or an array of arrays—to store the filename and caption for each image. If you find the concept of a multidimensional array difficult to understand in abstract terms, think of it as a large box with a lot of envelopes inside, and inside each envelope are the photos and captions. The box is the top-level array, and the envelopes inside are the subarrays.

The images are different sizes, but PHP conveniently provides a function called getimagesize(). Guess what it does.

This PHP solution builds on the previous one, so continue working with the same files.

1. Open random_image.php, and change the code like this:

```php
<?php
$images = array(
    array('file'    => 'kinkakuji',
          'caption' => 'The Golden Pavilion in Kyoto'),
    array('file'    => 'maiko',
          'caption' => 'Maiko&#8212;trainee geishas in Kyoto'),
    array('file'    => 'maiko_phone',
          'caption' => 'Every maiko should have one&#8212;a mobile, of course'),
    array('file'    => 'monk',
          'caption' => 'Monk begging for alms in Kyoto'),
    array('file'    => 'fountains',
          'caption' => 'Fountains in central Tokyo'),
    array('file'    => 'ryoanji',
          'caption' => 'Autumn leaves at Ryoanji temple, Kyoto'),
    array('file'    => 'menu',
          'caption' => 'Menu outside restaurant in Pontocho, Kyoto'),
    array('file'    => 'basin',
          'caption' => 'Water basin at Ryoanji temple, Kyoto')
);
$i = rand(0, count($images)-1);
$selectedImage = "images/{$images[$i]['file']}.jpg";
$caption = $images[$i]['caption'];
```

Although the code looks complicated, it's an ordinary indexed array that contains eight items, each of which is an associative array containing definitions for 'file' and 'caption'. The definition of the multidimensional array forms a single statement, so there are no semicolons until line 19. The closing parenthesis on that line matches the opening one on line 2. All the array elements in between are separated by commas. The deep indenting isn't necessary, but it makes the code a lot easier to read.

The variable used to select the image also needs to be changed, because $images[$i] no longer contains a string, but an array. To get the correct filename for the image, you need to use $images[$i]['file']. The caption for the selected image is contained in $images[$i]['caption'] and stored in a shorter variable.

2. You now need to amend the code in index.php to display the caption like this:

```php
<div id="pictureWrapper">
  <img src="<?php echo $selectedImage; ?>" alt="Random image" ➥
    class="picBorder">
  <p id="caption"><?php echo $caption; ?></p>
</div>
```

3. Save `index.php` and `random_image.php`, and load `index.php` into a browser. Most images will look fine, but there's an ugly gap to the right of the image of the trainee geisha with a mobile phone, as shown in Figure 4-11.

Ut enim ad minim veniam, quis nostrud exercitation consectetur adipisicing elit. Velit esse cillum dolore ullamco laboris nisi in reprehenderit in voluptate. Mollit anim id est laborum. Sunt in culpa duis aute irure dolor excepteur sint occaecat.

Eu fugiat nulla pariatur. Ut labore et dolore magna aliqua. Cupidatat non proident, quis nostrud exercitation ut enim ad minim veniam. Quis nostrud exercitation eu fugiat nulla pariatur. Ut labore et dolore magna aliqua. Sed do eiusmod tempor incididunt velit esse cillum dolore ullamco laboris nisi.

Every maiko should have one—a mobile, of course

Sed do eiusmod tempor incididunt ullamco laboris nisi consectetur adipisicing elit. Ut

Figure 4-11. The long caption protrudes beyond the image and shifts it too far left.

4. Add the following code at the end of `random_image.php`:

```
if (file_exists($selectedImage) && is_readable($selectedImage)) {
  $imageSize = getimagesize($selectedImage);
}
```

The `if` statement uses two functions, `file_exists()` and `is_readable()`, to make sure `$selectedImage` not only exists but also that it's accessible (it may be corrupted or have the wrong permissions). These functions return Boolean values (`true` or `false`), so they can be used directly as part of the conditional statement.

The single line inside the `if` statement uses the function `getimagesize()` to get the image's dimensions and stores them in `$imageSize`. You'll learn more about `getimagesize()` in Chapter 8. At the moment, you're interested in the following two pieces of information:

- `$imageSize[0]`: The width of the image in pixels
- `$imageSize[3]`: A string containing the image's height and width formatted for inclusion in an `<img>` tag

5. First of all, let's fix the code in the `<img>` tag. Change it like this:

```
<img src="<?php echo $selectedImage; ?>" alt="Random image" ➥
  class="picBorder" <?php echo $imageSize[3]; ?>>
```

This inserts the correct `width` and `height` attributes inside the `<img>` tag.

89

6. Although this sets the dimensions for the image, you still need to control the width of the caption. You can't use PHP inside an external style sheet, but there's nothing stopping you from creating a `<style>` block in the `<head>` of index.php. Insert the following code just before the closing `</head>` tag.

```php
<?php
if (isset($imageSize)) {
?>
<style>
#caption {
  width: <?php echo $imageSize[0]; ?>px;
}
</style>
<?php } ?>
```

This code consists of only nine short lines, but it's an odd mix of PHP and HTML. Let's start with the first three lines and the final one. If you strip away the PHP tags and replace the HTML `<style>` block with a comment, this is what you end up with:

```php
if (isset($imageSize)) {
  // do something if $imageSize has been set
}
```

In other words, if the variable `$imageSize` hasn't been set (defined), the PHP engine ignores everything between the curly braces. It doesn't matter that most of the code between the braces is HTML and CSS. If `$imageSize` hasn't been set, the PHP engine skips to the closing brace, and the intervening code isn't sent to the browser.

> *Many inexperienced PHP coders wrongly believe that they need to use echo or print to create HTML output inside a conditional statement. As long as the opening and closing braces match, you can use PHP to hide or display sections of HTML like this. It's a lot neater and involves a lot less typing than using echo all the time.*

If `$imageSize` has been set, the `<style>` block is created, and `$imageSize[0]` is used to set the correct width for the paragraph that contains the caption.

7. Save random_image.php and index.php, and reload index.php into a browser. Click the Reload button until the image of the trainee geisha with the mobile phone appears. This time, it should look like Figure 4-12. If you view the browser's source code, the style rule uses the correct width for the image.

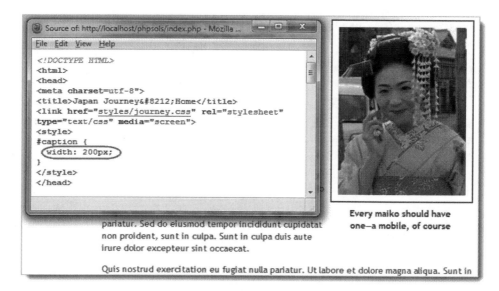

Figure 4-12. The ugly gap is removed by creating a style rule directly related to the image size.

If the caption still protrudes, make sure there's no gap between the closing PHP tag and px in the `<style>` block. CSS does not permit whitespace between the value and unit of measurement.

8. The code in `random_image.php` and the code you have just inserted prevent errors if the selected image can't be found, but the code that displays the image is devoid of similar checks. Temporarily change the name of one of the images, either in `random_image.php` or in the `images` folder. Reload `index.php` several times. Eventually, you should see an error message like that in Figure 4-13. It looks very unprofessional.

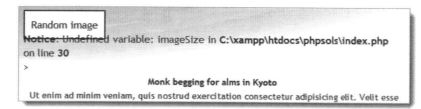

Figure 4-13. An error in an include file can destroy the look of your page.

9. The conditional statement at the foot of `random_image.php` sets `$imageSize` only if the selected image both exists and is readable, so if `$imageSize` has been set, you know it's all systems go. Add the opening and closing blocks of a conditional statement around the `<div>` that displays the image in `index.php` like this:

```
<?php if (isset($imageSize)) { ?>
<div id="pictureWrapper">
```

```
        <img src="<?php echo $selectedImage; ?>" alt="Random image" ➥
          class="picBorder" <?php echo $imageSize[3]; ?> />
        <p id="caption"><?php echo $caption; ?></p>
      </div>
      <?php } ?>
```

Images that exist will display normally, but you'll avoid any embarrassing error messages in case of a missing or corrupt file—a much more professional look. Don't forget to restore the name of the image you changed in the previous step. You can check your code against index_05.php and random_image_02.php in the ch04 folder.

Preventing errors with include files

Many hosting companies turn off error reporting for notices, so you probably wouldn't be aware of the problem shown in Figure 4-13 if you did all your testing on your remote server. However, it's important to eliminate all errors before deploying PHP pages on the Internet. Just because you can't see the error message, doesn't mean your page is OK.

Pages that use a server-side technology such as PHP deal with a lot of unknowns, so it's wise to code defensively, checking values before using them. This section describes measures you can take to prevent and troubleshoot errors with include files.

Checking the existence of variables

The lesson that can be drawn from PHP Solution 4-7 is that you should always use isset() to verify the existence of a variable that comes from an include file and wrap any code that uses it in a conditional statement. In this particular case, you know there's no image to display if $imageSize doesn't exist, so the pictureWrapper <div> is dropped. However, in other cases, you might be able to assign a default value to the variable like this:

```
if (!isset($someVariable)) {
  $someVariable = default value;
}
```

This uses the logical Not operator (see Table 3-6 in Chapter 3) to check if $someVariable has not been set. If $someVariable doesn't exist, it's assigned a default value, which can then be used later in your script. If it does exist, the code inside the conditional statement is skipped, and the original value is used.

Checking whether a function or class has been defined

Include files are frequently used to define custom functions or classes. Attempting to use a function or class that hasn't been defined triggers a fatal error. To check whether a function has been defined, pass the name of the function as a string to function_exists(). When passing the name of the function to function_exists(), omit the parentheses at the end of function name. For example, you check whether a function called doubleIt() has been defined like this:

```
if (function_exists('doubleIt')) {
  // use doubleIt()
}
```

To check whether a class has been defined, use `class_exists()` in the same way, passing a string containing the class name as the argument:

```
if (class_exists('MyClass')) {
  // use MyClass
}
```

Assuming you want to use the function or class, a more practical approach is to use a conditional statement to include the definition file if the function or class hasn't already been defined. For example, if the definition for `doubleIt()` is in a file called `utilities.inc.php`:

```
if (!function_exists('doubleIt')) {
  require_once('includes/utilities.inc.php');
}
```

Temporarily turning on error messages

Error messages are there to help the developer. Unfortunately, displaying them in a live website exposes information that could be useful to an attacker, which is why it's now common for hosting companies to turn off the display of error messages. Depending on the nature of the error, all you might see when accessing the page is a blank screen. This isn't very helpful when you need to find out what's wrong with a page that worked perfectly in your local testing environment.

Fortunately, it's easy to turn on the display of error messages temporarily for an individual page with `ini_set()`, which can be used to override some directives in `php.ini`, the server's PHP configuration file. Add the following code at the top of the page that's causing problems:

```
<?php ini_set('display_errors', '1'); ?>
```

Upload the file to your remote server, and reload the page in your browser. You should then be able to read the error message onscreen. Fix the problem, and test the page again. If the page displays correctly, remove the extra line of code.

> If you still see a blank screen, it means there's a syntax error in your PHP code. Using `ini_set()` has no effect if there's a parse error.

The most common cause of errors is forgetting to upload the include file to your remote server. Even if you have uploaded all the files, you might get an error message telling you that you don't have permission to access an include file. This is likely to happen in the following circumstances:

- **The server is running in safe mode**: If your hosting company is running PHP in a highly restricted way, you will see a warning that a safe mode restriction is in effect. Run `phpinfo()`, and check the value of `safe_mode_include_dir` in the Core section. All your include files must be stored in this location. Adjust your site structure accordingly. Safe mode is scheduled to be removed from the next major version of PHP, so this problem is less common.

- **The** `open_basedir` **directive has been set**: The `open_basedir` directive restricts your ability to include or open files. This should affect you only when the include file is outside your web server's document root. The warning message produced by PHP lists the allowed path(s). Move your include file to a permitted location, and adjust the path in the include command accordingly.

Dealing with missing include files

Assuming your include files are working normally on your remote server, that's probably all the error checking you need. However, if your remote server displays error messages, you should take steps to suppress them in case an include file is accidentally deleted or corrupted.

A rather crude, but effective way is to use the PHP **error control operator** (@), which suppresses error messages associated with the line of code in which it's used. You place the error control operator either at the beginning of the line or directly in front of the function or command that you think might generate an error like this:

```
@ include('./includes/random_image.php');
```

The problem with the error control operator is that it hides errors, rather than working around them. It's only one character, so it's easy to forget you have used it. Consequently, you can waste a lot of time looking for errors in the wrong part of your script. If you use the error control operator, the @ mark should be the first thing you remove when troubleshooting a problem.

The other drawback is that you need to use the error control operator in every line that might generate an error message, because it affects only the current line.

A better way of suppressing error messages in a live website is to turn off the `display_errors` directive in the web server's configuration. The most effective way is to edit `php.ini` if your hosting company gives you control over its settings. Alternatively, if your server runs on Apache and you have permission to change the configuration with an `.htaccess` file, you should add the following command to the `.htaccess` file in your server root folder:

```
php_flag display_errors Off
```

If neither option is available, add the following line at the top of any script that uses include files:

```
<?php ini_set('display_errors', '0'); ?>
```

All the techniques suggested so far only suppress error messages if an include file can't be found. If a page would be meaningless without the include file, you should redirect the user to an error page if the include file is missing.

One way to do so is to throw an exception like this:

```
$file = 'includes/menu.inc.php';
if (file_exists($file) && is_readable($file)) {
  include($file);
} else {
  throw new Exception("$file can't be found");
}
```

When using code that might throw an exception, you need to wrap it in a try block and create a catch block to handle the exception (see "Handling Exceptions" in Chapter 3). The next PHP solution shows how to do this.

PHP Solution 4-8: Redirecting when an include file can't be found

This PHP solution shows how to redirect users to a different page if an include file can't be found. If you have designed and tested your site thoroughly, this technique should not be necessary on most pages that use include files. However, this is by no means a pointless exercise. It demonstrates several important features of PHP: how to throw and catch exceptions and how to redirect to another page. As you'll see from the following instructions, redirection isn't always straightforward. This PHP solution shows how to overcome the most common problem.

Continue working with index.php from PHP Solution 4-7. Alternatively, use index_05.php from the ch04 folder.

1. Copy error.php from the ch04 folder to the site root. Don't update the links in the page if your editing program prompts you to do so. This is a static page that contains a generic error message and links back to the other pages.

2. Open index.php in your editing program. The navigation menu is the most indispensible include file, so edit the include command in index.php like this:

```
$file = 'includes/menu.inc.php';
if (file_exists($file) && is_readable($file)) {
  include($file);
} else {
  throw new Exception("$file can't be found");
}
```

Storing the path of the include file in a variable like this avoids the need to retype it four times, reducing the likelihood of spelling mistakes.

3. To redirect the user to another page, you use the header() function. However, redirection doesn't work if any output has been sent to the browser before you call header(). Unless there's a syntax error, the PHP engine normally processes a page from the top outputting the HTML until it reaches a problem. This means that output will have already begun by the time the PHP engine gets to this code. To prevent this from happening, start the try block before any output is generated. (This actually won't work, but bear with me, because it demonstrates an important point.)

Scroll to the top of the page, and edit the opening PHP code block like this:

```
<?php try {
  include('./includes/title.inc.php');
  include('./includes/random_image.php'); ?>
```

This opens the try block.

4. Scroll down to the bottom of the page, and add the following code after the closing `</html>` tag:

```
<?php } catch (Exception $e) {
  header('Location: http://localhost/phpsols/error.php');
} ?>
```

This closes the `try` block and creates a `catch` block to handle the exception. The code in the catch block uses `header()` to redirect the user to `error.php`.

The `header()` function is used to send any HTTP headers to the browser. It takes as its argument a string containing the header and its value separated by a colon. In this case, it uses the `Location` header to redirect the browser to the page specified by the URL following the colon. Adjust the URL to match your own setup if necessary.

5. Save `index.php`, and test the page in a browser. It should display as normal.

6. Change the value of `$file`, the variable you created in step 2, to point to a nonexistent include file, such as `menu.php`.

7. Save `index.php`, and reload it in your browser. Instead of being redirected to `error.php`, you're likely to see the following message:

This error message is probably responsible for more heads being banged against keyboards than any other. (I, too, bear the scars.) As mentioned earlier, the `header()` function cannot be used if output has been sent to the browser. So, what's happened?

The answer is in the error message, but it's not immediately obvious. It says the error happened on line 54, which is where the `header()` function is called. What you really need to know is where the output was generated. That information is buried here:

```
(output started at C:\xampp\htdocs\phpsols\index.php:9)
```

The number 9 after the colon is the line number. So, what's on line 9 of `index.php`?

```
1  <?php try {
2      include('./includes/title.inc.php');
3      include('./includes/random_image.php'); ?>
4  <!DOCTYPE HTML>
5  <html>
6  <head>
7  <meta charset=utf-8">
8  <title>Japan Journey
9  <?php if (isset($title)) {echo "&#8212;{$title}";} ?>
```

As you can see from the preceding screenshot, line 9 uses `echo` to display the value of `$title`. Because there's no error in the code up to this point, the PHP engine has already output the HTML. Once that has happened, `header()` can't redirect the page. However, even if you remove this line of PHP, the error message simply reports that output started on the next line that contains a PHP block. What's happening is that the web server is outputting all the HTML following the `DOCTYPE`, but the PHP engine needs to process a PHP code block before it can report a line number. This poses the problem of how to redirect a page after output has been sent to the browser. Fortunately, PHP provides the answer by allowing you to store the output in a buffer (the web server's memory).

8. Edit the code block at the top of `index.php` like this:

```php
<?php ob_start();
try {
  include('./includes/title.inc.php');
  include('./includes/random_image.php'); ?>
```

The `ob_start()` function turns on output buffering, preventing any output from being sent to the browser before the `header()` function is called.

9. The PHP engine automatically flushes the buffer at the end of the script, but it's better to do so explicitly. Edit the PHP code block at the foot of the page like this:

```php
<?php } catch (Exception $e) {
  ob_end_clean();
  header('Location: http://localhost/phpsols/error.php');
}
ob_end_flush();
?>
```

Two different functions have been added here. When redirecting to another page, you don't want the HTML stored in the buffer. So, inside the `catch` block, a call is made to `ob_end_clean()`, which turns off the buffer and discards its contents.

However, if an exception isn't thrown, you want to display the contents of the buffer, so `ob_end_flush()` is called at the end of the page after both the `try` and `catch` blocks. This flushes the contents of the buffer and sends it to the browser.

10. Save `index.php` and reload it in a browser. This time, you should be redirected to the error page:

97

11. Change the value of $file back to includes/menu.inc.php, and save index.php. When you click the **Home** link in the error page, index.php should display normally.

You can compare your code with index_06.php in the ch04 folder.

Redirecting the page when an error occurs improves the user experience, but you should also log the error. You'll learn how to do that in Chapter 6.

Choosing where to locate your include files

A useful feature of PHP include files is they can be located anywhere, as long as the page with the include command knows where to find them. Include files don't even need to be inside your web server root. This means that you can protect include files that contain sensitive information, such as passwords, in a private directory (folder) that cannot be accessed through a browser. So, if your hosting company provides a storage area outside your server root, you should seriously consider locating some, if not all, of your include files there.

An include command expects either a relative path or a fully qualified path. If neither is given, PHP automatically looks in the include_path specified in your PHP configuration. The following section explains how to change the folders PHP searches automatically for include files.

Adjusting your include_path

The advantage of locating include files in a folder specified in your web server's include_path is that you don't need to worry about getting the relative or absolute path correct. All you need is the filename. This can be very useful if you use a lot of includes or you have a site hierarchy several levels deep. There are three ways to change the include_path:

- **Edit the value in** php.ini: If your hosting company gives you access to php.ini, this is the best way to add a custom includes folder.
- **Use** .htaccess: If your remote web server runs on Apache and you are allowed to change the configuration with an .htaccess file, this is a good alternative.
- **Use** set_include_path(): Use this only if the previous options are not available to you, because it affects the include_path only for the current file.

The value of the include_path for your web server is listed in the Core section of the configuration details when you run phpinfo(). It normally begins with a period, which indicates the current folder, and is followed by the absolute path of each folder to be searched. On Linux and Mac OS X, each path is separated by a colon. On Windows, the separator is a semicolon.

On a Linux or Mac server your existing include_path directive might look like this:

.:/php/PEAR

On a Windows server, the equivalent would look like this:

.;C:\php\PEAR

Editing the include_path in php.ini

In php.ini, locate the include_path directive. To add a folder called includes in your own site, add a colon or semicolon—depending on your server's operating system—at the end of the existing value followed by the absolute path to the includes folder.

On a Linux or Mac server, use a colon like this:

```
include_path=".:/php/PEAR:/home/mysite/public_html/includes"
```

On a Windows server, use a semicolon:

```
include_path=".;C:\php\PEAR;C:\sites\mysite\www\includes"
```

Using .htaccess to change the include_path

If you can use .htaccess to change the server's configuration, you can adjust the include_path on Linux or Mac like this:

```
php_value include_path ".:/php/PEAR:/home/mysite/public_html/includes"
```

The command is the same on Windows, except that you separate the paths with a semicolon:

```
php_value include_path ".;C:\php\PEAR;C:\sites\mysite\www\includes"
```

> Do not insert an equal sign between include_path and the list of path names. Because .htaccess overrides the default include_path, make sure you copy the existing value from phpinfo() and add the new path to it.

If you're testing locally in XAMPP in a subfolder of the server root called phpsols, you can create an .htaccess file for this book like this:

```
php_value include_path ".;C:\xampp\php\PEAR;C:\xampp\htdocs\phpsols\includes"
```

If you're testing locally in MAMP, the file should look like this:

```
php_value include_path ".:/Applications/MAMP/bin/php5.3/lib/php:/Applications/ ↪
MAMP/htdocs/phpsols/includes"
```

These values are correct at the time of this writing, but you should check the actual value of include_path in your own setup and adjust the path accordingly if it's different.

> The best way to create an .htaccess file on your local computer is to use a dedicated web development program, such as Dreamweaver or Zend Studio. If you create an .htaccess file in a text editor on a Mac, it will disappear without trace in Finder. Mac OS X has the infuriating habit of hiding files with filenames that begin with a dot. Dedicated web development programs are more understanding.

Using set_include_path()

Although set_include_path() affects only the current page, you can easily create a code snippet and paste it into pages where you want to use it. PHP also makes it easy to get the existing include_path and combine it with the new one in a platform-neutral way.

Store the new path in a variable and then combine it with the existing include path like this:

```
$includes_folder = '/home/mysite/public_html/includes';
set_include_path(get_include_path() . PATH_SEPARATOR . $includes_folder);
```

It looks as though three arguments are being passed to set_include_path(), but it's only one, because the three elements are joined by the concatenation operator (a period), not commas. As you can imagine, get_include_path() gets the existing include_path. PATH_SEPARATOR is a PHP constant that automatically inserts a colon or semicolon depending on the operating system. The result is a string that contains both the original and new paths.

The problem with this approach is that the path to the new includes folder won't be the same on your remote and local testing servers. Fortunately, you can fix that with a conditional statement. The superglobal variable $_SERVER['HTTP_HOST'] contains the domain name of the website. So, if your domain is www.example.com, you can set the correct path for each server like this:

```
if ($_SERVER['HTTP_HOST'] == 'www.example.com') {
  $includes_folder = '/home/example/public_html/includes';
} else {
  $includes_folder = 'C:/xampp/htdocs/phpsols/includes';
}
set_include_path(get_include_path() . PATH_SEPARATOR . $includes_folder);
```

Using set_include_path() is probably not worthwhile for small websites that don't use many include files. Where it comes in really useful is if you use a third-party PHP library, such as Zend Framework (http://framework.zend.com/) or Symfony (www.symfony-project.org), which relies heavily on include files.

Why can't I use site-root-relative links with PHP includes?

Well, you can and you can't. For the sake of clarity, I'll begin by explaining the distinction between links relative to the document and to the site root. When you click a link to go to another page, the path in the `<a>` tag tells the browser how to get from the current page to the next one. Most web authoring tools specify the path relative to the current document. If the target page is in the same folder, just the filename is used. If it's one level higher than the current page, the filename is preceded by ../. This is known as a **document-relative path** or link. If you have a site with many levels of folders, this type of link can be difficult to understand—at least for humans.

The other type of link always begins with a forward slash, which is shorthand for the site root. The advantage of a **site-root-relative path** is that it doesn't matter how deep the current page is in the site hierarchy, the forward slash at the beginning guarantees the web server will start looking from the top level of the site. Although site-root-relative links are much easier to read, PHP include commands can't handle them. You must use a document-relative path, an absolute path, or specify the includes folder in your include_path directive.

Having said that, you can convert a site-root-relative path to an absolute one by concatenating the superglobal variable $_SERVER['DOCUMENT_ROOT'] to the beginning of the path like this:

```
include($_SERVER['DOCUMENT_ROOT'] . '/includes/filename.php');
```

Most servers support $_SERVER['DOCUMENT_ROOT'], but you should check the **PHP Variables** section at the bottom of the configuration details displayed by phpinfo() to make sure.

Now, this is the point that tends to confuse many people. Although you can't use a site-root-relative link to include a file, the links *inside* the include file should normally be relative to the site root. This is because an include file can be included at any level of the site hierarchy, so document-relative links break when a file is included at a different level.

> *You might have noticed a contradiction between the previous paragraph and the document-relative links in menu.inc.php. They have been deliberately left like that because, unless you have created a virtual host, the site root is localhost, not phpsols. This is a disadvantage of testing a site in a subfolder of the web server's document root. The Japan Journey site used throughout this book has only one level, so the document-relative links work. When developing a site that uses multiple levels of folders, use site-root-relative links inside your include files, and consider setting up a virtual host for testing (see Chapter 2 for details).*

Security considerations with includes

Include files are a very powerful feature of PHP. With that power come some serious security risks. As long as the external file is accessible, PHP includes it and incorporates any code into the main script. But, as mentioned in the previous section, include files can be located anywhere. Technically speaking, they can even be on a different server. However, this was considered such a security risk, a new configuration directive, allow_url_include, was introduced in PHP 5.2. The default setting is Off, so it's now impossible to include files from a different server unless you have complete control over your server's configuration. Unlike include_path, the allow_url_include directive cannot be overridden except by the server administrator.

Even if you control both servers yourself, you should never include a file from a different server. It's possible for an attacker to spoof the address and try to execute a malicious script on your site.

Chapter review

This chapter has plunged you headlong into the world of PHP, using includes, arrays, and multidimensional arrays. It has shown you how to extract the name of the current page, display a random image, and get the image's dimensions. You have also learned how to throw and catch exceptions and to redirect to a different page. There's a lot to absorb, so don't worry if it doesn't all sink in the first time. The more you use PHP, the more familiar you'll become with the basic techniques. In the next chapter, you'll learn how PHP processes input from online forms and will use that knowledge to send feedback from a website to your email inbox.

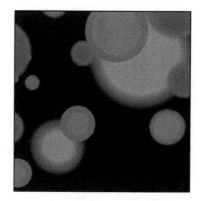

Chapter 5

Bringing Forms to Life

Forms lie at the very heart of working with PHP. You use forms for logging in to restricted pages, registering new users, placing orders with online stores, entering and updating information in a database, sending feedback . . . The list goes on. The same principles lie behind all these uses, so the knowledge you gain from this chapter will have practical value in most PHP applications. To demonstrate how to process information from a form, I'm going to show you how to gather feedback from visitors to your site and send it to your mailbox.

Unfortunately, user input can expose your site to malicious attacks. It's important to always check data submitted from a form before accepting it. Although HTML5 form elements validate user input in the most recent browsers, you still need to check the data on the server. HTML5 validation helps legitimate users avoid submitting a form with errors, but malicious users can easily sidestep checks performed in the browser. Server-side validation is not optional, but essential. The PHP solutions in this chapter show you how to filter out or block anything suspicious or dangerous. It doesn't take a lot of effort to keep marauders at bay. It's also a good idea to preserve user input and redisplay it if the form is incomplete or errors are discovered.

These solutions build a complete mail processing script that can be reused in different forms, so it's important to read them in sequence.

In this chapter, you'll learn about the following:

- Understanding how user input is transmitted from an online form
- Displaying errors without losing user input
- Validating user input and preventing spam with a CAPTCHA
- Sending user input by email

How PHP gathers information from a form

Although HTML contains all the necessary tags to construct a form, it doesn't provide any means to process the form when submitted. For that, you need a server-side solution, such as PHP.

The Japan Journey website contains a simple feedback form (see Figure 5-1). Other elements—such as radio buttons, check boxes, and drop-down menus—will be added later.

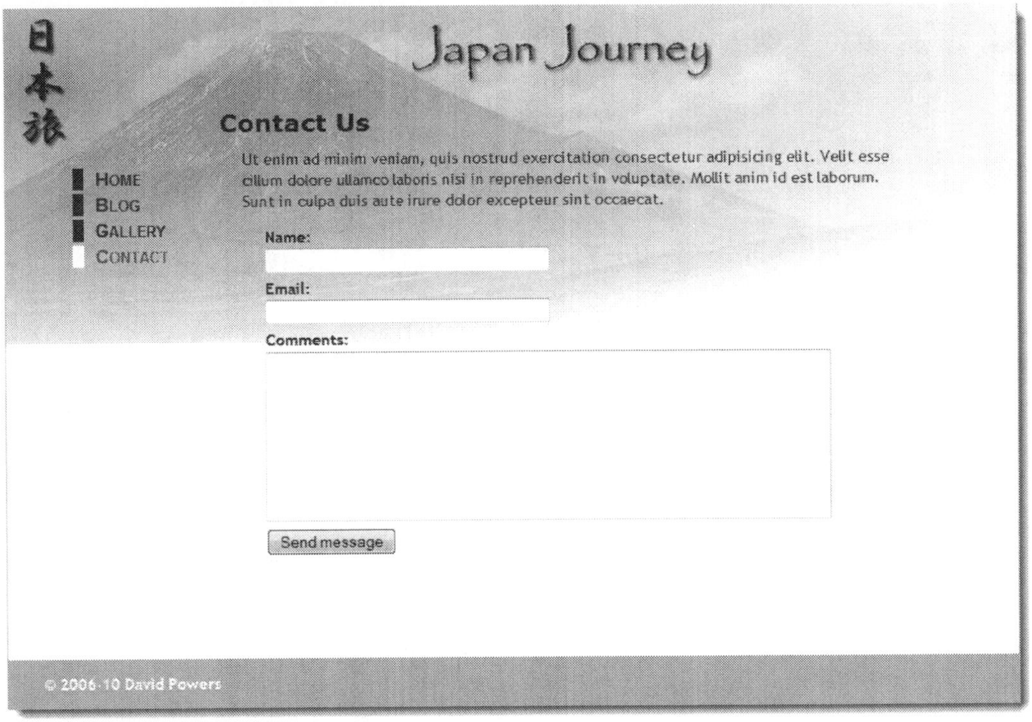

Figure 5-1. Processing a feedback form is one of the most popular uses of PHP.

First, let's take a look at the HTML code for the form (it's in contact_01.php in the ch05 folder):

```
<form id="feedback" method="post" action="">
  <p>
    <label for="name">Name:</label>
    <input name="name" id="name" type="text" class="formbox">
  </p>
  <p>
    <label for="email">Email:</label>
    <input name="email" id="email" type="text" class="formbox">
  </p>
  <p>
    <label for="comments">Comments:</label>
    <textarea name="comments" id="comments" cols="60" rows="8"></textarea>
  </p>
  <p>
    <input name="send" id="send" type="submit" value="Send message">
  </p>
</form>
```

The first thing to notice about this code is that the `<input>` and `<textarea>` tags contain both `name` and `id` attributes set to the same value. The reason for this duplication is that HTML, CSS, and JavaScript all refer to the `id` attribute. Form processing scripts, however, rely on the `name` attribute. So, although the `id` attribute is optional, you *must* use the `name` attribute for each element that you want to be processed.

Two other things to notice are the `method` and `action` attributes inside the opening `<form>` tag. The `method` attribute determines how the form sends data. It can be set to either `post` or `get`. The `action` attribute tells the browser where to send the data for processing when the submit button is clicked. If the value is left empty, as here, the page attempts to process the form itself.

> *I have deliberately avoided using any of the new HTML5 form features, such as `type="email"` and the `required` attribute. This makes it easier to test the PHP server-side validation scripts. After testing, update your forms to use the HTML5 validation features.*

Understanding the difference between post and get

The best way to demonstrate the difference between the `post` and `get` methods is with a real form. If you completed the previous chapter, you can continue working with the same files.

Otherwise, the `ch05` folder contains a complete set of files for the Japan Journey site with all the code from the last chapter incorporated in them. Make sure that the `includes` folder contains `title.inc.php`, `footer.inc.php` and `menu.inc.php`. Copy `contact_01.php` to the site root, and rename it `contact.php`.

1. Locate the opening `<form>` tag in `contact.php`, and change the value of the `method` attribute from `post` to `get` like this:

   ```
   <form id="feedback" method="get" action="">
   ```

2. Save `contact.php`, and load the page in a browser. Type your name, email address, and a short message into the form, and click **Send message**.

3. Look in the browser address bar. You should see the contents of the form attached to the end of the URL like this:

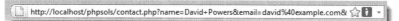

If you break up the URL, it looks like this:

```
http://localhost/phpsols/contact.php
?name=David+Powers
&email=david%40example.com
&comments=I+hope+you+get+this.+%3B-%29
&send=Send+message
```

Each line after the basic URL begins with the `name` attribute of one of the form elements, followed by an equal sign and the contents of the input fields. URLs cannot contain spaces or certain characters (such as my smiley), so the browser encodes them as hexadecimal values, a process known as **URL encoding** (for a full list of values, see `www.w3schools.com/tags/ref_urlencode.asp`).

The first `name` attribute is preceded by a question mark (?) and the others by an ampersand (&). You'll see this type of URL when using search engines, which helps explain why everything after the question mark is known as a **query string**.

4. Go back into the code of `contact.php`, and change `method` back to **post**, like this:

```
<form id="feedback" method="post" action="">
```

5. Save `contact.php`, and reload the page in your browser. Type another message, and click **Send message**. Your message should disappear, but nothing else happens. So where has it gone? It hasn't been lost, but you haven't done anything to process it yet.

6. In `contact.php`, add the following code immediately below the closing `</form>` tag:

```
<pre>
<?php if ($_POST) { print_r($_POST); } ?>
</pre>
```

This displays the contents of the `$_POST` superglobal array if any `post` data has been sent. As explained in Chapter 3, the `print_r()` function allows you to inspect the contents of arrays; the `<pre>` tags simply make the output easier to read.

7. Save the page, and click the **Refresh** button in your browser. You'll probably see a warning similar to the following. This tells you that the data will be resent, which is exactly what you want. Click **OK** or **Send** depending on your browser.

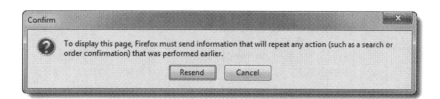

The code from step 6 should now display the contents of your message below the form as shown in Figure 5-2. Everything has been stored in one of PHP's superglobal arrays, $_POST, which contains data sent using the post method. The name attribute of each form element is used as the array key, making it easy to retrieve the content.

```
    Send message

        Array
    (
        [name] => David Powers
        [email] => david@example.com
        [comments] => So what does post do then?
        [send] => Send message
    )
```

Figure 5-2. The $_POST array contains form data with each element identified by its name attribute.

As you have just seen, the get method sends your data in a very exposed way, making it vulnerable to alteration. Also, Internet Explorer limits the maximum length of a URL to 2,048 characters, so the get method can be used only for small amounts of data. The post method is more secure and can be used for much larger amounts of data. By default, PHP permits up to 8MB of post data, although hosting companies may set a smaller limit.

Consequently, you should normally use the post method with forms. The get method is used mainly in conjunction with database searches and has the advantage that you can bookmark a search result because all the data is in the URL. We'll return to the get method later in the book. This chapter concentrates on the post method and its associated superglobal array, $_POST.

> Although the post method is more secure than get, you shouldn't assume that it's 100% safe. For secure transmission, you need to use encryption or the Secure Sockets Layer (SSL) with a URL that begins with https://.

Keeping safe with PHP superglobals

While I'm on the subject of security, it's worth explaining the background to the PHP superglobal arrays, which include $_POST and $_GET. The $_POST array contains data sent using the post method. So it should come as no surprise that data sent by the get method is in the $_GET array.

In the early days of PHP, you didn't need to use special arrays to access data submitted from a form. If the name of the form element was email, all that was necessary was to stick a dollar sign on the front, like this: $email. Bingo, you had instant access to the data. It was incredibly convenient. Unfortunately, it also left a gaping security hole. All that an attacker needed to do was view the source of your web page and pass values to your script through a query string.

Occasionally, you'll still see "advice" to turn on register_globals in php.ini to restore the old way of gathering form data. Turning on register_globals is foolish for the following reasons:

- It's totally insecure.
- Most hosting companies now disable register_globals. There is no way to override the setting for individual scripts, so any scripts that rely on it won't work.
- The register_globals setting will be removed completely from the next major version of PHP. Scripts that rely on register_globals won't work with that version, period.

It's very easy to write scripts that don't rely on register_globals. It just requires putting the name attribute of the form element in quotes between square brackets after $_POST or $_GET, depending on the form's method attribute. So email becomes $_POST['email'] if sent by the post method, and $_GET['email'] if sent by the get method. That's all there is to it.

You may come across scripts that use $_REQUEST, which avoids the need to distinguish between $_POST or $_GET. It's less secure. Always use $_POST or $_GET instead.

Old scripts may use $HTTP_POST_VARS or $HTTP_GET_VARS, which have the same meaning as $_POST and $_GET. The old versions don't work on most servers.

> Always use $_POST and $_GET when processing user input from a form.

Removing unwanted backslashes from form input

Some PHP servers automatically insert backslashes in front of quotes when a form is submitted. You should follow the instructions in Chapter 2 to check the value of magic_quotes_gpc on your remote server. If it's on, and you can't use php.ini or an .htaccess file to turn it off, you need to remove these backslashes with the script in nuke_magic_quotes.php.

> You can ignore PHP Solution 5-1 entirely if magic_quotes_gpc is off on your remote server.

PHP Solution 5-1: Using a script to eliminate magic quotes

This PHP solution is the least efficient way of dealing with magic quotes and should be used *only* if you cannot turn off magic_quotes_gpc on your remote server by any other means. To reproduce the same conditions as on your remote server, edit your local version of php.ini to turn on magic_quotes_gpc (Chapter 2 describes how to edit configuration directives in php.ini).

Continue working with the file from the previous exercise. Alternatively, use contact_02.php from the ch05 folder. Copy it to the site root and rename it contact.php.

1. Load contact.php into a browser. Enter some text that contains an apostrophe or some double quotes. Click **Send message**.

2. Check the contents of the $_POST array at the bottom of the screen. If magic quotes are on, you will see something like Figure 5-3. A backslash has been inserted in front of all single and double quotes (apostrophes are treated the same as single quotes). If magic quotes are off, you will see no change from your original text.

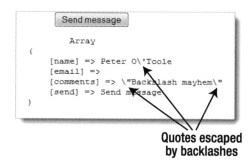

Quotes escaped by backlashes

Figure 5-3. PHP magic quotes automatically insert a backslash in front of quotes when a form is submitted.

3. If your remote server uses magic quotes, add the following code shown in bold at the end of the code block at the top of contact.php:

```php
<?php
include('./includes/title.inc.php');
if ($_POST) {
  include('./includes/nuke_magic_quotes.php');
}
?>
```

4. The conditional statement checks if the $_POST array contains any values. If it does, it includes the file nuke_magic_quotes.php, which contains a script from the PHP manual at http://docs.php.net/manual/en/security.magicquotes.disabling.php. The script removes backslashes from form data and cookies. You should always include this script at the beginning of any page that processes form data.

    In this case, I have wrapped the include command in a conditional statement that checks only the $_POST array. Obviously, if the form is submitted using the get method, you should check the $_GET array. If you're expecting data from multiple sources, you can omit the conditional statement, but it's slightly more efficient to use one, because it avoids running the script in nuke_magic_quotes.php unnecessarily.

    The script in nuke_magic_quotes.php automatically checks whether magic_quotes_gpc is on. If it's off, the form data is not touched, so your pages will continue to work correctly even if your hosting company changes the setting.

5. Save contact.php, and click the **Reload** button in your browser. Confirm that you want to resend the post data.

6. The $_POST array should now be clear of backslashes, as shown in Figure 5-4. You can check your code with contact_03.php in the ch05 folder.

```
        Send message

            Array
(

    [name] => Peter O'Toole
    [email] =>
    [comments] => "Backslash mayhem"
    [send] => Send message
)
```

Figure 5-4. The backslashes have been cleaned up from the $_POST array.

Since magic quotes are rapidly being phased out of PHP, the remaining PHP solutions and download files assume magic_quotes_gpc is off.

Processing and validating user input

The ultimate aim of this chapter is to send the input from the form in contact.php by email to your inbox. Using the PHP mail() function is relatively simple. It takes a minimum of three arguments: the address(es) the email is being sent to, a string containing the subject line, and a string containing the body of the message. You build the body of the message by concatenating (joining) the contents of the input fields into a single string.

Security measures implemented by most Internet service providers (ISPs) make it difficult—if not impossible—to test the mail() function in a local testing environment. Instead of jumping straight into the use of mail(), PHP Solutions 5-2 through 5-5 concentrate on validating user input to make sure required fields are filled in and displaying error messages. Implementing these measures makes your online forms more user-friendly and secure.

For many years, web designers have used JavaScript to check user input when the submit button is clicked. That role is being gradually taken over by browsers that support HTML5. This is called **client-side validation** because it happens on the user's computer (or client). It's useful because it's almost instantaneous and can alert the user to a problem without making an unnecessary round trip to the server. However, you should never rely on client-side validation alone because it's too easy to sidestep. All a malicious user has to do is turn off JavaScript in the browser, or submit data from a custom script, and your checks are rendered useless. It's vital to check user input on the server side with PHP, too.

Creating a reusable script

Email processing scripts are usually stored in a separate file that contains generic code capable of handling any form input. Information specific to the form, such as the destination address and subject line, must be added directly to the script or sent to it using hidden form fields. The location of the processing script is stored in the action attribute of the <form> tag, so the browser knows where to send the input data when the user clicks the submit button.

The ability to reuse the same script—perhaps with only a few edits—for multiple websites is a great timesaver. However, sending the input data to a separate file for processing makes it difficult to alert users to errors without losing their input. To get around this problem, the approach taken in this chapter is to use what's known as a **self-processing form**.

Instead of sending the data to a separate file, the page containing the form is reloaded, and the processing script is wrapped in a PHP conditional statement above the DOCTYPE declaration that checks if the form has been submitted. The advantage is that the form can be redisplayed with error messages and preserving the user's input if errors are detected by the server-side validation.

Parts of the script that are specific to the form will be embedded in the PHP code block above the DOCTYPE declaration. The generic, reusable parts of the script will be in a separate file that can be included in any page that requires an email processing script.

PHP Solution 5-2: Making sure required fields aren't blank

When required fields are left blank, you don't get the information you need, and the user may never get a reply, particularly if contact details have been omitted.

Continue using the same files. Alternatively, use contact_02.php from the ch05 folder. If your remote server has magic quotes turned on, use contact_03.php instead.

1. The processing script uses two arrays called $errors and $missing to store details of errors and required fields that haven't been filled in. These arrays will be used to control the display of error messages alongside the form labels. There won't be any errors when the page first loads, so initialize $errors and $missing as empty arrays in the PHP code block at the top of contact.php like this:

```php
<?php
include('./includes/title.inc.php');
$errors = array();
$missing = array();
?>
```

2. The email processing script should be executed only if the form has been submitted. As Figures 5-2 through 5-4 show, the $_POST array contains a name/value pair for the submit button, which is called send in contact.php. You can test whether the form has been submitted by creating a conditional statement and passing $_POST['send'] to isset(). If $_POST['send'] has been defined (set), the form has been submitted. Add the code highlighted in bold to the PHP block at the top of the page.

```php
<?php
include('./includes/title.inc.php');
$errors = array();
$missing = array();
// check if the form has been submitted
if (isset($_POST['send'])) {
  // email processing script
}
?>
```

Note that send is the value of the name attribute of the submit button in this form. If you give your submit button a different name, you need to use that name.

If your remote server has magic_quotes_gpc turned on, this is where you should include nuke_magic_quotes.php:

```
if (isset($_POST['send'])) {
  // email processing script
  include('./includes/nuke_magic_quotes.php');
}
```

You don't need to include nuke_magic_quotes.php if your remote server has turned off magic_quotes_gpc.

3. Although you won't be sending the email just yet, define two variables to store the destination address and subject line of the email. The following code goes inside the conditional statement that you created in the previous step:

```
if (isset($_POST['send'])) {
  // email processing script
  $to = 'david@example.com'; // use your own email address
  $subject = 'Feedback from Japan Journey';
}
```

4. Next, create two arrays: one listing the name attribute of each field in the form and the other listing all *required* fields. For the sake of this demonstration, make the email field optional, so that only the name and comments fields are required. Add the following code inside the conditional block immediately after the code that defines the subject line:

```
$subject = 'Feedback from Japan Journey';
// list expected fields
$expected = array('name', 'email', 'comments');
// set required fields
$required = array('name', 'comments');
}
```

Why is the $expected array necessary? It's to prevent an attacker from injecting other variables in the $_POST array in an attempt to overwrite your default values. By processing only those variables that you expect, your form is much more secure. Any spurious values are ignored.

5. The next section of code is not specific to this form, so it should go in an external file that can be included in any email processing script. Create a new PHP file called processmail.inc.php in the includes folder. Then include it in contact.php immediately after the code you entered in the previous step like this:

```
$required = array('name', 'comments');
```

```
require('./includes/processmail.inc.php');
}
```

6. The code in processmail.inc.php begins by checking the $_POST variables for required fields that have been left blank. Strip any default code inserted by your editor, and add the following to processmail.inc.php:

```php
<?php
foreach ($_POST as $key => $value) {
  // assign to temporary variable and strip whitespace if not an array
  $temp = is_array($value) ? $value : trim($value);
  // if empty and required, add to $missing array
  if (empty($temp) && in_array($key, $required)) {
    $missing[] = $key;
  } elseif (in_array($key, $expected)) {
    // otherwise, assign to a variable of the same name as $key
    ${$key} = $temp;
  }
}
```

In simple terms, this foreach loop goes through the $_POST array, strips out any whitespace from text fields, and assigns its contents to a variable with the same name (so $_POST['email'] becomes $email, and so on). If a required field is left blank, its name attribute is added to the $missing array.

7. Save processmail.inc.php. You'll add more code to it later, but let's turn now to the main body of contact.php. You need to display a warning if anything is missing. Add a conditional statement at the top of the page content between the <h2> heading and first paragraph like this:

```php
<h2>Contact us</h2>
<?php if ($missing || $errors) { ?>
  <p class="warning">Please fix the item(s) indicated.</p>
<?php } ?>
<p>Ut enim ad minim veniam . . . </p>
```

This checks $missing and $errors, which you initialized as empty arrays in step 1. PHP treats an empty array as false, so the paragraph inside the conditional statement isn't displayed when the page first loads. However, if a required field hasn't been filled in when the form is submitted, its name is added to the $missing array. An array with at least one element is treated as true. The || means "or," so this warning paragraph will be displayed if a required field is left blank or if an error is discovered. (The $errors array comes into play in PHP Solution 5-4.)

8. To make sure it works so far, save contact.php, and load it normally in a browser (don't click the Refresh button). The warning message is not displayed. Click **Send message** without filling in any of the fields. You should now see the message about missing items, as shown in the following screenshot.

9. To display a suitable message alongside each missing required field, add a PHP code block to display a warning as a `<span>` inside the `<label>` tag like this:

```
<label for="name">Name:
<?php if ($missing && in_array('name', $missing)) { ?>
  <span class="warning">Please enter your name</span>
<?php } ?>
</label>
```

The first condition checks the $missing array. If it's empty, the conditional statement fails, and the `<span>` is never displayed. But if $missing contains any values, the in_array() function checks if the $missing array contains the value name. If it does, the `<span>` is displayed as shown in Figure 5-5.

10. Insert similar warnings for the email and comments fields like this:

```
    <label for="email">Email:
<?php if ($missing && in_array('email', $missing)) { ?>
    <span class="warning">Please enter your email address</span>
<?php } ?>
    </label>
    <input name="email" id="email" type="text" class="formbox">
</p>
<p>
    <label for="comments">Comments:
<?php if ($missing && in_array('comments', $missing)) { ?>
    <span class="warning">Please enter your comments</span>
<?php } ?>
    </label>
```

The PHP code is the same except for the value you are looking for in the $missing array. It's the same as the name attribute for the form element.

11. Save `contact.php`, and test the page again, first by entering nothing into any of the fields. The page should look like Figure 5-5.

Figure 5-5. By validating user input, you can display warnings about required fields.

Although you added a warning to the `<label>` for the `email` field, it's not displayed, because `email` hasn't been added to the `$required` array. As a result, it's not added to the `$missing` array by the code in `processmail.inc.php`.

12. Add `email` to the `$required` array in the code block at the top of `comments.php` like this:

    $required = array('name', 'comments', **'email'**);

13. Click **Send message** again without filling in any fields. This time, you'll see a warning message alongside each label.

14. Type your name in the **Name** field. In the **Email** and **Comments** fields, just press the spacebar several times. Then click **Send message**. The warning message alongside the **Name** field disappears, but the other two warning messages remain. The code in `processmail.inc.php` strips whitespace from text fields, so it rejects attempts to bypass required fields by entering a series of spaces.

    If you have any problems, compare your code with `contact_04.php` and `processmail.inc_01.php` in the ch05 folder.

All you need to do to change the required fields is change the names in the `$required` array and add a suitable alert inside the `<label>` tag of the appropriate input element inside the form. It's easy to do, because you always use the `name` attribute of the form input element.

Preserving user input when a form is incomplete

Imagine you have spent ten minutes filling in a form. You click the submit button, and back comes the response that a required field is missing. It's infuriating if you have to fill in every field all over again. Since the content of each field is in the `$_POST` array, it's easy to redisplay it when an error occurs.

PHP Solution 5-3: Creating sticky form fields

This PHP solution shows how to use a conditional statement to extract the user's input from the $_POST array and redisplay it in text input fields and text areas.

Continue working with the same files as before. Alternatively, use contact_04.php and processmail.inc_01.php from the ch05 folder.

1. When the page first loads, you don't want anything to appear in the input fields. But you do want to redisplay the content if a required field is missing or there's an error. So that's the key: if the $missing or $errors arrays contain any values, you want the content of each field to be redisplayed. You set default text for a text input field with the value attribute of the <input> tag, so amend the <input> tag for name like this:

```
<input name="name" id="name" type="text" class="formbox"
<?php if ($missing || $errors) {
  echo 'value="' . htmlentities($name, ENT_COMPAT, 'UTF-8') . '"';
} ?>>
```

The line inside the curly braces contains a combination of quotes and periods that might confuse you. The first thing to realize is that there's only one semicolon—right at the end—so the echo command applies to the whole line. As explained in Chapter 3, a period is called the concatenation operator, which joins strings and variables. You can break down the rest of the line into three sections, as follows:

- 'value="' .
- htmlentities($name, ENT_COMPAT, 'UTF-8')
- . '"'

The first section outputs value=" as text and uses the concatenation operator to join it to the next section, which passes $name to a function called htmlentities(). I'll explain what the function does in a moment, but the third section uses the concatenation operator again to join the next section, which consists solely of a double quote. So, if $missing or $errors contain any values, and $_POST['name'] contains Joe, you'll end up with this inside the <input> tag:

```
<input name="name" id="name" type="text" class="formbox" value="Joe">
```

The $name variable contains the original user input, which was transmitted through the $_POST array. The foreach loop that you created in processmail.inc.php in PHP Solution 5-2 processes the $_POST array and assigns each element to a variable with the same name. This allows you to access $_POST['name'] simply as $name.

So, what's the htmlentities() function for? As the function name suggests, it converts certain characters to their equivalent HTML entity. The one you're concerned with here is the double quote. Let's say Elvis really is still alive and decides to send feedback through the form. If you use $name on its own, Figure 5-6 shows what happens when a required field is omitted and you don't use htmlentities().

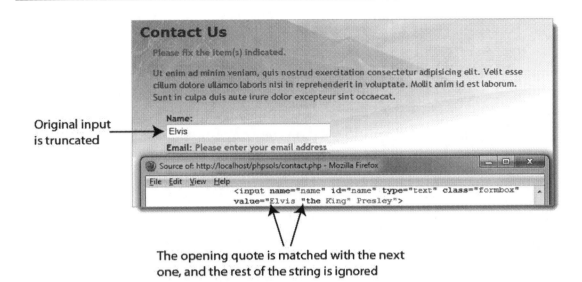

Figure 5-6. Quotes need special treatment before form fields can be redisplayed.

Passing the content of the $_POST array element to the htmlentities(), however, converts the double quotes in the middle of the string to ". And, as Figure 5-7 shows, the content is no longer truncated. What's cool about this is that the HTML entity " is converted back to double quotes when the form is resubmitted. As a result, there's no need for any further conversion before the email can be sent.

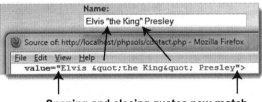

Opening and closing quotes now match

Figure 5-7. The problem is solved by passing the value to htmlentities() before it's displayed.

By default, htmlentities() uses the Latin1 (ISO-8859-1) character set, which doesn't support accented characters. To support Unicode (UTF-8) encoding, you need to pass three arguments to htmlentities():

- The string you want to convert

- A PHP constant indicating how to handle single quotes (ENT_COMPAT leaves them untouched; ENT_QUOTES converts them to ', the numeric entity for a single straight quote)

- A string containing one of the permitted character sets (encodings) listed at http://docs.php.net/manual/en/function.htmlentities.php

2. Edit the `email` field the same way, using `$email` instead of `$name`.

3. The `comments` text area needs to be handled slightly differently because `<textarea>` tags don't have a `value` attribute. You place the PHP block between the opening and closing tags of the text area like this (new code is shown in bold):

```
<textarea name="comments" id="comments" cols="60" rows="8"><?php
  if ($missing || $errors) {
    echo htmlentities($comments, ENT_COMPAT, 'UTF-8');
  } ?></textarea>
```

It's important to position the opening and closing PHP tags right up against the `<textarea>` tags. If you don't, you'll get unwanted whitespace inside the text area.

4. Save `contact.php`, and test the page in a browser. If any required fields are omitted, the form displays the original content along with any error messages.

You can check your code with `contact_05.php` in the `ch05` folder.

Using this technique prevents a form reset button from clearing any fields that have been changed by the PHP script. This is a minor inconvenience in comparison with the greater usability offered by preserving existing content when an incomplete form is submitted.

Filtering out potential attacks

A particularly nasty exploit known as **email header injection** seeks to turn online forms into spam relays. A simple way of preventing this is to look for the strings "Content-Type:", "Cc:", and "Bcc:", as these are email headers that the attacker injects into your script to trick it into sending HTML email with copies to many people. If you detect any of these strings in user input, it's a pretty safe bet that you're the target of an attack, so you should block the message. An innocent message may also be blocked, but the advantages of stopping an attack outweigh that small risk.

PHP Solution 5-4: Blocking emails that contain specific phrases

This PHP solution checks the user input for suspect phrases. If one is detected, a Boolean variable is set to `true`. This will be used later to prevent the email from being sent.

Continue working with the same page as before. Alternatively, use `contact_05.php` and `processmail.inc_01.php` from the `ch05` folder.

1. PHP conditional statements rely on a `true`/`false` test to determine whether to execute a section of code. So the way to filter out suspect phrases is to create a Boolean variable that is switched to `true` as soon as one of those phrases is detected. The detection is done using a search pattern or **regular expression**. Add the following code at the top of `processmail.inc.php` before the existing `foreach` loop:

```
// assume nothing is suspect
$suspect = false;
// create a pattern to locate suspect phrases
$pattern = '/Content-Type:|Bcc:|Cc:/i';

foreach ($_POST as $key => $value) {
```

The string assigned to $pattern will be used to perform a case-insensitive search for any of the following: "Content-Type:", "Bcc:", or "Cc:". It's written in a format called Perl-compatible regular expression (PCRE). The search pattern is enclosed in a pair of forward slashes, and the i after the final slash makes the pattern case-insensitive.

> For a basic introduction to regular expressions (regex), see my tutorial in the Adobe Developer Connection at www.adobe.com/devnet/dreamweaver/articles/regular_expressions_pt1.html. For a more in-depth treatment, Regular Expressions Cookbook by Jan Goyvaerts and Steven Levithan (O'Reilly, 2009, ISBN: 978-0-596-52068-7) is excellent.

2. You can now use the PCRE stored in $pattern to filter out any suspect user input from the $_POST array. At the moment, each element of the $_POST array contains only a string. However, multiple-choice form elements, such as check box groups, return an array of results. So you need to tunnel down any subarrays and check the content of each element separately. That's precisely what the following custom-built function isSuspect() does. Insert it immediately after the $pattern variable from step 1.

```
$pattern = '/Content-Type:|Bcc:|Cc:/i';

// function to check for suspect phrases
function isSuspect($val, $pattern, &$suspect) {
  // if the variable is an array, loop through each element
  // and pass it recursively back to the same function
  if (is_array($val)) {
    foreach ($val as $item) {
      isSuspect($item, $pattern, $suspect);
    }
  } else {
    // if one of the suspect phrases is found, set Boolean to true
    if (preg_match($pattern, $val)) {
      $suspect = true;
    }
  }
}

foreach ($_POST as $key => $value) {
```

The isSuspect() function is a piece of code that you may want to just copy and paste without delving too deeply into how it works. The important thing to notice is that the third argument has an ampersand (&) in front of it (&$suspect). This means that any changes made to the variable passed as the third argument to isSuspect() will affect the value of that variable elsewhere in the script.

This technique is known as **passing by reference**. As explained in "Passing values to functions" in Chapter 3, changes to a variable passed as an argument to a function normally have no effect on the variable's value outside the function unless you explicitly return the value and reassign it to the original variable. They're limited in scope. Prefixing an argument with an ampersand in the function definition overrides this limited scope. When you pass a value by reference, the changes are automatically reflected outside the function. There's no need to return the value and reassign it to the same variable. This technique isn't used very often, but it can be useful in some cases. The ampersand is used only when defining the function. When using the function, you pass arguments in the normal way.

The other feature of this function is that it's what's known as a **recursive function**. It keeps on calling itself until it finds a value that it can compare against the regex.

3. To call the function, pass it the $_POST array, the pattern, and the $suspect Boolean variable. Insert the following code immediately after the function definition:

```
// check the $_POST array and any subarrays for suspect content
isSuspect($_POST, $pattern, $suspect);
```

Note that you don't put an ampersand in front of $suspect this time. The ampersand is required only when you define the function in step 2, not when you call it.

4. If suspect phrases are detected, the value of $suspect changes to true. There's also no point in processing the $_POST array any further. Wrap the code that processes the $_POST variables in a conditional statement like this:

```
if (!$suspect) {
  foreach ($_POST as $key => $value) {
    // assign to temporary variable and strip whitespace if not an array
    $temp = is_array($value) ? $value : trim($value);
    // if empty and required, add to $missing array
    if (empty($temp) && in_array($key, $required)) {
      $missing[] = $key;
    } elseif (in_array($key, $expected)) {
      // otherwise, assign to a variable of the same name as $key
      ${$key} = $temp;
    }
  }
}
```

This processes the variables in the $_POST array only if $suspect is not true.

Don't forget the extra curly brace to close the conditional statement.

5. Add a new warning message at the top of page in contact.php like this:

```
<?php if ($_POST && $suspect) { ?>
  <p class="warning">Sorry, your mail could not be sent. Please try later.</p>
<?php } elseif ($missing || $errors) { ?>
  <p class="warning">Please fix the item(s) indicated.</p>
<?php } ?>
```

This sets a new condition that takes priority over the original warning message by being considered first. It checks if the $_POST array contains any elements—in other words, the form has been submitted—and if $suspect is true. The warning is deliberately neutral in tone. There's no point in provoking attackers. More important, it avoids offending anyone who may have innocently used a suspect phrase.

6. Save contact.php, and test the form by typing one of the suspect phrases in one of the fields. You should see the second warning message, but your input won't be preserved.

    You can check your code against contact_06.php and processmail.inc_02.php in the ch05 folder.

Sending email

Before proceeding any further, it's necessary to explain how the PHP mail() function works, because it will help you understand the rest of the processing script.

The PHP mail() function takes up to five arguments, all of them strings, as follows:

*   The address(es) of the recipient(s)
*   The subject line
*   The message body
*   A list of other email headers (optional)
*   Additional parameters (optional)

Email addresses in the first argument can be in either of the following formats:

```
'user@example.com'
'Some Guy <user2@example.com>'
```

To send to more than one address, use a comma-separated string like this:

```
'user@example.com, another@example.com, Some Guy <user2@example.com>'
```

The message body must be presented as a single string. This means that you need to extract the input data from the $_POST array and format the message, adding labels to identify each field. By default, the mail() function supports only plain text. New lines must use both a carriage return and newline character. It's also recommended to restrict the length of lines to no more than 78 characters. Although it sounds complicated, you can build the message body automatically with about 20 lines of PHP code, as you'll see in PHP Solution 5-6.

Adding other email headers is covered in detail in the next section.

Many hosting companies now make the fifth argument a requirement. It ensures that the email is sent by a trusted user, and it normally consists of your own email address prefixed by -f (without a space in between), all enclosed in quotes. Check your hosting company's instructions to see whether this is required and the exact format it should take.

Using additional email headers safely

You can find a full list of email headers at www.faqs.org/rfcs/rfc2076, but some of the most well-known and useful ones enable you to send copies of an email to other addresses (Cc and Bcc), or to change the encoding. Each new header, except the final one, must be on a separate line terminated by a carriage return and new line character. This means using the \r and \n escape sequences in double-quoted strings (see Table 3-4 in Chapter 3).

By default, mail() uses Latin1 (ISO-8859-1) encoding, which doesn't support accented characters. Web page editors these days frequently use Unicode (UTF-8), which supports most written languages, including the accents commonly used in European languages, as well as nonalphabetic scripts, such as Chinese and Japanese. To ensure that email messages aren't garbled, use the Content-Type header to set the encoding to UTF-8 like this:

```
$headers = "Content-Type: text/plain; charset=utf-8\r\n";
```

You also need to add UTF-8 as the charset attribute in a <meta> tag in the <head> of your web pages like this in HTML5:

```
<meta charset=utf-8">
```

In HTML 4.01, use this:

```
<meta http-equiv="Content-Type" content="text/html; charset=utf-8">
```

Let's say you also want to send copies of messages to other departments, plus a copy to another address that you don't want the others to see. Email sent by mail() is often identified as coming from nobody@yourdomain (or whatever username is assigned to the web server), so it's a good idea to add a more user-friendly "From" address. This is how you build those additional headers, using the combined concatenation operator (.=) to add each one to the existing variable:

```
$headers .= "From: Japan Journey<feedback@example.com>\r\n";
$headers .= "Cc: sales@example.com, finance@example.com\r\n";
$headers .= 'Bcc: secretplanning@example.com';
```

After building the set of headers you want to use, you pass the variable containing them as the fourth argument to mail() like this (assuming that the destination address, subject, and message body have already been stored in variables):

```
$mailSent = mail($to, $subject, $message, $headers);
```

Hard-coded additional headers like this present no security risk, but anything that comes from user input must be filtered before it's used. The biggest danger comes from a text field that asks for the user's email address. A widely used technique is to incorporate the user's email address into a Reply-To header, which enables you to reply directly to incoming messages by clicking the **Reply** button in your email program. It's very convenient, but attackers frequently try to pack an email input field with a large number of spurious headers.

Although email fields are the prime target for attackers, the destination address and subject line are both vulnerable if you let users change the value. User input should always be regarded as suspect. PHP Solution 5-4 performs only a basic test for suspect phrases. Before using external input directly in a header you need to apply a more rigorous test.

PHP Solution 5-5: Adding headers and automating the reply address

This PHP solution adds three headers to the email: `From`, `Content-Type` (to set the encoding to UTF-8), and `Reply-To`. Before adding the user's email address to the final header, it uses one of the filter functions introduced in PHP 5.2 to verify that the submitted value conforms to the format of a valid email address.

Continue working with the same page as before. Alternatively, use `contact_06.php` and `processmail.inc_02.php` from the `ch05` folder.

1. Headers are often specific to a particular website or page, so the `From` and `Content-Type` headers will be added to the script in `contact.php`. Add the following code to the PHP block at the top of the page just before `processmail.inc.php` is included:

```
$required = array('name', 'comments', 'email');
// create additional headers
$headers = "From: Japan Journey<feedback@example.com>\r\n";
$headers .= 'Content-Type: text/plain; charset=utf-8';
require('./includes/processmail.inc.php');
```

The `\r\n` at the end of the `From` header is an escape sequence that inserts a carriage return and newline character, so the string must be in double quotes. At the moment, `Content-Type` is the final header, so it isn't followed by a carriage return and newline character, and the string is in single quotes.

2. The purpose of validating the email address is to make sure it's in a valid format, but the field might be empty because you decide not to make it required or because the user simply ignored it. If the field is required but empty, it will be added to the `$missing` array, and the warning you added in PHP Solution 5-2 will be displayed. If the field isn't empty, but the input is invalid, you need to display a different message.

Switch to `processmail.inc.php`, and add this code at the bottom of the script:

```
// validate the user's email
if (!$suspect && !empty($email)) {
  $validemail = filter_input(INPUT_POST, 'email', FILTER_VALIDATE_EMAIL);
  if ($validemail) {
    $headers .= "\r\nReply-To: $validemail";
  } else {
    $errors['email'] = true;
  }
}
```

This begins by checking that no suspect phrases have been found and that the `email` field isn't empty. Both conditions are preceded by the logical Not operator (!), so they return `true` if `$suspect` and `empty($email)` are both `false`. The `foreach` loop you added in PHP Solution 5-2 assigns all expected elements in the `$_POST` array to simpler variables, so `$email` contains the same value as `$_POST['email']`.

The next line uses `filter_input()` to validate the email address. The first argument is a PHP constant, `INPUT_POST`, which specifies that the value must be in the `$_POST` array. The second argument is the name of the element you want to test. The final argument is another PHP constant that specifies you want to check the element conforms to the valid format for an email.

The `filter_input()` function returns the value being tested if it's valid. Otherwise, it returns `false`. So, if the value submitted by the user looks like a valid email address, `$validemail` contains the address. If the format is invalid, `$validemail` is `false`. The `FILTER_VALIDATE_EMAIL` constant accepts only a single email address, so any attempt to insert multiple email addresses will be rejected.

FILTER_VALIDATE_EMAIL checks only the format. It doesn't check that the address is genuine.

If `$validemail` isn't `false`, it's safe to incorporate into a `Reply-To` email header. Since the last value added to `$headers` in step 1 doesn't end with a carriage return and newline character, they're added before `Reply-To`. When building the `$headers` string, it doesn't matter whether you put the `\r\n` at the end of a header or at the beginning of the next one, as long as a carriage return and newline character separates them.

If `$validemail` is false, `$errors['email']` is added to the `$errors` array.

3. You now need to amend the `<label>` for the email field in `contact.php` like this:

```
<label for="email">Email:
<?php if ($missing && in_array('email', $missing)) { ?>
  <span class="warning">Please enter your email address</span>
<?php } elseif (isset($errors['email'])) { ?>
  <span class="warning">Invalid email address</span>
<?php } ?>
</label>
```

This adds an `elseif` clause to the first conditional statement and displays a different warning if the email address fails validation.

4. Save `contact.php`, and test the form by leaving all fields blank and clicking **Send message**. You'll see the original error message. Test it again by entering a value that isn't an email address in the **Email** field. This time, you'll see the invalid message. The same happens if you enter two email addresses.

You can check your code against `contact_07.php` and `processmail.inc_03.php` in the ch05 folder.

PHP Solution 5-6: Building the message body and sending the mail

Many PHP tutorials show how to build the message body manually like this:

```
$message = "Name: $name\r\n\r\n";
$message .= "Email: $email\r\n\r\n";
$message .= "Comments: $comments";
```

This adds a label to identify which field the input comes from and inserts two carriage returns and newline characters between each one. This is fine for a small number of fields, but it soon becomes tedious with more fields. As long as you give your form fields meaningful `name` attributes, you can build the message body automatically with a `foreach` loop, which is the approach taken in this PHP solution.

> *The* `name` *attribute must not contain any spaces. If you want to use multiple words to name your form fields, join them with an underscore or hyphen, for example:* `first_name` *or* `first-name`.

Continue working with the same files as before. Alternatively, use `contact_07.php` and `processmail.inc_03.php` from the ch05 folder.

1. Add the following code at the bottom of the script in `processmail.inc.php`:

    ```php
    $mailSent = false;
    ```

    This initializes a variable that will be used to redirect the user to a thank you page after the mail has been sent. It needs to be set to `false` until you know the `mail()` function has succeeded.

2. Now add that code that builds the message. It goes immediately after the variable you have just initialized.

    ```php
    // go ahead only if not suspect and all required fields OK
    if (!$suspect && !$missing && !$errors) {
      // initialize the $message variable
      $message = '';
      // loop through the $expected array
      foreach($expected as $item) {
        // assign the value of the current item to $val
        if (isset(${$item}) && !empty(${$item})) {
          $val = ${$item};
        } else {
          // if it has no value, assign 'Not selected'
          $val = 'Not selected';
        }
        // if an array, expand as comma-separated string
        if (is_array($val)) {
          $val = implode(', ', $val);
        }
        // replace underscores and hyphens in the label with spaces
        $item = str_replace(array('_', '-'), ' ', $item);
        // add label and value to the message body
        $message .= ucfirst($item).": $val\r\n\r\n";
      }

      // limit line length to 70 characters
      $message = wordwrap($message, 70);

      $mailSent = true;
    }
    ```

This is another complex block of code that you might prefer just to copy and paste. Still, you need to know what it does. In brief, the code checks that $suspect, $missing, and $errors are all false. If they are, it builds the message body by looping through the $expected array and stores the result in $message as a series of label/value pairs. The label is derived from the input field's name attribute. Underscores and hyphens in name attributes are replaced by spaces, and the first letter is set to uppercase.

If a field that's not specified as required is left empty, its value is set to "Not selected." The code also processes values from multiple-choice elements, such as check box groups and <select> lists, which are transmitted as subarrays of the $_POST array. The implode() function converts the subarrays into comma-separated strings.

After the message body has been combined into a single string, it's passed to the wordwrap() function to limit the line length to 70 characters. The code that sends the email still needs to be added, but for testing purposes, $mailSent has been set to true.

If you're interested in learning how the code in this block works, read the inline comments, which describe each stage of the process. The key to understanding it is in the following conditional statement:

```
if (isset(${$item}) && !empty(${$item})) {
  $val = ${$item};
}
```

The rather odd-looking ${$item} is what's known as a **variable variable** (the repetition is deliberate, not a misprint). Since the value of $item is name the first time the loop runs, ${$item} refers to $name. In effect, the conditional statement becomes this:

```
if (isset($name) && !empty($name)) {
  $val = $name;
}
```

On the next pass through the loop, ${$item} refers to $email, and so on.

> The vital point about this script is that it builds the message body only from items in the $expected array. You must list the names of all form fields in the $expected array for it to work.

3. Save processmail.inc.php. Locate this code block at the bottom of contact.php:

```
<pre>
<?php if ($_POST) {print_r($_POST);} ?>
</pre>
```

4. Change it to this:

```
<pre>
<?php if ($_POST && $mailSent) {
  echo htmlentities($message, ENT_COMPAT, 'UTF-8') . "\n";
  echo 'Headers: '. htmlentities($headers, ENT_COMPAT, 'UTF-8');
} ?>
</pre>
```

This checks that the form has been submitted and the mail is ready to send. It then displays the values in $message and $headers. Both values are passed to htmlentities() to ensure they display correctly in the browser.

5. Save contact.php, and test the form by entering your name, email address, and a brief comment. When you click **Send message**, you should see the message body and headers displayed at the bottom of the page, as shown in Figure 5-8.

```
Send message

        Message body

Name: David Powers

Email: david@example.com

Comments: This is a test of the mail processing script. If everything
is working, the message body and headers should be displayed at the
bottom of the page.


Headers

From: Japan Journey<feedback@example.com>
Content-Type: text/plain; charset=utf-8
Reply-To: david@example.com
```

Figure 5-8. Verifying that the message body and headers are correctly formed

Assuming that the message body and headers display correctly at the bottom of the page, you're ready to add the code to send the email. If your code didn't work, check it against contact_08.php and processmail.inc_04.php in the ch05 folder.

6. In processmail.inc.php, add the code to send the mail. Locate the following line:

```
$mailSent = true;
```

Change it to this:

```
$mailSent = mail($to, $subject, $message, $headers);
if (!$mailSent) {
  $errors['mailfail'] = true;
}
```

This passes the destination address, subject line, message body, and headers to the mail() function, which returns true if it succeeds in handing the email to the web server's mail transport agent (MTA). If it fails—perhaps because the mail server is down—$mailSent is set to false, and the conditional statement adds an element to the $errors array, allowing you to preserve the user's input when the form is redisplayed.

7. In the PHP block at the top of contact.php, add the following conditional statement immediately after the command that includes processmail.inc.php:

```
require('./includes/processmail.inc.php');
if ($mailSent) {
```

```
    header('Location: http://www.example.com/thank_you.php');
    exit;
  }
}
?>
```

Replace www.example.com with your own domain name. This checks if $mailSent is true. If it is, the header() function redirects the user to thank_you.php, a page acknowledging that the message has been sent. The exit command on the following line ensures that the script is terminated after the page has been redirected.

There's a copy of thank_you.php in the ch05 folder.

8. If $mailSent is false, contact.php is redisplayed, and you need to warn the user that the message couldn't be sent. Edit the conditional statement just after the <h2> heading like this:

```
<h2>Contact Us </h2>
<?php if (($_POST && $suspect) || ($_POST && isset($errors['mailfail']))) { ?>
  <p class="warning">Sorry, your mail could not be sent. Please try later.</p>
```

The original and new conditions have been wrapped in parentheses, so each pair is considered as a single entity. The warning about the message not being sent is displayed if the form has been submitted and suspect phrases have been found, *or* if the form has been submitted and $errors['mailfail'] has been set.

9. Delete the code block (including the <pre> tags) that displays the message body and headers at the bottom of contact.php.

10. Testing this locally is likely to result in the thank you page being shown, but the email never arriving. This is because most testing environments don't have an MTA. Even if you set one up, most mail servers reject mail from unrecognized sources. Upload contact.php and all related files, including processmail.inc.php and thank_you.php to your remote server, and test the contact form there.

You can check your code with contact_09.php and processmail.inc_05.php in the ch05 folder.

Troubleshooting mail()

It's important to understand that mail() isn't an email program. PHP's responsibility ends as soon as it passes the address, subject, message, and headers to the MTA. It has no way of knowing if the email is delivered to its intended destination. Normally, email arrives instantaneously, but network logjams can delay it by hours or even a couple of days.

If you're redirected to the thank you page after sending a message from contact.php, but nothing arrives in your inbox, check the following:

- Has the message been caught by a spam filter?
- Have you checked the destination address stored in $to? Try an alternative email address to see if it makes a difference.

- Have you used a genuine address in the `From` header? Using a fake or invalid address is likely to cause the mail to be rejected. Use a valid address that belongs to the same domain as your web server.
- Check with your hosting company to see if the fifth argument to `mail()` is required. If so, it should normally be a string composed of `-f` followed by your email address. For example, `david@example.com` becomes `'-fdavid@example.com'`.

If you still don't receive messages from `contact.php`, create a file with this simple script:

```php
<?php
ini_set('display_errors', '1');
$mailSent = mail('you@example.com', 'PHP mail test', 'This is a test email');
if ($mailSent) {
  echo 'Mail sent';
} else {
  echo 'Failed';
}
```

Replace `you@example.com` with your own email address. Upload the file to your website, and load the page into a browser.

If you see an error message about there being no `From` header, add one as a fourth argument to the `mail()` function like this:

```php
$mailSent = mail('you@example.com', 'PHP mail test', 'This is a test email', ↵
  'From: me@example.com');
```

It's usually a good idea to use a different address from the destination address in the first argument.

If your hosting company requires the fifth argument, adjust the `mail()` function like this:

```php
$mailSent = mail('you@example.com', 'PHP mail test', 'This is a test email', null, ↵
  '-fme@example.com');
```

Using the fifth argument normally replaces the need to supply a `From` header, so using `null` (without quotes) as the fourth argument indicates that it has no value.

If you see **Mail sent** and no mail arrives, or you see **Failed** after trying all five arguments, consult your hosting company for advice.

If you receive the test email from this script but not from `contact.php`, it means you have made a mistake in the code, or that you have forgotten to upload `processmail.inc.php`.

Keeping spam at bay

Validating user input on the server is an important weapon in the fight against spam. Unfortunately, spam merchants are resourceful and often find ways of circumventing measures designed to stop them. Opinions differ about the effectiveness of anti-spam techniques, but one that's worth considering is reCAPTCHA (`www.google.com/recaptcha/captcha`).

CAPTCHA stands for Completely Automated Public Turing Test to Tell Computers and Humans Apart. In its most common form, the user is presented with an image of random characters that need to be typed correctly into a text field. The images are designed to be unreadable by optical character recognition

(OCR) software, but humans often have equal difficulty in reading them. The downside of CAPTCHA tests is that they also present a barrier to the blind and people with poor eyesight.

What makes reCAPTCHA (see Figure 5-9) stand out among similar anti-spam measures is that it automatically provides an option to refresh the image if the user can't read it. Perhaps more important, it offers an audio alternative for people with visual difficulties.

Figure 5-9. Adding a reCAPTCHA widget to a form is an effective anti-spam measure.

Using reCAPTCHA actually has a double benefit. The images used by the reCAPTCHA service come from books and newspapers that have been digitized but which OCR software has difficulty in deciphering. The user is asked to type two words, one of which has been successfully deciphered by OCR. Success or failure is determined by the response to the known word, which could be on either the left or the right. The service collates responses to the unknown word, and uses them to improve the accuracy of OCR technology.

To use reCAPTCHA, you need to set up a Google account, which is free, and obtain a pair of software keys (random strings designed to prevent spammers from circumventing the test). Once you have set up an account, incorporating a reCAPTCHA widget into your contact form is easy.

PHP Solution 5-7: Incorporating a reCAPTCHA widget into your form

This PHP solution describes how to obtain a pair of software keys and add a reCAPTCHA widget to contact.php. Continue working with the same files as before. Alternatively, use contact_09.php and processmail.inc_05.php from the ch05 folder.

1. Go to www.google.com/recaptcha/whyrecaptcha, and click the **Sign up Now!** button. If you have a Gmail account, log in with your email address and password. If you don't have a Google account, you'll be prompted to create one.

2. To create the software keys, enter your website's domain name, select the check box if you want to enable them on all domains, and click **Create Key**. The public and private keys are random strings of characters. Copy and save them in a text file on your local computer.

3. You also need recaptchalib.php, which contains the PHP code to generate the reCAPTCHA widget. There's a copy in the includes folder. To get the most up-to-date version go to http://code.google.com/apis/recaptcha/docs/php.html, and click the link for the **reCAPTCHA PHP library**.

4. Include recaptchalib.php in contact.php. The file is needed both when the form first loads and when the mail processing script runs, so the include command needs to come before the conditional statement that runs only if the form has been submitted. You also need to create variables for the public and private keys. Edit the code at the top of contact.php like this (using your own public and private keys):

```php
<?php
include('./includes/title.inc.php');
require_once('./includes/recaptchalib.php');
$public_key = 'your_public_key';
$private_key = 'your_private_key';
$errors = array();
```

5. The code that checks the user's response must be run only when the form has been submitted. If you plan to use a reCAPTCHA widget on every site, you can put it in processmail.inc.php immediately after the code that validates the email address. However, it will trigger an error if you decide not to use reCAPTCHA, so I have put it in contact.php just before processmail.inc.php is included. The code looks like this:

```php
$headers .= 'Content-Type: text/plain; charset=utf-8';
$response = recaptcha_check_answer($private_key, $_SERVER['REMOTE_ADDR'], ↪
  $_POST['recaptcha_challenge_field'], $_POST['recaptcha_response_field']);
if (!$response->is_valid) {
  $errors['recaptcha'] = true;
}
require('./includes/processmail.inc.php');
```

The recaptcha_get_answer() function takes four arguments: your private key, a PHP superglobal variable that identifies the user's IP address, and two $_POST variables that contain the challenge and response. The result is stored in an object called $response.

The conditional statement checks the response by accessing the object's is_valid property. If the response is invalid, $errors['recaptcha'] is added to the $errors array, preventing processmail.inc.php from sending the email.

6. To display the reCAPTCHA widget in the contact form, add the following code above the submit button:

```php
<?php if (isset($errors['recaptcha'])) { ?>
  <p class="warning">The values didn't match. Try again.</p>
<?php }
echo recaptcha_get_html($public_key); ?>
<p>
  <input name="send" id="send" type="submit" value="Send message">
</p>
```

This adds a paragraph that displays an error message if the user's response was invalid, followed by the code to display the reCAPTCHA widget.

7. Upload the revised version of contact.php and recaptchalib.php to your remote server, and load the contact form into a browser. A reCAPTCHA widget should appear above the submit button as shown in Figure 5-9.

You can check your code against contact_10.php in the ch05 folder.

The code generated by reCAPTCHA creates a <div> with the ID recaptcha_widget_div, which you can use to create a CSS style rule to align the widget with other form elements.

You can find instructions on how to customize the look of a reCAPTCHA widget at http://code.google.com/apis/recaptcha/docs/customization.html. At the time of this writing, you can choose from four themes or create your own. You can also change the language. There are built-in translations for several languages, including French, Spanish, and Russian. If your language isn't supported, you can define your own custom translations.

Handling multiple-choice form elements

The form in contact.php uses only text input fields and a text area. To work successfully with forms, you also need to know how to handle multiple-choice elements, namely:

- Radio buttons
- Check boxes
- Drop-down option menus
- Multiple-choice lists

The principle behind them is the same as the text input fields you have been working with: the name attribute of the form element is used as the key in the $_POST array. However, there are some important differences:

- Check box groups and multiple-choice lists store selected values as an array, so you need to add an empty pair of square brackets at the end of the name attribute for these types of input. For example, for a check box group called interests, the name attribute in each <input> tag should be `name="interests[]"`. If you omit the square brackets, only the last item selected is transmitted through the `$_POST` array.

- The values of selected items in a check box group or multiple-choice list are transmitted as a subarray of the `$_POST` array. The code in PHP Solution 5-6 automatically converts these subarrays to comma-separated strings. However, when using a form for other purposes, you need to extract the values from the subarrays. You'll see how to do so in later chapters.

- Radio buttons, check boxes, and multiple-choice lists are *not* included in the `$_POST` array if no value is selected. So, it's vital to use `isset()` to check for their existence before attempting to access their values when processing the form.

Figure 5-10 shows `contact.php` with each type of input added to the original design.

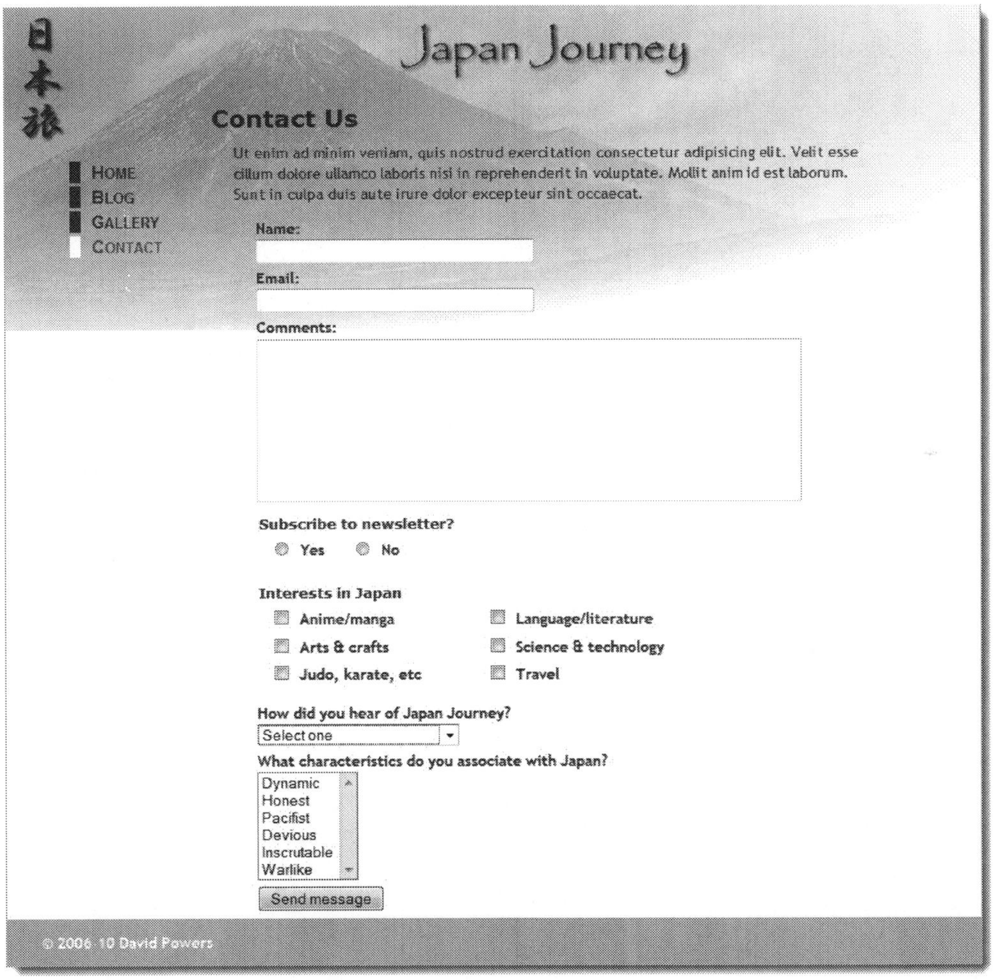

Figure 5-10. The feedback form with examples of multiple-choice form elements

The remaining PHP solutions in this chapter show how to handle multiple-choice form elements. Rather than go through each step in detail, I'll just highlight the important points. Bear the following points in mind when working through the rest of this chapter:

- Processing these elements relies on the code in processmail.inc.php.
- You must add the name attribute of each element to the $expected array for it to be added to the message body.
- To make a field required, add its name attribute to the $required array.
- If a field that's not required is left blank, the code in processmail.inc.php sets its value to "Not selected."

The completed code for the rest of the chapter is in contact_11.php. The reCAPTCHA widget has been omitted to simplify the page.

> HTML5 adds many new types of form input. They all use the name attribute and send values as text or as a subarray of the $_POST array, so you should be able to adapt the code accordingly.

PHP Solution 5-8: Handling radio button groups

Radio button groups let you pick only one value. Although it's common to set a default value in the HTML markup, it's not obligatory. This PHP solution shows how to handle both scenarios.

1. The simple way to deal with radio buttons is to make one of them the default. The radio group is always included in the $_POST array, because a value is always selected.

   The code for a radio group with a default value looks like this (the name attributes and PHP code are highlighted in bold):

```
<fieldset id="subscribe">
  <h2>Subscribe to newsletter?</h2>
  <p>
  <input name="subscribe" type="radio" value="Yes" id="subscribe-yes"
  <?php
  if ($_POST && $_POST['subscribe'] == 'Yes') {
    echo 'checked';
  } ?>>
  <label for="subscribe-yes">Yes</label>
  <input name="subscribe" type="radio" value="No" id="subscribe-no"
  <?php
  if (!$_POST || $_POST['subscribe'] == 'No') {
    echo 'checked';
  } ?>>
  <label for="subscribe-no">No</label>
  </p>
</fieldset>
```

   All members of the radio group share the same name attribute. Because only one value can be selected, the name attribute does *not* end with a pair of empty brackets.

The conditional statement in the **Yes** button checks $_POST to see if the form has been submitted. If it has and the value of $_POST['subscribe'] is "Yes," the checked attribute is added to the <input> tag.

In the **No** button, the conditional statement uses || (or). The first condition is !$_POST, which is true when the form hasn't been submitted. If true, the checked attribute is added as the default value when the page first loads. If false, it means the form has been submitted, so the value of $_POST['subscribe'] is checked.

2. When a radio button doesn't have a default value, it's not included in the $_POST array, so it isn't detected by the loop in processmail.inc.php that builds the $missing array. To ensure that the radio button element is included in the $_POST array, you need to test for its existence after the form has been submitted. If it isn't included, you need to set its value to an empty string like this:

```php
$required = array('name', 'comments', 'email', 'subscribe');
// set default values for variables that might not exist
if (!isset($_POST['subscribe'])) {
  $_POST['subscribe'] = '';
}
```

3. If the radio button group is required but not selected, you need to display an error message when the form reloads. You also need to change the conditional statements in the <input> tags to reflect the different behavior.

The following listing shows the subscribe radio button group from contact_11.php, with all the PHP code highlighted in bold:

```php
<fieldset id="subscribe">
  <h2>Subscribe to newsletter?
  <?php if ($missing && in_array('subscribe', $missing)) { ?>
    <span class="warning">Please make a selection</span>
  <?php } ?>
  </h2>
  <p>
  <input name="subscribe" type="radio" value="Yes" id="subscribe-yes"
  <?php
  if ($_POST && $_POST['subscribe'] == 'Yes') {
    echo 'checked';
  } ?>>
  <label for="subscribe-yes">Yes</label>
  <input name="subscribe" type="radio" value="No" id="subscribe-no"
  <?php
  if ($_POST && $_POST['subscribe'] == 'No') {
    echo 'checked';
  } ?>>
  <label for="subscribe-no">No</label>
  </p>
</fieldset>
```

The conditional statement that controls the warning message in the <h2> tag uses the same technique as for the text input fields. The message is displayed if the radio group is a required item and it's in the $missing array.

The conditional statement surrounding the checked attribute is the same in both radio buttons. It checks if the form has been submitted and displays the checked attribute only if the value in $_POST['subscribe'] matches.

PHP Solution 5-9: Handling check boxes and check box groups

Check boxes can be used in two ways:

- **Individually**: Each check box must have a unique name attribute. The value attribute is optional. If omitted, the default is "on."
- **As a group**: When used this way, all check boxes in the group share the same name attribute, which needs to end with an empty pair of square brackets for PHP to transmit the selected values as an array. To identify which check boxes have been selected, each one needs a unique value attribute.

This PHP solution shows how to deal with a check box group called interests. If no items are selected, the check box group is not included in the $_POST array. After the form has been submitted, you need to check the $_POST array to see if it contains a subarray for the check box group. If it doesn't, you need to create an empty subarray as the default value for the script in processmail.inc.php.

1. To save space, just the first two check boxes of the group are shown. The name attribute and PHP sections of code are highlighted in bold.

```
<fieldset id="interests">
<h2>Interests in Japan</h2>
<div>
  <p>
    <input type="checkbox" name="interests[]" value="Anime/manga" id="anime"
    <?php
    if ($_POST && in_array('Anime/manga', $_POST['interests'])) {
      echo 'checked';
    } ?>>
    <label for="anime">Anime/manga</label>
  </p>
  <p>
    <input type="checkbox" name="interests[]" value="Arts & crafts" id="art"
    <?php
    if ($_POST && in_array('Arts & crafts', $_POST['interests'])) {
      echo 'checked';
    } ?>>
    <label for="art">Arts &amp; crafts</label>
  </p>
. . .
</div>
</fieldset>
```

Each check box shares the same name attribute, which ends with an empty pair of square brackets, so the data is treated as an array. If you omit the brackets, $_POST['interests'] contains the value of only the first check box selected.

> Although the brackets must be added to the name attribute for multiple selections to be treated as an array, the subarray of selected values is in $_POST['interests'], not $_POST['interests[]'].

The PHP code inside each check box element performs the same role as in the radio button group, wrapping the checked attribute in a conditional statement. The first condition checks that the form has been submitted. The second condition uses the in_array() function to check whether the value associated with that check box is in the $_POST['interests'] subarray. If it is, it means the check box was selected.

2. After the form has been submitted, you need to check for the existence of $_POST['interests']. If it hasn't been set, you must create an empty array as the default value for the rest of the script to process. The code follows the same pattern as for the radio group:

```
$required = array('name', 'comments', 'email', 'subscribe', 'interests');
// set default values for variables that might not exist
if (!isset($_POST['subscribe'])) {
  $_POST['subscribe'] = '';
}
if (!isset($_POST['interests'])) {
  $_POST['interests'] = array();
}
```

When dealing with a single check box, use an empty string instead of an empty array.

3. To set a minimum number of required check boxes, use the count() function to check the number of values transmitted from the form. If it's less than the minimum required, add the group to the $errors array like this:

```
if (!isset($_POST['interests'])) {
  $_POST['interests'] = array();
}
// minimum number of required check boxes
$minCheckboxes = 2;
if (count($_POST['interests']) < $minCheckboxes) {
  $errors['interests'] = true;
}
```

The count() function returns the number of elements in an array, so this creates $errors['interests'] if fewer than two check boxes have been selected. You might be wondering why I have used a variable instead of the number like this:

```
if (count($_POST['interests']) < 2) {
```

This certainly works and it involves less typing, but $minCheckboxes can be reused in the error message. Storing the number in a variable means this condition and the error message always remain in sync.

4. The error message in the body of the form looks like this:

```
<h2>Interests in Japan
<?php if (isset($errors['interests'])) { ?>
  <span class="warning">Please select at least <?php echo $minCheckboxes; ↦
    ?></span>
<?php } ?>
</h2>
```

PHP Solution 5-10: Using a drop-down option menu

Drop-down option menus created with the <select> tag are similar to radio button groups in that they normally allow the user to pick only one option from several. Where they differ is one item is always selected in a drop-down menu, even if it's only the first item inviting the user to select one of the others. As a result, this means that the $_POST array always contains an element referring to a <select> menu, whereas a radio button group is ignored unless a default value is preset.

1. The following code shows the first two items from the drop-down menu in contact_11.php with the PHP code highlighted in bold. As with all multiple-choice elements, the PHP code wraps the attribute that indicates which item has been chosen. Although this attribute is called checked in radio buttons and check boxes, it's called selected in <select> menus and lists. It's important to use the correct attribute to redisplay the selection if the form is submitted with required items missing. When the page first loads, the $_POST array contains no elements, so you can select the first <option> by testing for !$_POST. Once the form is submitted, the $_POST array always contains an element from a drop-down menu, so you don't need to test for its existence.

```
<p>
  <label for="select">How did you hear of Japan Journey?</label>
  <select name="howhear" id="howhear">
    <option value="No reply"
    <?php
    if (!$_POST || $_POST['howhear'] == 'No reply') {
      echo 'selected';
    } ?>>Select one</option>
    <option value="foED"
    <?php
    if (isset($_POST && $_POST['howhear'] == 'foED') {
      echo 'selected';
    } ?>>friends of ED</option>
    . . .
  </select>
</p>
```

2. Even though an option is always selected in a drop-down menu, you might want to force users to make a selection other than the default. To do so, add the name attribute of the <select>

menu to the $required array, and set the value attribute and the $_POST array element for the default option to an empty string like this:

```php
<option value=""
<?php
if (!$_POST || $_POST['howhear'] == '') {
  echo 'selected';
} ?>>Select one</option>
```

The value attribute is not required in the <option> tag, but if you leave it out, the form uses the text between the opening and closing tags as the selected value. So, it's necessary to set the value attribute explicitly to an empty string. Otherwise, "Select one" is transmitted as the selected value.

3. The code that displays a warning message if no selection has been made follows the familiar pattern:

```php
<label for="select">How did you hear of Japan Journey?
<?php if ($missing && in_array('howhear', $missing)) { ?>
  <span class="warning">Please make a selection</span>
<?php } ?>
</label>
```

PHP Solution 5-11: Handling a multiple-choice list

Multiple-choice lists are similar to check boxes: they allow the user to choose zero or more items, so the result is stored in an array. If no items are selected, you need to add an empty subarray to the $_POST array in the same way as with a check box group.

1. The following code shows the first two items from the multiple-choice list in contact_11.php with the name attribute and PHP code highlighted in bold. Note that the name attribute needs a pair of square brackets on the end to store the results as an array. The code works in an identical way to the check boxes in PHP Solution 5-9.

```php
<p>
  <label for="select">What characteristics do you associate with ➡
    Japan?</label>
  <select name="characteristics[]" size="6" multiple="multiple" ➡
    id="characteristics">
  <option value="Dynamic"
  <?php
  if ($_POST && in_array('Dynamic', $_POST['characteristics'])) {
    echo 'selected';
  } ?>>Dynamic</option>
  <option value="Honest"
  <?php
  if ($_POST && in_array('Honest', $_POST['characteristics'])) {
    echo 'selected';
  } ?>>Honest</option>
  . . .
```

```
    </select>
  </p>
```

2. In the code that processes the message, set a default value for a multiple-choice list in the same way as for an array of check boxes.

```
if (!isset($_POST['interests'])) {
  $_POST['interests'] = array();
}
if (!isset($_POST['characteristics'])) {
  $_POST['characteristics'] = array();
}
```

3. To make a multiple-choice list required and set a minimum number of choices, use the same technique as for a check box group in PHP Solution 5-9.

Chapter review

A lot of work has gone into building processmail.inc.php, but the beauty of this script is that it works with any form. The only parts that need changing are the $expected and $required arrays and details specific to the form, such as the destination address, headers, and default values for multiple-choice elements that won't be included in the $_POST array if no value is selected.

I've avoided talking about HTML email because the mail() function handles only plain text email. The PHP online manual at www.php.net/manual/en/function.mail.php shows a way of sending HTML mail by adding an additional header. However, it's not a good idea, as HTML mail should always contain an alternative text version for email programs that don't accept HTML. If you want to send HTML mail or attachments, try PHPM@iler (http://phpmailer.worxware.com/) or Zend_Mail (http://zendframework.com/manual/en/zend.mail.html).

As you'll see in later chapters, online forms lie at the heart of just about everything you do with PHP. They're the gateway between the browser and the web server. You'll come back time and again to the techniques that you have learned in this chapter.

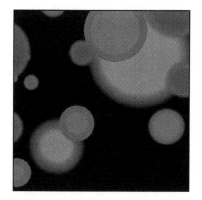

Chapter 6

Uploading Files

PHP's ability to handle forms isn't restricted to text. It can also be used to upload files to a server. For instance, you could build a real estate website for clients to upload pictures of their properties or a site for all your friends and relatives to upload their holiday photos. However, just because you can do it, doesn't necessarily mean that you should. Allowing others to upload material to your website could expose you to all sorts of problems. You need to make sure that images are the right size, that they're of suitable quality, and that they don't contain any illegal material. You also need to ensure that uploads don't contain malicious scripts. In other words, you need to protect your website just as carefully as your own computer.

PHP makes it relatively simple to restrict the type and size of files accepted. What it cannot do is check the suitability of the content. Think carefully about security measures, such as restricting uploads to registered and trusted users by placing the upload form in a password-protected area.

Until you learn how to restrict access to pages with PHP in Chapters 9 and 17, use the PHP solutions in this chapter only in a password-protected directory if deployed on a public website. Most hosting companies provide simple password protection through the site's control panel.

The first part of this chapter is devoted to understanding the mechanics of file uploads, which will make it easier to understand the code that follows. This is a fairly intense chapter, not a collection of quick solutions. But by the end of the chapter, you will have built a PHP class capable of handling single and multiple file uploads. You can then use the class in any form by writing only a few lines of code.

You'll learn about the following:

- Understanding the $_FILES array
- Restricting the size and type of uploads
- Preventing files from being overwritten
- Organizing uploads into specific folders
- Handling multiple uploads

How PHP handles file uploads

The term "upload" means moving a file from one computer to another, but as far as PHP is concerned, all that's happening is that a file is being moved from one location to another. This means you can test all the scripts in this chapter on your local computer without the need to upload files to a remote server.

PHP supports file uploads by default, but hosting companies can restrict the size of uploads or disable them altogether. Before going any further, it's a good idea to check the settings on your remote server.

Checking whether your server supports uploads

All the information you need is displayed in the main PHP configuration page that you can display by running phpinfo() on your remote server, as described in Chapter 2. Scroll down until you find file_uploads in the **Core** section, as shown in the following screenshot.

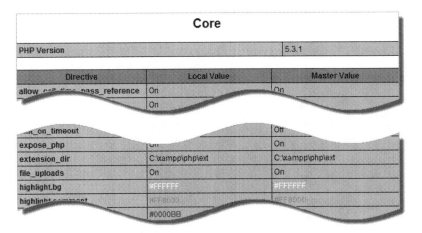

If the **Local Value** is **On**, you're ready to go, but you should also check the other configuration settings listed in Table 6-1.

Table 6-1. PHP configuration settings that affect file uploads

Directive	Default value	Description
max_execution_time	30	The maximum number of seconds that a PHP script can run. If the script takes longer, PHP generates a fatal error.
max_input_time	60	The maximum number of seconds that a PHP script is allowed to parse the $_POST and $_GET arrays and file uploads. Very large uploads are likely to run out of time.
post_max_size	8M	The maximum permitted size of all $_POST data, *including* file uploads. Although the default is 8MB, hosting companies may impose a smaller limit.

Directive	Default value	Description
upload_tmp_dir		This is where PHP stores uploaded files until your script moves them to a permanent location. If no value is defined in php.ini, PHP uses the system default temporary directory (C:\Windows\Temp or /tmp on Mac/Linux).
upload_max_filesize	2M	The maximum permitted size of a single upload file. Although the default is 2MB, hosting companies may impose a smaller limit. A number on its own indicates the number of bytes permitted. A number followed by K indicates the number of kilobytes permitted.

The default 8MB value of post_max_size includes the content of the $_POST array, so the total size of files that can be uploaded simultaneously is less than 8MB, with no single file greater than 2MB. These defaults can be changed by the server administrator, so it's important to check the limits set by your hosting company. If you exceed those limits, an otherwise perfect script will fail.

If the **Local Value** of file_uploads is **Off**, uploads have been disabled. There is nothing you can do about it, other than ask your hosting company if it offers a package with file uploading enabled. Your only alternatives are to move to a different host or to use a different solution, such as uploading files by FTP.

> *After using phpinfo() to check your remote server's settings, it's a good idea to remove the script or put it in a password-protected directory.*

Adding a file upload field to a form

Adding a file upload field to an HTML form is easy. Just add enctype="multipart/form-data" to the opening <form> tag, and set the type attribute of an <input> element to file. The following code is a simple example of an upload form (it's in file_upload_01.php in the ch06 folder):

```
<form action="" method="post" enctype="multipart/form-data" id="uploadImage">
  <p>
    <label for="image">Upload image:</label>
    <input type="file" name="image" id="image">
  </p>
  <p>
    <input type="submit" name="upload" id="upload" value="Upload">
  </p>
</form>
```

Although this is standard HTML, how it's rendered in a web page depends on the browser (see Figure 6-1). Some browsers insert a text input field with a **Browse** button on the right. In older browsers, the text input field is editable, but most modern browsers make it read-only or launch the operating system's file navigation panel as soon as you click inside the field. Browsers that use the WebKit engine, such as Safari and Google Chrome, display a **Choose File** button with a status message or name of the selected file on the right. These differences don't affect the operation of an upload form, but you need to take them into account when designing the layout.

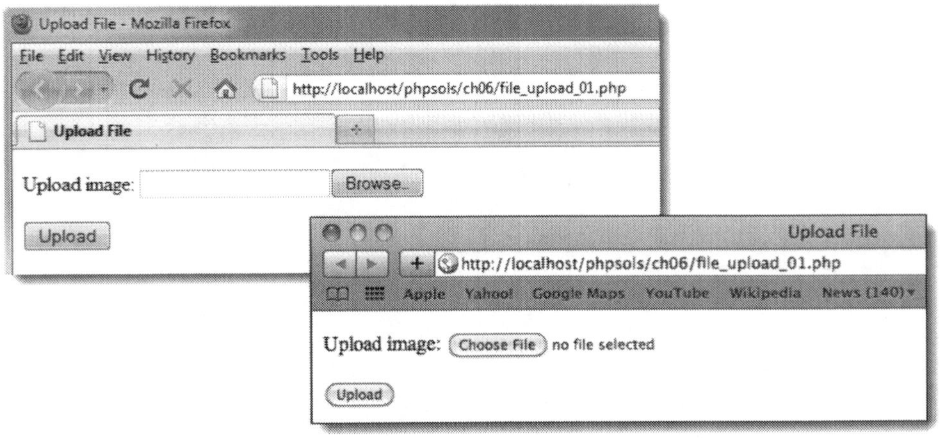

Figure 6-1. The look of a file input field depends on the browser.

Understanding the $_FILES array

What confuses many people is that their file seems to vanish after it has been uploaded. This is because you can't refer to an uploaded file in the $_POST array in the same way as with text input. PHP transmits the details of uploaded files in a separate superglobal array called, not unreasonably, $_FILES. Moreover, files are uploaded to a temporary folder and are deleted unless you explicitly move them to the desired location. Although this sounds like a nuisance, it's done for a very good reason: you can subject the file to security checks before accepting the upload.

Inspecting the $_FILES array

The best way to understand how the $_FILES array works is to see it in action. If you have installed a local test environment, you can test everything on your computer. It works in exactly the same way as uploading a file to a remote server.

1. Create a new folder called uploads in the phpsols site root. Create a new PHP file called file_upload.php in the uploads folder, and insert the code from the previous section. Alternatively, copy file_upload_01.php from the ch06 folder, and rename the file file_upload.php.

2. Insert the following code right after the closing </form> tag (it's also in file_upload_02.php):

```
</form>
<pre>
<?php
if (isset($_POST['upload'])) {
  print_r($_FILES);
```

```
}
?>
</pre>
</body>
```

This uses `isset()` to checks whether the `$_POST` array contains `upload`, the `name` attribute of the submit button. If it does, you know the form has been submitted, so you can use `print_r()` to inspect the `$_FILES` array. The `<pre>` tags make the output easier to read.

3. Save `file_upload.php`, and load it into a browser.

4. Click the **Browse** (or **Choose File**) button, and select a file on your hard disk. Click **Open** (or **Choose** on a Mac) to close the file selection dialog box, and then click **Upload**. You should see something similar to Figure 6-2.

    You can see that the `$_FILES` array is actually a multidimensional array—an array of arrays. The top-level array contains just one element, which gets its key (or index) from the `name` attribute of the file input field—in this case, `image`.

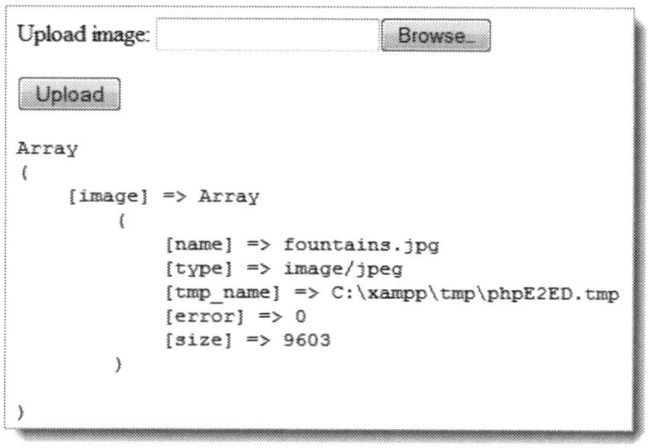

Figure 6-2. The `$_FILES` array contains the details of an uploaded file.

The `image` element contains another array (or subarray) that consists of five elements, namely:

*   `name`: The original name of the uploaded file

*   `type`: The uploaded file's MIME type

*   `tmp_name`: The location of the uploaded file

*   `error`: An integer indicating the status of the upload

*   `size`: The size of the uploaded file in bytes

Don't waste time searching for the temporary file indicated by `tmp_name`: it won't be there. If you don't save it immediately, PHP discards it.

5. Click **Upload** without selecting a file. The `$_FILES` array should look like Figure 6-3.

```
Upload image:                    Browse..

  Upload

Array
(
    [image] => Array
        (
            [name] =>
            [type] =>
            [tmp_name] =>
            [error] => 4
            [size] => 0
        )

)
```

Figure 6-3. The $_FILES array still exists when no file is uploaded.

An error level of 4 indicates that no file was uploaded; 0 means the upload succeeded. Table 6-2 later in this chapter lists all the error codes.

6. Select a program file, and click the **Upload** button. In many cases, the form will happily try to upload the program and display its type as application/zip or something similar. This is a warning that it's important to check the MIME type of uploaded files.

Establishing an upload directory

Another source of confusion is the question of permissions. An upload script that works perfectly locally may confront you with a message like this when you transfer it to your remote server:

```
Warning:  move_uploaded_file(/home/user/htdocs/testarea/kinkakuji.jpg)
[function.move-uploaded-file]: failed to open stream: Permission denied in ↦
 /home/user/htdocs/testarea/upload_test.php on line 3
```

Why is permission denied? Most hosting companies use Linux servers, which impose strict rules about the ownership of files and directories. In most cases, PHP doesn't run in *your* name, but as the web server—usually nobody or apache. Unless PHP has been configured to run in your name, you need to give global access (chmod 777) to every directory to which you want to upload files.

Since 777 is the least secure setting, begin by testing uploads with a setting of 700. If that doesn't work, try 770, and use 777 only as a last resort. The upload directory doesn't need to be within your site root. If your hosting company gives you a private directory outside the site root, create a subdirectory for uploads inside the private one. Alternatively, create a directory inside your site root, but don't link to it from any web pages. Give it an innocuous name, such as lastyear.

Creating an upload folder for local testing on Windows

For the following exercises, I suggest you create a folder called upload_test at the top level of the C drive. There are no permissions issues on Windows, so that's all that you need to do.

Creating an upload folder for local testing on Mac OS X

Mac users need to do a little more preparation, because file permissions are similar to Linux. Without changing the permissions, you'll be confronted with a screen like this:

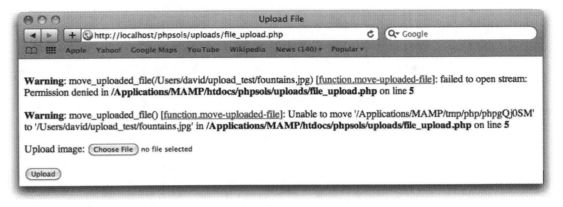

1. Create a folder called `upload_test` within your home folder.

2. Select `upload_test` in Finder, and select **File ➤ Get Info** (Cmd-I) to open its **Info panel**.

3. In **Sharing & Permissions**, click the padlock icon at the bottom right to unlock the settings, and change the setting for **everyone** from **Read only** to **Read & Write**, as shown in the following screenshot.

In older versions of Mac OS X, **Sharing & Permissions** is called **Ownership & Permissions**, and **everyone** is called **Others**.

4. Click the padlock icon again to preserve the new settings, and close the **Info** panel. Your `upload_test` folder is now ready for use.

Uploading files

Before building the file upload class, it's a good idea to create a simple file upload script to make sure that your system handles uploads correctly.

Moving the temporary file to the upload folder

The temporary version of an uploaded file has only a fleeting existence. If you don't do anything with the file, it's discarded immediately. You need to tell PHP where to move it and what to call it. You do this with the `move_uploaded_file()` function, which takes the following two arguments:

- The name of the temporary file
- The full pathname of the file's new location, including the filename itself

Obtaining the name of the temporary file itself is easy: it's stored in the `$_FILES` array as `tmp_name`. Because the second argument requires a full pathname, it gives you the opportunity to rename the file. For the moment, let's keep things simple and use the original filename, which is stored in the `$_FILES` array as `name`.

PHP Solution 6-1: Creating a basic file upload script

Continue working with the same file as in the previous exercise. Alternatively, use `file_upload_03.php` from the `ch06` folder. The final script for this PHP solution is in `file_upload_04.php`.

1. If you are using the file from the previous exercise, delete the code highlighted in bold between the closing `</form>` and `</body>` tags:

```
</form>
<pre>
<?php
if (isset($_POST['upload'])) {
  print_r($_FILES);
  }
?>
</pre>
</body>
```

2. In addition to the automatic limits set in the PHP configuration (see Table 6-1), you can specify a maximum size for an upload file in your HTML form. Add the following line highlighted in bold immediately before the file input field:

```
<label for="image">Upload image:</label>
<input type="hidden" name="MAX_FILE_SIZE" value="<?php echo $max; ?>">
<input type="file" name="image" id="image">
```

This is a hidden form field, so it won't be displayed onscreen. However, it's vital to place it *before* the file input field; otherwise, it won't work. The `name` attribute, `MAX_FILE_SIZE`, is fixed. The `value` attribute sets the maximum size of the upload file in bytes. Instead of specifying a numeric value, I have used a variable, which needs to be defined next. This value will also be used in the server-side validation of the file upload, so it makes sense to define it once, avoiding the possibility of changing it in one place, but forgetting to change it elsewhere.

3. Define the value of `$max` in a PHP block above the `DOCTYPE` declaration like this:

```
<?php
// set the maximum upload size in bytes
```

```
$max = 51200;
?>
<!DOCTYPE HTML>
```

This sets the maximum upload size to 50kB (51,200 bytes).

4. The code that moves the uploaded file from its temporary location to its permanent one needs to be run after the form has been submitted. Insert the following code in the PHP block you have just created at the top of the page:

```
$max = 51200;
if (isset($_POST['upload'])) {
  // define the path to the upload folder
  $destination = '/path/to/upload_test/';
  // move the file to the upload folder and rename it
  move_uploaded_file($_FILES['image']['tmp_name'], $destination . ↵
    $_FILES['image']['name']);
}
?>
```

Although the code is quite short, there's a lot going on. The entire code block is enclosed in a conditional statement that checks whether the **Upload** button has been clicked by checking to see if its key is in the $_POST array.

The value of $destination depends on your operating system and the location of the upload folder.

*   If you are using Windows, and you created the upload_test folder at the top level of the C drive, it should look like this:

    $destination = 'C:/upload_test/';

    Note that I have used forward slashes instead of the Windows convention of backslashes. You can use either, but if you use backslashes, the final one needs to be escaped by another backslash, like this (otherwise the backslash escapes the quote):

    $destination = 'C:\upload_test\\';

*   On a Mac, if you created the upload_test folder in your home folder, it should look like this (replace *username* with your Mac username):

    $destination = '/Users/*username*/upload_test/';

*   On a remote server, you need the fully qualified filepath as the second argument. On Linux, it will probably be something like this:

    $destination = '/home/user/private/upload_test/';

The final line inside the if statement moves the file with the move_uploaded_file() function. Since $_FILES['image']['name'] contains the name of the original file, the second argument, $destination . $_FILES['image']['name'], stores the uploaded file under its original name inside the upload folder.

149

> *You may come across scripts that use* copy() *instead of* move_uploaded_file()*. Without other checks in place,* copy() *can expose your website to serious security risks. For example, a malicious user could try to trick your script into copying files that it should not have access to, such as password files. Always use* move_uploaded_file()*; it's much more secure.*

5. Save file_upload.php, and load it into your browser. Click the **Browse** or **Choose File** button, and select a file from the images folder in the phpsols site. If you choose one from elsewhere, make sure it's less than 50kB. Click **Open** (**Choose** on a Mac) to display the filename in the form. In browsers that display a file input field, you might not be able to see the full path. That's a cosmetic matter that I'll leave you to sort out yourself with CSS. Click the **Upload** button. If you're testing locally, the form input field should clear almost instantly.

6. Navigate to the upload_test folder, and confirm that a copy of the image you selected is there. If there isn't, check your code against file_upload_04.php. Also check that the correct permissions have been set on the upload folder, if necessary.

> *The download files set* $destination *to* C:/upload_test/. *Adjust this to your own setup.*

7. If you get no error messages and cannot find the file, make sure that the image didn't exceed upload_max_filesize (see Table 6-1). Also check that you didn't leave the trailing slash off the end of $destination. Instead of myfile.jpg in upload_test, you may find upload_testmyfile.jpg one level higher in your disk structure.

8. Change the value of $max to 3000, save file_upload.php, and test it again by selecting a file bigger than 2.9kB to upload (any file in the images folder will do). Click the **Upload** button, and check the upload folder. The file shouldn't be there.

9. If you're in the mood for experimentation, move the MAX_FILE_SIZE hidden field below the file input field, and try it again. Make sure you choose a different file from the one you used in step 6, because move_uploaded_file() overwrites existing files of the same name. You'll learn later how to give files unique names.

   This time the file should be copied to your upload folder. Move the hidden field back to its original position before continuing.

The advantage of using MAX_FILE_SIZE is that PHP abandons the upload if the file is bigger than the stipulated value, avoiding unnecessary delay if the file is too big. Unfortunately, users can get around this restriction by faking the value submitted by the hidden field, so the script you'll develop in the rest of this chapter will check the actual size of the file on the server side, too.

Creating a PHP file upload class

As you have just seen, it takes just a few lines of code to upload a file, but this is not enough on its own. You need to make the process more secure by implementing the following steps:

- Check the error level.
- Verify on the server that the file doesn't exceed the maximum permitted size.
- Check that the file is of an acceptable type.
- Remove spaces from the filename.
- Rename files that have the same name as an existing one to prevent overwriting.
- Handle multiple file uploads automatically.
- Inform the user of the outcome.

You need to implement these steps every time you want to upload files, so it makes sense to build a script that can be reused easily. That's why I have chosen to use a custom class. Building PHP classes is generally regarded as an advanced subject, but don't let that put you off. I won't get into the more esoteric details of working with classes, and the code is fully explained. Although the class definition is long, using the class involves writing only a few lines of code.

A **class** is a collection of functions designed to work together. That's an oversimplification, but it's sufficiently accurate to give you the basic idea behind building a file upload class. Each function inside a class should normally focus on a single task, so you'll build separate functions to implement the steps outlined in the previous list. The code should also be generic, so it isn't tied to a specific web page. Once you have built the class, you can reuse it in any form.

If you're in a hurry, the finished class is in the `classes/completed` folder of the download files. Even if you don't build the script yourself, read through the descriptions so you have a clear understanding of how it works.

Defining a PHP class

Defining a PHP class is very easy. You use the `class` keyword followed by the class name and put all the code for the class between a pair of curly braces. By convention, class names normally begin with an uppercase letter and are stored in a separate file. It's also recommended to prefix class names with an uncommon combination of 3–4 letters followed by an underscore to prevent naming conflicts (see `http://docs.php.net/manual/en/userlandnaming.tips.php`). All custom classes in this book use `Ps2_`.

> *PHP 5.3 introduced the concept of namespaces to avoid naming conflicts. At the time of this writing, many hosting companies have not yet migrated to PHP 5.3, so namespaces may not be supported on your server. PHP Solution 6-7 converts the scripts to use namespaces.*

PHP Solution 6-2: Creating the basic file upload class

In this PHP solution, you'll create the basic definition for a class called `Ps2_Upload`, which stores the `$_FILES` array in an internal property ready to handle file uploads. You'll also create an instance of the class (a `Ps2_Upload` object), and use it to upload an image.

1. Create a subfolder called `Ps2` in the `classes` folder.

2. In the new `Ps2` folder, create a file called `Upload.php`, and insert the following code:

   ```php
   <?php
   ```

```
class Ps2_Upload {

}
```

That, believe it or not, is a valid class called `Ps2_Upload`. It doesn't do anything, so it's not much use yet, but it will be once you start adding code between the curly braces. This file will contain only PHP code, so you don't need a closing PHP tag.

3. In many ways, a class is like a car engine. Although you can strip down the engine to see its inner workings, most of the time, you're not interested in what goes on inside, as long as it powers your car. PHP classes hide their inner workings by declaring some variables and functions as protected. If you prefix a variable or function with the keyword `protected`, it can be accessed only inside the class. The reason for doing so is to prevent values from being changed accidentally.

> *Technically speaking, a protected variable or function can also be accessed by a subclass derived from the original class. To learn about classes in more depth, see my* PHP Object-Oriented Solutions *(friends of ED, 2008, ISBN: 978-1-4302-1011-5).*

The `Ps2_Upload` class needs protected variables for the following items:

*   `$_FILES` array
*   Path to the upload folder
*   Maximum file size
*   Messages to report the status of uploads
*   Permitted file types
*   A Boolean variable that records whether a filename has been changed

Create the variables by adding them inside the curly braces like this:

```
class Ps2_Upload {

    protected $_uploaded = array();
    protected $_destination;
    protected $_max = 51200;
    protected $_messages = array();
    protected $_permitted = array('image/gif',
                                  'image/jpeg',
                                  'image/pjpeg',
                                  'image/png');
    protected $_renamed = false;

}
```

I have begun the name of each protected variable (or **property**, as they're normally called inside classes) with an underscore. This is a common convention programmers use to remind themselves that a property is protected; but it's the `protected` keyword that restricts access to the property, not the underscore.

By declaring the properties like this, they can be accessed elsewhere in the class using `$this->`, which refers to the current object. For example, inside the class definition, you access `$_uploaded` as `$this->_uploaded`.

> *When you first declare a property inside a class, it begins with a dollar sign like any other variable. However, you omit the dollar sign from the property name after the -> operator.*

With the exception of `$_destination`, each protected property has been given a default value:

- `$_uploaded` and `$_messages` are empty arrays.

- `$_max` sets the maximum file size to 50kB (51200 bytes).

- `$_permitted` contains an array of image MIME types.

- `$_renamed` is initially set to `false`.

The value of `$_destination` will be set when an instance of the class is created. The other values will be controlled internally by the class, but you'll also create functions (or **methods**, as they're called in classes) to change the values of `$_max` and `$_permitted`.

4. When you create an instance of a class (an **object**), the class definition file automatically calls the class's constructor method, which initializes the object. The constructor method for all classes is called `__construct()` (with two underscores). Unlike the properties you defined in the previous step, the constructor needs to be accessible outside the class, so you precede its definition with the `public` keyword.

> *The public and protected keywords control the **visibility** of properties and methods. Public properties and methods can be accessed anywhere. Any attempt to access protected properties or methods outside the class definition or a subclass triggers a fatal error.*

The constructor for the `Ps2_Upload` class takes the path to the upload folder as an argument and assigns it to `$_destination`. It also assigns the `$_FILES` array to `$_uploaded`. The code looks like this:

```
protected $_renamed = false;

public function __construct($path) {
  if (!is_dir($path) || !is_writable($path)) {
    throw new Exception("$path must be a valid, writable directory.");
```

```
    }
    $this->_destination = $path;
    $this->_uploaded = $_FILES;
  }

}
```

The conditional statement inside the constructor passes $path to the is_dir() and is_writable() functions, which check that the value submitted is a valid directory (folder) that is writable. If either condition fails, the constructor throws an exception with a message indicating the problem.

If $path is OK, it's assigned the $_destination property of the current object, and the $_FILES array is assigned to $_uploaded.

Don't worry if this sounds mysterious. You'll soon see the fruits of your efforts.

5. With the $_FILES array stored in $_uploaded, you can access the file's details and move it to the upload folder with move_uploaded_file(). Create a public method called move() immediately after the constructor, but still inside the curly braces of the class definition. The code looks like this:

```
public function move() {
  $field = current($this->_uploaded);
  $success = move_uploaded_file($field['tmp_name'], $this->_destination . ↵
    $field['name']);
  if ($success) {
    $this->_messages[] = $field['name'] . ' uploaded successfully';
  } else {
    $this->_messages[] = 'Could not upload ' . $field['name'];
  }
}
```

To access the file in the $_FILES array in PHP Solution 6-1, you needed to know the name attribute of the file input field. The form in file_upload.php uses image, so you accessed the filename as $_FILES['image']['name']. But if the field had a different name, such as upload, you would need to use $_FILES['upload']['name']. To make the script more flexible, the first line of the move() method passes the $_uploaded property to the current() function, which returns the current element of an array—in this case, the first element of the $_FILES array. As a result, $field holds a reference to the first uploaded file regardless of name used in the form. This is the first benefit of building generic code. It takes more effort initially, but saves time in the end.

So, instead of using $_FILES['image']['tmp_name'] and $_FILES['image']['name'] in move_uploaded_file(), you refer to $field['tmp_name'] and $field['name']. If the upload succeeds, move_uploaded_file() returns true. Otherwise, it returns false. By storing the result in $success, you can control which message is assigned to the $_messages array.

6. Since $_messages is a protected property, you need to create a public method to retrieve the contents of the array. Add this to the class definition after the move() method:

```php
public function getMessages() {
  return $this->_messages;
}
```

This simply returns the contents of the $_messages array. Since that's all it does, why not make the array public in the first place? Public properties can be accessed—and changed—outside the class definition. This ensures that the contents of the array cannot be altered, so you know the message has been generated by the class. This might not seem such a big deal with a message like this, but it becomes very important when you start working with more complex scripts or in a team.

7. Save Upload.php, and change the code at the top of file_upload.php like this:

```php
<?php
// set the maximum upload size in bytes
$max = 51200;
if (isset($_POST['upload'])) {
  // define the path to the upload folder
  $destination = 'C:/upload_test/';
  require_once('../classes/Ps2/Upload.php');
  try {
    $upload = new Ps2_Upload($destination);
    $upload->move();
    $result = $upload->getMessages();
  } catch (Exception $e) {
    echo $e->getMessage();
  }
}
?>
```

This includes the Ps2_Upload class definition and creates an instance of the class called $upload by passing it the path to the upload folder. It then calls the $upload object's move() and getMessages() methods, storing the result of getMessages() in $result. Because the object might throw an exception, the code is wrapped in a try/catch block.

At the moment, the value of $max in file_upload.php affects only MAX_FILE_SIZE in the hidden form field. Later, you'll also use $max to control the maximum file size permitted by the class.

8. Add the following PHP code block above the form to display any messages returned by the $upload object:

```php
<body>
<?php
if (isset($result)) {
  echo '<ul>';
  foreach ($result as $message) {
```

```
        echo "<li>$message</li>";
    }
  echo '</ul>';
  }
  ?>
  <form action="" method="post" enctype="multipart/form-data" id="uploadImage">
```

This is a simple `foreach` loop that displays the contents of `$result` as an unordered list. When the page first loads, `$result` isn't set, so this code runs only after the form has been submitted.

9. Save `file_upload.php`, and test it in a browser. As long as you choose an image that's less than 50kB, you should see confirmation that the file was uploaded successfully, as shown in Figure 6-4.

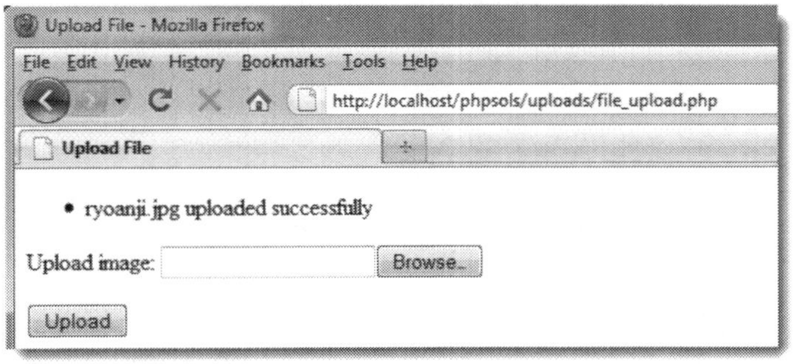

Figure 6-4. The `Ps2_Upload` class reports a successful upload.

You can compare your code with `file_upload_05.php` and `Upload_01.php` in the `ch06` folder.

The class does exactly the same as PHP Solution 6-1: it uploads a file, but it requires a lot more code to do so. However, you have laid the foundation for a class that's going to perform a series of security checks on uploaded files. This is code that you'll write once. When you use the class, you won't need to write this code again.

If you haven't worked with objects and classes before, some of the concepts might seem strange. Think of the `$upload` object simply as a way of accessing the functions (methods) you have defined in the `Ps2_Upload` class. You often create separate objects to store different values, for example, when working with `DateTime` objects. In this case, a single object is sufficient to handle the file upload.

Checking upload errors

As it stands, the `Ps2_Upload` class uploads any type of file indiscriminately. Even the 50kB maximum size can be circumvented, because the only check is made in the browser. Before handing the file to `move_uploaded_file()`, you need to run a series of checks to make sure the file is OK. And if a file is rejected, you need to let the user know why.

PHP Solution 6-3: Testing the error level, file size, and MIME type

This PHP solution shows how to create a series of internal (protected) methods for the class to verify that the file is OK to accept. If a file fails for any reason, an error message reports the reason to the user.

Continue working with Upload.php. Alternatively, use Upload_01.php in the ch06 folder, and rename it Upload.php. (Always remove the underscore and number from partially completed files.)

1. The first test you should run is on the error level. As you saw in the exercise at the beginning of this chapter, level 0 indicates the upload was successful and level 4 that no file was selected.

   Table 6-2 shows a full list of error levels. Error level 8 is the least helpful, because PHP has no way of detecting which PHP extension was responsible for stopping the upload. Fortunately, it's rarely encountered.

Table 6-2. Meaning of the different error levels in the $_FILES array

Error level*	Meaning
0	Upload successful
1	File exceeds maximum upload size specified in php.ini (default 2MB)
2	File exceeds size specified by MAX_FILE_SIZE (see PHP Solution 6-1)
3	File only partially uploaded
4	Form submitted with no file specified
6	No temporary folder
7	Cannot write file to disk
8	Upload stopped by an unspecified PHP extension

Error level 5 is not currently defined.

2. Add the following code after the definition of getMessages() in Upload.php:

```
protected function checkError($filename, $error) {
  switch ($error) {
    case 0:
      return true;
    case 1:
    case 2:
      $this->_messages[] = "$filename exceeds maximum size: " . ➥
        $this->getMaxSize();
      return true;
    case 3:
```

```
      $this->_messages[] = "Error uploading $filename. Please try again.";
      return false;
    case 4:
      $this->_messages[] = 'No file selected.';
      return false;
    default:
      $this->_messages[] = "System error uploading $filename. Contact ➥
        webmaster.";
      return false;
  }
}
```

Preceding the definition with the `protected` keyword means this method can be accessed only inside the class. The `checkError()` method will be used internally by the `move()` method to determine whether to save the file to the upload folder.

It takes two arguments, the filename and the error level. The method uses a `switch` statement (see "Using the switch statement for decision chains" in Chapter 3). Normally, each `case` in a `switch` statement is followed by the `break` keyword, but that's not necessary here, because `return` is used instead.

Error level 0 indicates a successful upload, so it returns `true`.

Error levels 1 and 2 indicate the file is too big, and an error message is added to the `$_messages` array. Part of the message is created by a method called `getMaxSize()`, which converts the value of `$_max` from bytes to kB. You'll define `getMaxSize()` shortly. Note the use of `$this->`, which tells PHP to look for the method definition in this class.

Logic would seem to demand that `checkError()` should return `false` if a file's too big. However, setting it to `true` gives you the opportunity to check for the wrong MIME type, too, so you can report both errors.

Error levels 3 and 4 return `false` and add the reason to the `$_messages` array. The `default` keyword catches other error levels, including any that might be added in future, and adds a generic reason.

3. Before using the `checkError()` method, let's define the other tests. Add the definition for the `checkSize()` method, which looks like this:

```
protected function checkSize($filename, $size) {
  if ($size == 0) {
    return false;
  } elseif ($size > $this->_max) {
    $this->_messages[] = "$filename exceeds maximum size: " . ➥
      $this->getMaxSize();
    return false;
  } else {
    return true;
  }
}
```

Like `checkError()`, this takes two arguments—the filename and the size of the file as reported by the `$_FILES` array—and returns `true` or `false`.

The conditional statement starts by checking if the reported size is zero. This happens if the file is too big or no file was selected. In either case, there's no file to save and the error message will have been created by `checkError()`, so the method returns `false`.

Next, the reported size is compared with the value stored in `$_max`. Although `checkError()` should pick up files that are too big, you still need to make this comparison in case the user has managed to sidestep `MAX_FILE_SIZE`. The error message also uses `getMaxSize()` to display the maximum size.

If the size is OK, the method returns `true`.

4. The third test checks the MIME type. Add the following code to the class definition:

```
protected function checkType($filename, $type) {
  if (!in_array($type, $this->_permitted)) {
    $this->_messages[] = "$filename is not a permitted type of file.";
    return false;
  } else {
    return true;
  }
}
```

This follows the same pattern of accepting the filename and the value to be checked as arguments and returning `true` or `false`. The conditional statement checks the type reported by the `$_FILES` array against the array stored in `$_permitted`. If it's not in the array, the reason for rejection is added to the `$_messages` array.

5. The `getMaxSize()` method used by the error messages in `checkError()` and `checkSize()` converts the raw number of bytes stored in `$_max` into a friendlier format. Add the following definition to the class file:

```
public function getMaxSize() {
  return number_format($this->_max/1024, 1) . 'kB';
}
```

This uses the `number_format()` function, which normally takes two arguments: the value you want to format and the number of decimal places you want the number to have. The first argument is `$this->_max/1024`, which divides `$_max` by 1024 (the number of bytes in a kB). The second argument is 1, so the number is formatted to one decimal place. The `. 'kB'` at the end concatenates kB to the formatted number.

The `getMaxSize()` method has been declared public in case you want to display the value in another part of a script that uses the `Ps2_Upload` class.

6. You can now check the validity of the file before handing it to `move_uploaded_file()`. Amend the `move()` method like this:

```
public function move() {
  $field = current($this->_uploaded);
  $OK = $this->checkError($field['name'], $field['error']);
  if ($OK) {
    $success = move_uploaded_file($field['tmp_name'], $this->_destination ↵
      . $field['name']);
    if ($success) {
      $this->_messages[] = $field['name'] . ' uploaded successfully';
    } else {
      $this->_messages[] = 'Could not upload ' . $field['name'];
    }
  }
}
```

The arguments passed to the checkError() method are the filename and the error level reported by the $_FILES array. The result is stored in $OK, which a conditional statement uses to control whether move_uploaded_file() is called.

7. The next two tests go inside the conditional statement. Both pass the filename and relevant element of the $_FILES array as arguments. The results of the tests are used in a new conditional statement to control the call to move_uploaded_file() like this:

```
public function move() {
  $field = current($this->_uploaded);
  $OK = $this->checkError($field['name'], $field['error']);
  if ($OK) {
    $sizeOK = $this->checkSize($field['name'], $field['size']);
    $typeOK = $this->checkType($field['name'], $field['type']);
    if ($sizeOK && $typeOK) {
      $success = move_uploaded_file($field['tmp_name'], $this->_destination ↵
        . $field['name']);
      if ($success) {
        $this->_messages[] = $field['name'] . ' uploaded successfully';
      } else {
        $this->_messages[] = 'Could not upload ' . $field['name'];
      }
    }
  }
}
```

8. Save Upload.php, and test it again with file_upload.php. With images smaller than 50kB, it works the same as before. But if you try uploading a file that's too big and of the wrong MIME type, you get a result similar to Figure 6-5.

You can check your code against Upload_02.php in the ch06 folder.

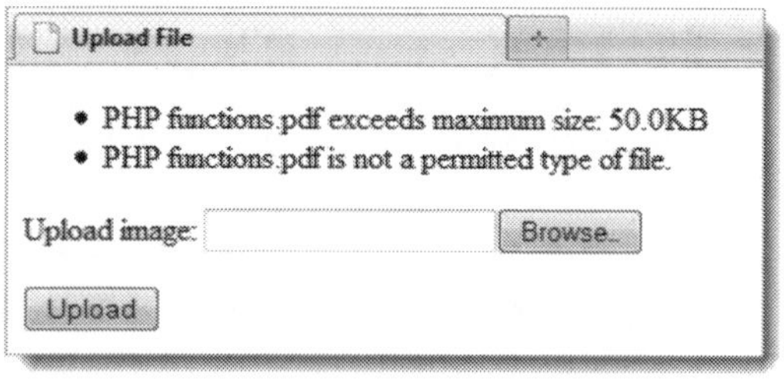

Figure 6-5. The class now reports errors with invalid size and MIME types.

Changing protected properties

The $_permitted property restricts uploads to images, but you might want to allow different types. Instead of diving into the class definition file every time you have different requirements, you can create public methods that allow you to make changes to protected properties on the fly.

You can find definitions of recognized MIME types at www.iana.org/assignments/media-types. Table 6-3 lists some of the most commonly used ones.

Table 6-3. Commonly used MIME types

Category	MIME type	Description
Documents	application/pdf	PDF document
	text/plain	Plain text
	text/rtf	Rich text format
Images	image/gif	GIF format
	image/jpeg	JPEG format (includes .jpg files)
	image/pjpeg	JPEG format (nonstandard, used by Internet Explorer)
	image/png	PNG format
	image/tiff	TIFF format

An easy way to find other MIME types not listed in Table 6-3 is to use file_upload_02.php and see what value is displayed for $_FILES['image']['type'].

PHP Solution 6-4: Allowing different types and sizes to be uploaded

This PHP solution shows you how to add one or more MIME types to the existing $_permitted array and how to reset the array completely. To keep the code relatively simple, the class checks the validity of only a few MIME types. Once you understand the principle, you can expand the code to suit your own requirements. You'll also add a public method to change the maximum permitted size.

Continue working with Upload.php from the previous PHP solution. Alternatively, use Upload_02.php in the ch06 folder.

1. The Ps2_Upload class already defines four permitted MIME types for images, but there might be occasions when you want to permit other types of documents to be uploaded as well. Rather than listing all permitted types again, it's easier to add the extra ones. Add the following method definition to the class file:

```
public function addPermittedTypes($types) {
  $types = (array) $types;
  $this->isValidMime($types);
  $this->_permitted = array_merge($this->_permitted, $types);
}
```

This takes a single argument, $types, which is checked for validity and then merged with the $_permitted array. The first line inside the method looks like this:

```
$types = (array) $types;
```

The highlighted code is what's known as a **casting operator** (see "Explicitly changing a data type" after this PHP solution). It forces the following variable to be a specific type—in this case, an array. This is because the final line of code passes $types to the array_merge() function, which expects both arguments to be arrays. As the function name indicates, it merges the arrays and returns the combined array.

The advantage of using the casting operator here is that it allows you to use either an array or a string as an argument to addPermittedTypes(). For example, to add multiple types, you use an array like this:

```
$upload->addPermittedTypes(array('application/pdf', 'text/plain'));
```

But to add one new type, you can use a string like this:

```
$upload->addPermittedTypes('application/pdf');
```

Without the casting operator, you would need an array for even one item like this:

```
$upload->addPermittedTypes(array('application/pdf'));
```

The middle line calls an internal method isValidMime(), which you'll define shortly.

2. On other occasions, you might want to replace the existing list of permitted MIME types entirely. Add the following definition for setPermittedTypes() to the class file:

```
public function setPermittedTypes($types) {
  $types = (array) $types;
  $this->isValidMime($types);
  $this->_permitted = $types;
}
```

This is quite simple. The first two lines are the same as addPermittedTypes(). The final line assigns $types to the $_permitted property, replacing all existing values.

3. Both methods call isValidMime(), which checks the values passed to them as arguments. Define the method now. It looks like this:

```
protected function isValidMime($types) {
  $alsoValid = array('image/tiff',
                     'application/pdf',
                     'text/plain',
                     'text/rtf');
  $valid = array_merge($this->_permitted, $alsoValid);
  foreach ($types as $type) {
    if (!in_array($type, $valid)) {
      throw new Exception("$type is not a permitted MIME type");
    }
  }
}
```

The method begins by defining an array of valid MIME types not already listed in the $_permitted property. Both arrays are then merged to produce a full list of valid types. The foreach loop checks each value in the user-submitted array by passing it to the in_array() function. If a value fails to match those listed in the $valid array, the isValidMime() method throws an exception, preventing the script from continuing.

4. The public method for changing the maximum permitted size needs to check that the submitted value is a number and assign it to the $_max property. Add the following method definition to the class file:

```
public function setMaxSize($num) {
  if (!is_numeric($num)) {
    throw new Exception("Maximum size must be a number.");
  }
  $this->_max = (int) $num;
}
```

This passes the submitted value to the is_numeric() function, which checks that it's a number. If it isn't, an exception is thrown.

The final line uses another casting operator—this time forcing the value to be an integer—before assigning the value to the $_max property. The is_numeric() function accepts any type of number, including a hexadecimal one or a string containing a numeric value. So, this ensures that the value is converted to an integer.

PHP also has a function called is_int() that checks for an integer. However, the value cannot be anything else. For example, it rejects '102400' even though it's a numeric value because the quotes make it a string.

5. Save `Upload.php`, and test `file_upload.php` again. It should continue to upload images smaller than 50kB as before.

6. Amend the code in `file_upload.php` to change the maximum permitted size to 3000 bytes like this:

```
$max = 3000;
if (isset($_POST['upload'])) {
// define the path to the upload folder
$destination = 'C:/upload_test/';
require_once('../classes/Ps2/Upload.php');
try {
  $upload = new Ps2_Upload($destination);
  $upload->setMaxSize($max);
  $upload->move();
```

By changing the value of $max and passing it as the argument to `setMaxSize()`, you affect both `MAX_FILE_SIZE` in the form's hidden field and the maximum value stored inside the class. Note that the call to `setMaxSize()` *must* come before you use the `move()` method. There's no point changing the maximum size in the class after the file has already been saved.

7. Save `file_upload_php`, and test it again. Select an image you haven't used before, or delete the contents of the `upload_test` folder. The first time you try it, you should see a message that the file is too big. If you check the `upload_test` folder, you'll see it hasn't been transferred.

8. Try it again. This time, you should see a result similar to Figure 6-6.

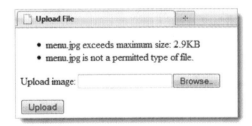

Figure 6-6. The size restriction is working, but there's an error in checking the MIME type.

What's going on? The reason you probably didn't see the message about the permitted type of file the first time is because the value of `MAX_FILE_SIZE` in the hidden field isn't refreshed until you reload the form in the browser. The error message appears the second time because the updated value of `MAX_FILE_SIZE` prevents the file from being uploaded. As a result, the type element of the `$_FILES` array is empty. You need to tweak the `checkType()` method to fix this problem.

9. In `Upload.php`, amend the `checkType()` definition like this:

```
protected function checkType($filename, $type) {
  if (empty($type)) {
```

```
      return false;
   } elseif (!in_array($type, $this->_permitted)) {
      $this->_messages[] = "$filename is not a permitted type of file.";
      return false;
   } else {
      return true;
   }
}
```

This adds a new condition that returns `false` if $type is empty. It needs to come before the other condition, because there's no empty value in the $_permitted array, which is why the false error message was generated.

10. Save the class definition, and test `file_upload.php` again. This time, you should see only the message about the file being too big.

11. Reset the value of $max at the top of `file_upload.php` to **51200**. You should now be able to upload the image. If it fails the first time, it's because MAX_FILE_SIZE hasn't been refreshed in the form.

12. Test the `addPermittedTypes()` method by adding an array of MIME types like this:

```
$upload->setMaxSize($max);
$upload->addPermittedTypes(array('application/pdf', 'text/plain'));
$upload->move();
```

MIME types must always be in lowercase.

13. Try uploading a PDF file. Unless it's smaller than 50kB, it won't be uploaded. Try a small text document. It should be uploaded. Change the value of $max to a suitably large number, and the PDF should also be uploaded.

14. Replace the call to `addPermittedTypes()` with `setPermittedTypes()` like this:

```
$upload->setMaxSize($max);
$upload->setPermittedTypes('text/plain');
$upload->move();
```

You can now upload only text files. All other types are rejected.

If necessary, check your class definition against `Upload_03.php` in the `ch06` folder.

Hopefully, by now you should be getting the idea of how a PHP class is built from functions (methods) that are dedicated to doing a single job. Fixing the incorrect error message about the image not being a permitted type was made easier by the fact that the message could only have come from the `checkType()` method. Most of the code used in the method definitions relies on built-in PHP functions. Once you learn which functions are the most suited to the task in hand, building a class—or any other PHP script—becomes much easier.

Explicitly changing a data type

Most of the time, you don't need to worry about the data type of a variable or value. Strictly speaking, all values submitted through a form are strings, but PHP silently converts numbers to the appropriate data type. This automatic **type juggling**, as it's called, is very convenient. There are times, though, when you want to make sure a value is a specific data type. In such cases, you can **cast** (or change) a value to the desired type by preceding it with the name of the data type in parentheses. You saw two examples of this in PHP Solution 6-4, casting a string to an array and a numeric value to an integer. This is how the value assigned to $types was converted to an array:

```
$types = (array) $types;
```

If the value is already of the desired type, it remains unchanged. Table 6-4 lists the casting operators used in PHP.

Table 6-4. PHP casting operators

Operator	Alternatives	Converts to
(array)		Array
(bool)	(boolean)	Boolean (true or false)
(float)	(double), (real)	Floating-point number
(int)	(integer)	Integer
(object)		Object
(string)		String
(unset)		Null

To learn more about what happens when casting between certain types, see the online documentation at http://docs.php.net/manual/en/language.types.type-juggling.php.

Preventing files from being overwritten

As the script stands, PHP automatically overwrites existing files without warning. That may be exactly what you want. On the other hand, it may be your worst nightmare. The class needs to offer a choice of whether to overwrite an existing file or to give it a unique name.

PHP Solution 6-5: Checking an uploaded file's name before saving it

This PHP solution improves the Ps2_Upload class by adding the option to insert a number before the filename extension of an uploaded file to avoid overwriting an existing file of the same name. By default, this option is turned on. At the same time, all spaces in filenames are replaced with underscores. Spaces should never be used in file and folder names on a web server, so this feature isn't optional.

Continue working with the same class definition file as before. Alternatively, use `Upload_03.php` in the ch06 folder.

1. Both operations are performed by the same method, which takes two arguments: the filename and a Boolean variable that determines whether to overwrite existing files. Add the following definition to the class file:

```
protected function checkName($name, $overwrite) {
  $nospaces = str_replace(' ', '_', $name);
  if ($nospaces != $name) {
    $this->_renamed = true;
  }
  if (!$overwrite) {
    // rename the file if it already exists
  }
  return $nospaces;
}
```

This first part of the method definition takes the filename and replaces spaces with underscores using the `str_replace()` function, which takes the following three arguments:

- The character(s) to replace—in this case, a space

- The replacement character(s)—in this case, an underscore

- The string you want to update—in this case, $name

The result is stored in `$nospaces`, which is then compared to the original value in `$name`. If they're not the same, the filename has been changed, so the `$_renamed` property is reset to `true`. If the original name didn't contain any spaces, `$nospaces` and `$name` are the same, and the `$_renamed` property—which is initialized when the `Ps2_Upload` object is created—remains `false`.

The next conditional statement controls whether to rename the file if one with the same name already exists. You'll add that code in the next step.

The final line returns `$nospaces`, which contains the name that will be used when the file is saved.

2. Add the code that renames the file if another with the same name already exists:

```
protected function checkName($name, $overwrite) {
  $nospaces = str_replace(' ', '_', $name);
  if ($nospaces != $name) {
    $this->_renamed = true;
  }
  if (!$overwrite) {
    // rename the file if it already exists
    $existing = scandir($this->_destination);
    if (in_array($nospaces, $existing)) {
      $dot = strrpos($nospaces, '.');
      if ($dot) {
```

```
        $base = substr($nospaces, 0, $dot);
        $extension = substr($nospaces, $dot);
    } else {
        $base = $nospaces;
        $extension = '';
    }
    $i = 1;
    do {
        $nospaces = $base . '_' . $i++ . $extension;
    } while (in_array($nospaces, $existing));
    $this->_renamed = true;
    }
}
return $nospaces;
}
```

The first line of new code uses the scandir() function, which returns an array of all the files and folders in a directory (folder), and stores it in $existing.

The conditional statement on the next line passes $nospaces to the in_array() function to determine if the $existing array contains a file with the same name. If there's no match, the code inside the conditional statement is ignored, and the method returns $nospaces without any further changes.

If $nospaces is found the $existing array, a new name needs to be generated. To insert a number before the filename extension, you need to split the name by finding the final dot (period). This is done with the strrpos() function (note the double-r in the name), which finds the position of a character by searching from the end of the string.

It's possible that someone might upload a file that doesn't have a filename extension, in which case strrpos() returns false.

If a dot is found, the following line extracts the part of the name up to the dot and stores it in $base:

```
$base = substr($nospaces, 0, $dot);
```

The substr() function takes two or three arguments. If three arguments are used, it returns a substring from the position specified by the second argument and uses the third argument to determine the length of the section to extract. PHP counts the characters in strings from 0, so this gets the part of the filename without the extension.

If two arguments are used, substr() returns a substring from the position indicated by the second argument to the end of the string. So this line gets the filename extension:

```
$extension = substr($nospaces, $dot);
```

If $dot is false, the full name is stored in $base, and $extension is an empty string.

The section that does the renaming looks like this:

```
$i = 1;
```

```
do {
  $nospaces = $base . '_' . $i++ . $extension;
} while (in_array($nospaces, $existing));
```

It begins by initializing $i as 1. Then a do. . . while loop builds a new name from $base, an underscore, $i, and $extension. Let's say you're uploading a file called menu.jpg, and there's already a file with the same name in the upload folder. The loop rebuilds the name as menu_1.jpg and assigns the result to $nospaces. The loop's condition then uses in_array() to check whether menu_1.jpg is in the $existing array.

If menu_1.jpg already exists, the loop continues, but the increment operator (++) has increased $i to 2, so $nospaces becomes menu_2.jpg, which is again checked by in_array(). The loop continues until in_array() no longer finds a match. Whatever value remains in $nospaces is used as the new filename.

Finally, $_renamed is set to true.

Phew! The code is relatively short, but it has a lot of work to do.

3. Now you need to amend the move() method to call checkName(). The revised code looks like this:

```
public function move($overwrite = false) {
  $field = current($this->_uploaded);
  $OK = $this->checkError($field['name'], $field['error']);
  if ($OK) {
    $sizeOK = $this->checkSize($field['name'], $field['size']);
    $typeOK = $this->checkType($field['name'], $field['type']);
    if ($sizeOK && $typeOK) {
      $name = $this->checkName($field['name'], $overwrite);
      $success = move_uploaded_file($field['tmp_name'], $this->_destination ➝
        . $name);
      if ($success) {
        $message = $field['name'] . ' uploaded successfully';
        if ($this->_renamed) {
          $message .= " and renamed $name";
        }
        $this->_messages[] = $message;
      } else {
        $this->_messages[] = 'Could not upload ' . $field['name'];
      }
    }
  }
}
```

The first change adds $overwrite = false as an argument to the method. Assigning a value to an argument in the definition like this sets the default value and makes the argument optional. So, using $upload->move() automatically results in the checkName() method assigning a unique name to the file if necessary.

The checkName() method is called inside the conditional statement that runs only if the previous checks have all been positive. It takes as its arguments the filename transmitted through the $_FILES array and $overwrite. The result is stored in $name, which now needs to be used as part of the second argument to move_uploaded_file() to ensure the new name is used when saving the file.

The final set of changes assign the message reporting successful upload to a temporary variable $message. If the file has been renamed, $_renamed is true and a string is added to $message reporting the new name. The complete message is then assigned to the $_messages array.

4. Save Upload.php, and test the revised class in file_upload.php. Start by amending the call to the move() method by passing true as the argument like this:

```
$upload->move(true);
```

5. Upload the same image several times. You should receive a message that the upload has been successful, but when you check the contents of the upload_test folder, there's only one copy of the image. It has been overwritten each time.

6. Remove the argument from the call to move():

```
$upload->move();
```

7. Save file_upload.php, and repeat the test, uploading the same image several times. Each time you upload the file, you should see a message that it has been renamed.

8. Repeat the test with an image that has a space in its filename. The space is replaced with an underscore, and a number is inserted in the name after the first upload.

9. Check the results by inspecting the contents of the upload_test folder. You should see something similar to Figure 6-7.

You can check your code, if necessary, against Upload_04.php in the ch06 folder.

Figure 6-7. The class removes spaces from filenames and prevents files from being overwritten.

Uploading multiple files

You now have a flexible class for file uploads, but it can handle only one file at a time. Adding the `multiple` attribute to the file field's `<input>` tag permits the selection of multiple files in an HTML5-compliant browser. Older browsers also support multiple uploads if you add extra file fields to your form.

The final stage in building the `Ps2_Upload` class is to adapt it to handle multiple files. To understand how the code works, you need to see what happens to the `$_FILES` array when a form allows multiple uploads.

How the $_FILES array handles multiple files

Since `$_FILES` is a multidimensional array, it's capable of handling multiple uploads. In addition to adding the `multiple` attribute to the `<input>` tag, you need to add an empty pair of square brackets to the `name` attribute like this:

```
<input type="file" name="image[]" id="image" multiple>
```

Support for the `multiple` attribute is available in Firefox 3.6, Safari 4, Chrome 4, and Opera 10. At the time of this writing, it is not supported in any version of Internet Explorer, but that might change once the final version of IE9 is released. If you need to support older browsers, omit the `multiple` attribute, and create separate file input fields for however many files you want to upload simultaneously, Give each `<input>` tag the same `name` attribute followed by square brackets.

As you learned in Chapter 5, adding square brackets to the `name` attribute submits multiple values as an array. You can examine how this affects the `$_FILES` array by using `file_upload_06.php` or `file_upload_07.php` in the `ch06` folder. Figure 6-8 shows the result of selecting four files in an HTML5-

compliant browser. The structure of the $_FILES array is the same when a form uses separate input fields that share the same name attribute.

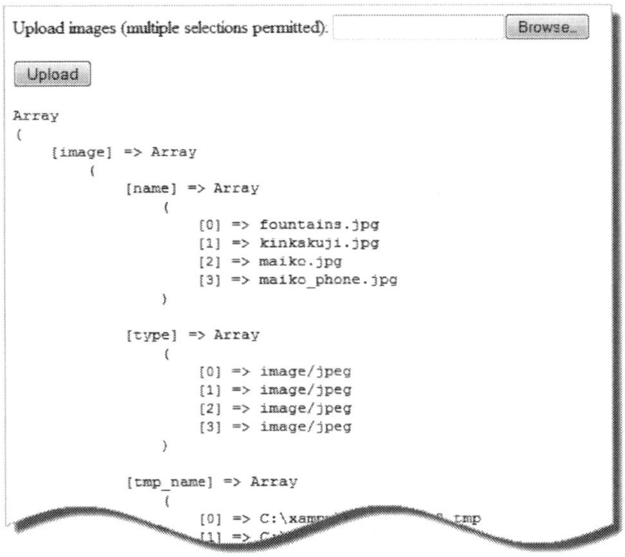

Figure 6-8. The $_FILES array can upload multiple files in a single operation.

Although this structure is not as convenient as having the details of each file stored in a separate subarray, the numeric keys keep track of the details that refer to each file. For example, $_FILES['image']['name'][2] relates directly to $_FILES['image']['tmp_name'][2], and so on.

When you use the HTML5 multiple attribute on file input fields, older browsers upload a single file using the same structure, so the name of the file is stored as $_FILES['image']['name'][0].

PHP Solution 6-6: Adapting the class to handle multiple uploads

This PHP solution shows how to adapt the move() method of the Ps2_Upload class to handle multiple file uploads. The class detects automatically when the $_FILES array is structured like Figure 6-8 and uses a loop to handle however many files are uploaded.

Continue working with your existing class file. Alternatively, use Upload_04.php in the ch06 folder.

1. When you upload a file from a form designed to handle only single uploads, the $_FILES array stores the name like this (see Figure 6-2 earlier in this chapter):

    $_FILES['image']['name']

    When you upload a file from a form capable of handling multiple uploads the name of the first file is stored like this (see Figure 6-8):

    $_FILES['image']['name']**[0]**

In Figures 6-2 and 6-8, both refer to fountains.jpg. $_FILES['image']['name'] is a string in Figure 6-2, but in Figure 6-8 it's an array.

So, by detecting whether the name element is an array, you can decide how to process the $_FILES array. If it's an array, you need to loop through it, passing the appropriate values to the checkError(), checkSize(), checkType(), and checkName() protected methods before passing it to move_uploaded_file(). The problem is that you need to add the index number for a multiple upload, but not for a single upload.

One solution is to require the upload form to use square brackets at the end of the name attribute, even for single uploads. This forces the form to submit the $_FILES array in the same format as shown in Figure 6-8. However, that's far from ideal.

The solution I have adopted is to split the move() method into two.

2. In the move() method select the code highlighted in bold, and cut it to your clipboard.

```
public function move($overwrite = false) {
  $field = current($this->_uploaded);
  $OK = $this->checkError($field['name'], $field['error']);
  if ($OK) {
    $sizeOK = $this->checkSize($field['name'], $field['size']);
    $typeOK = $this->checkType($field['name'], $field['type']);
    if ($sizeOK && $typeOK) {
      $name = $this->checkName($field['name'], $overwrite);
      $success = move_uploaded_file($field['tmp_name'], ↪
        $this->_destination . $name);
      if ($success) {
        $message = $field['name'] . ' uploaded successfully';
        if ($this->_renamed) {
          $message .= " and renamed $name";
        }
        $this->_messages[] = $message;
      } else {
        $this->_messages[] = 'Could not upload ' . $field['name'];
      }
    }
  }
}
```

3. Create a new protected method called processFile(), and paste the code from the move() method between the curly braces like this:

```
protected function processFile() {
  $OK = $this->checkError($field['name'], $field['error']);
  if ($OK) {
    $sizeOK = $this->checkSize($field['name'], $field['size']);
    $typeOK = $this->checkType($field['name'], $field['type']);
    if ($sizeOK && $typeOK) {
      $name = $this->checkName($field['name'], $overwrite);
```

```
      $success = move_uploaded_file($field['tmp_name'], ⮐
        $this->_destination . $name);
      if ($success) {
        $message = $field['name'] . ' uploaded successfully';
        if ($this->_renamed) {
          $message .= " and renamed $name";
        }
        $this->_messages[] = $message;
      } else {
        $this->_messages[] = 'Could not upload ' . $field['name'];
      }
    }
  }
}
```

At the moment, this new method won't do anything because the arguments to checkError(), checkSize(), and so on are dependent on the move() method. To activate the processFile() method, you need to call it from the move() method, and pass the following values as arguments:

- $field['name']

- $field['error']

- $field['size']

- $field['type']

- $field['tmp_name']

- $overwrite

4. Amend the move() method like this:

```
public function move($overwrite = false) {
  $field = current($this->_uploaded);
  $this->processFile($field['name'], $field['error'], $field['size'], ⮐
                     $field['type'], $field['tmp_name'], $overwrite);
}
```

5. Next, fix the arguments in the processFile() definition. Although, you could use the same variables, the code is cleaner and easier to understand if you change them both in the arguments declared between the parentheses and in the body of the method. Amend the code like this:

```
protected function processFile($filename, $error, $size, $type, ⮐
                               $tmp_name, $overwrite) {
  $OK = $this->checkError($filename, $error);
  if ($OK) {
    $sizeOK = $this->checkSize($filename, $size);
    $typeOK = $this->checkType($filename, $type);
    if ($sizeOK && $typeOK) {
      $name = $this->checkName($filename, $overwrite);
```

```
          $success = move_uploaded_file($tmp_name, $this->_destination . $name);
          if ($success) {
            $message = "$filename uploaded successfully";
            if ($this->_renamed) {
              $message .= " and renamed $name";
            }
            $this->_messages[] = $message;
          } else {
            $this->_messages[] = "Could not upload $filename";
          }
        }
      }
    }
```

In other words, $field['name'] has been converted to $filename, $field['error'] to $error, and so on.

6. Splitting the functionality like this gives you a method that handles individual files. You can now use it inside a loop to handle multiple files one by one. Update the move() method like this:

```
public function move($overwrite = false) {
  $field = current($this->_uploaded);
  if (is_array($field['name'])) {
    foreach ($field['name'] as $number => $filename) {
      // process multiple upload
      $this->_renamed = false;
      $this->processFile($filename, $field['error'][$number], ↪
                    $field['size'][$number], $field['type'][$number], ↪
                    $field['tmp_name'][$number], $overwrite);
    }
  } else {
    $this->processFile($field['name'], $field['error'], $field['size'], ↪
                    $field['type'], $field['tmp_name'], $overwrite);
  }
}
```

The conditional statement checks if $field['name'] is an array ($field is the current element of the $_FILES array, so $field['name'] stores $_FILES['image']['name']). If it is an array, a foreach loop is created to handle each uploaded file. The key of each element is assigned to $number. The value of each element is assigned to $filename. These two variables give you access to each file and its details. Using the example in Figure 6-8, the first time the loop runs, $number is 0 and $filename is fountains.jpg. The next time, $number is 1 and $filename is kinkakuji.jpg, and so on.

Each time the loop runs, the $_renamed property needs to be reset to false. The values extracted from the current element of the $_FILES array are then passed to the processFile() method.

The existing code is wrapped in an else block that runs when a single file is uploaded. Don't forget the extra curly brace to close the else block.

7. Save `Upload.php`, and test it with `file_upload.php`. It should work the same as before.

8. If you're using an HTML5-compliant browser, add a pair of square brackets at the end of the `name` attribute in the file field, and insert the `multiple` attribute like this:

```
<input type="file" name="image[]" id="image" multiple>
```

You don't need to make any changes to the PHP code above the `DOCTYPE` declaration. The code is the same for both single and multiple uploads.

9. Save `file_upload.php`, and reload it in your browser. Test it by selecting multiple files. When you click **Upload**, you should see messages relating to each file. Files that meet your criteria are uploaded. Those that are too big or of the wrong type are rejected.

You can check your code against `Upload_05.php` in the `ch06` folder.

Using namespaces in PHP 5.3 and later

Prefixing the class names with `Ps2_` to avoid potential name clashes is a minor inconvenience when you're using only a handful of classes. But third-party libraries of PHP classes, such as the Zend Framework (`http://framework.zend.com/`), often consist of thousands of files in hundreds of folders. Naming the classes can become a major headache. The Zend Framework uses the convention of naming classes after the folder structure, so you can end up with unwieldy class names such as `Zend_File_Transfer_Adapter_Http`.

This led to the decision to implement namespaces in PHP 5.3. The idea is to prevent name collisions and very long class names. Instead of using underscores to indicate the folder structure, namespaces uses backslashes. So, instead of `Ps2_Upload`, the namespaced class name becomes `Ps2\Upload`. Although that doesn't sound like much of a gain, the advantage is that instead of referring all the time to `Ps2\Upload`, you can shorten it to `Upload`.

To declare a namespace, just use the `namespace` keyword followed by the name like this:

```
namespace Ps2;
```

This *must* be the first line of code after the opening PHP tag.

PHP Solution 6-7: Converting the class to use a namespace

This PHP solution shows how to convert the `Ps2_Upload` class to use a namespace. Your server must be running PHP 5.3 or later. It will not work in earlier versions of PHP.

1. Open your copy of `Upload.php` in the `Ps2` folder.

2. Declare the `Ps2` namespace immediately after the opening PHP tag, and change the class name from `Ps2_Upload` to `Upload` like this:

```
<?php
namespace Ps2;
class Upload {
```

3. Save `Upload.php`. That's all you need to do to the class definition.

4. Open `file_upload.php` in the `uploads` folder.

5. Locate the following line:

```
$upload = new Ps2_Upload($destination);
```

Change it to this:

```
$upload = new Ps2\Upload($destination);
```

6. Save `file_upload.php`, and test it. It should work as before.

7. Add the namespace declaration immediately after the opening PHP tag in `file_upload.php`:

```
<?php
namespace Ps2;
```

8. Change the code that instantiates the upload object like this:

```
$upload = new Upload($destination);
```

9. Save `file_upload.php`, and test it again. It should continue to work as before.

You can find examples of the code in `file_upload_ns.php` and `Upload_ns.php` in the `ch06` folder.

This has been a relatively trivial example, which sidesteps many subtleties of using namespaces. To learn more about using namespaces, see `www.phparch.com/2010/03/29/namespaces-in-php/`, as well as `http://docs.php.net/manual/en/language.namespaces.faq.php`.

Using the upload class

The `Ps2_Upload` class is simple to use. Just include the class definition in your script, and create a `Ps2_Upload` object by passing the file path to the upload folder as an argument like this:

```
$destination = 'C:/upload_test/';
$upload = new Ps2_Upload($destination);
```

The path to the upload folder must end in a trailing slash.

The class has the following public methods:

- `setMaxSize()`: Takes an integer and sets the maximum size for each upload file, overriding the default 51200 bytes (50kB). The value must be expressed as bytes.
- `getMaxSize()`: Reports the maximum size in kB formatted to one decimal place.
- `addPermittedTypes()`: Takes an array of MIME types, and adds them to the types of file accepted for upload. A single MIME type can be passed as a string.
- `setPermittedTypes()`: Similar to `addPermittedTypes()`, but replaces existing values.
- `move()`: Saves the file(s) to the destination folder. Spaces in filenames are replaced by underscores. By default, files with the same name as an existing file are renamed by inserting a number in front of the filename extension. To overwrite files, pass `true` as an argument.
- `getMessages()`: Returns an array of messages reporting the status of uploads.

Points to watch with file uploads

Uploading files from a web form is easy with PHP. The main causes of failure are not setting the correct permissions on the upload directory or folder, and forgetting to move the uploaded file to its target destination before the end of the script. Letting other people upload files to your server, however, exposes you to risk. In effect, you're allowing visitors the freedom to write to your server's hard disk. It's not something you would allow strangers to do on your own computer, so you should guard access to your upload directory with the same degree of vigilance.

Ideally, uploads should be restricted to registered and trusted users, so the upload form should be in a password-protected part of your site. Also, the upload folder does not need to be inside your site root, so locate it in a private directory whenever possible unless you want uploaded material to be displayed immediately in your web pages. Remember, though, there is no way PHP can check that material is legal or decent, so immediate public display entails risks that go beyond the merely technical. You should also bear the following security points in mind:

- Set a maximum size for uploads both in the web form and on the server side.
- Restrict the types of uploaded files by inspecting the MIME type in the $_FILES array.
- Replace spaces in filenames with underscores or hyphens.
- Inspect your upload folder on a regular basis. Make sure there's nothing in there that shouldn't be, and do some housekeeping from time to time. Even if you limit file upload sizes, you may run out of your allocated space without realizing it.

Chapter review

This chapter has introduced you to creating a PHP class. If you're new to PHP or programming, you might have found it tough going. Don't be disheartened. The Ps2_Upload class contains more than 170 lines of code, and some of it is complex, although I hope the descriptions have explained what the code is doing at each stage. Even if you don't understand all the code, the Ps2_Upload class will save you a lot of time. It implements the main security measures necessary for file uploads, yet using it involves as little as ten lines of code:

```php
if (isset($_POST['upload'])) {
  require_once('classes/Ps2/Upload.php');
  try {
    $upload = new Ps2_Upload('C:/upload_test/');
    $upload->move();
    $result = $upload->getMessages();
  } catch (Exception $e) {
    echo $e->getMessage();
  }
}
```

If you found this chapter a struggle, come back to it later when you have more experience, and you should find the code easier to understand.

In the next chapter, you'll learn some techniques for inspecting the contents of files and folders, including how to use PHP to read and write text files.

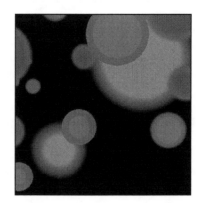

Chapter 7

Using PHP to Manage Files

PHP has a huge range of functions designed to work with the server's file system, but finding the right one for the job isn't always easy. This chapter cuts through the tangle to show you some practical uses of these functions, such as reading and writing text files to store small amounts of information without a database. Loops play an important role in inspecting the contents of the file system, so you'll also explore some of the Standard PHP Library (SPL) iterators that are designed to make loops more efficient.

As well as opening local files, PHP can read public files, such as news feeds, on other servers. News feeds are normally formatted as XML (Extensible Markup Language). In the past, extracting information from an XML file was tortuous process, but that's no longer the case thanks to the very aptly named SimpleXML that was introduced in PHP 5. In this chapter, I'll show you how to create a drop-down menu that lists all images in a folder, create a function to select files of a particular type from a folder, pull in a live news feed from another server, and prompt a visitor to download an image or PDF file rather than open it in the browser. As an added bonus, you'll learn how to change the time zone of a date retrieved from another website.

This chapter covers the following subjects:

- Reading and writing files
- Listing the contents of a folder
- Inspecting files with the `SplFileInfo` class
- Controlling loops with SPL iterators
- Using SimpleXML to extract information from an XML file
- Consuming an RSS feed
- Creating a download link

Checking that PHP has permission to open a file

As I explained in the previous chapter, PHP runs on most Linux servers as nobody or apache. Consequently, a folder must have minimum access permissions of 755 for scripts to open a file. To create or alter files, you normally need to set global access permissions of 777, the least secure setting. If PHP is configured to run in your own name, you can be more restrictive, because your scripts can create and write to files in any folder for which you have read, write, and execute permissions. On a Windows server, you need write permission to create or update a file. If you need assistance with changing permissions, consult your hosting company.

Configuration settings that affect file access

Hosting companies can impose further restrictions on file access through php.ini. To find out what restrictions have been imposed, run phpinfo() on your website, and check the settings in the **Core** section. Table 7-1 lists the settings you need to check. Unless you run your own server, you normally have no control over these settings.

Table 7-1. PHP configuration settings that affect file access

Directive	Default value	Description
allow_url_fopen	**On**	Allows PHP scripts to open public files on the Internet.
allow_url_include	**Off**	Controls the ability to include remote files.
open_basedir	**no value**	Restricts accessible files to the specified directory tree. Even if no value is set, restrictions may be set directly in the server configuration.
safe_mode	**Off**	Mainly restricts the ability to use certain functions (for details, see www.php.net/manual/en/features.safe-mode.functions.php). This feature has been deprecated since PHP 5.3 and will be removed at a future date.
safe_mode_include_dir	**no value**	If safe_mode is enabled, user and group ID checks are skipped when files are included from the specified directory tree.

Accessing remote files

Arguably the most important setting in Table 7-1 is allow_url_fopen. If it's disabled, you cannot access useful external data sources, such as news feeds and public XML documents. Prior to PHP 5.2, allow_url_fopen also allowed you to include remote files in your pages. This represented a major security risk, prompting many hosting companies to disabled allow_url_fopen. The security risk was eliminated in PHP 5.2 by the introduction of a separate setting for including remote files: allow_url_include, which is disabled by default.

After PHP 5.2 was released, not all hosting companies realized that allow_url_fopen had changed, and continued to disable it. Hopefully, by the time you read this, the message will have sunk in that allow_url_fopen allows you to read remote files, but not to include them directly in your scripts. If your hosting company still disables allow_url_fopen, ask it to turn it on. Otherwise, you won't be able to use

PHP Solution 7-5. If the hosting company refuses, you should consider moving to one with a better understanding of PHP.

Configuration settings that affect local file access

If the **Local Value** column for open_basedir or safe_mode_include_dir displays **no value**, you can ignore this section. However, if it does have a value, the meaning depends on whether the value ends with a trailing slash, like this:

/home/includes/

In this example, you can open or include files only from the includes directory or any of its subdirectories.

If the value doesn't have a trailing slash, the value after the last slash acts as a prefix. For example, /home/inc gives you access to /home/inc, /home/includes, /home/incredible, and so on— assuming, of course, that they exist or you have the right to create them. PHP Solution 7-1 shows what happens when you try to access a file outside the limits imposed by open_basedir.

Creating a file storage folder for local testing

Storing data inside your site root is highly insecure, particularly if you need to set global access permissions on the folder. If you have access to a private folder outside the site root, create your data store as a subfolder and give it the necessary permissions.

For the purposes of this chapter, I suggest that Windows users create a folder called private on their C drive. Mac users should create a private folder inside their home folder and then set **Read & Write** permissions in the folder's **Info** panel as described in the previous chapter.

Reading and writing files

The restrictions described in the previous section reduce the attraction of reading and writing files with PHP. Using a database is more convenient and offers greater security. However, that assumes you have access to a database and the necessary knowledge to administer it. So, for small-scale data storage and retrieval, working directly with text files is worth considering.

Reading files in a single operation

The simplest way to read the contents of a text file is to use file_get_contents() or readfile().

PHP Solution 7-1: Getting the contents of a text file

This PHP solution demonstrates how to use file_get_contents() and readfile(), and explains how they differ.

1. Create a text file in your private folder, type some text into it, and save it as filetest_01.txt (or use the version in the ch07 folder).

2. Create a new folder called filesystem in your phpsols site root, and create a PHP file called get_contents.php in the new folder. Insert the following code inside a PHP block

(get_contents_01.php in the ch07 folder shows the code embedded in a web page, but you can use just the PHP code for testing purposes):

```
echo file_get_contents('C:/private/filetest_01.txt');
```

If you're on a Mac, amend the pathname like this, using your own Mac username:

```
echo file_get_contents('/Users/username/private/filetest_01.txt');
```

If you're testing on a remote server, amend the pathname accordingly.

For brevity, the remaining examples in this chapter show only the Windows pathname.

3. Save get_contents.php, and view it in a browser. Depending on what you wrote in filetest_01.txt, you should see something like the following screenshot.

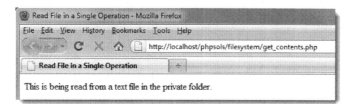

You shouldn't see any error messages on your local system, unless you typed the code incorrectly or you didn't set the correct permissions on a Mac. However, on a remote system, you may see error messages similar to this:

Warning: file_get_contents() [function.file-get-contents]: open_basedir restriction in effect. File(C:/private/filetest_01.txt) is not within the allowed path(s): (c:/xampp/htdocs;C:/dpowers) in **C:\xampp\htdocs\phpsols\filesystem\get_contents.php** on line 10

Warning: file_get_contents(C:/private/filetest_01.txt) [function.file-get-contents]: failed to open stream: Operation not permitted in **C:\xampp\htdocs\phpsols\filesystem\get_contents.php** on line 10

The error messages in the preceding screenshot were created on a local system to demonstrate what happens when open_basedir has been set either in php.ini or on the server. They mean you're trying to access a file outside your permitted file structure. The first error message should indicate the allowed paths. On a Windows server, each path is separated by a semicolon. On Linux, the separator is a colon.

4. Change the code in get_contents.php like this (it's in get_contents_02.php):

```
readfile('C:/private/filetest_01.txt');
```

5. Save `get_contents.php`, and reload it in your browser. The contents of the text file are displayed as before.

So, what's the difference? The original code uses `echo` to display the contents of the file. The amended code doesn't use `echo`. In other words, `file_get_contents()` simply gets the contents of a file, but `readfile()` also displays it immediately. The advantage of `file_get_contents()` is that you can assign the file contents to a variable and process it in some way before deciding what to do with it.

6. Change the code in `get_contents.php` like this (or use `get_contents_03.php`), and load the page into a browser:

```
// get the contents of the file
$contents = file_get_contents('C:/private/filetest_01.txt');
// split the contents into an array of words
$words = explode(' ', $contents);
// extract the first four elements of the array
$first = array_slice($words, 0, 4);
// join the first four elements and display
echo implode(' ', $first);
```

This stores the contents of `filetest_01.txt` in a variable, which is passed to the `explode()` function. This alarmingly named function "blows apart" a string and converts it into an array, using the first argument to determine where to break the string. In this case, a space is used, so the contents of the text file are split into an array of words.

The array of words is then passed to the `array_slice()` function, which takes a slice out of an array starting from the position specified in the second argument. The third argument specifies the length of the slice. PHP counts arrays from 0, so this extracts the first four words.

Finally, `implode()` does the opposite of `explode()`, joining the elements of an array and inserting the first argument between each one. The result is displayed by `echo`, producing the following outcome:

Instead of displaying the entire contents of the file, the script now displays only the first four words. The full string is still stored in `$contents`.

7. If you need to extract the first few words from a string on a regular basis, you could create a custom function like this:

```
function getFirstWords($string, $number) {
```

```
$words = explode(' ', $string);
$first = array_slice($words, 0, $number);
return implode(' ', $first);
}
```

You can extract the first seven words like this (the code is in get_contents_04.php):

```
$contents = file_get_contents('C:/private/filetest_01.txt');
echo getFirstWords($contents, 7);
```

8. Among the dangers with accessing external files are that the file might be missing or its name misspelled. Change the code like this (it's in get_contents_05.php):

```
$contents = file_get_contents('C:/private/filetest_01.txt');
if ($contents === false) {
  echo 'Sorry, there was a problem reading the file.';
} else {
  echo $contents;
}
```

If the file_get_contents() function can't open the file, it returns false. Often, you can test for false by using the logical Not operator like this:

```
if (!$contents) {
```

If the file is empty or contains only the number 0, $contents is implicitly false. To make sure the returned value is explicitly false, you need to use the **identical operator** (three equal signs).

9. Test the page in a browser, and it should display the contents of the text file as before.

10. Replace the contents of filetest_01.txt with the number 0. Save the text file, and reload get_contents.php in the browser. The number displays correctly.

11. Delete the number in the text file, and reload get_contents.php. You should get a blank screen, but no error message. The file loads, but doesn't contain anything.

12. Change the code in get_contents.php so that it attempts to load a nonexistent file. When you load the page, you should see an ugly error message like this:

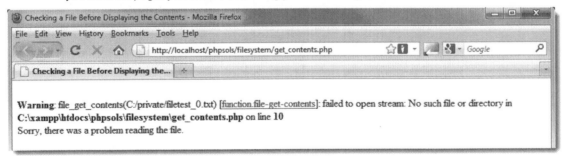

"Failed to open stream" means it couldn't open the file.

13. This is an ideal place to use the error control operator (see Chapter 4). Insert an @ mark immediately in front of the call to `file_get_contents()` like this (the code is in `get_contents_07.php`):

```
$contents = @ file_get_contents('C:/private/filetest0.txt');
```

14. Test `get_contents.php` in a browser. You should now see only the following custom error message:

> *Always add the error control operator only after testing the rest of a script. When developing, you need to see error messages to understand why something isn't working the way you expect.*

Text files can be used as a **flat-file database**—where each record is stored on a separate line, with a tab, comma, or other delimiter between each field (see `http://en.wikipedia.org/wiki/Flat_file_database`). With this sort of file, it's more convenient to store each line individually in an array to process with a loop. The `file()` function builds the array automatically.

PHP Solution 7-2: Reading a text file into an array

To demonstrate the `file()` function, this PHP solution uses `filetest_02.txt`, which contains just two lines as follows:

```
david, codeslave
chris, bigboss
```

This will be used as the basis for a simple login system to be developed further in Chapter 9.

1. Create a PHP file called `file.php` inside the `filesystem` folder. Insert the following code (or use `file_01.php` from the `ch07` folder):

```php
<?php
// read the file into an array called $users
$users = file('C:/private/filetest_02.txt');
?>
<pre>
<?php print_r($users); ?>
</pre>
```

This draws the contents of `filetest_02.txt` into an array called `$users` and then passes it to `print_r()` to display the contents of the array. The `<pre>` tags simply make the output easier to read in a browser.

2. Save the page, and load it in a browser. You should see the following output:

It doesn't look very exciting, but now that each line is a separate array element, you can loop through the array to process each line individually.

3. You need to use a counter to keep track of each line; a `for` loop is the most convenient (see "The versatile for loop" in Chapter 3). To find out how many times the loop should run, pass the array to the `count()` function to get its length. Amend the code in `file.php` like this (or use `file_02.php`):

```php
<?php
// read the file into an array called $users
$users = file('C:/private/filetest03.txt');

// loop through the array to process each line
for ($i = 0; $i < count($users); $i++) {
  // separate each element and store in a temporary array
  $tmp = explode(', ', $users[$i]);
  // assign each element of the temporary array to a named array key
  $users[$i] = array('name' => $tmp[0], 'password' => $tmp[1]);
}
?>
<pre>
<?php print_r($users); ?>
</pre>
```

The `count()` function returns the length of an array, so in this case, the value of `count($users)` is 2. This means the first line of the loop is equivalent to this:

```php
for ($i = 0; $i < 2; $i++) {
```

The loop continues running while `$i` is less than 2. Since arrays are always counted from 0, this means the loop runs twice before stopping.

Inside the loop, the current array element (`$users[$i]`) is passed to the `explode()` function. In this case, the separator is defined as a comma followed by a space (`', '`). However, you can use any character or sequence of characters: using `"\t"` (see Table 3-4 in Chapter 3) as the first argument to `explode()` turns a tab-separated string into an array.

The first line in `filetest 02.txt` looks like this:

```
david, codeslave
```

When this line is passed to `explode()`, the result is saved in `$tmp`, so `$tmp[0]` is `david`, and `$tmp[1]` is `codeslave`. The final line inside the loop reassigns `$tmp[0]` to `$users[0]['name']`, and `$tmp[1]` to `$users[0]['password']`.

The next time the loop runs, `$tmp` is reused, and `$users[1]['name']` becomes `chris`, and `$users[1]['password']` becomes `bigboss`.

4. Save `file.php`, and view it in a browser. The result looks like this:

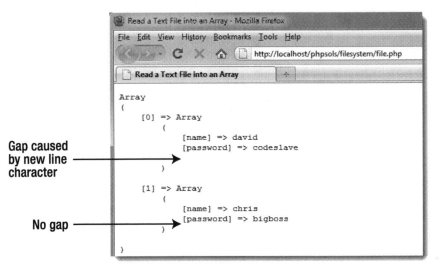

5. Take a close look at the gap between **codeslave** and the closing parenthesis of the first subarray. The `file()` function doesn't remove newline characters or carriage returns, so you need to do it yourself. Pass the final item of `$tmp` to `rtrim()` like this:

```
$users[$i] = array('name' => $tmp[0], 'password' => rtrim($tmp[1]));
```

The `rtrim()` function removes whitespace (spaces, tabs, newline characters, and carriage returns) from the end of a string. It has two companions: `ltrim()` which removes whitespace from the beginning of a string, and `trim()`, which removes whitespace from both ends of a string.

> If you're working with each line as a whole, pass the entire line to `rtrim()`.

6. As always, you need to check that the file is accessible before attempting to process its contents, so wrap the main PHP block in a conditional statement like this (see `file_03.php`):

```
$textfile = 'C:/private/filetest_02.txt';
if (file_exists($textfile) && is_readable($textfile)) {
  // read the file into an array called $users
  $users = file($textfile);

  // loop through the array to process each line
  for ($i = 0; $i < count($users); $i++) {
    // separate each element and store in a temporary array
    $tmp = explode(', ', $users[$i]);
    // assign each element of the temporary array to a named array key
    $users[$i] = array('name' => $tmp[0], 'password' => rtrim($tmp[1]));
  }
} else {
  echo "Can't open $textfile";
}
```

To avoid typing out the file pathname each time, begin by storing it in a variable.

This simple script extracts a useful array of names and associated passwords. You could also use this with a series of sports statistics or any data that follows a regular pattern.

Opening and closing files for read/write operations

The functions we have looked at so far do everything in a single pass. However, PHP also has a set of functions that allow you to open a file, read it and/or write to it, and then close the file. The following are the most important functions used for this type of operation:

- fopen(): Opens a file
- fgets(): Reads the contents of a file, normally one line at a time
- fread(): Reads a specified amount of a file
- fwrite(): Writes to a file
- feof(): Determines whether the end of the file has been reached
- rewind(): Moves an internal pointer back to the top of the file
- fclose(): Closes a file

The first of these, fopen(), is the most difficult to understand, mainly because you need to specify how the file is to be used once it's open: fopen() has one read-only mode, three write-only modes, and four read/write modes. Sometimes, you want to overwrite the existing content. At other times, you may want to append new material. At yet other times, you may want PHP to create a file if it doesn't already exist.

The other thing you need to understand is where each mode places the internal pointer when it opens the file. It's like the cursor in a word processor: PHP starts reading or writing from wherever the pointer happens to be when you call fread() or fwrite().

Table 7-2 brings order to the confusion.

Table 7-2. Read/write modes used with fopen()

Type	Mode	Description
Read-only	r	Internal pointer initially placed at beginning of file.
Write-only	w	Existing data deleted before writing. Creates a file if it doesn't already exist.
	a	Append mode. New data added at end of file. Creates a file if it doesn't already exist.
	x	Creates a file only if it doesn't already exist, so no danger of deleting existing data.
Read/write	r+	Read/write operations can take place in either order and begin wherever the internal pointer is at the time. Pointer initially placed at beginning of file. File must already exist for operation to succeed.
	w+	Existing data deleted. Data can be read back after writing. Creates a file if it doesn't already exist.
	a+	Opens a file ready to add new data at end of file. Also permits data to be read back after internal pointer has been moved. Creates a file if it doesn't already exist.
	x+	Creates a new file, but fails if a file of the same name already exists. Data can be read back after writing.

Choose the wrong mode, and you could end up deleting valuable data. You also need to be careful about the position of the internal pointer. If the pointer is at the end of the file, and you try to read the contents, you end up with nothing. On the other hand, if the pointer is at the beginning of the file, and you start writing, you overwrite the equivalent amount of any existing data. "Moving the internal pointer" later in this chapter explains this in more detail with a practical example.

You work with fopen() by passing it the following two arguments:

- The path to the file you want to open
- One of the modes listed in Table 7-2

The fopen() function returns a reference to the open file, which can then be used with any of the other read/write functions. So, this is how you would open a text file for reading:

```
$file = fopen('C:/private/filetest_02.txt', 'r');
```

Thereafter, you pass $file as the argument to other functions, such as fgets() and fclose(). Things should become clearer with a few practical demonstrations. Rather than building the files yourself, you'll probably find it easier to use the files in the ch07 folder. I'll run quickly through each mode.

Mac users need to adjust the path to the private folder in the example files to match their setup.

Reading a file with fopen()

The file `fopen_read.php` contains the following code:

```
// store the pathname of the file
$filename = 'C:/private/filetest_02.txt';
// open the file in read-only mode
$file = fopen($filename, 'r');
// read the file and store its contents
$contents = fread($file, filesize($filename));
// close the file
fclose($file);
// display the contents
echo nl2br($contents);
```

If you load this into a browser, you should see the following output:

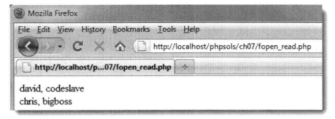

Unlike `file_get_contents()`, the function `fread()` needs to know how much of the file to read. So you need to supply a second argument indicating the number of bytes. This can be useful if you want, say, only the first 100 characters of a text file. However, if you want the whole file, you need to pass the file's pathname to `filesize()` to get the correct figure.

The `nl2br()` function in the final line converts new line characters to HTML `<br />` tags.

The other way to read the contents of a file with `fopen()` is to use the `fgets()` function, which retrieves one line at a time. This means that you need to use a `while` loop in combination with `feof()` to read right through to the end of the file. This is done by replacing this line:

```
$contents = fread($file, filesize($filename));
```

with this (the full script is in `fopen_readloop.php`):

```
// create variable to store the contents
$contents = '';
// loop through each line until end of file
while (!feof($file)) {
  // retrieve next line, and add to $contents
  $contents .= fgets($file);
}
```

The `while` loop uses `fgets()` to retrieve the contents of the file one line at a time—`!feof($file)` is the same as saying until the end of `$file`—and stores them in `$contents`.

Both methods are more long-winded than `file()` or `file_get_contents()`. However, you need to use either `fread()` or `fgets()` if you want to read and write to a file at the same time.

Replacing content with fopen()

The first of the write-only modes (`w`) deletes any existing content in a file, so it's useful for working with files that need to be updated frequently. You can test the `w` mode with `fopen_write.php`, which has the following PHP code above the `DOCTYPE` declaration:

```php
<?php
// if the form has been submitted, process the input text
if (isset($_POST['contents'])) {
  // open the file in write-only mode
  $file = fopen('C:/private/filetest_03.txt', 'w');
  // write the contents
  fwrite($file, $_POST['contents']);
  // close the file
  fclose($file);
}
?>
```

There's no need to use a loop this time: you're just writing the value of `$contents` to the opened file. The function `fwrite()` takes two arguments: the reference to the file and whatever you want to write to it.

> In other books or scripts on the Internet, you may come across `fputs()` instead of `fwrite()`. The two functions are identical: `fputs()` is a synonym for `fwrite()`.

If you load `fopen_write.php` into a browser, type something into the text area, and click **Write to file**, PHP creates `filetest_03.txt` and inserts whatever you typed into the text area. Since this is just a demonstration, I've omitted any checks to make sure that the file was successfully written. Open `filetest_03.txt` to verify that your text has been inserted. Now, type something different into the text area and submit the form again. The original content is deleted from `filetest_03.txt` and replaced with the new text. The deleted text is gone forever.

Appending content with fopen()

The append mode is one of the most useful ways of using `fopen()`, because it adds new content at the end, preserving any existing content. The main code in `fopen_append.php` is the same as `fopen_write.php`, apart from those elements highlighted here in bold:

```php
// open the file in append mode
$file = fopen('C:/private/filetest_03.txt', 'a');
// write the contents after inserting new line
fwrite($file, PHP_EOL . $_POST['contents']);
// close the file
fclose($file);
```

Notice that I have concatenated PHP_EOL to the beginning of $_POST['contents'] . This is a PHP constant that represents a new line on any operating system. On Windows, new lines require a carriage return and newline character, but Macs traditionally use only a carriage return, while Linux uses only a newline character. PHP_EOL gets round this nightmare by automatically choosing the correct characters depending on the server's operating system.

If you load fopen_append.php into a browser and insert some text, it should now be added to the end of the existing text, as shown in the following screenshot.

This is a very easy way of creating a flat-file database. We'll come back to append mode in Chapter 9.

Writing a new file with fopen()

Although it can be useful to have a file created automatically with the same name, it may be exactly the opposite of what you want. To make sure you're not overwriting an existing file, you can use fopen() with x mode. The main code in fopen_exclusive.php looks like this (changes are highlighted in bold):

```
// create a file ready for writing only if it doesn't already exist
$file = fopen('C:/private/filetest_04.txt', 'x');
// write the contents
fwrite($file, $_POST['contents']);
// close the file
fclose($file);
```

If you load fopen_exclusive.php into a browser, type some text, and click **Write to file**, the content should be written to filetest_04.txt in your target folder.

If you try it again, you should get a series of error messages telling you that the file already exists.

Combined read/write operations with fopen()

By adding a plus sign (+) after any of the previous modes, the file is opened for both reading and writing. You can perform as many read or write operations as you like—and in any order—until the file is closed. The difference between the combined modes is as follows:

- r+: The file must already exist; a new one will not be automatically created. The internal pointer is placed at the beginning, ready for reading existing content.
- w+: Existing content is deleted, so there is nothing to read when the file is first opened.
- a+: The file is opened with the internal pointer at the end, ready to append new material, so the pointer needs to be moved back before anything can be read.
- x+: Always creates a new file, so there's nothing to read when the file is first opened.

Reading is done with fread() or fgets() and writing with fwrite() exactly the same as before. What's important is to understand the position of the internal pointer.

Moving the internal pointer

Reading and writing operations always start wherever the internal pointer happens to be, so you normally want it to be at the beginning of the file for reading, and at the end of the file for writing.

To move the pointer to the beginning of a file, pass the file reference to rewind() like this:

```
rewind($file);
```

Moving the pointer to the end of a file is more complex. You need to use fseek(), which moves the pointer to a location specified by an offset and a PHP constant. The constant that represents the end of the file is SEEK_END, so an offset of 0 bytes places the pointer at the end. You also need to pass fseek() a reference to the open file, so all three arguments together look like this:

```
fseek($file, 0, SEEK_END);
```

SEEK_END is a constant, so it doesn't need quotes, and it must be in uppercase. You can also use fseek() to move the internal pointer to a specific position or relative to its current position. For details, see http://docs.php.net/manual/en/function.fseek.php.

The file fopen_pointer.php uses the fopen() r+ mode to demonstrate combining several read and write operations, and the effect of moving the pointer. The main code looks like this:

```
$filename = 'C:/private/filetest_04.txt';
// open a file for reading and writing
$file = fopen($filename, 'r+');

// the pointer is at the beginning, so existing content is overwritten
fwrite($file, $_POST['contents'] );

// read the contents from the current position
$readRest = '';
while (!feof($file)) {
  $readRest .= fgets($file);
}

// reset internal pointer to the beginning
rewind($file);

// read the contents from the beginning (nasty gotcha here)
$readAll = fread($file, filesize($filename));

// pointer now at the end, so write the form contents again
fwrite($file, $_POST['contents']);

// read immediately without moving the pointer
$readAgain = '';
while (!feof($file)) {
  $readAgain .= fgets($file);
}
```

```
// close the file
fclose($file);
```

The version of this file in the ch07 folder contains code that displays the values of $readRest, $readAll, and $readAgain to show what happens at each stage of the read/write operations. The existing content in filetest_04.txt was This works only the first time. When I typed **New content.** in fopen_pointer.php and clicked **Write to file**, I got the results shown here:

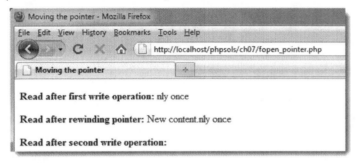

Table 7-3 describes the sequence of events.

Table 7-3. Sequence of read/write operations in fopen_pointer.php

Command	Position of pointer	Result
`$file = fopen($filename,'r+');`	Beginning of file	File opened for processing
`fwrite($file, $_POST['contents']);`	End of write operation	Form contents overwrites beginning of existing content

`while (!feof($file)) {`
`  $readRest .= fgets($file);`
`}`
	End of file	Remainder of existing content read

`rewind($file);`	Beginning of file	Pointer moved back to beginning of file
`$readAll = fread($file, ➥` `filesize($filename));`	See text	Content read from beginning of file
`fwrite($file, $_POST['contents']);`	At end of previous operation	Form contents added at current position of pointer

`while (!feof($file)) {`
`  $readAgain .= fgets($file);`
`}`
	End of file	Nothing read because pointer was already at end of file

`fclose($file);`	Not applicable	File closed and all changes saved

When I opened `filetest_04.txt`, this is what it contained:

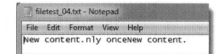

If you study the code in `fopen_pointer.php`, you'll notice that the second read operation uses `fread()`. It works perfectly with this example but contains a nasty surprise. Change the code in `fopen_pointer.php` to add the following line after the external file has been opened (it's commented out in the download version):

```
$file = fopen($filename, 'r+');
fseek($file, 0, SEEK_END);
```

This moves the pointer to the end of the file before the first write operation. Yet, when you run the script, `fread()` ignores the text added at the end of the file. This is because the external file is still open, so `filesize()` reads its original size. Consequently, you should always use a `while` loop with `!feof()` and `fgets()` if your read operation takes place after any new content has been written to a file.

> *The changes to a file with read and write operations are saved only when you call `fclose()` or when the script comes to an end. Although PHP saves the file if you forget to use `fclose()`, you should always close the file explicitly. Don't get into bad habits; one day they may cause your code to break and lose valuable data.*

When you create or open a file in a text editor, you can use your mouse to highlight and delete existing content, or position the insertion point exactly where you want. You don't have that luxury with a PHP script, so you need to give it precise instructions. On the other hand, you don't need to be there when the script runs. Once you have designed it, it runs automatically every time.

Exploring the file system

PHP's file system functions can also open directories (folders) and inspect their contents. You put one of these functions to practical use in PHP Solution 6-5 by using `scandir()` to create an array of existing filenames in the `images` folder and looping through the array to create a unique name for an uploaded file. From the web developer's point of view, other practical uses of the file system functions are building drop-down menus displaying the contents of a folder and creating a script that prompts a user to download a file, such as an image or PDF document.

Inspecting a folder with scandir()

Let's take a closer look at the `scandir()` function, which you used in PHP Solution 6-5. It returns an array consisting of the files and folders within a specified folder. Just pass the pathname of the folder (directory) as a string to `scandir()`, and store the result in a variable like this:

```
$files = scandir('../images');
```

You can examine the result by using print_r() to display the contents of the array, as shown in the following screenshot (the code is in scandir.php in the ch07 folder):

As you can see, the array returned by scandir() doesn't contain only files. The first two items are known as dot files, which represent the current and parent folders. The third item is a folder called _notes, and the penultimate item is a folder called thumbs.

The array contains only the names of each item. If you want more information about the contents of a folder, it's better to use the DirectoryIterator class.

Inspecting the contents of a folder with DirectoryIterator

The DirectoryIterator class is part of the Standard PHP Library (SPL), which has been part of PHP since PHP 5.0. The SPL offers a mind-boggling assortment of specialized iterators that allow you to create sophisticated loops with very little code. As the name suggests, the DirectoryIterator class lets you loop through the contents of a directory or folder.

Because it's a class, you instantiate a DirectoryIterator object with the new keyword and pass the path of the folder you want to inspect to the constructor like this:

```
$files = new DirectoryIterator('../images');
```

Unlike scandir(), this doesn't return an array of filenames—although you can loop through $files in the same way as an array. Instead, it returns an SplFileInfo object that gives you access to a lot more information about the folder's contents than just the filenames. Because it's an object, you can't use print_r() to display its contents.

However, if all you want to do is to display the filenames, you can use a foreach loop like this (the code is in iterator_01.php in the ch07 folder):

```
$files = new DirectoryIterator('../images');
foreach ($files as $file) {
  echo $file . '<br>';
}
```

This produces the following result:

Although using echo in the foreach loop displays the filenames, the value stored in $file each time the loop runs is not a string. In fact, it's another SplFileInfo object. Table 7-4 lists the main SplFileInfo methods that can be used to extract useful information about files and folders.

Table 7-4. File information accessible through SplFileInfo methods

Method	Returns
getFilename()	The name of the file
getPath()	The current object's relative path minus the filename, or minus the folder name if the current object is a folder
getPathName()	The current object's relative path, including the filename or folder name, depending on the current type
getRealPath()	The current object's full path, including filename if appropriate
getSize()	The size of the file or folder in bytes
isDir()	True, if the current object is a folder (directory)
isFile()	True, if the current object is a file
isReadable()	True, if the current object is readable
isWritable()	True, if the current object is writable

The `RecursiveDirectoryIterator` class burrows down into subfolders. To use it, you wrap it in the curiously named `RecursiveIteratorIterator` like this (the code is in `iterator_03.php`):

```
$files = new RecursiveIteratorIterator(new RecursiveDirectoryIterator('../images'));
foreach ($files as $file) {
  echo $file->getRealPath() . '<br>';
}
```

As the following screenshot shows, the `RecursiveDirectoryIterator` inspects the contents of all subfolders, revealing the contents of the `thumbs` and `_notes` folders, in a single operation:

However, what if you want to find only certain types of files? Cue another iterator. . . .

Restricting file types with the RegexIterator

The `RegexIterator` acts as a wrapper to another iterator, filtering its contents using a regular expression (regex) as a search pattern. To restrict the search to the most commonly used types of image files, you need to look for any of the following filename extensions: `.jpg`, `.png`, or `.gif`. The regex used to search for these filename extensions looks like this:

```
'/\.(?:jpg|png|gif)$/i'
```

In spite of its similarity to Vogon poetry, this regex matches image filename extensions in a case-insensitive manner. The code in `iterator_04.php` has been modified like this:

```
$files = new RecursiveIteratorIterator(new RecursiveDirectoryIterator('../images'));
$images = new RegexIterator($files, '/\.(?:jpg|png|gif)$/i');
foreach ($images as $file) {
  echo $file->getRealPath() . '<br>';
}
```

The original $files object is passed to the RegexIterator constructor, with the regex as the second argument, and the filtered set is stored in $images. The result is this:

Only image files are now listed. The folders and other miscellaneous files have been removed. Before PHP 5, the same result would have involved many more lines of complex looping.

> To learn more about the mysteries of regular expressions (regexes), see my two-part tutorial at www.adobe.com/devnet/dreamweaver/articles/regular_expressions_pt1.html. As you progress through this book, you'll see I make frequent use of regexes. They're a useful tool to add to your skill set.

I expect that by this stage, you might be wondering if this can be put to any practical use. OK, let's build a drop-down menu of images in a folder.

PHP Solution 7-3: Building a drop-down menu of files

When you work with a database, you often need a list of images or other files in a particular folder. For instance, you may want to associate a photo with a product detail page. Although you can type the name of the image into a text field, you need to make sure that the image is there and that you spell its name correctly. Get PHP to do the hard work by building a drop-down menu automatically. It's always up-to-date, and there's no danger of misspelling the name.

1. Create a PHP page called imagelist.php in the filesystem folder. Alternatively, use imagelist_01.php in the ch07 folder.

2. Create a form inside `imagelist.php`, and insert a `<select>` element with just one `<option>` like this (the code is already in `imagelist_01.php`):

```
<form id="form1" name="form1" method="post" action="">
<select name="pix" id="pix">
  <option value="">Select an image</option>
</select>
</form>
```

This `<option>` is the only static element in the drop-down menu.

3. Amend the form like this:

```
<form id="form1" name="form1" method="post" action="">
<select name="pix" id="pix">
  <option value="">Select an image</option>
<?php
$files = new DirectoryIterator('../images');
$images = new RegexIterator($files, '/\.(?:jpg|png|gif)$/i');
foreach ($images as $image) {
?>
<option value="<?php echo $image; ?>"><?php echo $image; ?></option>
<?php } ?>
</select>
</form>
```

4. Make sure that the path to the `images` folder is correct for your site's folder structure.

5. Save `imagelist.php`, and load it into a browser. You should see a drop-down menu listing all the images in your `images` folder, as shown in Figure 7-1.

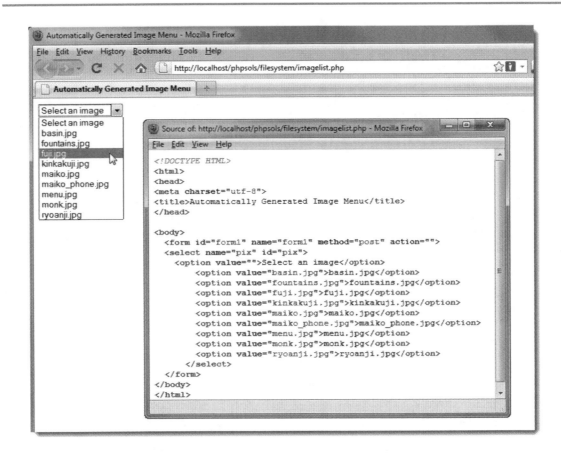

Figure 7-1. PHP makes light work of creating a drop-down menu of images in a specific folder.

When incorporated into an online form, the filename of the selected image appears in the $_POST array identified by the name attribute of the <select> element—in this case, $_POST['pix']. That's all there is to it!

You can compare your code with imagelist_02.php in the ch07 folder.

PHP Solution 7-4: Creating a generic file selector

The previous PHP solution relies on an understanding of regular expressions. Adapting it to work with other filename extensions isn't difficult, but you need to be careful that you don't accidentally delete a vital character. Unless regexes or Vogon poetry are your specialty, it's probably easier to wrap the code in a function that can be used to inspect a specific folder and create an array of filenames of specific types. For example, you might want to create an array of PDF document filenames or one that contains both PDFs and Word documents. Here's how you do it.

1. Create a new file called buildlist.php in the filesystem folder. The file will contain only PHP code, so delete any HTML inserted by your editing program.

2. Add the following code to the file:

```
function buildFileList($dir, $extensions) {
  if (!is_dir($dir) || !is_readable($dir)) {
    return false;
  } else {
    if (is_array($extensions)) {
      $extensions = implode('|', $extensions);
    }
  }
}
```

This defines a function called `buildFileList()`, which takes two arguments:

- `$dir`: The path to the folder from which you want to get the list of filenames.

- `$extensions`: This can be either a string containing a single filename extension or an array of filename extensions. To keep the code simple, the filename extensions should not include a leading period.

The function begins by checking whether `$dir` is a folder and is readable. If it isn't, the function returns `false`, and no more code is executed.

If `$dir` is OK, the `else` block is executed. It also begins with a conditional statement that checks whether `$extensions` is an array. If it is, it's passed to `implode()`, which joins the array elements with a vertical pipe (|) between each one. A vertical pipe is used in regexes to indicate alternative values. Let's say the following array is passed to the function as the second argument:

```
array('jpg', 'png', 'gif')
```

The conditional statement converts it to `jpg|png|gif`. So, this looks for `jpg`, or `png`, or `gif`. However, if the argument is a string, it remains untouched.

3. You can now build the regex search pattern and pass both arguments to the `DirectoryIterator` and `RegexIterator` like this:

```
function buildFileList($dir, $extensions) {
  if (!is_dir($dir) || !is_readable($dir)) {
    return false;
  } else {
    if (is_array($extensions)) {
      $extensions = implode('|', $extensions);
    }
    $pattern = "/\.(?:{$extensions})$/i";
    $folder = new DirectoryIterator($dir);
    $files = new RegexIterator($folder, $pattern);
  }
}
```

The regex pattern is built using a string in double quotes and wrapping $extensions in curly braces to make sure it's interpreted correctly by the PHP engine. Take care when copying the code. It's not exactly easy to read.

4. The final section of the code extracts the filenames to build an array, which is sorted and then returned. The finished function definition looks like this:

```
function buildFileList($dir, $extensions) {
  if (!is_dir($dir) || !is_readable($dir)) {
    return false;
  } else {
    if (is_array($extensions)) {
      $extensions = implode('|', $extensions);
    }
    // build the regex and get the files
    $pattern = "/\.(?:{$extensions})$/i";
    $folder = new DirectoryIterator($dir);
    $files = new RegexIterator($folder, $pattern);
    // initialize an array and fill it with the filenames
    $filenames = array();
    foreach ($files as $file) {
      $filenames[] = $file->getFilename();
    }
    // sort the array and return it
    natcasesort($filenames);
    return $filenames;
  }
}
```

This initializes an array and uses a foreach loop to assign the filenames to it with the getFilename() method. Finally, the array is passed to natcasesort(), which sorts it in a natural, case-insensitive order. What "natural" means is that strings that contain numbers are sorted in the same way as a person would. For example, a computer normally sorts img12.jpg before img2.jpg, because the 1 in 12 is lower than 2. Using natcasesort() results in img2.jpg preceding img12.jpg.

5. To use the function, use as arguments the path to the folder and the filename extensions of the files you want to find. For example, you could get all Word and PDF documents from a folder like this:

```
$docs = buildFileList('folder_name', array('doc', 'docx', 'pdf'));
```

The code for the buildFileList() function is in buildlist.php in the ch07 folder.

Accessing remote files

Reading, writing, and inspecting files on your local computer or on your own website is useful. But allow_url_fopen also gives you access to publicly available documents anywhere on the Internet. You can't directly include files from other servers—not unless allow_url_include is on—but you can read the content, save it to a variable, and manipulate it with PHP functions before incorporating it in your own pages or saving the information to a database. You can also write to documents on a remote server as long as the owner sets the appropriate permissions.

A word of caution is in order here. When extracting material from remote sources for inclusion in your own pages, there's a potential security risk. For example, a remote page might contain malicious scripts embedded in <script> tags or hyperlinks. Unless the remote page supplies data in a known format from a trusted source—such as product details from the Amazon.com database, weather information from a government meteorological office, or a newsfeed from a newspaper or broadcaster—sanitize the content by passing it to htmlentities() (see PHP Solution 5-3). As well as converting double quotes to ", htmlentities() converts < to < and > to >. This displays tags in plain text, rather than treating them as HTML.

If you want to permit some HTML tags, use the strip_tags() function instead. If you pass a string to strip_tags(), it returns the string with all HTML tags and comments stripped out. It also removes PHP tags. A second, optional argument is a list of tags that you want preserved. For example, the following strips out all tags except paragraphs and first- and second-level headings:

```
$stripped = strip_tags($original, '<p><h1><h2>');
```

> For an in-depth discussion of security issues, see Pro PHP Security by Chris Snyder and Michael Southwell (Apress, 2005, ISBN: 978-1-59059-508-4).

Consuming news and other RSS feeds

Some of the most useful remote sources of information that you might want to incorporate in your sites come from RSS feeds. RSS stands for Really Simple Syndication, and it's a dialect of XML. XML is similar to HTML in that it uses tags to mark up content. Instead of defining paragraphs, headings, and images, XML tags are used to organize data in a predictable hierarchy. XML is written in plain text, so it's frequently used to share information between computers that might be running on different operating systems.

Figure 7-2 shows the typical structure of an RSS 2.0 feed. The whole document is wrapped in a pair of <rss> tags. This is the root element, similar to the <html> tags of a web page. The rest of the document is wrapped in a pair of <channel> tags, which always contains the following three elements that describe the RSS feed: <title>, <description>, and <link>.

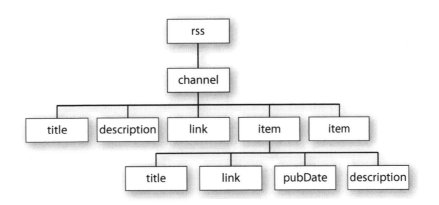

Figure 7-2. The main contents of an RSS feed are in the item elements.

In addition to the three required elements, the <channel> can contain many other elements, but the interesting material is to be found in the <item> elements. In the case of a news feed, this is where the individual news items can be found. If you're looking at the RSS feed from a blog, the <item> elements normally contain summaries of the blog posts.

Each <item> element can contain several elements, but those shown in Figure 7-2 are the most common—and usually the most interesting:

- <title>: The title of the item
- <link>: The URL of the item
- <pubDate>: Date of publication
- <description>: Summary of the item

This predictable format makes it easy to extract the information from an RSS feed using SimpleXML.

You can find the full RSS Specification at www.rssboard.org/rss-specification. Unlike most technical specifications, it's written in plain language, and easy to read.

Using SimpleXML

As long as you know the structure of an XML document, SimpleXML does what it says on the tin: it makes extracting information from XML simple. The first step is to pass the URL of the XML document to simplexml_load_file(). You can also load a local XML file by passing the path as an argument. For example, this gets the world news feed from the BBC:

```
$feed = simplexml_load_file('http://feeds.bbci.co.uk/news/world/rss.xml');
```

This creates an instance of the SimpleXMLElement class. All the elements in the feed can now be accessed as properties of the $feed object, using the names of the elements. With an RSS feed, the <item> elements can be accessed as $feed->channel->item.

To display the `<title>` of each `<item>`, create a `foreach` loop like this:

```
foreach ($feed->channel->item as $item) {
  echo $item->title . '<br>';
}
```

If you compare this with Figure 7-2, you can see that you access elements by chaining the element names with the `->` operator until you reach the target. Since there are multiple `<item>` elements, you need to use a loop to tunnel further down. Alternatively, use array notation like this:

```
$feed->channel->item[2]->title
```

This gets the `<title>` of the third `<item>` element. Unless you want only a specific value, it's simpler to use a loop.

With that background out of the way, let's use SimpleXML to display the contents of a news feed.

PHP Solution 7-5: Consuming an RSS news feed

This PHP solution shows how to extract the information from a live news feed using SimpleXML and display it in a web page. It also shows how to format the `<pubDate>` element to a more user-friendly format and how to limit the number of items displayed using the `LimitIterator` class.

1. Create a new page called `newsfeed.php` in the `filesystem` folder. This page will contain a mixture of PHP and HTML.

2. The news feed chosen for this PHP solution is the BBC World News. A condition of using most news feeds is that you acknowledge the source. So add **The Latest from BBC News** formatted as an `<h1>` heading at the top of the page.

> See *http://news.bbc.co.uk/1/hi/help/rss/4498287.stm* for the full terms and conditions of using a BBC news feed on your own site.

3. Create a PHP block below the heading, and add the following code to load the feed:

    ```
    $url = 'http://feeds.bbci.co.uk/news/world/rss.xml';
    $feed = simplexml_load_file($url);
    ```

4. Use a `foreach` loop to access the `<item>` elements and display the `<title>` of each one:

    ```
    foreach ($feed->channel->item as $item) {
      echo $item->title . '<br>';
    }
    ```

5. Save `newsfeed.php`, and load the page in a browser. You should see a long list of news items similar to Figure 7-3.

Figure 7-3. The news feed contains a large number of items.

6. The normal feed often contains 50 or more items. That's fine for a news site, but you probably want a shorter selection in your own site. Use another SPL iterator to select a specific range of items. Amend the code like this:

```php
$url = 'http://feeds.bbci.co.uk/news/world/rss.xml';
$feed = simplexml_load_file($url, 'SimpleXMLIterator');
$filtered = new LimitIterator($feed->channel->item, 0 , 4);
foreach ($filtered as $item) {
  echo $item->title . '<br>';
}
```

To use SimpleXML with an SPL iterator, you need to supply the name of the SimpleXMLIterator class as the second argument to simplexml_load_file(). You can then pass the SimpleXML element you want to affect to an iterator constructor.

In this case, $feed->channel->item is passed to the LimitIterator constructor. The LimitIterator takes three arguments: the object you want to limit, the starting point (counting from 0), and the number of times you want the loop to run. This code starts at the first item and limits the number of items to four.

The foreach loop now loops over the $filtered result. If you test the page again, you'll see just four titles, as shown in Figure 7-4. Don't be surprised if the selection of headlines is different from before. The BBC News website is updated every minute.

Figure 7-4. The `LimitIterator` restricts the number of items displayed.

7. Now that you have limited the number of items, amend the `foreach` loop to wrap the `<title>` elements in a link to the original article, and display the `<pubDate>` and `<description>` items. The loop looks like this:

```
foreach ($filtered as $item) { ?>
  <h2><a href="<?php echo $item->link; ?>"><?php echo $item->title; ↰
  ?></a></h2>
  <p class="datetime"><?php echo $item->pubDate; ?></p>
  <p><?php echo $item->description; ?></p>
<?php } ?>
```

8. Save the page, and test it again. The links take you directly to the relevant news story on the BBC website. The news feed is now functional, but the `<pubDate>` format follows the format laid down in the RSS specification, as shown in the next screenshot:

> ### Middle East peace talks to resume
>
> Fri, 20 Aug 2010 16:47:35 GMT

9. To format the date and time in a more user-friendly way, pass `$item->pubDate` to the `DateTime` class constructor, and then use the `DateTime format()` method to display it.

10. Change the code in the `foreach` loop like this:

```
<p class="datetime"><?php $date= new DateTime($item->pubDate);
echo $date->format('M j, Y, g:ia'); ?></p>
```

This reformats the date like this:

> ### Middle East peace talks to resume
>
> Aug 20, 2010, 4:47pm

The mysterious PHP formatting strings for dates are explained in Chapter 14.

11. That looks a lot better, but the time is still expressed in GMT (London time). If most of your site's visitors live on the East Coast of the United States, you probably want to show the local time. That's no problem with a DateTime object. Use the setTimezone() method to change to New York time. You can even automate the display of EDT (Eastern Daylight Time) or EST (Eastern Standard Time) depending on whether daylight saving time is in operation. Amend the code like this:

```
<p class="datetime"><?php $date = new DateTime($item->pubDate);
$date->setTimezone(new DateTimeZone('America/New_York'));
$offset = $date->getOffset();
$timezone = ($offset == -14400) ? ' EDT' : ' EST';
echo $date->format('M j, Y, g:ia') . $timezone; ?></p>
```

To create a DateTimeZone object, you pass it as an argument one of the time zones listed at `http://docs.php.net/manual/en/timezones.php`. This is the only place that the DateTimeZone object is needed, so it has been created directly as the argument to the setTimezone() method.

There isn't a dedicated method that tells you whether daylight saving time is in operation, but the getOffset() method returns the number of seconds the time is offset from Coordinated Universal Time (UTC). The following line determines whether to display EDT or EST:

```
$timezone = ($offset == -14400) ? ' EDT' : ' EST';
```

This uses the value of $offset with the conditional operator. In summer, New York is 4 hours behind UTC (–14440 seconds). So, if $offset is –14400, the condition equates to true, and EDT is assigned to $timezone. Otherwise, EST is used.

Finally, the value of $timezone is concatenated to the formatted time. The string used for $timezone has a leading space to separate the time zone from the time. When the page is loaded, the time is adjusted to the East Coast of the United States like this:

> **Middle East peace talks to resume**
>
> Aug 20, 2010, 12:47pm EDT

12. All the page needs now is smartening up with CSS. Figure 7-5 shows the finished news feed styled with newsfeed.css in the styles folder.

You can learn more about SPL iterators and SimpleXML in my PHP Object-Oriented Solutions *(friends of ED, 2008, ISBN: 978-1-4302-1011-5).*

Figure 7-5. The live news feed requires only a dozen lines of PHP code.

Although I have used the BBC News feed for this PHP solution, it should work with any RSS 2.0 feed. For example, you can try it locally with `http://rss.cnn.com/rss/edition.rss`. Using a CNN news feed in a public website requires permission from CNN. Always check with the copyright holder for terms and conditions before incorporating a feed into a website.

Creating a download link

A question that crops up regularly in online forums is, "How do I create a link to an image (or PDF file) that prompts the user to download it?" The quick solution is to convert the file into a compressed format, such as ZIP. This frequently results in a smaller download, but the downside is that inexperienced users may not know how to unzip the file, or they may be using an older operating system that doesn't include an extraction facility. With PHP file system functions, it's easy to create a link that automatically prompts the user to download a file in its original format.

PHP Solution 7-6: Prompting a user to download an image

The script in this PHP solution sends the necessary HTTP headers, opens the file, and outputs its contents as a binary stream.

1.   Create a PHP file called `download.php` in the `filesystem` folder. The full listing is given in the next step. You can also find it in `download.php` in the `ch07` folder.

2. Remove any default code created by your script editor, and insert the following code:

```php
<?php
// define error page
$error = 'http://localhost/phpsols/error.php';
// define the path to the download folder
$filepath = 'C:/xampp/htdocs/phpsols/images/';

$getfile = NULL;

// block any attempt to explore the filesystem
if (isset($_GET['file']) && basename($_GET['file']) == $_GET['file']) {
  $getfile = $_GET['file'];
} else {
  header("Location: $error");
  exit;
}

if ($getfile) {
  $path = $filepath . $getfile;
  // check that it exists and is readable
  if (file_exists($path) && is_readable($path)) {
    // get the file's size and send the appropriate headers
    $size = filesize($path);
    header('Content-Type: application/octet-stream');
    header('Content-Length: '. $size);
    header('Content-Disposition: attachment; filename=' . $getfile);
    header('Content-Transfer-Encoding: binary');
    // open the file in read-only mode
    // suppress error messages if the file can't be opened
    $file = @fopen($path, 'r');
    if ($file) {
      // stream the file and exit the script when complete
      fpassthru($file);
      exit;
    } else {
      header("Location: $error");
    }
  } else {
    header("Location: $error");
}
```

The only two lines that you need to change in this script are highlighted in bold type. The first defines $error, a variable that contains the URL of your error page. The second line that needs to be changed defines the path to the folder where the download file is stored.

The script works by taking the name of the file to be downloaded from a query string appended to the URL and saving it as $getfile. Because query strings can be easily tampered with,

`$getfile` is initially set to `NULL`. This is an important security measure. If you fail to do this, you could give a malicious user access to any file on your server.

The opening conditional statement uses `basename()` to make sure that an attacker cannot request a file, such as one that stores passwords, from another part of your file structure. As explained in Chapter 4, `basename()` extracts the filename component of a path, so if `basename($_GET['file'])` is different from `$_GET['file']`, you know there's an attempt to probe your server, and you can stop the script from going any further by using the `header()` function to redirect the user to the error page.

After checking that the requested file exists and is readable, the script gets the file's size, sends the appropriate HTTP headers, and opens the file in read-only mode using `fopen()`. Finally, `fpassthru()` dumps the file to the output buffer. But if the file can't be opened or doesn't exist, the user is redirected to the error page.

3. Test the script by creating another page and add a couple of links to `download.php`. Add a query string at the end of each link with `file=` followed by the name a file to be downloaded. You'll find a page called `getdownloads.php` in the `ch07` folder, which contains the following two links:

```
<p><a href="download.php?file=maiko.jpg">Download image 1</a></p>
<p><a href="download.php?file=basin.jpg">Download image 2</a></p>
```

4. Click one of the links, and the browser should present you with a dialog box prompting you to download the file or choose a program to open it, as shown in Figure 7-6.

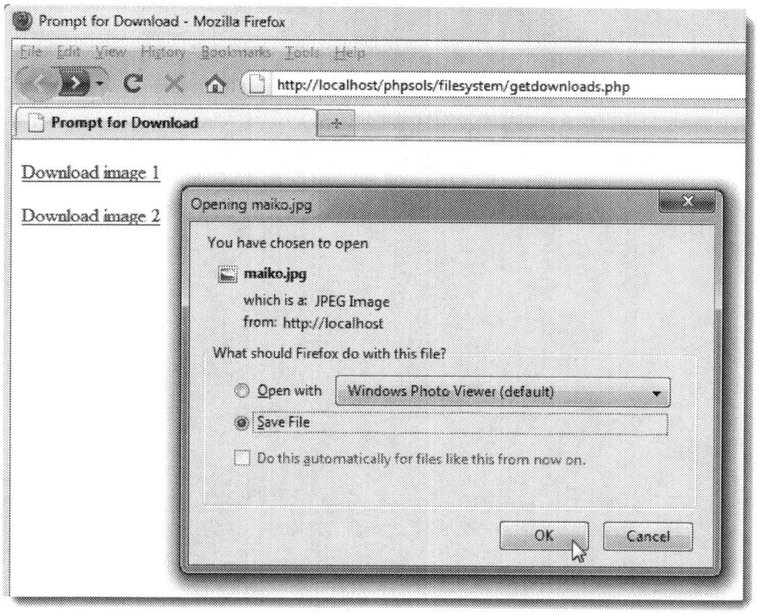

Figure 7-6. The browser prompts the user to download the image, rather than opening it directly.

5. Select **Save File**, and click **OK**, and the file should be saved rather than displayed. Click **Cancel** to abandon the download. Whichever button you click, the original page remains in the browser window. The only time download.php should load into the browser is if the file cannot be opened. That's why it's important to send the user to an error page if there's a problem.

I've demonstrated download.php with image files, but it can be used for any type of file because the headers send the file as a binary stream.

This script relies on header() to send the appropriate HTTP headers to the browser. It is vital to ensure that there are no new lines or whitespace ahead of the opening PHP tag. If you have removed all whitespace and still get an error message saying "headers already sent," your editor may have inserted invisible control characters at the beginning of the file. Some editing programs insert the byte order mark (BOM), which is known to cause problems with the ability to use the header() function. Check your program preferences to make sure the option to insert the BOM is deselected.

Chapter review

The file system functions aren't particularly difficult to use, but there are many subtleties that can turn a seemingly simple task into a complicated one. It's important to check that you have the right permissions. Even when handling files in your own website, PHP needs permission to access any folder where you want to read files or write to them.

The SPL DirectoryIterator and RecursiveDirectoryIterator classes make it easy to examine the contents of folders. Used in combination with the SplFileInfo methods and the RegexIterator, you can quickly find files of a specific type within a folder or folder hierarchy.

When dealing with remote data sources, you need to check that allow_url_fopen hasn't been disabled. One of the most common uses of remote data sources is extracting information from RSS news feeds or XML documents, a task that takes only a few lines of code thanks to SimpleXML.

In the next two chapters, we'll put some of the PHP solutions from this chapter to further practical use when working with images and building a simple user authentication system.

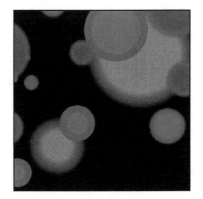

Chapter 8

Generating Thumbnail Images

PHP has an extensive range of functions designed to work with images. You've already met one of them, getimagesize(), in Chapter 4. As well as providing useful information about an image's dimensions, PHP can manipulate images by resizing or rotating them. It can also add text dynamically without affecting the original; it can even create images on the fly.

To give you just a taste of PHP image manipulation, I'm going to show you how to generate a smaller copy of an uploaded image. Most of the time, you'll want to use a dedicated graphics program, such as Photoshop or Fireworks, to generate thumbnail images because it gives you much better quality control. However, automatic thumbnail generation with PHP can be very useful if you want to allow registered users to upload images, but make sure they conform to a maximum size. You can save just the resized copy, or the copy along with the original.

In Chapter 6, you built a PHP class to handle file uploads. In this chapter, you'll create two classes: one to generate thumbnail images, the other to upload and resize images in a single operation. Rather than build the second class from scratch, you'll base it on the Ps2_Upload class from Chapter 6. A great advantage of using classes is that they're extensible—a class based on another can inherit the functionality of its parent class. Building the classes to upload images and generate thumbnails from them involves a lot of code. But once you have defined the classes, using them involves only a few lines of script. If you're in a rush or writing a lot of code makes you break out in a cold sweat, you can just use the finished classes. Come back later to learn how the code works. It uses many basic PHP functions that you'll find useful in other situations.

In this chapter you'll learn about the following:

- Scaling an image
- Saving a rescaled image
- Automatically resizing and renaming uploaded images
- Creating a subclass by extending an existing one

Checking your server's capabilities

Working with images in PHP relies on the GD extension. Originally GD stood for GIF Draw, but problems with the GIF patent led to support for GIF files being dropped in 1999, but the name GD stuck. The problematic patent expired in 2004, and GIF is once again supported. The all-in-one PHP packages recommended in Chapter 2 support GD by default, but you need to make sure the GD extension has also been enabled on your remote web server.

As in previous chapters, run `phpinfo()` on your website to check the server's configuration. Scroll down until you reach the section shown in the following screenshot (it should be about halfway down the page).

gd	
GD Support	enabled
GD Version	bundled (2.0.34 compatible)
FreeType Support	enabled
FreeType Linkage	with freetype
FreeType Version	2.3.11
T1Lib Support	enabled
GIF Read Support	enabled
GIF Create Support	enabled
JPEG Support	enabled
libJPEG Version	7
PNG Support	enabled
libPNG Version	1.2.40
WBMP Support	enabled
XBM Support	enabled
JIS-mapped Japanese Font Support	enabled

Directive	Local Value	Master Value
gd.jpeg_ignore_warning	0	0

If you can't find this section, the GD extension isn't enabled, so you won't be able to use any of the scripts in this chapter on your website. Ask for it to be enabled or move to a different host.

> *Strictly for abbreviation/acronym freaks: GIF stands for Graphics Interchange Format, JPEG is the standard created by the Joint Photographic Experts Group, and PNG is short for Portable Network Graphics. Although JPEG is the correct name for the standard, the "E" is frequently dropped, particularly when used as a filename extension.*

Manipulating images dynamically

The GD extension allows you to generate images entirely from scratch or work with existing images. Either way, the underlying process always follows four basic steps:

1. Create a resource for the image in the server's memory while it's being processed.

2. Process the image.

3. Display and/or save the image.

4. Remove the image resource from the server's memory.

This process means that you are always working on an image in memory only and not on the original. Unless you save the image to disk before the script terminates, any changes are discarded. Working with images requires a lot of memory, so it's vital to destroy the image resource as soon as it's no longer needed. If a script runs very slowly or crashes, it probably indicates that the original image is too large.

Making a smaller copy of an image

The aim of this chapter is to show you how to resize images automatically on upload. This involves extending the `Ps2_Upload` class from Chapter 6. However, to make it easier to understand how to work with PHP's image manipulation functions, I propose to start by using images already on the server, and create a separate class to generate the thumbnail images.

Getting ready

The starting point is the following simple form, which uses PHP Solution 7-3 to create a drop-down menu of the photos in the `images` folder. You can find the code in `create_thumb_win01.php` and `create_thumb_mac01.php` in the `ch08` folder. Copy it to a new folder called `gd` in the `phpsols` site root, and rename it `create_thumb.php`.

```
<form id="form1" name="form1" method="post" action="">
  <p>
    <select name="pix" id="pix">
      <option value="">Select an image</option>
      <?php
      $files = new DirectoryIterator('../images');
      $images = new RegexIterator($files, '/\.(?:jpg|png|gif)$/i');
      foreach ($images as $image) {
      ?>
        <option value="C:/xampp/htdocs/phpsols/images/<?php echo $image; ?>"> ↵
          <?php echo $image; ?></option>
      <?php } ?>
    </select>
  </p>
  <p>
    <input type="submit" name="create" id="create" value="Create Thumbnail">
  </p>
</form>
```

The `Win` and `Mac` versions contain the fully qualified path to the images folder in default installations of XAMPP and MAMP. If necessary, change the path (highlighted in bold) to match your setup. When loaded into a browser, the drop-down menu should display the names of the photos in the `images` folder. This makes it easier to pick images quickly for testing.

Inside the upload_test folder that you created in Chapter 6, create a new folder called thumbs, and make sure it has the necessary permissions for PHP to write to it. Refer to "Establishing an upload directory" in Chapter 6 if you need to refresh your memory.

Building the Ps2_Thumbnail class

To generate a thumbnail image, the class needs to execute the following steps:

1. Get the dimensions of the original image.

2. Get the image's MIME type.

3. Calculate the scaling ratio.

4. Create an image resource of the correct MIME type for the original image.

5. Create an image resource for the thumbnail.

6. Create the resized copy.

7. Save the resized copy to the destination folder using the correct MIME type.

8. Destroy the image resources to free memory.

In addition to generating a thumbnail image, the class automatically inserts _thb before the filename extension, but a public method allows you to alter this value. The class also needs public methods to set the destination folder and the maximum size of the thumbnail, and to retrieve messages generated by the class. To keep the calculations simple, the maximum size controls only the larger of the thumbnail's dimensions.

There's a lot to do, so I'll break up the code into sections. They're all part of the same class definition, but presenting the script this way should make it easier to understand, particularly if you want to use some of the code in a different context.

PHP Solution 8-1: Getting the image details

This PHP Solution describes how to get the dimensions and MIME type of the original image.

1. Create a new page called Thumbnail.php in the classes/Ps2 folder. The file will contain only PHP, so strip out any HTML code inserted by your editing program.

2. The class needs to keep track of quite a few properties. Begin the class definition by listing them like this:

```php
<?php
class Ps2_Thumbnail {
  protected $_original;
  protected $_originalwidth;
  protected $_originalheight;
  protected $_thumbwidth;
  protected $_thumbheight;
  protected $_maxSize = 120;
  protected $_canProcess = false;
  protected $_imageType;
```

```
    protected $_destination;
    protected $_name;
    protected $_suffix = '_thb';
    protected $_messages = array();
}
```

As in the Ps2_Upload class, all the properties have been declared as protected, which means they can't be changed accidentally outside the class definition. Again, I have followed the convention of beginning protected property names with an underscore. The names are descriptive, so they need little explanation. The $_maxSize property has been given a default value of 120 (pixels). This determines the maximum size of the thumbnail's longer dimension.

The $_canProcess Boolean is initially set to false. This is to prevent the script from attempting to process a file that isn't an image. The value will be reset to true if the MIME type matches that of an image. You can also use it to prevent the generation of a thumbnail if another error occurs.

3. The constructor takes one argument, the path to an image. Add the constructor definition after the list of protected properties, but inside the the closing curly brace:

```
    protected $_messages = array();

    public function __construct($image) {
      if (is_file($image) && is_readable($image)) {
        $details = getimagesize($image);
      } else {
        $details = null;
        $this->_messages[] = "Cannot open $image.";
      }
      // if getimagesize() returns an array, it looks like an image
      if (is_array($details)) {
        $this->_original = $image;
        $this->_originalwidth = $details[0];
        $this->_originalheight = $details[1];
        // check the MIME type
        $this->checkType($details['mime']);
      } else {
        $this->_messages[] = "$image doesn't appear to be an image.";
      }
    }
}
```

The constructor begins with a conditional statement that checks that $image is a file and is readable. If it is, it's passed to getimagesize() and the result is stored in $details. Otherwise, $details is set to null, and an error message is added to the $_messages property.

When you pass an image to getimagesize(), it returns an array containing the following elements:

- 0: width (in pixels)

- 1: height

- 2: an integer indicating the type of image

- 3: a string containing the correct width and height attributes ready for insertion in an <img> tag

- mime: the image's MIME type

- channels: 3 for RGB, and 4 for CMYK images

- bits: the number of bits for each color

If the value passed as an argument to getimagesize() isn't an image, it returns false. Consequently, if $details is an array, you know you're dealing with an image. The image's path is stored in the $_original property, and its width and height are stored in $_originalWidth and $_originalHeight respectively.

However, the image might not be a suitable type, so the final check is to pass its MIME type to an internal method called checkType(), which you'll define next.

4. The checkType() method compares the MIME type with an array of acceptable image types. If it finds a match, it resets the $_canProcess property to true, and stores the type in the $_imageType property. The method is used internally, so it needs to be declared as protected. Add the following code to the class definition:

```
protected function checkType($mime) {
  $mimetypes = array('image/jpeg', 'image/png', 'image/gif');
  if (in_array($mime, $mimetypes)) {
    $this->_canProcess = true;
    // extract the characters after 'image/'
    $this->_imageType = substr($mime, 6);
  }
}
```

There are many types of images, but only JPEG, PNG, and GIF are used in web pages, so the $_canProcess property is set to true only if the image's MIME type matches one of those listed in the $mimetypes array. If the MIME type isn't in the list $_canProcess remains false, which later prevents the class from attempting to create a thumbnail.

All image MIME types begin with image/. To make the value easier to use later, the substr() function extracts the characters after the slash and stores them in the $_imageType property. When used with two arguments, substr() starts at the position (counting from 0) specified in the second argument, and returns the rest of the string.

5. It's a good idea to test your code as you build the class. Catching errors early is much easier than hunting for a problem in a long script. To test the code, create a new public method called test() inside the class definition.

It doesn't matter which order your methods appear inside the class definition, but it's common practice to keep all public methods together after the constructor and to put protected methods at the bottom of the file. This makes the code easier to maintain.

Insert the following definition between the constructor and the `checkType()` definition:

```php
public function test() {
  echo 'File: ' . $this->_original . '<br>';
  echo 'Original width: ' . $this->_originalwidth . '<br>';
  echo 'Original height: ' . $this->_originalheight . '<br>';
  echo 'Image type: ' . $this->_imageType . '<br>';
  if ($this->_messages) {
    print_r($this->_messages);
  }
}
```

This uses `echo` and `print_r()` to display the value of the properties.

6. To test the class definition so far, save `Thumbnail.php`, and add the following code block above the `DOCTYPE` declaration in `create_thumb.php` (the code is in `create_thumb_win02.php` and `create_thumb_mac02.php` in the `ch08` folder):

```php
<?php
if (isset($_POST['create'])) {
  require_once('../classes/Ps2/Thumbnail.php');
  try {
    $thumb = new Ps2_Thumbnail($_POST['pix']);
    $thumb->test();
  } catch (Exception $e) {
    echo $e->getMessage();
  }
}
?>
```

The name of the submit button in `create_thumb.php` is `create`, so this code runs only when the form has been submitted. It includes the `Ps2_Thumbnail` class definition, creates an instance of the class, passing the selected value from the form as an argument, and calls the `test()` method.

7. Save `create_thumb.php`, and load it into a browser. Select an image, and click **Create Thumbnail**. This produces output similar to Figure 8-1.

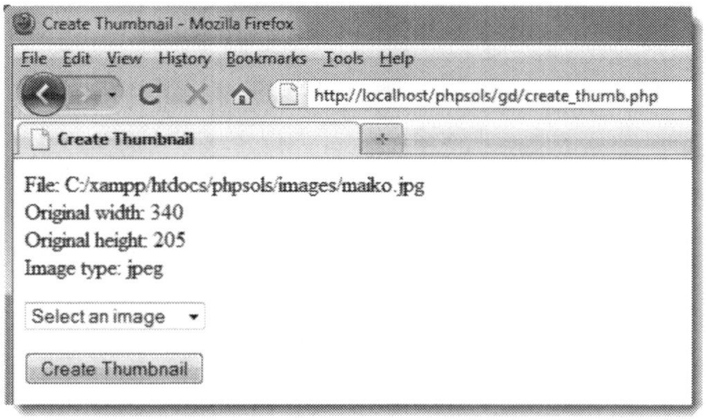

Figure 8-1. Displaying the details of the selected image confirms the code is working.

If necessary, check your code against `Thumbnail_01.php` in the `ch08` folder.

Although some properties have default values, you need to provide the option to change them by creating public methods to set the maximum size of the thumbnail image, and the suffix applied to the base of the filename. You also need to tell the class where to create the thumbnail. The formal term for this type of method is a **mutator method**. However, because it sets a value, it's commonly referred to as a **setter method**. The next stage is to create the setter methods.

PHP Solution 8-2: Creating the setter methods

In addition to setting the value of protected properties, setter methods play an important role in ensuring the validity of the value being assigned. Continue working with the same class definition. Alternatively, use `Thumbnail_01.php` in the `ch08` folder.

1. Begin by creating the setter method for the folder where the thumbnail is to be created. Add the following code to `Thumbnail.php` after the constructor definition.

```php
public function setDestination($destination) {
  if (is_dir($destination) && is_writable($destination)) {
    // get last character
    $last = substr($destination, -1);
    // add a trailing slash if missing
    if ($last == '/') || $last == '\\') {
      $this->_destination = $destination;
    } else {
      $this->_destination = $destination . DIRECTORY_SEPARATOR;
    }
  } else {
    $this->_messages[] = "Cannot write to $destination.";
  }
}
```

This begins by checking that $destination is a folder (directory) and that it's writable. If it isn't, the error message in the else clause at the end of the method definition is added to the $_messages property. Otherwise, the rest of the code is executed.

Before assigning the value of $destination to the $_destination property, the code checks whether the value submitted ends in a forward slash or backslash. It does this by extracting the final character in $destination, using the substr() function. The second argument to substr() determines the position from which to start the extract. A negative number counts from the end of the string. If the third argument is omitted, the function returns the rest of the string. So, $last = substr($destination, -1) has the effect of extracting the last character, and storing it in $last.

The conditional statement checks whether $last is a forward slash or a backslash. Two backslashes are needed because PHP uses a backslash to escape quotes (see "Understanding when to use quotes" and "Using escape sequences" in Chapter 3).

It's necessary to check for both forward slashes and backslashes in $destination because a Windows user might use backslashes out of habit. If the conditional statement confirms that the final character is a forward slash or a backslash, $destination is assigned to the $_destination property. Otherwise, the else clause concatenates the PHP constant DIRECTORY_SEPARATOR to the end of $destination before assigning it to the $_destination property. The DIRECTORY_SEPARATOR constant automatically chooses the right type of slash depending on the operating system.

> *PHP treats forward slashes or backslashes equally in a path. Even if this results in adding the opposite type of slash, the path remains valid as far as PHP is concerned.*

2. The setter method for the maximum size of the thumbnail simply needs to check that the value is a number. Add the following code to the class definition:

```php
public function setMaxSize($size) {
  if (is_numeric($size)) {
    $this->_maxSize = abs($size);
  }
}
```

The is_numeric() function checks that the submitted value is a number. If it is, it's assigned to the $_maxSize property. As a precaution, the value is passed to the abs() function, which converts a number to its absolute value. In other words, a negative number is converted into a positive one.

If the submitted value isn't a number, nothing happens. The property's default value remains unchanged.

3. The setter function for the suffix inserted in the filename needs to make sure the value doesn't contain any special characters. The code looks like this:

```
public function setSuffix($suffix) {
  if (preg_match('/^\w+$/', $suffix)) {
    if (strpos($suffix, '_') !== 0) {
      $this->_suffix = '_' . $suffix;
    } else {
      $this->_suffix = $suffix;
    }
  } else {
    $this->_suffix = '';
  }
}
```

This uses `preg_match()`, which takes a regular expression as its first argument and searches for a match in the value passed as the second argument. Regular expressions need to be wrapped in a pair of matching delimiter characters—normally forward slashes, as used here. Stripped of the delimiters, the regex looks like this:

`^\w+$`

In this context, the caret (^) tells the regex to start at the beginning of the string. The \w matches any alphanumeric character or an underscore. The + means match one or more of the preceding character, and the $ means match the end of the string. In other words, the regex matches a string that contains only alphanumeric characters and underscores. If the string contains spaces or special characters, it won't match.

> As mentioned before, regexes can be difficult to learn, but they're extremely useful in PHP, JavaScript, and other web-related languages.

If the match fails, the `else` clause at the end of the method definition sets the `$_suffix` property to an empty string. Otherwise, this conditional statement is executed.

`if (strpos($suffix, '_') !== 0) {`

The condition equates to `true` if the first character of `$suffix` is *not* an underscore. It uses the `strpos()` function to find the position of the first underscore. If the first character is an underscore, the value returned by `strpos()` is 0. However, if `$suffix` doesn't contain an underscore, `strpos()` returns `false`. As explained in Chapter 3, 0 is treated by PHP as `false`, so the condition needs to use the "not identical" operator (with two equal signs). So, if the suffix doesn't begin with an underscore, one is added. Otherwise, the original value is preserved.

> Don't confuse `strpos()` and `strrpos()`. The former finds the position of the first matching character. The latter searches the string in reverse.

4. Update the `test()` method to display the values of the properties for which you have just created setter methods. The revised code looks like this:

```php
public function test() {
  echo 'File: ' . $this->_original . '<br>';
  echo 'Original width: ' . $this->_originalwidth . '<br>';
  echo 'Original height: ' . $this->_originalheight . '<br>';
  echo 'Image type: ' . $this->_imageType . '<br>';
  echo 'Destination: ' . $this->_destination . '<br>';
  echo 'Max size: ' . $this->_maxSize . '<br>';
  echo 'Suffix: ' . $this->_suffix . '<br>';
  if ($this->_messages) {
    print_r($this->_messages);
  }
}
```

5. Test the updated class by using the new setter methods in `create_thumb.php` like this:

```php
$thumb = new Ps2_Thumbnail($_POST['pix']);
$thumb->setDestination('C:/upload_test/thumbs/');
$thumb->setMaxSize(100);
$thumb->setSuffix('small');
$thumb->test();
```

6. Save both pages, and select an image from the list in `create_thumb.php`. You should see results similar to Figure 8-2.

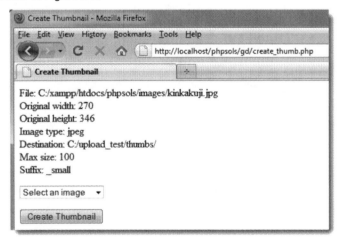

Figure 8-2. Verifying that the setter methods work

7. Try a number of tests, omitting the trailing slash from the value passed to `setDestination()` or selecting a nonexisting folder. Also pass invalid values to the setters for the maximum size and suffix. An invalid destination folder produces an error message, but the others fail silently, using the default value for the maximum size or an empty string for the suffix.

If necessary, compare your code with `Thumbnail_02.php` in the ch08 folder.

You might not agree with my decision to fail silently when the values passed as arguments are invalid. By now, though, you should have sufficient experience of conditional statements to adapt the code to your own requirements. For example, if you want the setter method for the thumbnail's maximum size to return an error message instead of failing silently, check that the value is greater than zero, and add an `else` clause to generate the error message. The `else` clause should also set the `$_canProcess` property to `false` to prevent the class from attempting to create a thumbnail image. This is how you would adapt the `setMaxSize()` method:

```
public function setMaxSize($size) {
    if (is_numeric($size) && $size > 0) {
    $this->_maxSize = $size;
} else {
    $this->_messages[] = 'The value for setMaxSize() must be a positive number.';
    $this->_canProcess = false;
    }
}
```

Before you can create the thumbnail image, you need to calculate its size. The value set in the `$_maxSize` property determines the width or height, depending which is larger. To avoid distorting the thumbnail, you need to calculate the scaling ratio for the shorter dimension. The ratio is calculated by dividing the maximum thumbnail size by the larger dimension of the original image.

For example, the original image of the Golden Pavilion (`kinkakuji.jpg`) is 270 × 346 pixels. If the maximum size is set at 120, dividing 120 by 346 produces a scaling ratio of 0.3468. Multiplying the width of the original image by this ratio fixes the thumbnail's width at 94 pixels (rounded up to the nearest whole number), maintaining the correct proportions. Figure 8-3 shows how the scaling ratio works.

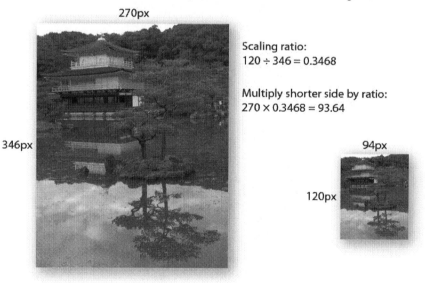

Figure 8-3. Working out the scaling ratio for a thumbnail image.

The base filename also needs to be split from the filename extension in preparation for inserting the suffix indicating it's a thumbnail.

PHP Solution 8-3: Final preparations for generating the thumbnail

This PHP solution adds three new methods to the Ps2_Thumbnail class: a public method that initiates the generation of the thumbnail image, and two internal methods that calculate the thumbnail's dimensions and split the image's base name from its filename extension. In PHP Solution 6-5, isolating the filename extension was done by searching for a dot or period in the filename. This time, you know the file types in advance, so a regular expression is used.

Continue working with your existing class definition. Alternatively, use Thumbnail_02.php in the ch08 folder.

1. Calculating the thumbnail dimensions doesn't require any further user input, so it can be handled by an internal method. Add the following code to the class definition. It's a protected method, so put it at the end of the file, just inside the closing curly brace.

```
protected function calculateSize($width, $height) {
  if ($width <= $this->_maxSize && $height <= $this->_maxSize) {
    $ratio = 1;
  } elseif ($width > $height) {
    $ratio = $this->_maxSize/$width;
  } else {
    $ratio = $this->_maxSize/$height;
  }
  $this->_thumbwidth = round($width * $ratio);
  $this->_thumbheight = round($height * $ratio);
}
```

The dimensions of the original image are stored as properties of the Ps2_Thumbnail object, so you could refer to them directly as $this->_originalWidth and $this->_originalHeight. However, the method needs to refer to these values often, so I decided to pass them as arguments to make the code easier to read and type.

The conditional statement begins by checking if the width and height of the original image are less than or equal to the maximum size. If they are, the image doesn't need to be resized, so the scaling ratio is set to 1.

The elseif clause checks if the width is greater than the height. If it is, the width is used to calculate the scaling ratio. The else clause is invoked if the height is greater or both sides are equal. In either case, the height is used to calculate the scaling ratio.

The last two lines multiply the original width and height by the scaling ratio, and assign the results to the $_thumbwidth and $_thumbheight properties. The calculation is wrapped in the round() function, which rounds the result to the nearest whole number.

2. Next, add the method that gets the filename and strips off the filename extension. The code looks like this:

```
protected function getName() {
```

227

```
$extensions = array('/\.jpg$/i', '/\.jpeg$/i', '/\.png$/i', '/\.gif$/i');
$this->_name = preg_replace($extensions, '', basename($this->_original));
}
```

The code inside the method is only two lines, but there's a lot going on. The first line creates an array of regular expressions. As mentioned earlier, regexes are wrapped in delimiter characters, normally forward slashes. The i after the closing slash of each regex tells it to peform a case-insensitive search.

A period normally represents any character, but escaping it with a backslash makes the regex look only for a period. The $ matches the end of the string. Everything else matches a literal character. In other words, these regexes match .jpg, .jpeg, .png, and .gif in a case-insensitive manner.

The second line uses the preg_replace() function, which performs a find and replace operation using a regex or array of regexes. The first argument is the value(s) you want to replace. The second argument is the replacement text—in this case, an empty string. The third argument is the subject of the search and replace operation.

Here, the third argument is the value of the $_original property, which has been passed to the basename() function. You met basename() in PHP Solution 4-3. It extracts the filename from a path. So, the code in the second line searches the filename for an image filename extension and replaces it with nothing. In other words, it strips off the filename extension, and assigns the result to the $_name property.

3. These two methods need to be called by the method that creates the thumbnail image. Add the following public method to the class definition above the protected methods:

```
public function create() {
  if ($this->_canProcess && $this->_originalwidth != 0) {
    $this->calculateSize($this->_originalwidth, $this->_originalheight);
    $this->getName();
  } elseif ($this->_originalwidth == 0) {
    $this->_messages[] = 'Cannot determine size of ' . $this->_original;
  }
}
```

This checks that $_canProcess is true and that the width of the original image is not 0. The second test is necessary because getimagesize() sets the width and height to 0 if it can't determine the size. This usually happens if the image format contains multiple images. The method then calls the two internal methods you have just created. If the $_originalwidth property is 0, an error message is added to the $_messages property.

4. To test the new methods, amend the test() method like this:

```
public function test() {
  echo 'File: ' . $this->_original . '<br>';
  echo 'Original width: ' . $this->_originalwidth . '<br>';
  echo 'Original height: ' . $this->_originalheight . '<br>';
  echo 'Image type: ' . $this->_imageType . '<br>';
```

```
    echo 'Destination: ' . $this->_destination . '<br>';
    echo 'Max size: ' . $this->_maxSize . '<br>';
    echo 'Suffix: ' . $this->_suffix . '<br>';
    echo 'Thumb width: ' . $this->_thumbwidth . '<br>';
    echo 'Thumb height: ' . $this->_thumbheight . '<br>';
    echo 'Base name: ' . $this->_name . '<br>';
    if ($this->_messages) {
      print_r($this->_messages);
    }
  }
}
```

5. The call to `create()` needs to come before the `test()` method. Otherwise, the new values won't have been generated. Amend the code in `create_thumb.php` like this:

```
$thumb = new Ps2_Thumbnail($_POST['pix']);
$thumb->setDestination('C:/upload_test/thumbs/');
$thumb->setMaxSize(100);
$thumb->setSuffix('small');
$thumb->create();
$thumb->test();
```

6. Test the updated class by selecting an image in `create_thumb.php` and clicking **Create Thumbnail**. You should see the values displayed onscreen, as shown in Figure 8-4.

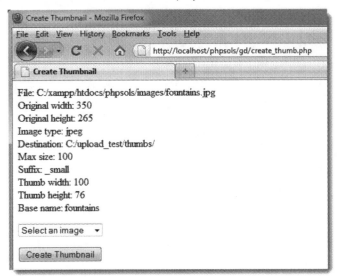

Figure 8-4. The class is now generating all the values needed to create the thumbnail image.

If necessary, check your code against `Thumbnail_03.php` in the `ch08` folder.

After you have gathered all the necessary information, you can generate a thumbnail image from a larger one. This involves creating image resources for the original image and the thumbnail. For the original image, you need to use one of these functions specific to the image's MIME type:

- `imagecreatefromjpeg()`
- `imagecreatefrompng()`
- `imagecreatefromgif()`

The functions take a single argument: the path to the file. Because the thumbnail doesn't yet exist, you use a different function, `imagecreatetruecolor()`, which takes two arguments—the width and height (in pixels).

The function that creates a resized copy of an image is `imagecopyresampled()`, which takes no fewer than ten arguments—all of them required. The arguments fall into five pairs as follows:

- References to the two image resources—copy first, original second
- The x and y coordinates of where to position the top-left corner of the copied image
- The x and y coordinates of the top-left corner of the original
- The width and height of the copy
- The width and height of the area to copy from the original

Figure 8-5 shows how the last four pairs of arguments can be used to extract a specific area, rather than copy the whole image, using the following arguments to `imagecopyresampled()`:

```
imagecopyresampled($thumb, $source, 0, 0, 170, 20, $thbwidth,$thbheight, 170, 102);
```

Figure 8-5. The `imagecopyresampled()` function allows you to copy part of an image.

The x and y coordinates of the area to copy are measured in pixels from the top left of the image. The x and y axes begin at 0 at the top left, and increase to the right and down. By setting the width and height of the area to copy to 170 and 102, respectively, PHP extracts the area outlined in white.

So, now you know how websites manage to crop uploaded images. They calculate the coordinates dynamically using JavaScript or Flash, both of which are beyond the scope of this book. For the `Ps2_Thumbnail` class, you'll use the whole of the original image to generate the thumbnail.

After creating the copy with `imagecopyresampled()`, you need to save it, again using a function specific to the MIME type, namely:

- `imagejpeg()`

- imagepng()
- imagegif()

Each function takes as its first two arguments: the image resource and the path to where you want to save it.

The imagejpeg() and imagepng() functions take an optional third argument to set the image quality. For imagejpeg(), you set quality by specifying a number in the range of 0 (worst) to 100 (best). If you omit the argument, the default is 75. For imagepng(), the range is 0 to 9. Confusingly, 0 produces the best quality (no compression).

Finally, once you have saved the thumbnail, you need to destroy the image resources by passing them to imagedestroy(). In spite of its destructive name, this function has no effect on the original image or the thumbnail. It simply frees the server memory by destroying the image resources required during processing.

PHP Solution 8-4: Generating the thumbnail image

This PHP Solution completes the Ps2_Thumbnail class by creating the image resources, copying the thumbnail, and saving it in the destination folder.

Continue working with your existing class definition. Alternatively, use Thumbnail_03.php in the ch08 folder.

1. The image resource for the original image needs to be specific to its MIME type, so start by creating an internal method to select the correct type. Add the following code to the class definition. It's a protected method, so put it at the bottom of the page (but inside the class's closing curly brace).

```
protected function createImageResource() {
  if ($this->_imageType == 'jpeg') {
    return imagecreatefromjpeg($this->_original);
  } elseif ($this->_imageType == 'png') {
    return imagecreatefrompng($this->_original);
  } elseif ($this->_imageType == 'gif') {
    return imagecreatefromgif($this->_original);
  }
}
```

   The checkType() method that you created in PHP Solution 8-1 stores the MIME type as jpeg, png, or gif. So, the conditional statement checks the MIME type, matches it to the appropriate function, and passes the original image as an argument. The method then returns the resulting image resource.

2. Now it's time to define the internal method that does all the hard work. It contains a lot of code, so I'll break it into sections. Start by defining the createThumbnail() method like this:

```
protected function createThumbnail() {
  $resource = $this->createImageResource();
  $thumb = imagecreatetruecolor($this->_thumbwidth, $this->_thumbheight);
}
```

This calls the `createImageResource()` method that you created in step 1, and then creates an image resource for the thumbnail, passing the thumbnail's width and height to `imagecreatetruecolor()`.

3. The next stage in creating the thumbnail involves passing both image resources to `imagecopyresampled()` and setting the coordinates and dimensions. Amend the `createThumbnail()` method like this:

```
protected function createThumbnail() {
  $resource = $this->createImageResource();
  $thumb = imagecreatetruecolor($this->_thumbwidth, $this->_thumbheight);
  imagecopyresampled($thumb, $resource, 0, 0, 0, 0, $this->_thumbwidth, ↪
    $this->_thumbheight, $this->_originalwidth, $this->_originalheight);
}
```

The first two arguments are the image resources you have just created for the thumbnail and original image. The next four arguments set the x and y coordinates for both the copy and the original to the top left corner. Next come the width and height calculated for the thumbnail, followed by the original image's width and height. By setting arguments 3–6 to the top left corner and both sets of dimensions to the full amounts, this copies the whole original image to the whole of the thumbnail. In other words, it creates a smaller copy of the original.

Note that you don't need to assign the result of `imagecopyresampled()` to a variable. The scaled down image is now stored in `$thumb`, but you still need to save it.

4. Complete the definition of `createThumbnail()` like this:

```
protected function createThumbnail() {
  $resource = $this->createImageResource();
  $thumb = imagecreatetruecolor($this->_thumbwidth, $this->_thumbheight);
  imagecopyresampled($thumb, $resource, 0, 0, 0, 0, $this->_thumbwidth, ↪
    $this->_thumbheight, $this->_originalwidth, $this->_originalheight);
  $newname = $this->_name . $this->_suffix;
  if ($this->_imageType == 'jpeg') {
    $newname .= '.jpg';
    $success = imagejpeg($thumb, $this->_destination . $newname, 100);
  } elseif ($this->_imageType == 'png') {
    $newname .= '.png';
    $success = imagepng($thumb, $this->_destination . $newname, 0);
  } elseif ($this->_imageType == 'gif') {
    $newname .= '.gif';
    $success = imagegif($thumb, $this->_destination . $newname);
  }
  if ($success) {
    $this->_messages[] = "$newname created successfully.";
  } else {
    $this->_messages[] = "Couldn't create a thumbnail for " . ↪
      basename($this->_original);
  }
  imagedestroy($resource);
```

```
  imagedestroy($thumb);
}
```

The first line of new code concatenates the suffix to the filename stripped of its filename extension. So, if the original file is called menu.jpg and the default _thb suffix is used, $newname becomes menu_thb.

The conditional statement checks the image's MIME type and appends the appropriate filename extension. In the case of menu.jpg, $newname becomes menu_thb.jpg. The scaled down image is then passed to the appropriate function to save it, using the destination folder and $newname as the path where it is saved. For JPEG and PNG images, the optional quality argument is set to the highest level: 100 for JPEG and 0 for PNG.

The result of the save operation is stored in $success. Depending on the outcome, $success is either true or false, and an appropriate message is added to the $_messages property.

Finally, imagedestroy() frees the server memory by destroying the resources used to create the thumbnail image.

5. Update the definition of the create() method to call the createThumbnail() method:

```
public function create() {
  if ($this->_canProcess && $this->_originalwidth != 0) {
    $this->calculateSize($this->_originalwidth, $this->_originalheight);
    $this->getName();
    $this->createThumbnail();
  } elseif ($this->_originalwidth == 0) {
    $this->_messages[] = 'Cannot determine size of ' . $this->_original;
  }
}
```

6. You no longer need the test() method. You can either delete it from the class definition or comment it out. If you plan to experiment further or make enhancements to the class, commenting it out saves the effort of creating it again from scratch.

7. Up to now, you have used the test() method to display error messages. Create a public method to get the messages:

```
public function getMessages() {
  return $this->_messages;
}
```

8. Save Thumbnail.php. In create_thumb.php, replace the call to the test() method with a call to getMessages(), and assign the result to a variable like this:

```
$thumb->create();
$messages = $thumb->getMessages();
```

9. Add a PHP code block just after the opening <body> tag to display any messages:

```
<?php
if (isset($messages) && !empty($messages)) {
```

```
    echo '<ul>';
    foreach ($messages as $message) {
      echo "<li>$message</li>";
    }
    echo '</ul>';
  }
  ?>
```

You've seen this code in previous chapters, so it needs no explanation.

10. Save `create_thumb.php`, load it in a browser, and test it by selecting an image from the list and clicking **Create Thumbnail**. If all goes well, you should see a message reporting the creation of the thumbnail, and confirm its existence in the `thumbs` subfolder of `upload_test`, as shown in Figure 8-6.

Figure 8-6. The thumbnail has been successfully created in the destination folder.

11. If the thumbnail isn't created, the error message generated by the `Ps2_Thumbnail` class should help you detect the source of the problem. Also, check your code carefully against `Thumbnail_04.php` in the `ch08` folder. If the tests in the previous PHP solutions worked, the error is likely to be in the `create()`, `createImageResource()`, or `createThumbnail()` method definitions. The other place to check is, of course, your PHP configuration. The class depends on the GD extension being enabled. Although GD is widely supported, it's not always on by default.

Resizing an image automatically on upload

Now that you have a class that creates a thumbnail from a larger image, it's relatively simple to adapt the Ps2_Upload class from Chapter 6 to generate a thumbnail from an uploaded image—in fact, not only from a single image, but also from multiple images.

Instead of changing the code in the Ps2_Upload class, it's more efficient to extend the class and create a subclass. You then have the choice of using the original class to perform uploads of any type of file, or the subclass to create thumbnail images on upload. The subclass also needs to provide the option to save or discard the larger image after the thumbnail has been created.

Before diving into the code, let's take a quick look at how you create a subclass.

Extending a class

A major advantage of using classes is that they're extensible. To extend a class, you simply include the original class definition and define the subclass using the extends keyword like this:

```
require_once('OriginalClass.php');
class MyNewClass extends OriginalClass {
  // subclass definition
}
```

This creates a new **subclass** or **child class** called MyNewClass from the original or **parent class**, OriginalClass. The parent-child analogy is apposite, because the child inherits all the features of its parent, but can adapt some of them and acquire new ones of its own. This means that MyNewClass shares the same properties and methods as OriginalClass, but you can add new properties and methods. You can also redefine (or **override**) some of the parent's methods and properties. This simplifies the process of creating a class to perform a more specialized task. The Ps2_Upload class you created in Chapter 6 performs basic file uploads. In this chapter, you'll extend it to create a child class called Ps2_ThumbnailUpload that uses the basic upload features of its parent, but adds specialized features that create thumbnail images.

Like all children, a child class often needs to borrow from its parent. This frequently happens when you override a method in the child class, but need to use the original version as well. To refer to the parent version, you prefix it with the parent keyword followed by two colons like this:

```
parent::originalMethod();
```

You'll see how this works in PHP Solution 8-5, because the child class defines its own constructor to add an extra argument, but also needs to use the parent constructor.

This description of inheritance covers only the bare minimum you need to understand PHP Solution 8-5. For a more detailed insight into PHP classes, see my PHP Object-Oriented Solutions *(friends of ED, 2008, ISBN: 978-1-4302-1011-5).*

So, let's create a class capable of uploading images and generating thumbnails at the same time.

PHP Solution 8-5: Creating the Ps2_ThumbnailUpload class

This PHP solution extends the `Ps2_Upload` class from Chapter 6 and uses it in conjunction with the `Ps2_Thumbnail` class to upload and resize images. It demonstrates how to create a child class and override parent methods. To create the child class, you need `Upload.php` from Chapter 6 and `Thumbnail.php` from this chapter. Copies of both files are in the `classes/completed` folder.

1. Create a new file called `ThumbnailUpload.php` in the `classes/Ps2` folder. It will contain only PHP code, so strip out any HTML inserted by your script editor, and add the following code:

```php
<?php
require_once('Upload.php');
require_once('Thumbnail.php');

class Ps2_ThumbnailUpload extends Ps2_Upload {

}
```

This includes the definitions of the `Ps2_Upload` and `Ps2_Thumbnail` classes, and declares that the `Ps2_ThumbnailUpload` class extends `Ps2_Upload`. All subsequent code needs to be inserted between the curly braces.

2. The child class needs three properties: for the folder where the thumbnail is to be saved, a Boolean that determines whether to delete the original image, and for the suffix to be added to the thumbnail. The last of these is required in case you don't want to use the default suffix defined in `Ps2_Thumbnail`. Add the following property definitions inside the curly braces:

```php
protected $_thumbDestination;
protected $_deleteOriginal;
protected $_suffix = '_thb';
```

3. When you extend a class, the only time you need to define a constructor method is when you want to change how the constructor works. The `Ps2_ThumbnailUpload` class takes an extra argument that determines whether to delete the original image, giving you the option to retain only the thumbnail or to keep both versions of the image. When testing locally, a `Ps2_Thumbnail` object can access the original image on your own hard drive. But generating the thumbnail is a server-side operation, so it won't work on a website without first uploading the original image to the server.

The constructor also needs to call the parent constructor to define the path to the upload folder. Add the following definition to the class:

```php
public function __construct($path, $deleteOriginal = false) {
  parent::__construct($path);
  $this->_thumbDestination = $path;
  $this->_deleteOriginal = $deleteOriginal;
}
```

The constructor takes two arguments: the path to the upload folder and a Boolean variable that determines whether to delete the original image. The second argument is set to `false` in the constructor signature, making it optional.

The first line of code inside the constructor passes `$path` to the parent constructor to set the destination folder for the file uploads. The second line also assigns `$path` to the `$_thumbDestination` property, making the same folder the default for both images.

The final line assigns the value of the second argument to the `$_deleteOriginal` property. Because the second argument is optional, it's automatically set to `false` and both images are retained unless you set it explicitly to `true`.

4. Create the setter method for the thumbnail destination folder like this:

```
public function setThumbDestination($path) {
  if (!is_dir($path) || !is_writable($path)) {
    throw new Exception("$path must be a valid, writable directory.");
  }
  $this->_thumbDestination = $path;
}
```

This takes a path as its only argument, checks that it's a folder (directory) and is writable, and assigns the value to the `$_thumbDestination` property. If the value passed as an argument is invalid, the class throws an exception.

Instead of creating a setter method for the thumbnail destination folder, I could have added an extra argument to the constructor. However, my choice simplifies the constructor for occasions when you want to save the thumbnail and original image in the same folder. Also, I could have silently used the original upload folder instead of throwing an exception if there's a problem with the thumbnail destination. I decided that a problem with the destination folder is too serious to ignore. Decisions like this are an integral part of writing any script, not just designing a class.

5. Apart from the name, the setter method for the thumbnail suffix is identical to the one in `Thumbnail.php`. It looks like this:

```
public function setThumbSuffix($suffix) {
  if (preg_match('/\w+/', $suffix)) {
    if (strpos($suffix, '_') !== 0) {
      $this->_suffix = '_' . $suffix;
    } else {
      $this->_suffix = $suffix;
    }
  } else {
    $this->_suffix = '';
  }
}
```

You need to define the method here because the class inherits from `Ps2_Upload`, not `Ps2_Thumbnail`. A PHP class can have only a single parent.

6. Next, create a protected method to generate the thumbnail using the following code:

```
protected function createThumbnail($image) {
  $thumb = new Ps2_Thumbnail($image);
  $thumb->setDestination($this->_thumbDestination);
  $thumb->setSuffix($this->_suffix);
  $thumb->create();
  $messages = $thumb->getMessages();
  $this->_messages = array_merge($this->_messages, $messages);
}
```

This takes a single argument, the path to an image, and creates a `Ps2_Thumbnail` object. The code is similar to `create_thumb.php`, so it shouldn't need explanation.

The final line uses `array_merge()` to merge any messages generated by the `Ps2_Thumbnail` object with the `$_messages` property of the `Ps2_ThumbnailUpload` class. Although the properties you defined in step 2 don't include a `$_messages` property, the child class automatically inherits it from its parent.

7. In the parent class, the `processFile()` method saves an uploaded file to its target destination. The thumbnail needs to be generated from the original image, so you need to override the parent's `processFile()` method, and use it to call the `createThumbnail()` method that you have just defined. Copy the `processFile()` method from `Upload.php`, and amend it by adding the code highlighted in bold.

```
protected function processFile($filename, $error, $size, $type, ↩
                               $tmp_name, $overwrite) {
  $OK = $this->checkError($filename, $error);
  if ($OK) {
    $sizeOK = $this->checkSize($filename, $size);
    $typeOK = $this->checkType($filename, $type);
    if ($sizeOK && $typeOK) {
      $name = $this->checkName($filename, $overwrite);
      $success = move_uploaded_file($tmp_name, $this->_destination . $name);
      if ($success) {
        // don't add a message if the original image is deleted
        if (!$this->_deleteOriginal) {
          $message = $filename . ' uploaded successfully';
          if ($this->_renamed) {
            $message .= " and renamed $name";
          }
          $this->_messages[] = $message;
        }
        // create a thumbnail from the uploaded image
        $this->createThumbnail($this->_destination . $name);
        // delete the uploaded image if required
        if ($this->_deleteOriginal) {
```

```
        unlink($this->_destination . $name);
      }
    } else {
      $this->_messages[] = 'Could not upload ' . $filename;
    }
  }
}
}
```

If the original image has been uploaded successfully, the new code adds a conditional statement to generate the message only if $_deleteOriginal is false. It then calls the createThumbnail() method, passing it the uploaded image as the argument. Finally, if $_deleteOriginal has been set to true, it uses unlink() to delete the uploaded image, leaving only the thumbnail.

8. Save ThumbnailUpload.php. To test it, copy create_thumb_upload_01.php from the ch08 folder to the gd folder, and save it as create_thumb_upload.php. The file contains a simple form with a file field and a PHP block that displays messages. Add the following PHP code block above the DOCTYPE declaration:

```php
if (isset($_POST['upload'])) {
  require_once('../classes/Ps2/ThumbnailUpload.php');
  try {
    $upload = new Ps2_ThumbnailUpload('C:/upload_test/');
    $upload->setThumbDestination('C:/upload_test/thumbs/');
    $upload->move();
    $messages = $upload->getMessages();
  } catch (Exception $e) {
    echo $e->getMessage();
  }
}
```

Adjust the paths in the constructor and setThumbDestination() method, if necessary.

9. Save create_thumb_upload.php, and load it in an HTML5-compliant browser. Click the **Browse** or **Choose File** button, and select multiple images. When you click the **Upload** button, you should see messages informing you of the successful upload and creation of the thumbnails. Check the destination folders, as shown in Figure 8-7.

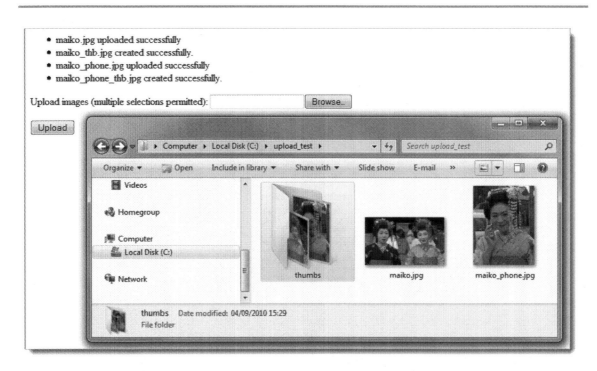

- maiko.jpg uploaded successfully
- maiko_thb.jpg created successfully.
- maiko_phone.jpg uploaded successfully
- maiko_phone_thb.jpg created successfully.

Upload images (multiple selections permitted): [   ] [Browse...]

[Upload]

Figure 8-7. The thumbnails are created in the same operation as the images are uploaded.

10. Test the `Ps2_ThumbnailUpload` class by uploading the same images again. This time, the original images and thumbnails should be renamed in the same way as in Chapter 6 through the addition of a number before the filename extension.

11. Try different tests, changing the suffix inserted into the thumbnail names, or deleting the original image after the thumbnail has been created. If you run into problems, check your code carefully against `ThumbnailUpload.php` in the `ch08` folder.

> *In older browsers that don't support the multiple attribute on form fields, the class uploads a single image and creates a thumbnail from it. To support multiple uploads from older browsers, create multiple file fields in the form, and give them all the same name attribute followed by an empty pair of square brackets like this: name="image[]".*

Using the Ps2_ThumbnailUpload class

The Ps2_ThumbnailUpload class is easy to use. Just include the class definition in your file, and pass the path to the upload folder to the constructor as an argument like this:

```
$upload = new Ps2_ThumbnailUpload('C:/upload_test/');
```

If you want to delete the original image after the thumbnail has been created, pass `true` as the second argument to the constructor like this:

```
$upload = new Ps2_ThumbnailUpload('C:/upload_test/', true);
```

The class has the following public methods:

- `setThumbDestination()`: This sets the path to the folder where the thumbnail images are to be saved. If you don't call this method, the thumbnails are stored in the same folder as the original images.
- `setThumbSuffix()`: Use this to change the suffix inserted into the thumbnail names. The default is `_thb`.
- `move()`: This uploads the original image(s) and generates the thumbnail(s). By default, images that have the same name as an existing one are renamed. To overwrite existing images, pass `true` as an argument to this method.

It also inherits the following methods from the parent `Ps2_Upload` class:

- `getMessages()`: Retrieves messages generated by the upload and the thumbnail.
- `getMaxSize()`: Gets the maximum upload size. The default is 50kB.
- `setMaxSize()`: Changes the maximum upload size. The argument should be expressed as the number of bytes permitted.
- `addPermittedTypes()`: This allows you to add other MIME types to the upload. The `Ps2_Thumbnail` class rejects MIME types that it doesn't recognize, but the files are uploaded as normal to the main destination folder.

The `Ps2_ThumbnailUpload` class wasn't designed with mixed uploads in mind, so refine the messages generated by the `Ps2_Thumbnail` class if you want to use the inherited `addPermittedTypes()` method.

Because the `Ps2_ThumbnailUpload` class is dependent on the `Ps2_Upload` and `Ps2_Thumbnail` classes, you need to upload all three class definition files to your remote web server when using this class on a live website.

Chapter summary

This has been quite an intense chapter, showing not only how to generate thumbnails from larger images, but also introducing you to extending an existing class and overriding inherited methods. Designing and extending classes can be confusing at first, but it becomes less intimidating if you concentrate on what each method is doing. A key principle of class design is to break large tasks down into small, manageable units. Ideally, a method should perform a single task, such as creating the image resource for the original image. This isn't always possible. For example, the `createThumbnail()` and `processFile()` methods perform multiple operations.

The real advantage of using classes is the time and effort they save once you have defined them. Instead of typing dozens of lines of code each time you want to add file or thumbnail upload functionality to a website, calling the class involves just a few simple lines. Also don't just think of the code in this chapter as being for creating and uploading thumbnail images. Many of the subroutines in the class files could be adapted for use in other situations.

In the next chapter, you'll learn all about PHP sessions, which preserve information related to a specific user and play a vital role in password-protecting web pages.

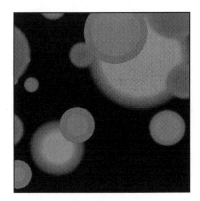

Chapter 9

Pages That Remember:
Simple Login and Multipage Forms

The Web is a brilliant illusion. When you visit a well-designed website, you get a great feeling of continuity, as though flipping through the pages of a book or a magazine. Everything fits together as a coherent entity. The reality is quite different. Each part of an individual page is stored and handled separately by the web server. Apart from needing to know where to send the relevant files, the server has no interest in who you are. Each time a PHP script runs, the variables exist only in the server's memory and are normally discarded as soon as the script finishes. Even variables in the $_POST and $_GET arrays have only a brief life span. Their value is passed once to the next script and then removed from memory unless you do something with it, such as store the information in a hidden form field. Even then, it persists only if the form is submitted.

To get around these problems, PHP uses **sessions**. After briefly describing how sessions work, I'll show you how you can use session variables to create a simple file-based login system and pass information from one page to another without the need to use hidden form fields.

In this chapter, you'll learn about the following:

- Understanding what sessions are and how to create them
- Creating a file-based login system
- Checking password strength with a custom-built class
- Setting a time limit for sessions
- Using sessions to keep track of information over multiple pages

What sessions are and how they work

A session ensures continuity by storing a random identifier—the session ID—on the web server and on the visitor's computer (as a cookie). The web server uses the cookie to recognize that it's communicating with the same person (or, to be more precise, with the same computer). Figures 9-1 through 9-3 show the details of a simple session created in my local testing environment.

As Figure 9-1 shows, the cookie stored in the browser is called PHPSESSID, and the content is a jumble of letters and numbers. This random string is the session's ID.

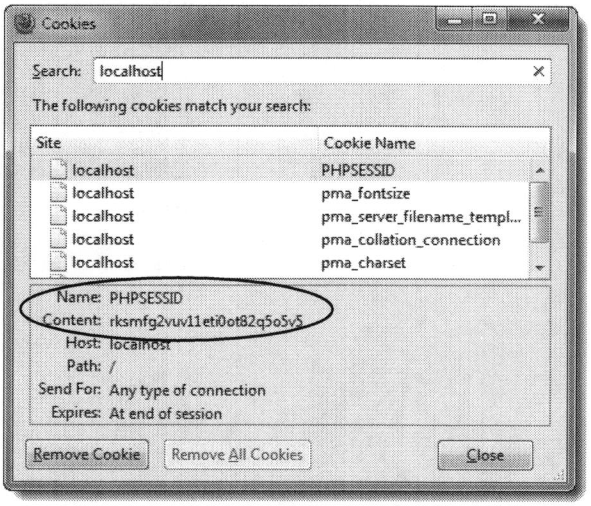

Figure 9-1. PHP sessions store a unique identifier as a cookie in the browser.

A matching file, which contains the same jumble of letters and numbers as part of its filename, is created on the web server, as shown in Figure 9-2.

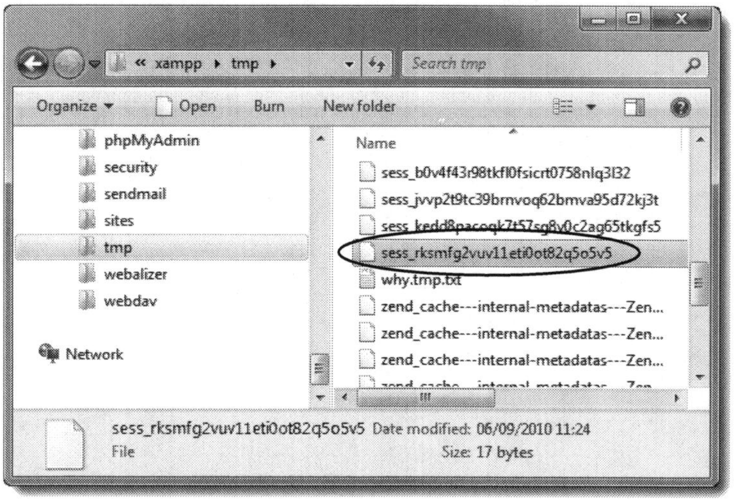

Figure 9-2. The content of the cookie identifies the session data stored on the web server.

When a session is initiated, the server stores information in session variables that can be accessed by other pages as long as the session remains active (normally until the browser is closed). Because the session ID is unique to each visitor, the information stored in session variables cannot be seen by anyone else. This means sessions are ideal for user authentication, although they can be used for any situation where you want to preserve information for the same user when passing from one page to the next, such as with a multipage form or a shopping cart.

The only information stored on the user's computer is the cookie that contains the session ID, which is meaningless by itself. This means there is no danger of private information being exposed through someone examining the contents of a cookie on a shared computer.

The session variables and their values are stored on the web server. Figure 9-3 shows the contents of a simple session file. As you can see, it's in plain text, and the content isn't difficult to decipher. The session shown in the figure has one variable: name. The variable's name is followed by a vertical pipe, then the letter "s", a colon, a number, another colon, and the variable's value in quotes. The "s" stands for string, and the number indicates how many characters the string contains. So, this session variable contains my name as a string, which is five characters long.

```
Start Page   sess_rksmfg2vuv11eti0ot82q5o5v5 {Generic Document}
name|s:5:"David";
```

Figure 9-3. The details of the session are stored on the server in plain text.

This setup has several implications. The cookie containing the session ID normally remains active until the browser is closed. So, if several people share the same computer, they all have access to each other's sessions unless they always close the browser before handing over to the next person, something over which you have no control. So, it's important to provide a logout mechanism to delete both the cookie and the session variables, keeping your site secure. You can also create a timeout mechanism, which automatically prevents anyone from regaining access after a certain period of inactivity.

Storing session variables in plain text on the web server is not, in itself, a cause for concern. As long as the server is correctly configured, the session files cannot be accessed through a browser. Inactive files are also routinely deleted by PHP (in theory, the lifetime is 1,440 seconds—24 minutes—but this cannot be relied upon). Nevertheless, it should be obvious that, if an attacker manages to compromise the server or hijack a session, the information could be exposed. So, although sessions are generally secure enough for password protecting parts of a website or working with multipage forms, you should never use session variables to store sensitive information, such as passwords or credit card details. As you'll see in "Using sessions to restrict access" later in this chapter, although a password is used to gain access to a protected site, the password itself is stored (preferably encrypted) in a separate location, and not as a session variable.

Sessions are supported by default, so you don't need any special configuration. However, sessions won't work if cookies are disabled in the user's browser. It is possible to configure PHP to send the session ID through a query string, but this is considered a security risk.

Creating PHP sessions

Just put the following command in every PHP page that you want to use in a session:

```
session_start();
```

This command should be called only once in each page, and it must be called before the PHP script generates any output, so the ideal position is immediately after the opening PHP tag. If any output is generated before the call to session_start(), the command fails and the session won't be activated for that page. (See "The 'Headers already sent' error" section later for an explanation.)

Creating and destroying session variables

You create a session variable by adding it to the $_SESSION superglobal array in the same way you would assign an ordinary variable. Say you want to store a visitor's name and display a greeting. If the name is submitted in a login form as $_POST['name'], you assign it like this:

```
$_SESSION['name'] = $_POST['name'];
```

$_SESSION['name'] can now be used in any page that begins with session_start(). Because session variables are stored on the server, you should get rid of them as soon as they are no longer required by your script or application. Unset a session variable like this:

```
unset($_SESSION['name']);
```

To unset *all* session variables—for instance, when you're logging someone out—set the $_SESSION superglobal array to an empty array, like this:

```
$_SESSION = array();
```

> Do not be tempted to try unset($_SESSION). It works all right—but it's a little too effective. It not only clears the current session but also prevents any further session variables from being stored.

Destroying a session

By itself, unsetting all the session variables effectively prevents any of the information from being reused, but you should also invalidate the session cookie like this:

```
if (isset($_COOKIE[session_name()])) {
  setcookie(session_name(), '', time()-86400, '/');
}
```

This uses the function session_name() to get the name of the session dynamically and resets the session cookie to an empty string and to expire 24 hours ago (86400 is the number of seconds in a day). The final argument ('/') applies the cookie to the whole domain.

Finally, destroy the session with the following command:

```
session_destroy();
```

By destroying a session like this, there is no risk of an unauthorized person gaining access either to a restricted part of the site or to any information exchanged during the session. However, a visitor may forget to log out, so it's not always possible to guarantee that the session_destroy() command will be triggered, which is why it's so important not to store sensitive information in a session variable.

> You may find session_register() and session_unregister() in old scripts. These functions are deprecated. Use $_SESSION['variable_name'] and unset($_SESSION['variable_name']) instead.

Regenerating the session ID

When a user changes status, such as after logging in, it's recommended as a security measure to regenerate the session ID. This changes the random string of letters and numbers that identify the session, but preserves all the information stored in session variables. In *PHP Pro Security* (Apress, 2005, ISBN 978-1-59059-508-4), Chris Snyder and Michael Southwell explain that "the goal of generating a fresh session ID is to remove the possibility, however slight, that an attacker with knowledge of the low-level security session might be able to perform high-security tasks."

To regenerate the session ID, simply call `session_regenerate_id()` and redirect the user to another page or reload the same one.

The "Headers already sent" error

Although using PHP sessions is very easy, there's one problem that causes beginners a great deal of head banging. Instead of everything working the way you expect, you see the following message:

Warning: Cannot add header information - headers already sent

I've mentioned this problem several times before in conjunction with the `header()` function. It affects `session_start()` and `setcookie()` as well. In the case of `session_start()`, the solution is simple: make sure that you put it immediately after the opening PHP tag (or very soon thereafter), and check that there's no whitespace before the opening tag.

Sometimes, the problem occurs even if there is no whitespace ahead of the PHP tag. This is usually caused by editing software inserting the byte order mark (BOM) at the beginning of the script. If this happens, open your script editor's preferences and disable the use of the BOM in PHP pages.

When using `setcookie()` to destroy the session cookie, though, it's quite likely that you may need to send output to the browser before calling the function. In this case, PHP lets you save the output in a buffer using `ob_start()`. You then flush the buffer with `ob_end_flush()` after `setcookie()` has done its job. You'll see how to do this in PHP Solution 9-2.

Using sessions to restrict access

The first words that probably come to mind when thinking about restricting access to a website are "username" and "password." Although these generally unlock entry to a site, neither is essential to a session. You can store any value as a session variable and use it to determine whether to grant access to a page. For instance, you could create a variable called `$_SESSION['status']` and give visitors access to different parts of the site depending on its value, or no access at all if it hasn't been set.

A little demonstration should make everything clear and show you how sessions work in practice.

PHP Solution 9-1: A simple session example

This should take only a few minutes to build, but you can also find the complete code in `session_01.php`, `session_02.php`, and `session_03.php`, in the `ch09` folder.

1. Create a page called `session_01.php` in a new folder called `sessions` in the `phpsols` site root. Insert a form with a text field called `name` and a submit button. Set the `method` to `post` and `action` to `session_02.php`. The form should look like this:

```
<form id="form1" method="post" action="session_02.php">
  <p>
    <label for="name">Name:</label>
    <input type="text" name="name" id="name">
  </p>
  <p>
    <input type="submit" name="Submit" value="Submit">
  </p>
</form>
```

2. In another page called `session_02.php`, insert this above the DOCTYPE declaration:

```php
<?php
// initiate session
session_start();
// check that form has been submitted and that name is not empty
if ($_POST && !empty($_POST['name'])) {
  // set session variable
  $_SESSION['name'] = $_POST['name'];
}
?>
```

The inline comments explain what's going on. The session is started, and as long as `$_POST['name']` isn't empty, its value is assigned to `$_SESSION['name']`.

3. Insert the following code between the `<body>` tags in `session_02.php`:

```php
<?php
// check session variable is set
if (isset($_SESSION['name'])) {
  // if set, greet by name
  echo 'Hi, ' . $_SESSION['name'] . '. <a href="session_03.php">Next</a>';
} else {
  // if not set, send back to login
  echo 'Who are you? <a href="session_01.php">Login</a>';
}
?>
```

4. If `$_SESSION['name']` has been set, a welcome message is displayed along with a link to `session_03.php`. Otherwise, the page tells the visitor that it doesn't recognize who's trying to gain access, and provides a link back to the first page.

Take care when typing the following line:

echo 'Hi, ' . $_SESSION['name'] . '. <a href="session03.php">Next</a>';

The first two periods (surrounding $_SESSION['name']) are the PHP concatenation operator. The third period (immediately after a single quote) is an ordinary period that will be displayed as part of the string.

5. Create `session_03.php`. Type the following above the `DOCTYPE` to initiate the session:

```php
<?php session_start(); ?>
```

6. Insert the following code between the `<body>` tags of `session_03.php`:

```php
<?php
// check whether session variable is set
if (isset($_SESSION['name'])) {
  // if set, greet by name
  echo 'Hi, ' . $_SESSION['name'] . '. See, I remembered your name!<br>';
  // unset session variable
  unset($_SESSION['name']);
  // invalidate the session cookie
  if (isset($_COOKIE[session_name()])) {
    setcookie(session_name(), '', time()-86400, '/');
  }
  // end session
  session_destroy();
  echo '<a href="session_02.php">Page 2</a>';
} else {
  // display if not recognized
  echo "Sorry, I don't know you.<br>";
  echo '<a href="session_01.php">Login</a>';
}
?>
```

If `$_SESSION['name']` has been set, the page displays it, then unsets it and invalidates the current session cookie. By placing `session_destroy()` at the end of the first code block, the session and its associated variables cease to be available.

7. Load `session_01.php` into a browser, type your name in the text field, and click **Submit**.

You should see something like the following screenshot. At this stage, there is no apparent difference between what happens here and in an ordinary form.

8. When you click **Next**, the power of sessions begins to show. The page remembers your name, even though the $_POST array is no longer available to it. There's a problem, though, with that **headers already sent** error message. You'll fix that later.

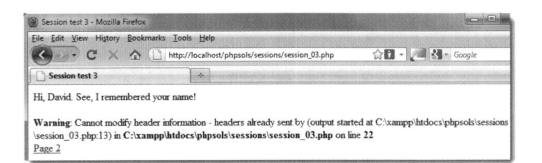

9. Click the link to Page 2 (just below the error message). The session has been destroyed, so this time `session_02.php` has no idea who you are.

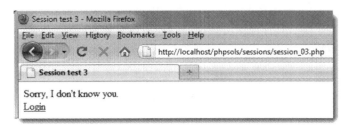

10. Type the address of `session_03.php` in the browser address bar and load it. It, too, has no recollection of the session and displays an appropriate message.

You need to get rid of the warning message in step 8, not only because it looks bad but also because it means `setcookie()` can't invalidate the session cookie. Even though `session_start()` comes immediately after the opening PHP tag in `session_03.php`, the warning message is triggered by the `DOCTYPE` declaration, the `<head>`, and other HTML being output before `setcookie()`.

PHP Solution 9-2: Buffering the output with ob_start()

Although you could put `setcookie()` in the PHP block above the `DOCTYPE` declaration, you would also need to assign the value of `$_SESSION['name']` to an ordinary variable, because it ceases to exist after the session is destroyed. Rather than pull the whole script apart, the answer is to buffer the output with `ob_start()`.

Continue working with `session_03.php` from the previous section.

1. Amend the PHP block above the `DOCTYPE` declaration like this:

```php
<?php
session_start();
ob_start();
?>
```

This turns on output buffering and prevents output being sent to the browser until the end of the script, or until you specifically flush the output with ob_end_flush().

2. Flush the output immediately after invalidating the session cookie like this:

```php
// invalidate the session cookie
if (isset($_COOKIE[session_name()])) {
  setcookie(session_name(), '', time()-86400, '/');
  }
ob_end_flush();
```

3. Save session_03.php, and test the sequence again. This time, there should be no warning. More importantly, the session cookie is no longer valid.

Using file-based authentication

As you have just seen, the combination of session variables and conditional statements lets you present completely different pages to a visitor depending on whether a session variable has been set. All you need to do is add a password checking system, and you have a basic user authentication system.

In PHP Solution 7-2, I showed you how to use the file() function to read each line of a text file into an array. You can now adapt that script to create a simple login system using sessions. Each person's username and password is separated by a comma and recorded on a new line of a text file like this:

```
david, codeslave
chris, bigboss
```

I'll use the same text file as before: filetest_02.txt, which is in the private folder that was set up in Chapter 7. Refer to Chapter 7 if you haven't set up a folder for PHP to read and write files.

PHP Solution 9-3: Building the login page

This PHP solution shows how to submit a username and password through the post method and check the submitted values against those stored in an external text file. It uses the file() function to inspect the external file one line at a time. If a match is found, the script sets a session variable and then redirects the user to another page.

1. Create a file called login.php in the sessions folder, and insert a form with a text input field each for username and password, plus a submit button named login, like this (alternatively, use login_01.php in the ch09 folder):

```html
<form id="form1" method="post" action="">
<p>
  <label for="username">Username:</label>
  <input type="text" name="username" id="username">
  </p>
  <p>
```

```
      <label for="pwd">Password:</label>
      <input type="password" name="pwd" id="pwd">
    </p>
    <p>
      <input name="login" type="submit" id="login" value="Log in">
    </p>
  </form>
```

It's a simple form, nothing fancy.

2. Add the following code in a PHP block above the DOCTYPE declaration:

```php
$error = '';
if (isset($_POST['login'])) {
  session_start();
  $username = $_POST['username'];
  $password = $_POST['pwd'];
  // location of usernames and passwords
  $userlist = 'C:/private/filetest_02.txt;
  // location to redirect on success
  $redirect = 'http://localhost/phpsols/sessions/menu.php';
  require_once('../includes/authenticate.inc.php');
}
```

This initializes a variable called $error as an empty string. If the login fails, this will be used to display an error message informing the user of the reason.

The conditional statement then checks whether the $_POST array contains an element named login. If it does, the form has been submitted, and the code inside the curly braces initiates a PHP session and stores the values passed through the $_POST array in $username and $password. Then, it creates $userlist, which defines the location of the file that contains the registered usernames and passwords, and $redirect, the URL of the page the user will be sent to after logging in successfully.

Finally, the code inside the conditional statement includes authenticate.inc.php, which you'll create next.

Adjust the value of $userlist to match the location in your own setup, if necessary.

3. Create a file called `authenticate.inc.php` in the `includes` folder. It will contain only PHP code, so strip out any HTML inserted by your script editor, and insert the following code:

```php
<?php
if (!file_exists($userlist) || !is_readable($userlist)) {
  $error = 'Login facility unavailable. Please try later.';
} else {
  // read the file into an array called $users
  $users = file($userlist);
  // loop through the array to process each line
  for ($i = 0; $i < count($users); $i++) {
    // separate each element and store in a temporary array
    $tmp = explode(', ', $users[$i]);
    // assign each element of the temp array to a named array key
    $users[$i] = array('name' => $tmp[0], 'password' => rtrim($tmp[1]));
  }
}
```

This is almost identical to the code that you used in `file.php` in PHP Solution 7-2. The only differences are the use of `$userlist` instead of `$textfile` and the conditional statement. Rather than testing that the file exists and is readable, the conditions check for a nonexistent file or one that can't be read. This has been done to make the code easier to read. If there's a problem with `$userfile`, the error message is created immediately. Otherwise, the main code in the `else` clause is executed.

The main code works exactly the same as in PHP Solution 7-2. It extracts the content of the text file into an array and loops through it, creating a multidimensional array containing the name and password of each registered user. The names and passwords in `filetest_02.txt` produce the following values:

```php
$users[0]['name']     = 'david';
$users[0]['password'] = 'codeslave';
$users[1]['name']     = 'chris';
$users[1]['password'] = 'bigboss';
```

4. To authenticate the user, you need to check the submitted values against those stored in the text file. Add the highlighted code to the `for` loop:

```php
for ($i = 0; $i < count($users); $i++) {
  // separate each element and store in a temporary array
  $tmp = explode(', ', $users[$i]);
  // assign each element of the temp array to a named array key
  $users[$i] = array('name' => $tmp[0], 'password' => rtrim($tmp[1]));
  // check for a matching record
  if ($users[$i]['name'] == $username && $users[$i]['password'] == ↵
    $password) {
```

```
    $_SESSION['authenticated'] = 'Jethro Tull';
    session_regenerate_id();
    break;
  }
}
```

If the record matches $username and $password, the script creates a variable called
$_SESSION['authenticated'] and assigns it the name of one of the great folk-rock bands of
the '70s. There's nothing magic about either of these (apart from Jethro Tull's music); I've
chosen the name and value of the variable arbitrarily. All that matters is a session variable is
created. As soon as a match is found, the session ID is regenerated, and break exits the loop.

5. Take a closer look at these two lines:

```
$users[$i] = array('name' => $tmp[0], 'password' => rtrim($tmp[1]));
if ($users[$i]['name'] == $username && $users[$i]['password'] == $password) {
```

The first one assigns $tmp[0] to $users[$i]['name'] and rtrim($tmp[1]) to
$users[$i]['password']. The next line compares the values in the $users array with
$username and $password. That's all the $users array is ever used for. Creating the array
made sense in PHP Solution 7-2, because you wanted to inspect the entire contents of the
file. However, all you need here is to compare $tmp[0] with $username and rtrim($tmp[1])
with $password.

Delete the first of these two lines, and amend the second one like this:

```
if ($tmp[0] == $username && rtrim($tmp[1]) == $password) {
```

6. If the login is successful, the header() function needs to redirect the user to the URL stored
in $redirect, and exit the script. Otherwise, an error message needs to be created, informing
the user that the login failed. The complete script looks like this:

```
<?php
if (!file_exists($userlist) || !is_readable($userlist)) {
  $error = 'Login facility unavailable. Please try later.';
} else {
  // read the file into an array called $users
  $users = file($userlist);
  // loop through the array to process each line
  for ($i = 0; $i < count($users); $i++) {
    // separate each element and store in a temporary array
    $tmp = explode(', ', $users[$i]);
    // check for a matching record
    if ($tmp[0] == $username && rtrim($tmp[1]) == $password) {
      $_SESSION['authenticated'] = 'Jethro Tull';
      session_regenerate_id();
      break;
    }
  }
  // if the session variable has been set, redirect
  if (isset($_SESSION['authenticated'])) {
```

```
    header("Location: $redirect");
    exit;
  } else {
    $error = 'Invalid username or password.';
  }
}
```

7. In login.php, add the following short code block just after the opening <body> tag to display any error messages:

```
<body>
<?php
if ($error) {
  echo "<p>$error</p>";
}
?>
<form id="form1" method="post" action="">
```

Before you can test login.php, you need to create menu.php and restrict access with a session.

PHP Solution 9-4: Restricting access to a page with a session

This PHP solution demonstrates how to restrict access to a page by checking for the existence of a session variable that indicates the user's credentials have been authenticated. If the variable hasn't been set, the header() function redirects the user to the login page.

1. Create two pages in the sessions folder called menu.php and secretpage.php. It doesn't matter what they contain, as long as they link to each other. Alternatively, use menu_01.php and secretpage_01.php in the ch09 folder.

2. Protect access to each page by inserting the following above the DOCTYPE declaration:

```
<?php
session_start();
// if session variable not set, redirect to login page
if (!isset($_SESSION['authenticated'])) {
    header('Location: http://localhost/phpsols/sessions/login.php');
    exit;
}
?>
```

After starting the session, the script checks whether $_SESSION['authenticated'] has been set. If it hasn't, it redirects the user to login.php and exits. That's all there is to it! The script doesn't need to know the value of $_SESSION['authenticated'], although you could make doubly sure by amending line 4 like this:

```
if (!isset($_SESSION['authenticated']) || $_SESSION['authenticated'] ➥
            != 'Jethro Tull')  {
```

This now also rejects a visitor if $_SESSION['authenticated'] has the wrong value.

3. Save `menu.php` and `secretpage.php`, and try to load either of them into a browser. You should always be redirected to `login.php`.

4. Enter a valid username and password in `login.php`, and click Log in. You should be redirected immediately to `menu.php`, and the link to `secretpage.php` should also work.

5. All you need to do to protect any page on your site is add the eight lines of code in step 2 above the DOCTYPE declaration.

PHP Solution 9-5: Creating a reusable logout button

As well as logging into a site, users should be able to log out. This PHP solution shows how to create a logout button that can be inserted in any page.

Continue working with the files from the preceding section.

1. Create a logout button in the `<body>` of `menu.php` by inserting the following form:

```
<form id="logoutForm" method="post" action="">
<input name="logout" type="submit" id="logout" value="Log out">
</form>
```

The page should look similar to the following screenshot:

2. You now need to add the script that runs when the logout button is clicked. Amend the code above the DOCTYPE declaration like this (the code is in `menu_02.php`):

```
<?php
session_start();
// if session variable not set, redirect to login page
if (!isset($_SESSION['authenticated'])) {
  header('Location: http://localhost/phpsols/sessions/login.php');
  exit;
}
// run this script only if the logout button has been clicked
if (isset($_POST['logout'])) {
  // empty the $_SESSION array
  $_SESSION = array();
  // invalidate the session cookie
```

```php
  if (isset($_COOKIE[session_name()])) {
    setcookie(session_name(), '', time()-86400, '/');
  }
  // end session and redirect
  session_destroy();
  header('Location: http://localhost/phpsols/sessions/login.php');
  exit;
}
?>
```

This is the same code as in "Destroying a session" earlier in this chapter. The only differences are that it's enclosed in a conditional statement so that it runs only when the logout button is clicked, and it uses header() to redirect the user to login.php.

3. Save menu.php, and test it by clicking **Log out**. You should be redirected to login.php. Any attempt to return to menu.php or secretpage.php will bring you back to login.php.

4. You can put the same code in every restricted page, but PHP is all about saving work, not making it. It makes sense to turn this into an include file. Create a new file called logout.inc.php in the includes folder. Cut and paste the new code from steps 1 and 2 into the new file like this (it's in logout.inc.php in the ch09 folder):

```php
<?php
// run this script only if the logout button has been clicked
if (isset($_POST['logout'])) {
  // empty the $_SESSION array
  $_SESSION = array();
  // invalidate the session cookie
  if (isset($_COOKIE[session_name()])) {
  setcookie(session_name(), '', time()-86400, '/');
  }
  // end session and redirect
  session_destroy();

  header('Location: http://localhost/phpsols/sessions/login.php');
  exit;
}
?>
<form id="logoutForm" method="post" action="">
  <input name="logout" type="submit" id="logout" value="Log out">
</form>
```

5. At the same point in menu.php from which you cut the code for the form, include the new file like this:

```php
<?php include('../includes/logout.inc.php'); ?>
```

6. Including the code from an external file like this means that there will be output to the browser before the calls to setcookie() and header(). So you need to buffer the output, as shown in PHP Solution 9-2.

Add `ob_start();` immediately after the call to `session_start()` at the top of `menu.php`. There's no need to use `ob_end_flush()` or `ob_end_clean()`. PHP automatically flushes the buffer at the end of the script if you haven't already done so explicitly.

7. Save `menu.php`, and test the page. It should look and work exactly the same as before.

8. Repeat steps 5 and 6 with `secretpage.php`. You now have a simple, reusable logout button that can be incorporated in any restricted page.

9. You can check your code against `menu_03.php`, `secretpage_02.php`, and `logout.inc.php` in the `ch09` folder.

Making passwords more secure

Although this file-based user authentication setup is adequate for restricting access to web pages, all the passwords are stored in plain text. For greater security, it's advisable to encrypt passwords. PHP provides a simple and effective way to encrypt passwords, using the SHA-1 (US Secure Hash Algorithm 1; for more info, see `www.faqs.org/rfcs/rfc3174`), which produces a 40-digit hexadecimal number. When encrypted with SHA-1, `codeslave` turns into this:

`fe228bd899980a7e23fd08082afddb74a467e467`

SHA-1 performs one-way encryption. This means that even if your password file is exposed, no one will be able to work out what the passwords are. It also means that you have no way of converting `fe228bd899980a7e23fd08082afddb74a467e467` back to `codeslave`. In one respect, this is unimportant: when a user logs in, you encrypt the password again and compare the two encrypted versions. The disadvantage is that there is no way that you can send users password reminders if they forget them; you must generate a new password. Nevertheless, good security demands encryption.

Another precaution that's worth taking is adding a **salt** to the password before encrypting it. This is a random value that's added to make decryption even harder. Even if two people choose the same password, adding a unique value to the password before encryption ensures that the encrypted values are different.

Encryption is no protection against the most common problem with passwords: ones that are easy to guess or use common words. Many registration systems now enforce the use of stronger passwords by requiring a mixture of alphanumeric characters and symbols.

To improve the basic login system developed so far, you need to create a user registration form that checks the following:

- The password and username contain a minimum number of characters.
- The password matches minimum strength criteria, such as containing a mixture of numbers, uppercase and lowercase characters, and symbols.
- The password matches a second entry in a confirmation field.
- The username isn't already in use.

PHP Solution 9-6: Creating a password strength checker

This PHP solution shows how to create a class that checks whether a password meets certain requirements, such as no spaces, a minimum number of characters, and a combination of different types of characters. By default, the class checks only that the password has no spaces and contains a minimum number of characters. Optional methods allow you to set tougher conditions, such as using a combination of uppercase and lowercase characters, numbers, and nonalphanumeric symbols.

This PHP solution starts by building the user registration form that will also be used in PHP Solution 9-7.

1. Create a page called register.php in the sessions folder, and insert a form with three text input fields and a submit button. Lay out the form, and name the input elements as shown in the following screenshot. If you want to save time, use register_01.php in the ch09 folder.

2. As always, you want the processing script to run only if the form has been submitted, so everything needs to be enclosed in a conditional statement that checks whether the name attribute of the submit button is in the $_POST array. Then, you need to check that the input meets your minimum requirements. Insert the following code in a PHP block above the DOCTYPE declaration:

```php
if (isset($_POST['register'])) {
  $username = trim($_POST['username']);
  $password = trim($_POST['pwd']);
  $retyped = trim($_POST['conf_pwd']);
  require_once('../classes/Ps2/CheckPassword.php');
}
```

The code inside the conditional statement passes the input from the three text fields to trim() to remove whitespace from the beginning and end, and assigns the results to simple variables. It then includes the file that will contain the class that checks the password, which you'll define next.

3. Create a file called CheckPassword.php in the classes/Ps2 folder. It will contain only PHP script, so strip out any HTML, and add the following code:

```php
<?php
class Ps2_CheckPassword{
```

```php
  protected $_password;
  protected $_minimumChars;
  protected $_mixedCase = false;
  protected $_minimumNumbers = 0;
  protected $_minimumSymbols = 0;
  protected $_errors = array();

  public function __construct($password, $minimumChars = 8) {
    $this->_password = $password;
    $this->_minimumChars = $minimumChars;
  }

  public function check() {
    if (preg_match('/\s/', $this->_password)) {
      $this->_errors[] = 'Password cannot contain spaces.';
    }
    if (strlen($this->_password) < $this->_minimumChars) {
      $this->_errors[] = "Password must be at least $this->_minimumChars ➥
        characters.";
    }
    return $this->_errors ? false : true;
  }

  public function getErrors() {
    return $this->_errors;
  }

}
```

This defines the basic `Ps2_CheckPassword` class, which initially checks only whether the password contains any spaces and whether it has the required minimum number of characters. You'll add the other features shortly.

The class begins by defining six protected properties. The first two are for the password and minimum number of characters. The `$_mixedCase`, `$_minimumNumbers`, and `$_minimumSymbols` properties will be used to add strength to the password but are initially set to `false` or 0. The `$_errors` property will be used to store an array of error messages if the password fails any of the checks.

The constructor method takes two arguments—the password and minimum number of characters—and assigns them to the relevant properties. By default, the minimum number of characters is set to 8, making this an optional argument.

The `check()` method contains two conditional statements. The first uses `preg_match()` with a regular expression that searches for whitespace characters inside the password. The second conditional statement uses `strlen()`, which returns the length of a string, and compares the result with `$_minimumChars`.

If the password fails either test or both, the $_errors property contains at least one element, which PHP treats as intrinsicly true. The final line in the check() method uses the $_errors property as the condition with the ternary operator. If any errors are found, the check() method returns false indicating that the password failed validation. Otherwise, it returns true.

The getErrors() public method simply returns the array of error messages.

4. Save CheckPassword.php, and switch to register.php.

5. In register.php, create a Ps2_CheckPassword object, passing $password as the argument. Then call the check() method and handle the result like this:

```
require_once('../classes/Ps2/CheckPassword.php');
$checkPwd = new Ps2_CheckPassword($password);
$passwordOK = $checkPwd->check();
if ($passwordOK) {
  $result = array('Password OK');
} else {
  $result = $checkPwd->getErrors();
}
```

6. The second argument to the Ps2_CheckPassword constructor is optional, so leaving it out sets the minimum number of characters to the default 8. The result of the check() method is assigned to $passwordOK. If it returns true, a single-element array reporting that the password is OK is assigned to $result. Otherwise, the getErrors() method is used to retrieve the array of errors from the $checkPwd object.

> The single-element array will be used only to test the class. Once testing is complete, it will be replaced by the script that registers the user.

7. Add the following PHP code block just above the form in the body of the page:

```
<h1>Register User</h1>
<?php
if (isset($result)) {
  echo '<ul>';
  foreach ($result as $item) {
    echo "<li>$item</li>";
  }
  echo '</ul>';
}
?>
<form action="" method="post" id="form1">
```

This displays the results of the password test as an unordered list after the form has been submitted.

8. Save `register.php`, and load it in a browser. Test the `Ps2_CheckPassword` class by clicking the **Register** button without filling in any of the fields. You should see a message informing you that the password requires a minimum of eight characters.

9. Try it with a password that contains eight characters. You should see **Password OK**.

10. Try a password with at least eight characters but insert a space in the middle. You'll be warned that no spaces are permitted.

11. Try one with fewer than eight characters but with a space in the middle. You'll see the following warnings:

12. Change the code in `register.php` to pass the optional second argument to the `Ps2_CheckPassword` constructor, and set the minimum number of characters to 10:

```
$checkPwd = new Ps2_CheckPassword($password, 10);
```

13. Save and test the page again. If you encounter any problems, compare your code with `register_02.php` and `CheckPassword_01.php` in the `ch09` folder.

14. Assuming that your code is working, add to the class definition in `CheckPassword.php` the public methods to set the password strength. Where you put them inside the class makes no difference technically (as long as they're inside the curly braces), but my preference is to put public methods in the same order as they're used. You need to set the options before calling the `check()` method, so insert the following code between the constructor and `check()` method definitions:

```
public function requireMixedCase() {
  $this->_mixedCase = true;
}

public function requireNumbers($num = 1) {
  if (is_numeric($num) && $num > 0) {
    $this->_minimumNumbers = (int) $num;
  }
}

public function requireSymbols($num = 1) {
```

```
    if (is_numeric($num) && $num > 0) {
      $this->_minimumSymbols = (int) $num;
    }
  }
}
```

The code is pretty straightforward. The requireMixedCase() method takes no arguments and resets the $_mixedCase property to true. The other two methods take one argument, check that it's a number greater that 0, and assign it to the relevant property. The (int) casting operator ensures that it's an integer. You first met the casting operator in PHP Solution 6-4. The value of $num sets the minimum amount of numbers or nonalphanumeric symbols the password must contain. By default, the value is set to 1, making the argument optional.

15. The check() method needs to be updated to perform the necessary checks for these strength criteria. Amend the code like this:

```
public function check() {
  if (preg_match('/\s/', $this->_password)) {
    $this->_errors[] = 'Password cannot contain spaces.';
  }
  if (strlen($this->_password) < $this->_minimumChars) {
    $this->_errors[] = "Password must be at least $this->_minimumChars ➥
      characters.";
  }
  if ($this->_mixedCase) {
    $pattern = '/(?=.*[a-z])(?=.*[A-Z])/';
    if (!preg_match($pattern, $this->_password)) {
      $this->_errors[] = 'Password should include uppercase and lowercase ➥
        characters.';
    }
  }
  if ($this->_minimumNumbers) {
    $pattern = '/\d/';
    $found = preg_match_all($pattern, $this->_password, $matches);
    if ($found < $this->_minimumNumbers) {
      $this->_errors[] = "Password should include at least ➥
        $this->_minimumNumbers number(s).";
    }
  }
  if ($this->_minimumSymbols) {
    $pattern = "/[-!$%^&*(){}<>[\]'" . '"|#@:;.,?+=_\/\~]/';
    $found = preg_match_all($pattern, $this->_password, $matches);
    if ($found < $this->_minimumSymbols) {
      $this->_errors[] = "Password should include at least ➥
        $this->_minimumSymbols nonalphanumeric character(s).";
    }
  }
  return $this->_errors ? false : true;
}
```

Each of the three new conditional statements is run only if the equivalent public method is called before the check() method. Each one stores a regular expression as $pattern and then uses preg_match() or preg_match_all() to test the password.

If the $_mixedCase property is set to true, the regular expression and password are passed to preg_match() to look for at least one lowercase letter and one uppercase letter in any position in the password.

The $_minimumNumbers and $_minimumSymbols properties are set to 0 by default. If they're reset to a positive number, the regular expression and password are passed to the preg_match_all() function to find how many times the regex matches. The function requires three arguments: the regex, the string to be searched, and a variable to store the matches. And it returns the number of matches found. In this case, all you're interested in is the number of matches. The variable that stores the matches is discarded.

The horrendous $pattern in the last conditional statement is actually a regex created by concatenating a single-quoted string to a double-quoted one. This is necessary to include single and double quotation marks in the permitted symbols. I have included most nonalphanumeric symbols on an English keyboard. If you want to add others, put them just before the final closing square bracket like this:

```
$pattern = "/[-!$%^&*(){}<>[\]'" . '"|#@:;.,?+=_\/\~£¦]/';
```

16. Save CheckPassword.php, and test the updated class by calling the new methods in register.php. For example, the following requires the password to have a minimum of 10 characters, at least one uppercase and one lowercase letter, two numbers, and one nonalphanumeric symbol:

```
$checkPwd = new Ps2_CheckPassword($password, 10);
$checkPwd->requireMixedCase();
$checkPwd->requireNumbers(2);
$checkPwd->requireSymbols();
$passwordOK = $checkPwd->check();
```

It doesn't matter which order you call the new methods, as long as they're after the constructor and before the call to the check() method. Use a variety of combinations to enforce different strengths of password.

If necessary, check your code against register_03.php and CheckPassword_02.php in the ch09 folder.

When developing the code for this chapter, I originally designed the password checker as a function. The basic code inside the function was the same, but I decided to convert it into a class to make it more flexible and easier to use. The problem with the function was that it needed a large number of arguments to set the different options, and it was difficult to remember which order they came in. There was also the difficulty of handling the result. If there were no errors, the function returned true; but if any errors were found, it returned the array of error messages. Since PHP treats an array with elements as implicitly true, this meant using the identical operator (three equal signs—see Table 3-5) to check whether the result was a Boolean true.

Converting the code to a class eliminated these problems. The public methods to set the options have intuitive names and can be set in any order—or not at all. And the result is always a Boolean `true` or `false`, because a separate method retrieves the array of error messages. It involved writing more code, but the improvements made it worthwhile.

PHP Solution 9-7: Creating a file-based user registration system

This PHP solution creates a simple user registration system that encrypts passwords with SHA-1 and a salt. It uses the `Ps2_CheckPassword` class from PHP Solution 9-6 to enforce minimum strength requirements. Further checks ensure that the username contains a minimum number of characters and that the user has retyped the password correctly in a second field.

The user credentials are stored in a plain text file, which must be outside the web server's document root. The instructions assume you have set up a private folder that PHP has write access to, as described in Chapter 7. It's also assumed you're familiar with "Appending content with fopen()" in the same chapter.

Continue working with the files from the preceding PHP solution. Alternatively, use `register_03.php` in the `ch09` folder and `CheckPassword.php` in the `classes/completed` folder.

1. Create a file called `register_user_text.inc.php` in the `includes` folder, and strip out any HTML inserted by your script editor.

2. Cut the following code from `register.php` (it doesn't matter if your settings for the `Ps2_CheckPassword` object are different):

    ```php
    require_once('../classes/Ps2/CheckPassword.php');
    $checkPwd = new Ps2_CheckPassword($password, 10);
    $checkPwd->requireMixedCase();
    $checkPwd->requireNumbers(2);
    $checkPwd->requireSymbols();
    $passwordOK = $checkPwd->check();
    if ($passwordOK) {
      $result = array('Password OK');
    } else {
      $result = $checkPwd->getErrors();
    }
    ```

3. At the end of the remaining script above the DOCTYPE declaration in `register.php`, create a variable for the location of the text file that will be used to store the user credentials, and include `register_user_text.inc.php`. The code in the PHP block at the top of `register.php` should now look like this:

    ```php
    if (isset($_POST['register'])) {
      $username = trim($_POST['username']);
      $password = trim($_POST['pwd']);
      $retyped = trim($_POST['conf_pwd']);
      $userfile = 'C:/private/encrypted.txt';
      require_once('../includes/register_user_text.inc.php');
    }
    ```

The text file for the user credentials doesn't exist yet. It will be created automatically when the first user is registered. Amend the path to the private folder to match your own setup if necessary.

4. In register_user_text.inc.php, paste the code you cut from register.php in step 2, and add the following code immediately after the command that includes the class definition:

```
require_once('../classes/Ps2/CheckPassword.php');
$usernameMinChars = 6;
$errors = array();
if (strlen($username) < $usernameMinChars) {
  $errors[] = "Username must be at least $usernameMinChars characters.";
}
if (preg_match('/\s/', $username)) {
  $errors[] = 'Username should not contain spaces.';
}
$checkPwd = new Ps2_CheckPassword($password, 10);
```

The first two lines of new code specify the minimum number of characters in the username and initialize an empty array for error messages. The rest of the new code checks the length of the username and tests whether it contains any spaces. The conditional statements use the same code as in the Ps2_CheckPassword class.

5. Amend the code at the bottom of register_user_text.inc.php like this:

```
$passwordOK = $checkPwd->check();
if (!$passwordOK) {
  $errors = array_merge($errors, $checkPwd->getErrors());
}
if ($password != $retyped) {
  $errors[] = "Your passwords don't match.";
}
if ($errors) {
  $result = $errors;
} else {
  $result = array('All OK');
}
```

This adds the logical Not operator to the conditional statement that tests the value of $passwordOK. If the password fails to validate, array_merge() is used to merge the result of $checkPwd->getErrors() with the existing $errors array.

The next conditional statement compares $password with $retyped and adds an error message to the $errors array if they don't match.

If any errors are discovered, the final conditional statement assigns the $errors array to $result. Otherwise, a single-element array is assigned to $result, reporting that all is OK. Again, this is only for testing purposes. Once you have checked your code, the script that registers the user will replace the final conditional statement.

6. Save `register_user_text.inc.php` and `register.php`, and test the form again. Leave all the fields blank and click **Register**. You should see the following error messages:

Register User

- Username must be at least 6 characters.
- Password must be at least 10 characters.
- Password should include uppercase and lowercase characters.
- Password should include at least 2 number(s).
- Password should include at least 1 nonalphanumeric character(s).

7. Try a variety of tests to make sure your validation code is working.

If you have problems, compare your code with `register_user_text.inc_01.php` and `register_04.php` in the `ch09` folder.

Assuming that your code is working, you're ready to create the registration part of the script. Let's pause to consider what the main script needs to do. First, you need to encrypt the password by combining it with the username as a salt. Then, before writing the details to a text file, you must check whether the username is unique. This presents a problem of which mode to use with `fopen()`.

> The various `fopen()` modes are described in Chapter 7.

Ideally, you want the internal pointer at the beginning of the file so that you can loop through existing records. The r+ mode does this, but the operation fails unless the file already exists. You can't use w+, because it deletes existing content. You can't use x+ either, because it fails if a file of the same name already exists. That leaves a+ as the only option with the flexibility you need: it creates the file if necessary and lets you read and write.

The file is empty the first time you run the script (you can tell because the `filesize()` function returns 0), so you can go ahead and write the details. If `filesize()` doesn't return 0, you need to reset the internal pointer and loop through the records to see if the username is already registered. If there's a match, you break out of the loop and prepare an error message. If there isn't a match by the end of the loop, you not only know it's a new username, you also know you're at the end of the file. So, you write a new line followed by the new record. Now that you understand the flow of the script, you can insert it into `register_user_text.inc.php`.

8. Delete the following code at the bottom of `register_user_text.inc.php`:

```
if ($errors) {
  $result = $errors;
} else {
  $result = array('All OK');
}
```

9. Replace it with the following code:

```
if (!$errors) {
  // encrypt password, using username as salt
```

```php
$password = sha1($username.$password);
// open the file in append mode
$file = fopen($userfile, 'a+');
// if filesize is zero, no names yet registered
// so just write the username and password to file
if (filesize($userfile) === 0) {
  fwrite($file, "$username, $password");
  $result = "$username registered.";
} else {
  // if filesize is greater than zero, check username first
  // move internal pointer to beginning of file
  rewind($file);
  // loop through file one line at a time
  while (!feof($file)) {
    $line = fgets($file);
    // split line at comma, and check first element against username
    $tmp = explode(', ', $line);
    if ($tmp[0] == $username) {
      $result = "$username taken - choose a different username.";
      break;
    }
  }
  // if $result not set, username is OK
  if (!isset($result)) {
    // insert line break followed by username, comma, and password
    fwrite($file, PHP_EOL . "$username, $password");
    $result = "$username registered.";
  }
  // close the file
  fclose($file);
}
}
```

The preceding explanation and inline comments should help you follow the script.

10. Windows, Mac OS X, and Linux use different characters to create a new line, so the script uses the PHP_EOL constant introduced in Chapter 7 to insert a line break in a platform-neutral way. The registration script stores the outcome as a string in $result. Amend the code in the body of register.php to display the result or the error messages like this:

```php
<?php
if (isset($result) || isset($errors)) {
  echo '<ul>';
  if (!empty($errors)) {
    foreach ($errors as $item) {
      echo "<li>$item</li>";
    }
  } else {
    echo "<li>$result</li>";
```

```
    }
  echo '</ul>';
}
?>
```

This loops through the $errors array if it's not empty. Otherwise, it displays the value of $result as a single bulleted item.

11. Save both register_user_text.inc.php and register.php, and test the registration system. Try registering the same username more than once. You should see a message informing you the username is taken and asking you to choose another.

12. Open encrypted.txt. You should see the usernames in plain text, but the passwords have been encrypted. Even if you choose the same password for two different users, the encrypted version is different because of the password being combined with the username as a salt. Figure 9-4 shows two users that were both registered with the password Ps2_Chapter9.

Figure 9-4. Using a salt produces completely different encryptions of the same password.

If necessary, check your code against register_user_text.inc_02.php and register_05.php in the ch09 folder.

Most of the code in register_user_text.php is generic. All you need to do to use it with any registration form is define $username, $password, $retyped, and $userfile before including it, and capture the results using $errors and $result. The only changes you might need to make to the external file are in setting the minimum number of characters in the username and the password strength. Those settings are defined at the top of the file, so they're easy to access and adjust.

PHP Solution 9-8: Using an encrypted login

Now that you have encrypted passwords, you need to change the login form to handle the new setup. All that's necessary is to select the text file that contains the encrypted passwords and to encrypt the password before comparing it with the one stored in the file.

1. Open login.php from PHP Solution 9-3, or use login_01.php from the ch09 folder. Amend the code like this:

```
$username = trim($_POST['username']);
$password = sha1($username . $_POST['pwd']);
// location of usernames and passwords
$userlist = 'C:/private/encrypted.txt';
```

This trims whitespace from the username. The next line adds the username to the front of the password before passing it to sha1() for encryption. Finally, the file that stores the user credentials is changed to the encrypted version.

2. Save login.php, and test it. It should work the same as before but be more secure. Check your code if necessary with login_02.php in the ch09 folder.

PHP Solutions 9-3 to 9-8 build a simple, yet effective, user authentication system that doesn't require a database back end. However, it does have its limitations. Above all, it's essential that the text file containing the usernames and passwords be outside the server root. Even though the passwords are encrypted, knowing the usernames reduces the effort that an attacker needs to try to break through your security. Another weakness is that the salt is the username. Ideally, you should create a random salt for each password, but you need to store it somewhere. If it's in the same file as the usernames, they would both be exposed at the same time.

Using a database for user authentication gets around many of these problems. It involves more work, but is likely to be more secure. Also, once you get more than a few records, querying a database is usually much faster than looping through a text file line by line. Chapter 17 covers user authentication with a database.

Setting a time limit on sessions

By default, PHP sets the lifetime of the session cookie on the user's computer to 0, which keeps the session active until the user logs out or the browser is closed. You can make the session timeout earlier through a call to ini_set(), the function that allows you to change some PHP configuration directives on the fly. As soon as the session starts, pass the directive session.cookie_lifetime as the first argument and a string containing the number of seconds you want the cookie to remain active as the second argument. For example, you could limit the session cookie's lifetime to ten minutes like this:

```
session_start();
ini_set('session.cookie_lifetime', '600');
```

Although this is effective, it has two drawbacks. First, the expiration is set relative to the time on the server, not the user's computer. If the user's computer clock is wrong, the cookie might be out of date immediately, or it might persist much longer than you anticipate. The other problem is that the user might be automatically logged out without explanation. The next PHP solution offers a user-friendlier approach.

PHP Solution 9-9: Ending a session after a period of inactivity

This PHP solution shows how to end a session if a user doesn't do anything that triggers a page to load after a specified period. When the session first starts, typically when the user logs in, the current time is stored in a session variable. Each time the user loads a page, the session variable is compared with the current time. If the difference is greater than a predetermined limit, the session and its variables are destroyed. Otherwise, the variable is updated to the current time.

These instructions assume you have set up the login system in PHP Solutions 9-3 to 9-8.

1. You need to store the current time after the user's credentials have been authenticated but before the script redirects the user to the restricted part of the site. Locate the following section of code in authenticate.inc.php (around lines 12–16), and insert the new code highlighted in bold as follows:

```
if ($tmp[0] == $username && rtrim($tmp[1]) == $password) {
  $_SESSION['authenticated'] = 'Jethro Tull';
  $_SESSION['start'] = time();
```

```php
session_regenerate_id();
break;
}
```

The `time()` function returns a current timestamp. By storing it in `$_SESSION['start']`, it becomes available to every page that begins with `session_start()`.

2. When a session times out, just dumping a user unceremoniously back at the login screen isn't very friendly, so it's a good idea to explain what's happened. In `login.php`, add the code highlighted in bold to the PHP block immediately after the opening `<body>` tag (around lines 22–26):

```php
<?php
if ($error) {
  echo "<p>$error</p>";
} elseif (isset($_GET['expired'])) {
?>
<p>Your session has expired. Please log in again.</p>
<?php } ?>
```

The message is shown if the URL contains a variable called `expired` in a query string.

3. Open `menu.php`, cut the code in the PHP block above the `DOCTYPE` declaration, and paste it into a new blank file.

4. Save the file as `session_timeout.inc.php` in the `includes` folder, and edit the code like this:

```php
<?php
session_start();
ob_start();
// set a time limit in seconds
$timelimit = 15;
// get the current time
$now = time();
// where to redirect if rejected
$redirect = 'http://localhost/phpsols/sessions/login.php';
// if session variable not set, redirect to login page
if (!isset($_SESSION['authenticated'])) {
  header("Location: $redirect");
  exit;
} elseif ($now > $_SESSION['start'] + $timelimit) {
  // if timelimit has expired, destroy session and redirect
  $_SESSION = array();
  // invalidate the session cookie
  if (isset($_COOKIE[session_name()])) {
    setcookie(session_name(), '', time()-86400, '/');
  }
  // end session and redirect with query string
  session_destroy();
  header("Location: {$redirect}?expired=yes");
```

```
    exit;
} else {
// if it's got this far, it's OK, so update start time
$_SESSION['start'] = time();
}
```

The inline comments explain what is going on, and you should recognize most of the `elseif` clause from PHP Solution 9-5. PHP measures time in seconds, and I've set $timelimit (in line 5) to a ridiculously short 15 seconds purely to demonstrate the effect. To set a more reasonable limit of, say, 15 minutes, change this later like this:

```
$timelimit = 15 * 60; // 15 minutes
```

You could, of course, set $timelimit to 900, but why bother when PHP can do the hard work for you?

If the sum of $_SESSION['start'] plus $timelimit is less than the current time (stored as $now), you end the session and redirect the user to the login page. The line that performs the redirect adds a query string to the end of the URL like this:

```
http://localhost/phpsols/sessions/login.php?expired=yes
```

The code in step 2 takes no notice of the value of expired; adding yes as the value just makes it look user-friendlier in the browser address bar.

If the script gets as far as the final else, it means that $_SESSION['authenticated'] has been set and that the time limit hasn't been reached, so $_SESSION['start'] is updated to the current time, and the page displays as normal.

5. Include session_timeout.inc.php above the DOCTYPE declaration in menu.php. The include command should be the only code in the PHP block:

```
<?php
require_once('../includes/session_timeout.inc.php');
?>
<!DOCTYPE HTML>
```

6. Replace the code above the DOCTYPE declaration in secretpage.php in the same way.

7. Save all the pages you have edited, and load either menu.php or secretpage.php into a browser. If the page displays, click **Log out**. Then log back in, and navigate back and forth between menu.php and secretpage.php. Once you have verified that the links work, wait 15 seconds or more, and try to navigate back to the other page. You should be automatically logged out and presented with the following screen:

If necessary, check your code against `authenticate.inc_02.php`, `login_03.php`, `session_timeout.inc.php`, `menu_04.php`, and `secretpage_03.php` in the ch09 folder.

Passing information through multipage forms

Variables passed through the $_POST and $_GET arrays have only a fleeting existence. Once they have been passed to a page, they're gone, unless you save their values in some way. The usual method of preserving information that's passed from one form to another is to extract its value from the $_POST array and store it in a hidden field in HTML like this:

```
<input type="hidden" name="address" id="address" value="<?php echo ➥
  $_POST['address']; ?>">
```

As their name suggests, hidden fields are part of a form's code, but nothing is displayed onscreen. Hidden fields are fine for one or two items, but say you have a survey that's spread over four pages. If you have 10 items on a page, you need a total of 60 hidden fields (10 on the second page, 20 on the third, and 30 on the fourth). Session variables can save you all that coding. They can also make sure that visitors always start on the right page of a multipage form.

PHP Solution 9-10: Using sessions for a multipage form

In this PHP solution, you'll build a script for use in multipage forms that gathers data from the $_POST array and assigns it to session variables. The script automatically redirects the user to the first page of the form if an attempt is made to access any other part of the form first.

1. Copy `multiple_01.php`, `multiple_02.php`, `multiple_03.php`, and `multiple_04.php` from the ch09 folder to the sessions folder. The first three pages contain simple forms that ask for the user's name, age, and address. The action attribute of each `<form>` tag is empty, so the forms are self-processing, but they don't yet contain any processing script. The final page is where the data from the first three pages will eventually be displayed.

2. Add the following code in a PHP block above the DOCTYPE declaration in `multiple_01.php`:

```
if (isset($_POST['next'])) {
  session_start();
  // set a variable to control access to other pages
```

```
    $_SESSION['formStarted'] = true;
    // set required fields
    $required = 'first_name';
    $firstPage = 'multiple_01.php';
    $nextPage = 'multiple_02.php';
    $submit = 'next';
    require_once('../includes/multiform.inc.php');
}
```

The name attribute of the submit button is next, so the code in this block runs only if the form has been submitted. It initiates a session and creates a session variable that will be used to control access to the other form pages.

Next come four variables that will be used by the script that processes the multipage form:

* $required: This is an array of the name attributes of required fields in the current page. If only one field is required, a string can be used instead of an array. If no fields are required, it can be omitted.

* $firstPage: The filename of the first page of the form.

* $nextPage: The filename of the next page in the form.

* $submit: The name of the submit button in the current page.

Finally, the code includes the script that processes the multipage form.

3. Create a file called multiform.inc.php in the includes folder. Delete any HTML markup, and insert the following code:

```
<?php
if (!isset($_SESSION)) {
  session_start();
}
$filename = basename($_SERVER['SCRIPT_FILENAME']);
$current = 'http://' . $_SERVER['HTTP_HOST'] . $_SERVER['PHP_SELF'];
```

Each page of the multipage form needs to call session_start(), but calling it twice on the same page generates an error, so the conditional statement first checks whether the $_SESSION superglobal variable is accessible. If it isn't, it initiates the session for the page.

After the conditional statement, $_SERVER['SCRIPT_FILENAME'] is passed to the basename() function to extract the filename of the current page. This is the same technique that you used in PHP Solution 4-3. $_SERVER['SCRIPT_FILENAME'] contains the path of the parent file, so when this script is included in multiple_01.php, the value of $filename will be multiple_01.php, *not* multiform.inc.php.

The next line builds the URL for the current page from the string http:// and the values of $_SERVER['HTTP_HOST'], which contains the current domain name, and $_SERVER['PHP_SELF'], which contains the path of the current file minus the domain name. If you're testing locally, when you load the first page of the multipage form $current is http://localhost/phpsols/sessions/multiple_01.php.

4. Now that you have both the name of the current file and its URL, you can use str_replace() to create the URLs for the first and next pages like this:

```
$redirectFirst = str_replace($filename, $firstPage, $current);
$redirectNext = str_replace($filename, $nextPage, $current);
```

The first argument to str_replace() is the string you want to replace, the second is the replacement string, and the third argument is the target string. In step 2, you set $firstPage to multiple_01.php and $nextPage to multiple_02.php. As a result, $redirectFirst becomes http://localhost/phpsols/sessions/multiple_01.php, and $redirectNext is http://localhost/phpsols/sessions/multiple_02.php.

5. To prevent users from accessing the multipage form without starting at the beginning, add a conditional statement that checks the value of $filename. If it's not the same as the first page and $_SESSION['formStarted'] hasn't been created, the header() function redirects to the first page like this:

```
if ($filename != $firstPage && !isset($_SESSION['formStarted'])) {
  header("Location: $redirectFirst");
  exit;
}
```

6. The rest of the script loops through the $_POST array, checking for required fields that are blank and adding them to a $missing array. If nothing is missing, the header() function redirects the user to the next page of the multipage form. The complete script for multiform.inc.php looks like this:

```
<?php
if (!isset($_SESSION)) {
  session_start();
}
$filename = basename($_SERVER['SCRIPT_FILENAME']);
$current = 'http://' . $_SERVER['HTTP_HOST'] . $_SERVER['PHP_SELF'];
$redirectFirst = str_replace($filename, $firstPage, $current);
$redirectNext = str_replace($filename, $nextPage, $current);
if ($filename != $firstPage && !isset($_SESSION['formStarted'])) {
  header("Location: $redirectFirst");
  exit;
}

if (isset($_POST[$submit])) {
  // create empty array for any missing fields
  $missing = array();
  // create $required array if not set
  if (!isset($required)) {
    $required = array();
  } else {
    // using casting operator to turn single string to array
    $required = (array) $required;
  }
```

```
    // process the $_POST variables and save them in the $_SESSION array
    foreach ($_POST as $key => $value) {
      // skip submit button
      if ($key == $submit) continue;
      // assign to temporary variable and strip whitespace if not an array
      $temp = is_array($value) ? $value : trim($value);
      // if empty and required, add to $missing array
      if (empty($temp) && in_array($key, $required)) {
        $missing[] = $key;
      } else {
        // otherwise, assign to a variable of the same name as $key
        $_SESSION[$key] = $temp;
      }
    }
    // if no required fields are missing, redirect to next page
    if (!$missing) {
      header("Location: $redirectNext");
      exit;
    }
  }
}
```

The code is very similar to that used in Chapter 5 to process the feedback form, so the inline comments should be sufficient to explain how it works. The conditional statement wrapped around the new code uses $_POST[$submit] to check if the form has been submitted. I have used a variable rather than hard-coding the name of the submit button to make the code more flexible. Although this script is included in the first page only after the form has been submitted, it's included directly in the other pages, so it's necessary to add the conditional statement here.

The name and value of the submit button are always included in the $_POST array, so the foreach loop uses the continue keyword to skip to the next item if the key is the same as the submit button's name. This avoids adding the unwanted value to the $_SESSION array. See "Breaking out of a loop" in Chapter 3 for a description of continue.

7. Add the following code in a PHP block above the DOCTYPE declaration in multiple_02.php:

```
$firstPage = 'multiple_01.php';
$nextPage = 'multiple_03.php';
$submit = 'next';
require_once('../includes/multiform.inc.php');
```

This sets the values of $firstPage, $nextPage, and $submit, and includes the processing script you have just created. The form in this page contains only one field, which is optional, so the $required variable isn't needed. The processing script automatically creates an empty array if it isn't set in the main page.

8. In multiple_03.php, add the following in a PHP code block above the DOCTYPE declaration:

```
// set required fields
$required = array('city', 'country');
```

```
$firstPage = 'multiple_01.php';
$nextPage = 'multiple_04.php';
$submit = 'next';
require_once('../includes/multiform.inc.php');
```

Two fields are required, so their name attributes are listed as an array and assigned to $required. The other code is the same as in the previous page.

9. Add the following code above the <form> tag in multiple_01.php, multiple_02.php, and multiple_03.php:

```
<?php if (isset($missing)) { ?>
<p> Please fix the following required fields:</p>
  <ul>
  <?php
  foreach ($missing as $item) {
    echo "<li>$item</li>";
  }
  ?>
  </ul>
<?php } ?>
```

This displays a list of required items that haven't been filled in.

10. In multiple_04.php, add the following code in a PHP block above the DOCTYPE declaration to redirect users to the first page if they didn't enter the form from there:

```
session_start();
if (!isset($_SESSION['formStarted'])) {
  header('Location: http://localhost/phpsols/sessions/multiple_01.php');
  exit;
}
```

11. In the body of the page, add the following code to the unordered list to display the results:

```
<ul>
<?php
$expected = array('first_name', 'family_name', 'age',
                  'address', 'city', 'country');
// unset the formStarted variable
unset($_SESSION['formStarted']);
foreach ($expected as $key) {
  echo "<li>$key: $_SESSION[$key]</li>";
  // unset the session variable
  unset($_SESSION[$key]);
}
?>
</ul>
```

This lists the name attributes of the form fields as an array and assigns it to $expected. This is a security measure to ensure you don't process bogus values that might have been injected into the $_POST array by a malicious user.

The code then unsets $SESSION['formStarted']$ and loops through the $expected array using each value to access the relevant element of the $SESSION array and display it in the unordered list. The session variable is then deleted. Deleting the session variables individually leaves intact any other session-related information.

12. Save all the pages, and try to load one of the middle pages of the form or the last one into a browser. You should be taken to the first page. Click **Next** without filling in either field. You'll be asked to fill in the first_name field. Fill in the required fields, and click **Next** on each page. The results should be displayed on the final page, as shown in Figure 9-5.

Figure 9-5. The session variables preserved the input from multiple pages.

You can check your code against multiple_01_done.php, multiple_02_done.php, multiple_03_done.php, multiple_04_done.php, and multiform.inc.php in the ch09 folder.

This is just a simple demonstration of a multipage form. In a real-world application, you would need to preserve the user input when required fields are left blank.

The script in multiform.inc.php can be used with any multipage form by creating $SESSION['formStarted'] on the first page after the form has been submitted, and using $required, $firstPage, $nextPage, and $submit on each page. Use the $missing array to handle required fields that aren't filled in.

Chapter review

If you started this book with little or no knowledge of PHP, you're no longer in the beginners' league, but are leveraging the power PHP in a lot of useful ways. Hopefully, by now, you'll have begun to appreciate that the same or similar techniques crop up again and again. Instead of just copying code, you should start to recognize techniques that you can adapt to your needs and experiment on your own.

The rest of this book continues to build on your knowledge, but brings a new factor into play: the MySQL relational database, which will take your PHP skills to a higher level. The next chapter offers an introduction to MySQL and shows you how to set it up for the remaining chapters.

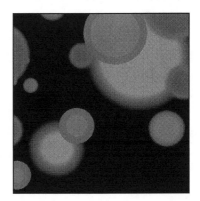

Chapter 10

Getting Started with MySQL

Dynamic websites take on a whole new meaning in combination with a database. Drawing content from a database allows you to present material in ways that would be impractical—if not impossible—with a static website. Examples that spring to mind are online stores, such as Amazon.com; news sites, such as the BBC (www.bbcnews.com); and the big search engines, including Google and Yahoo! Database technology allows these websites to present thousands, sometimes millions, of unique pages. Even if your ambitions are nowhere near as grandiose, a database can increase your website's richness of content with relatively little effort.

PHP supports all major databases, including Microsoft SQL Server, Oracle, and PostgreSQL, but it's most frequently used in conjunction with the open source MySQL database, which is the choice for this book. MySQL is actually a database management system that consists of several components: a database server, a client program for accessing individual databases and records, and utility programs for various administrative tasks. What comes as a shock to many people is that MySQL doesn't have a glossy graphical user interface (UI). The traditional way to work with MySQL is on the command line—through the Command Prompt on Windows or Terminal on a Mac. However, several third-party graphical UIs are available. I'll discuss some of them in this chapter, but the one I'll concentrate on is phpMyAdmin, a web-based interface. It's free. It's installed by default with XAMPP and MAMP, and many hosting companies offer it as the default interface to MySQL.

In this chapter, you'll learn about the following:

- The main features of MySQL
- How a database stores information
- Choosing a graphical interface for MySQL
- Creating MySQL user accounts
- Defining a database table with the appropriate data types
- Backing up and transferring data to another server

Why MySQL?

Of all the available databases, why choose MySQL? The following reasons should convince you:

- **Cost**: The MySQL Community Edition is free under the open source GPL license (www.gnu.org/copyleft/gpl.html).
- **Powerful:** The same basic database system as the Community Edition is used by leading organizations such as YouTube, Wikipedia, NASA, Flickr, and Facebook. It's feature-rich and fast.
- **Widespread availability:** MySQL is the most popular open source database. Most hosting companies automatically offer MySQL in combination with PHP.
- **Cross-platform compatibility**: MySQL runs on Windows, Mac OS X, and Linux. A database requires no conversion when transferred from one system to another.
- **Open source**: Although there is a commercial version, the code and features in the Community Edition are identical. New features are being added constantly.
- **Security**: Bugs, when found, are dealt with quickly.

Older versions of MySQL lacked several features considered as standard by its main commercial rivals, Microsoft SQL Server and Oracle, and the open source PostgreSQL (www.postgresql.org). However, MySQL 5.0 and later offers an excellent range of features, and certainly everything you'll need for this book. MySQL's great strengths lie in speed and efficiency. It's particularly suited to web-based applications.

MySQL was originally developed by MySQL AB in Sweden, but the company was sold to Sun Microsystems in 2008. Sun was acquired two years later by Oracle, a major commercial database supplier. Many regarded this as a threat to MySQL's continued survival as a free, open source database. However, Oracle is on record as saying "MySQL is integral to Oracle's complete, open and integrated strategy." The difference between the free Community Edition and the commercial one is that the latter provides paying customers with automatic updates and service packs. Otherwise, the software is the same.

Which version?

At the time of this writing, the current version of MySQL is 5.1, and MySQL 5.5 is in an advanced stage of development. Unfortunately, hosting companies are often slow to update. Although the code in this book works on MySQL 4.1 or later, official support for MySQL 4.1 ended in 2009, and support for MySQL 5.0 ends in 2011 (see http://www.mysql.com/about/legal/lifecycle/).

Even if you don't need the advanced features offered by the latest version, it's important to use a version that's still officially supported to ensure you benefit from security updates. If your hosting company is offering an outdated version and refuses to upgrade, it's time to move.

How a database stores information

All the data in MySQL is stored in tables, very much in the same way as in a spreadsheet, with information organized into rows and columns. Figure 10-1 shows the database table that you will build later in this chapter, as displayed in phpMyAdmin.

Figure 10-1. A database table stores information in rows and columns like in a spreadsheet.

Each **column** has a name (image_id, filename, and caption) indicating what it stores.

The rows aren't labeled, but the first column (image_id) contains a unique value known as a **primary key**, which identifies the data associated with the row. Each row contains an individual **record** of related data.

The intersection of a row and a column, where the data is stored, is called a **field**. For instance, the caption field for the third record in Figure 10-1 contains the value "The Golden Pavilion in Kyoto" and the primary key for that record is 3.

> The terms "field" and "column" are often used interchangeably, particularly by phpMyAdmin. A field holds one piece of information for a single record, whereas a column contains the same field for all records.

How primary keys work

Although Figure 10-1 shows image_id as a consecutive sequence from 1 to 8, they're not row numbers. Figure 10-2 shows the same table with the captions sorted in alphabetical order. The field highlighted in Figure 10-1 has moved to the seventh row, but it still has the same image_id and filename.

image_id	filename	caption ⌃
8	ryoanji.jpg	Autumn leaves at Ryoanji temple, Kyoto
5	maiko_phone.jpg	Every maiko should have one—a mobile, of cou...
2	fountains.jpg	Fountains in central Tokyo
4	maiko.jpg	Maiko—trainee geishas in Kyoto
6	menu.jpg	Menu outside restaurant in Pontocho, Kyoto
7	monk.jpg	Monk begging for alms in Kyoto
3	kinkakuji.jpg	The Golden Pavilion in Kyoto
1	basin.jpg	Water basin at Ryoanji temple, Kyoto

Now in the seventh row, but image_id → remains unchanged

Figure 10-2. The primary key identifies the row even when the table is sorted in a different order.

Although the primary key is rarely displayed, it identifies the record and all the data stored in it. Once you know the primary key of a record, you can update it, delete it, or use it to display data in a separate page. Don't worry about how you find the primary key. It's easily done using Structured Query Language (SQL), the standard means of communicating with all major databases. The important thing to remember is to assign a primary key to every record.

- A primary key doesn't need to be a number, but *it must be unique.*
- Social security, staff ID, or product numbers make good primary keys. They may consist of numbers, letters, and other characters but are always different.
- MySQL can generate a primary key for you automatically.
- Once a primary key has been assigned, it should never—repeat, never—be changed.

Because a primary key must be unique, MySQL doesn't normally reuse the number when a record is deleted. This leaves holes in the sequence. *Don't even think about renumbering.* Gaps in the sequence are of no importance whatsoever. The purpose of the primary key is to identify the record, and by changing the numbers to close the gaps, you put the integrity of your database at serious risk.

Some people want to remove gaps in the sequence to keep track of the number of records in a table. It's not necessary, as you'll discover in the next chapter.

Linking tables with primary and foreign keys

Unlike a spreadsheet, most databases store data in several smaller tables, rather than in one huge table. This prevents duplication and inconsistency. Let's say you're building a database of your favorite quotations. Instead of typing out the name of the author each time, it's more efficient to put the authors' names in a separate table, and store a reference to an author's primary key with each quotation. As you can see in Figure 10-3, every record in the left-hand table identified by `author_id` 32 is a quotation from William Shakespeare.

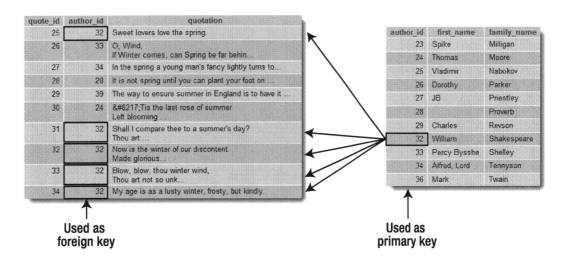

Used as foreign key

Used as primary key

Figure 10-3. Foreign keys are used to link information stored in separate tables.

Because the name is stored in only one place, it guarantees that it's always spelled correctly. And if you do make a spelling mistake, just a single correction is all that's needed to ensure that the change is reflected throughout the database.

Storing a primary key from one table in another table is known as creating a **foreign key**. Using foreign keys to link information in different tables is one of the most powerful aspects of a relational database. It can also be difficult to grasp in the early stages, so we'll work with single tables until Chapter 15 and 18, which cover foreign keys in detail. In the meantime, bear the following points in mind:

- When used as the primary key of a table, the value must be unique within the column. So each author_id in the table on the right of Figure 10-3 is used only once.
- When used as a foreign key, there can be multiple references to the same value. So 32 appears several times in the author_id column in the table on the left.

> As long as author_id remains unique in the table where it's the primary key, you know that it always refers to the same person.

Breaking down information into small chunks

You may have noticed that the table on the right in Figure 10-3 has separate columns for each author's first name and family name. This is an important principle of a relational database: *break down complex information into its component parts, and store each part separately.*

It's not always easy to decide how far to go with this process. In addition to first and last name, you might want separate columns for title (Mr., Mrs., Ms., Dr., and so on) and for middle names or initials. Addresses are best broken down into street, town, county, state, zip code, and so on. Although it may be a nuisance to break down information into small chunks, you can always use SQL and/or PHP to join them together again. However, once you have more than a handful of records, it's a major undertaking to try to separate complex information stored in a single field.

Checkpoints for good database design

There is no *right* way to design a database—each one is different. However, the following guidelines should point you in the right direction:

- Give each record in a table a unique identifier (primary key).
- Put each group of associated data in a table of its own.
- Cross-reference related information by using the primary key from one table as the foreign key in other tables.
- Store only one item of information in each field.
- Stay DRY (don't repeat yourself).

In the early stages, you are likely to make design mistakes that you later come to regret. Try to anticipate future needs, and make your table structure flexible. You can add new tables at any time to respond to new requirements.

That's enough theory for the moment. Let's get on with something more practical by building a database for the Japan Journey website from Chapters 4 and 5.

Using MySQL with a graphical interface

Rather than working with MySQL in a Command Prompt window or Terminal, it's a lot easier to use a graphic interface. In addition to phpMyAdmin, there are several others to choose from, both commercial and free. Among the free offerings is MySQL Workbench (http://dev.mysql.com/downloads/ workbench/), which is created by MySQL itself. Two other graphical front ends for MySQL worthy of note are Navicat (www.navicat.com), and SQLyog (www.webyog.com), which are available in both commercial and free versions.

MySQL Workbench seems aimed at the professional database administrator. Navicat (see Figure 10-4) and SQLyog are particularly popular among web developers, because the commercial versions are capable of performing scheduled backups of databases from a remote server to your local computer. They also help you build SQL queries in a visual and intuitive manner. The free versions have fewer features. MySQL Workbench and Navicat are available for both Windows and Mac OS X. There's also a version of Navicat for Linux. SQLyog runs on Windows only.

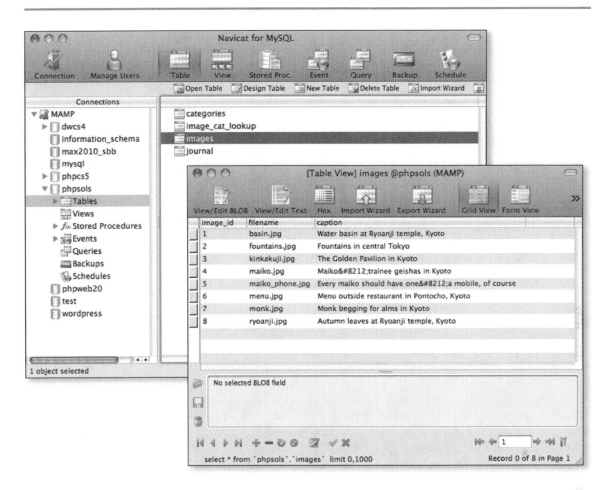

Figure 10-4. Navicat is one of the most popular graphical UIs for MySQL.

Because phpMyAdmin (www.phpmyadmin.net) is installed automatically with XAMPP and MAMP, it's the UI chosen for this book. It's a browser-based application (see Figure 10-5), so it doesn't have the glossy interface of MySQL Workbench, Navicat, or SQLyog, but it's easy to use and has all the basic functionality required for setting up and administering MySQL databases. It works on Windows, Mac OS X, and Linux. Version 3.x of phpMyAdmin requires PHP 5.2 and MySQL 5.0 or later. Many hosting companies provide it as the standard interface to MySQL.

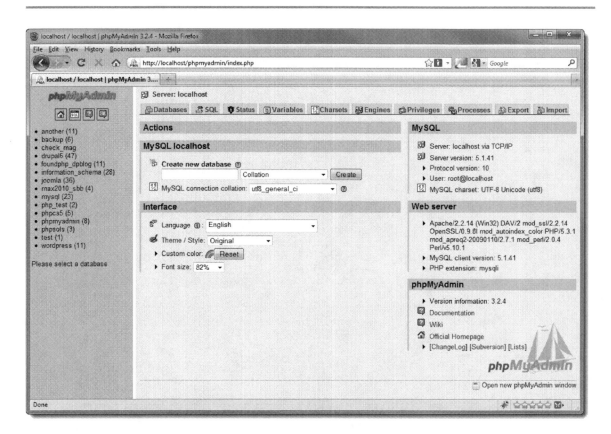

Figure 10-5. phpMyAdmin is a free graphical interface to MySQL that runs in your browser.

If you work with databases on a regular basis, you may want to explore the other graphical interfaces later. However, since phpMyAdmin is free, you have nothing to lose—and you may find it does everything you want.

Launching phpMyAdmin

If you're running XAMPP on Windows, there are three ways to launch phpMyAdmin:

- Enter http://localhost/phpMyAdmin/ in the browser address bar.
- Click the MySQL **Admin** button in the XAMPP Control Panel.
- Click the **phpMyAdmin** link under **Tools** in the XAMPP administration page (http://localhost/xampp/).

If you installed MAMP on Mac OS X, click the **phpMyAdmin** tab in the menu at the top of the MAMP start page (click **Open start page** in the MAMP control widget).

If you installed phpMyAdmin manually, enter the appropriate address in your browser address bar (normally http://localhost/phpmyadmin/).

> *If you get a message saying that the server is not responding or that the socket is not correctly configured, make sure that the MySQL server is running.*

If you installed XAMPP, you might be presented with a screen asking for a username and password. If so, log into phpMyAdmin as the root superuser. Enter **root** as the username, and use the password you created for root when setting up XAMPP.

Setting up the phpsols database

In a local testing environment, there's no limit to the number of databases that you can create in MySQL, and you can call them whatever you like. I am going to assume that you are working in a local testing environment and will show you how to set up a database called phpsols, together with two user accounts called psread and pswrite.

> *On shared hosting, you may be limited to just one database set up by the hosting company. If you're testing on a remote server and don't have the freedom to set up a new database and user accounts, substitute the name and username allocated by your hosting company for phpsols and pswrite respectively throughout the rest of this book.*

MySQL naming rules

The basic MySQL naming rules for databases, tables, and columns are as follows:

- Names can be up to 64 characters long.
- Legal characters are numbers, letters, the underscore, and $.
- Names can begin with a number, but cannot consist exclusively of numbers.

Some hosting companies seem blissfully ignorant of these rules and assign clients databases that contain one or more hyphens (an illegal character) in their name. If a database, table, or column name contains spaces or illegal characters, you must always surround it by backticks (`) in SQL queries. Note that this is not a single quote ('), but a separate character. On my Windows keyboard, it's directly above the Tab key. On my Mac keyboard, it's next to the left Shift key on the same key as the tilde (~).

When choosing names, you might accidentally choose one of MySQL's many reserved words (http://dev.mysql.com/doc/refman/5.1/en/reserved-words.html), such as date or time. One technique to avoid this is to use compound words, such as arrival_date, arrival_time, and so on. Alternatively, surround all names with backticks. phpMyAdmin does this automatically, but you need to do this manually when writing your own SQL in a PHP script.

> *Because so many people have used date, text, time, and timestamp as column names, MySQL permits their use without backticks. However, you should avoid using them. It's bad practice and is unlikely to work if you migrate your data to a different database system.*

Case sensitivity of names

Windows and Mac OS X treat MySQL names as case-insensitive. However, Linux and Unix servers respect case sensitivity. To avoid problems when transferring databases and PHP code from your local computer to a remote server, I strongly recommend that you use lowercase exclusively in database, table, and column names. When building names from more than one word, join them with an underscore.

Using phpMyAdmin to create a new database

Creating a new database in phpMyAdmin is easy.

1. Launch phpMyAdmin.

2. Type the name of the new database (**phpsols**) into the field labeled **Create new database**. Leave the **Collation** drop-down menu at its default setting, and click **Create**, as shown in the following screenshot:

Collation determines the sort order of records according to the rules of the language being used. Unless you are using a language other than English, Swedish, or Finnish, you never need to change its value. Collation is not supported in MySQL 3.23 or 4.0.

3. The next screen should confirm that the database has been created and offer you the opportunity to create your first table. Before creating any tables in a new database, it's a good idea to create user accounts for it. Leave phpMyAdmin open, as you'll continue using it in the next section.

Creating database-specific user accounts

A new installation of MySQL normally has only one registered user—the superuser account called "root," which has complete control over everything. (XAMPP also creates a user account called "pma," which phpMyAdmin uses for advanced features not covered by this book.) The root user should *never* be used for anything other than top-level administration, such as the creation and removal of databases, creating user accounts, and exporting and importing data. Each individual database should have at least one— preferably two—dedicated user accounts with limited privileges.

When you put a database online, you should grant users the least privileges they need, and no more. There are four important privileges—all named after the equivalent SQL commands:

- SELECT: Retrieves records from database tables
- INSERT: Inserts records into a database

- UPDATE: Changes existing records
- DELETE: Deletes records, but not tables or databases (the command for that is DROP)

Most of the time, visitors need only to retrieve information, so the psread user account will have just the SELECT privilege and be read-only. However, for user registration or site administration, you need all four privileges. These will be made available to the pswrite account.

Granting user privileges

1. Return to the main phpMyAdmin screen by clicking either the little house icon at the top left of the left frame or **Server: localhost** at the top left of the main frame.

2. Click the **Privileges** tab at the top of the page to open the **User overview** page.

Most links and tabs in phpMyAdmin are context-sensitive. It's important to click the Privileges tab on the welcome page rather than at the top of the previous screen. The tab on the welcome page lets you set up new user accounts. The Privileges tab at the top of any other page only provides information about existing accounts.

3. Click the **Add a new User** link halfway down the page.

4. In the page that opens, enter **pswrite** (or the name of the user account that you want to create) in the **User name** field. Select **Local** from the **Host** drop-down menu. This automatically enters **localhost** in the field alongside. Selecting this option allows the pswrite user to connect to MySQL only from the same computer. Then enter a password in the **Password** field, and type it again for confirmation in the **Re-type** field.

In the example files for this book, I've used 0Ch@Nom1$u as the password. MySQL passwords are case-sensitive.

5. Beneath the **Login Information** table is one labeled **Global privileges**. These give a user privileges on all databases, including the mysql one, which contains sensitive information. Granting such extensive privileges is insecure, so leave the **Global privileges** table unchecked, and click the **Go** button right at the bottom of the page.

6. The next page confirms that the pswrite user has been created and displays many options, beginning with the **Global privileges** table again. Scroll down below this to the section labeled **Database-specific privileges**. Activate the drop-down menu to display a list of all databases on your system. Select **phpsols**.

MySQL has three default databases: *information_schema*, a read-only, virtual database that contains details of all other databases on the same server; *mysql*, which contains details of all user accounts and privileges; and *test*, which is empty. You should never edit the *mysql* database directly unless you're sure what you're doing.

A rather annoying quirk of phpMyAdmin is the way the drop-down menu inserts a backslash in front of underscores in database names, such as *information_schema*. You don't need the backslash when inserting a name that uses an underscore.

7. The next screen allows you to set the privileges for this user on just the phpsols database. You want pswrite to have all four privileges listed earlier, so click the check boxes next to **SELECT**, **INSERT**, **UPDATE**, and **DELETE**. (If you hover your mouse pointer over each option, phpMyAdmin displays a tooltip describing what the option is for, as shown.) After selecting the four privileges, click the top **Go** button. (Always click the **Go** button at the foot of or alongside the section with the options you want to set.)

> **Edit Privileges: User** *'pswrite'@'localhost'* **- Database** *phpsols*
>
> ─Database-specific privileges (Check All / Uncheck All)─
>
> Note: MySQL privilege names are expressed in English
>
> ┌Data─────┐ ┌Structure──────────────┐ ┌Administration───┐
> ☑ SELECT   ☐ CREATE   ☐ GRANT
> ☑ INSERT   ☐ ALTER   ☐ LOCK TABLES
> ☑ U[Allows reading data.]   ☐ REFERENCES
> ☑ DELETE   ☐ DROP
>   ☐ CREATE TEMPORARY TABLES
>   ☐ SHOW VIEW
>   ☐ CREATE ROUTINE
>   ☐ ALTER ROUTINE
>   ☐ EXECUTE
>   ☐ CREATE VIEW
>   ☐ EVENT
>   ☐ TRIGGER
>
> [Go]

8. phpMyAdmin presents you with confirmation that the privileges have been updated for the pswrite user account: the page displays the **Database-specific privileges** table again, in case you need to change anything. Click the **Privileges** tab at the top of the page. You should now see pswrite listed the **User overview**.

9. If you ever need to make any changes to a user's privileges, click the **Edit Privileges** icon to the right of the listing, as shown.

 ◄─── **Edit privileges**

10. To delete a user, select the check box to the left of the account's username, and then click **Go** in the **Remove selected users** section.

11. Click **Add a new User**, and repeat steps 4 through 8 to create a second user account called `psread`. This user will have much more restricted privileges, so when you get to step 7, check only the **SELECT** option. The password used for `psread` in the example files is `K1y0mi$u`.

Creating a database table

Now that you have a database and dedicated user accounts, you can begin creating tables. Let's begin by creating a table to hold the details of images, as shown in Figure 10-1. Before you can start entering data, you need to define the table structure. This involves deciding the following:

- The name of the table
- How many columns it will have
- The name of each column
- What type of data will be stored in each column
- Whether the column must always have data in each field
- Which column contains the table's primary key

If you look at Figure 10-1, you can see that the table contains three columns: `image_id` (primary key), `filename`, and `caption`. Because it contains details of images, that's a good name to use for the table. There's not much point in storing a filename without a caption, so every column must contain data. Great! Apart from the data type, all the decisions have been made. I'll explain the data types as we go along.

Defining the images table

These instructions show how to define a table in phpMyAdmin. If you prefer to use Navicat, SQLyog, or a different UI for MySQL, use the settings in Table 10-1.

1. Launch phpMyAdmin, if it's not already open, and select **phpsols** from the **Database** drop-down menu in the left frame. Type the name of the new table (`images`) in the field labeled **Create new table on database phpsols**, and enter **3** as the **Number of fields**. (As mentioned before, phpMyAdmin refers to columns as fields. What it means is how many fields each record has.) Then click the **Go** button.

2. The next screen is where you define the table. Because the `images` table contains only three columns, the options for each column are listed vertically. When you define a table with more than three columns, the options are displayed horizontally. There are a lot of options, but not all of them need to be filled in. Table 10-1 lists the settings for the `images` table.

Table 10-1. Settings for the `images` table

Field	Type	Length/Values	Attributes	Null	Index	AUTO_INCREMENT
image_id	INT		UNSIGNED	Deselected	PRIMARY	Selected
filename	VARCHAR	25		Deselected		
caption	VARCHAR	120		Deselected		

The first column, image_id, is defined as type INT, which stands for integer. Its attribute is set to UNSIGNED, which means that only positive numbers are allowed. Its index is declared as PRIMARY, and the AUTO_INCREMENT check box is selected, so MySQL automatically inserts in this column the next available number (starting at 1) whenever a new record is inserted.

The next column, filename, is defined as type VARCHAR with a length of 25. This means it accepts up to 25 characters of text.

The final column, caption, is also VARCHAR with a length of 120, so it accepts up to 120 characters of text.

The **Null** check box for all columns is deselected, so they must always contain something. However, that "something" can be as little as an empty string. I'll describe the column types in more detail in "Choosing the right column type in MySQL" later in this chapter.

The following screenshot shows the options after they have been set in phpMyAdmin:

3. Toward the bottom of the screen is an option for **Storage Engine**. This determines the format used internally by MySQL to store the database files. MyISAM is the default storage engine in MySQL 3.23 through 5.1. However, it has been announced that an improved version of the InnoDB storage engine will become the default in MySQL 5.5. At the time of this writing, many hosting companies don't support InnoDB or offer it only on premium hosting plans. I'll explain the differences between these storage engines in Chapter 16. In the meantime, use MyISAM. Converting from one storage engine to another is very simple.

4. When you have finished, click the **Save** button at the bottom of the screen.

> *If you click **Go** instead of **Save**, phpMyAdmin adds an extra column for you to define. If this happens, give the new column a dummy name, and set the **Type** option to **INT**. You can then delete the extra column by clicking the Delete icon (a red cross) in the relevant row in the **Structure** table that appears in the next screen.*

5. The next screen displays the SQL query that phpMyAdmin used to define the images table. Beneath that, you'll see the structure of the table displayed like this:

Field	Type	Collation	Attributes	Null	Default	Extra	Action
image_id	int(10)		UNSIGNED	No	None	auto_increment	
filename	varchar(25)	latin1_swedish_ci		No	None		
caption	varchar(120)	latin1_swedish_ci		No	None		

Don't be alarmed by the fact that **Collation** displays **latin1_swedish_ci**. MySQL was originally developed in Sweden, and Swedish uses the same sort order as English (and Finnish). The underlining of image_id indicates that it's the table's primary key. To change any settings, click the pencil-like icon in the appropriate row. This opens a version of the previous screen and allows you to change the values. If you made a complete mess and want to start again, click the **Drop** tab at the top right of the screen, and confirm that you want to drop the table. (In SQL, *delete* refers only to records. You *drop* a table or a database.)

Inserting records into a table

Now that you have a table, you need to put some data into it. Eventually, you'll need to build your own content management system using HTML forms, PHP, and SQL; but the quick and easy way to do it is with phpMyAdmin.

Using phpMyAdmin to insert records manually

These instructions show how to add individual records to the images table through the phpMyAdmin interface.

1. If phpMyAdmin is still displaying the structure of the images table as at the end of the previous section, skip to step 2. Otherwise, launch phpMyAdmin, and select the phpsols database from the drop-down menu in the left frame. Then click the **Structure** icon alongside **images**, as shown in the following screenshot:

> The breadcrumb trail at the top of the main frame provides the context for the tabs across the head of the page. The *Structure* tab at the top left of the preceding screenshot refers to the structure of the *phpsols* database. At the moment, it contains only one table, *images*. To access the structure of an individual table, click the *Structure* icon alongside its name. Use your mouse pointer to reveal tooltips for each icon. Some, such as *Browse*, are grayed out because there are no records in the table.

2. Click the **Insert** tab in the center top of the page. This displays the following screen, ready for you to insert up to two records:

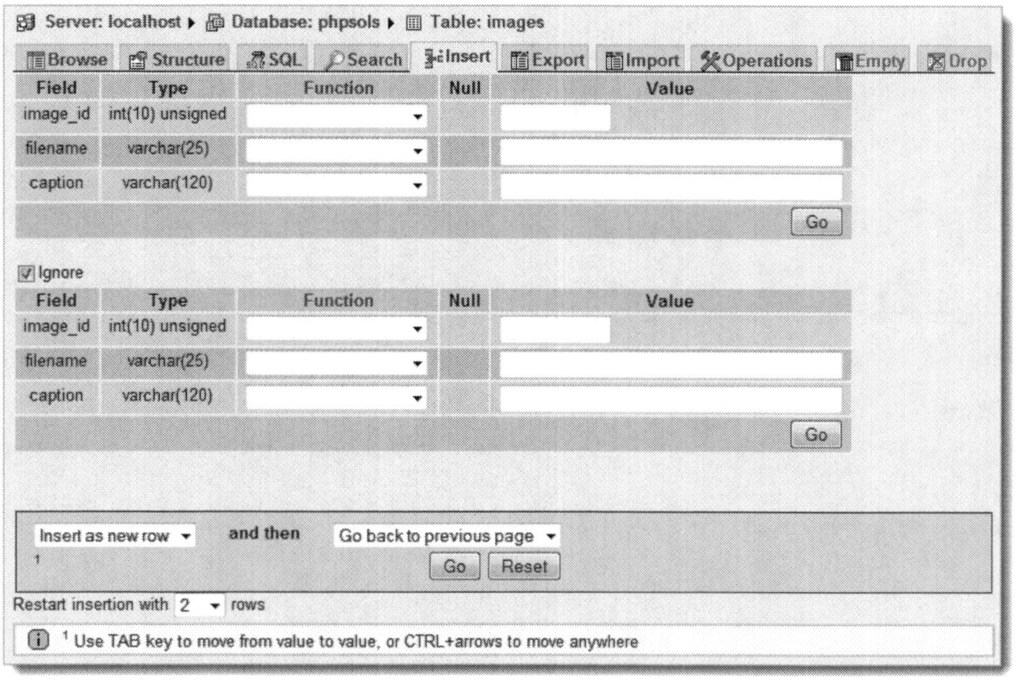

3. The forms display the names and details of each column. You can ignore the **Function** fields. MySQL has a large number of functions that you can apply to the values being stored in your

table. You'll learn more about them in the following chapters. The **Value** field is where you enter the data you want to insert in the table.

Because you have defined `image_id` as `AUTO_INCREMENT`, MySQL inserts the next available number automatically. So you *must l*eave the `image_id` **Value** field blank. Fill in the next two **Value** fields as follows:

- `filename`: **basin.jpg**
- `caption`: **Water basin at Ryoanji temple, Kyoto**

4. In the second form, leave the **Value** field for `image_id` blank, and fill in the next two fields like this:

- `filename`: **fountains.jpg**
- `caption`: **Fountains in central Tokyo**

Normally, the `Ignore` check box is automatically deselected when you add values to the second form, but deselect it if necessary.

5. Click **Go**. The SQL used to insert the records is displayed at the top of the page, together with a report that two rows have been inserted. I'll explain the basic SQL commands in the remaining chapters, but studying the SQL that phpMyAdmin displays is a good way to learn how to build your own queries. SQL is closely based on human language, so it isn't all that difficult to learn.

6. Click the **Browse** tab at the top left of the page. You should now see the first two entries in the `images` table, as shown here:

	image_id	filename	caption
☐ ✏ ✕	1	basin.jpg	Water basin at Ryoanji temple, Kyoto
☐ ✏ ✕	2	fountains.jpg	Fountains in central Tokyo

As you can see, MySQL has automatically inserted **1** and **2** in the `image_id` fields.

You could continue typing out the details of the remaining six images, but let's speed things up a bit by using a SQL file that contains all the necessary data.

Loading the images records from a SQL file

Because the primary key of the `images` table has been set to `AUTO_INCREMENT`, it's necessary to drop the original table and all its data. The SQL file does this automatically and builds the table from scratch. These instructions assume that phpMyAdmin is open at the page in step 6 of the previous section.

1. If you're happy to overwrite the data in the `images` table, skip to step 2. However, if you have entered data that you don't want to lose, copy your data to a different table. Click the **Operations** tab at the top of the page, type the name of the new table in the blank field in the section titled **Copy table to (database.table)**, and click **Go**. The following screenshot shows the settings for copying the `images` table to `images_backup`:

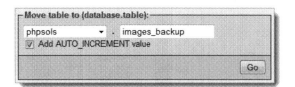

2. After clicking **Go**, you should see confirmation that the table has been copied. The breadcrumb trail at the top of the page indicates that phpMyAdmin is still in the images table, so you can proceed to step 2, even though you have a different page onscreen.

3. Click the **Import** tab at the top right of the page. In the next screen, click the **Browse** (or **Choose File**) button in **File to import**, and navigate to images.sql in the ch10 folder. Leave all options at their default setting, and click **Go** at the foot of the page.

4. phpMyAdmin drops the original table, creates a new version, and inserts all the records. When you see confirmation that the file has been imported, click the **Browse** button at the top left of the page. You should now see the same data as shown in Figure 10-1 at the beginning of the chapter.

If you open the images.sql in a text editor, you'll see that it contains the SQL commands that create the images table and populate it with data. This is how the table is built:

```
DROP TABLE IF EXISTS `images`;
CREATE TABLE IF NOT EXISTS `images` (
  `image_id` int(10) unsigned NOT NULL AUTO_INCREMENT,
  `filename` varchar(25) NOT NULL,
  `caption` varchar(120) NOT NULL,
  PRIMARY KEY (`image_id`)
) ENGINE=MyISAM  DEFAULT CHARSET=latin1 AUTO_INCREMENT=9 ;
```

Importing data from a SQL file like this is how you transfer data from your local testing environment to the remote server where your website is located. Assuming that your hosting company provides phpMyAdmin to administer your remote database, all you need to do to transfer the data is to launch the version of phpMyAdmin on your remote server, click the **Import** tab, select the SQL file on your local computer, and click **Go**.

The next section describes how to create the SQL file.

Creating a SQL file for backup and data transfer

MySQL doesn't store your database in a single file that you can simply upload to your website. Even if you find the right files (on Windows, they're located in C:\Program Files\MySQL\MySQL Server 5.1\data), you're likely to damage them unless the MySQL server is turned off. Anyway, most hosting companies won't permit you to upload the raw files because it would also involve shutting down their server, causing a great deal of inconvenience for everyone.

Nevertheless, moving a database from one server to another is very easy. All it involves is creating a backup **dump** of the data and loading it into the other database with phpMyAdmin or any other database administration program. The dump is a text file that contains all the necessary SQL commands to populate an individual table or even an entire database elsewhere. phpMyAdmin can create backups of your entire MySQL server, individual databases, selected tables, or individual tables. To keep things simple, these instructions show you how to back up only a single database.

1. In phpMyAdmin, select the phpsols database from the drop-down menu in the navigation frame. If the database was already selected, click the **Database: phpsols** breadcrumb at the top of the screen, as shown here:

2. Select **Export** from the tabs along the top of the screen.

3. The rather fearsome looking screen shown in Figure 10-6 opens. In spite of all the options, you need to concern yourself with only a few.

   - The **Export** section on the left of the screen lists all the tables in your database. Click **Select All,** and leave the radio buttons on the default **SQL**.
   - If the database has *never* been transferred to the other server before, the only option that you need to set on the right side of the screen is the drop-down menu labeled **SQL export compatibility**. If the other server is running MySQL 3.23, choose **MYSQL323**. If the other server is running MySQL 4.0, choose **MYSQL40**. Otherwise, choose **NONE**.
   - If the database has *already* been transferred on a previous occasion, select **Add DROP TABLE** in the **Structure** section. The existing contents of each table are dropped and are replaced with the data in the backup file.

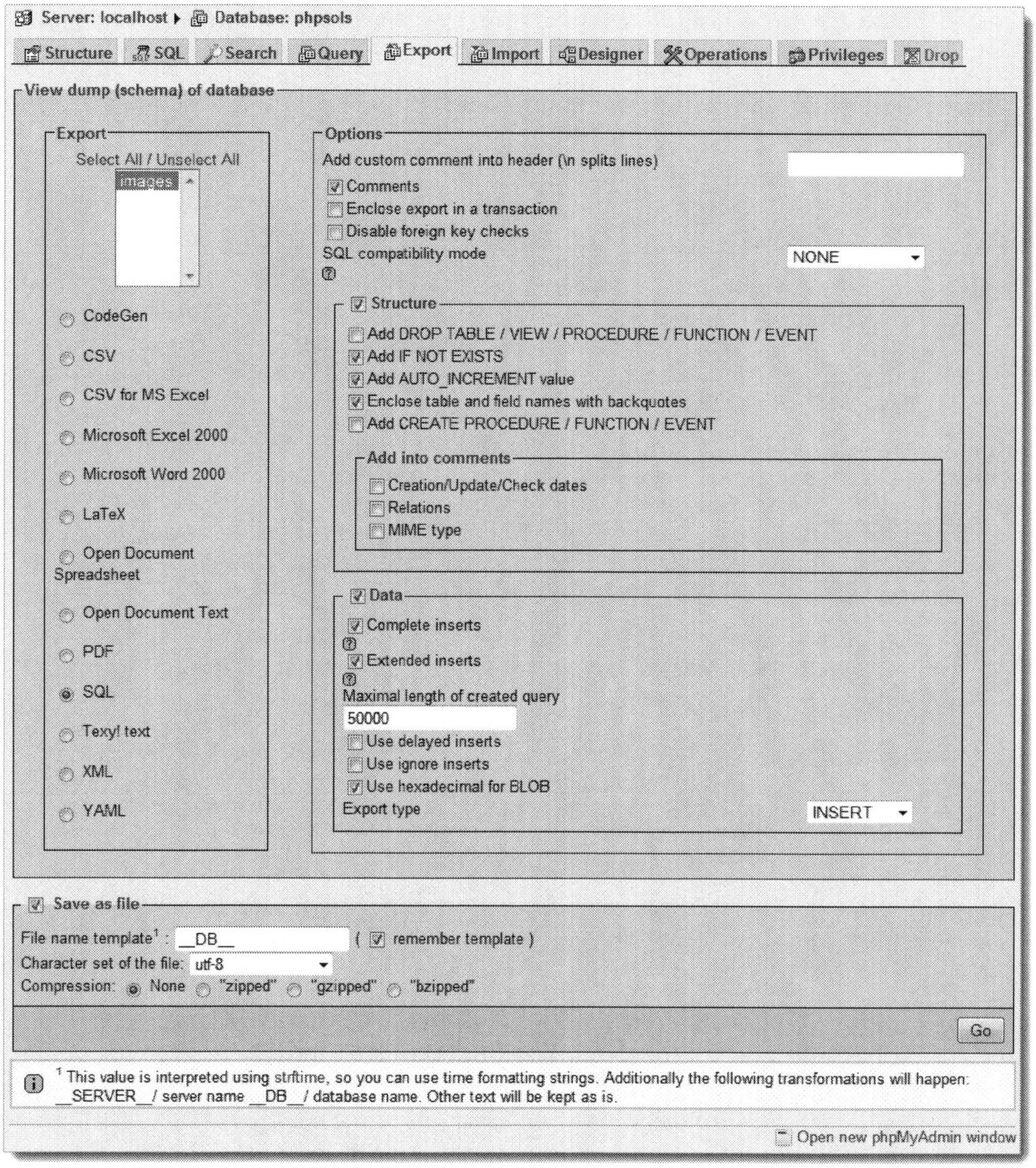

Figure 10-6. phpMyAdmin offers a wide range of choices when exporting data from MySQL.

4. Make sure the check box labeled **Save as file** at the bottom of the screen is selected. The default setting in **File name template** is __DB__, which automatically gives the backup file the same name as your database. So, in this case, it becomes phpsols.sql. If you add anything after the final double underscore, phpMyAdmin adds this to the name. For instance,

you might want to indicate the date of the backup, so you could add **2011-11-11** for a backup made on November 11, 2011. The file would then be named `phpsols2011-11-11.sql`.

5. If your database contains a lot of data, select a compression format from one of the radio buttons at the bottom of the page. When you import the file to another server, phpMyAdmin automatically decompresses it.

6. Click **Go**, and save the SQL file to your local hard disk. You now have a backup that can be used to transfer the contents of your database to another server.

> The file created by phpMyAdmin contains the SQL commands only to create and populate the database tables. It does not include the command to create the database. This means you can import the tables into any database. It does not need to have the same name as the one in your local testing environment.

Choosing the right data type in MySQL

You may have received a bit of a shock when selecting **Type** for the `image_id` column. phpMyAdmin lists all available data types—there are nearly 40 in MySQL 5.1. Rather than confuse you with unnecessary details, I'll explain just the most commonly used. You can find full details of all data types in the MySQL documentation at `http://dev.mysql.com/ doc/refman/5.1/en/data-types.html`.

Storing text

The difference between the main text data types boils down to the maximum number of characters that can be stored in an individual field, the treatment of trailing spaces, and whether you can set a default value.

- `CHAR`: A fixed-length string. You must specify the required length in the **Length/Values** field. The maximum permitted value is 255. Internally, strings are right-padded with spaces to the specified length, but the trailing spaces are stripped when you retrieve the value. You can define a default.
- `VARCHAR`: A variable-length string. You must specify the maximum number of characters you plan to use (in phpMyAdmin, enter the number in the **Length/Values** field). Prior to MySQL 5.0, the limit was 255. This was increased to 65,535 in MySQL 5.0. If a string is stored with trailing spaces, they are preserved on retrieval. Accepts a default value.
- `TEXT`: Stores text up to a maximum of 65,535 characters (approximately 50% longer than this chapter). Cannot define a default value.

`TEXT` is convenient because you don't need to specify a maximum size (in fact, you can't). Although the maximum length of `VARCHAR` is the same as `TEXT` in MySQL 5.0 and later, other factors may limit the actual amount that can be stored.

> Keep it simple: use VARCHAR for short text items and TEXT for longer ones.

Storing numbers

The most frequently used numeric column types are as follows:

- INT: Any whole number (integer) between –2,147,483,648 and 2,147,483,647. If the column is declared as UNSIGNED, the range is from 0 to 4,294,967,295.
- FLOAT: A floating-point number. You can optionally specify two comma-separated numbers to limit the range. The first number specifies the maximum number of digits, and the second specifies how many of those digits should come after the decimal point. Since PHP will format numbers after calculation, I recommend that you use FLOAT without the optional parameters.
- DECIMAL: A number with a fraction containing a fixed number of digits after the decimal point. When defining the table, you need to specify the maximum number of digits and how many of those digits should come after the decimal point. In phpMyAdmin, enter the numbers separated by a comma in the **Length/Values** field. For example, 6,2 permits numbers in the range from –9999.99 to 9999.99. If you don't specify the size, the decimal fraction is truncated when values are stored in this type of column.

The difference between FLOAT and DECIMAL is accuracy. Floating-point numbers are treated as approximate values and are subject to rounding errors (for a detailed explanation, see http://dev.mysql.com/doc/refman/5.1/en/problems-with-float.html).

Use DECIMAL to store currencies. However, it's important to note that prior to MySQL 5.0.3, the DECIMAL data type was stored as a string, so could not be used with SQL functions, such as SUM(), to perform calculations inside the database. If your remote server is running an older version of MySQL, store currencies in an INT column as cents; for pounds, use pence. Then use PHP to divide the result by 100, and format the currency as desired. Better still, move to a server that runs MySQL 5.0 or higher.

> Don't use commas or spaces as the thousands-separator. Apart from numerals, the only characters permitted in numbers are the negative operator (-) and the decimal point (.).

Storing dates and times

MySQL stores dates in one format only: YYYY-MM-DD. It's the standard approved by the ISO (International Organization for Standardization) and avoids the ambiguity inherent in different national conventions. I'll return to the subject of dates in Chapter 14. The most important column types for dates and times are as follows:

- DATE: A date stored as YYYY-MM-DD. The range is 1000-01-01 to 9999-12-31.
- DATETIME: A combined date and time displayed in the format YYYY-MM-DD HH:MM:SS.
- TIMESTAMP: A timestamp (normally generated automatically by the computer). Legal values range from the beginning of 1970 to partway through January 2038.

MySQL timestamps are based on a human-readable date and, since MySQL 4.1, use the same format as DATETIME. As a result, they are incompatible with Unix and PHP timestamps, which are based on the number of seconds elapsed since January 1, 1970. Don't mix them.

Storing predefined lists

MySQL lets you store two types of predefined list that could be regarded as the database equivalents of radio button and check box states:

- ENUM: This column type stores a single choice from a predefined list, such as "yes, no, don't know" or "male, female." The maximum number of items that can be stored in the predefined list is a mind-boggling 65,535—some radio-button group!
- SET: This column type stores zero or more choices from a predefined list. The list can hold a maximum of 64 choices.

While ENUM is quite useful, SET tends to be less so, mainly because it violates the principle of storing only one piece of information in a field. The type of situation where it can be useful is when recording optional extras on a car or multiple choices in a survey.

Storing binary data

Storing binary data, such as images, isn't a good idea. It bloats your database, and you can't display images directly from a database. However, the following column types are designed for binary data:

- TINYBLOB: Up to 255 bytes
- BLOB: Up to 64kB
- MEDIUMBLOB: Up to 16MB
- LONGBLOB: Up to 4GB

With such whimsical names, it's a bit of a letdown to discover that BLOB stands for **binary large object**.

Chapter review

Much of this chapter has been devoted to theory, explaining the basic principles of good database design. Instead of putting all the information you want to store in a single, large table like a spreadsheet, you need to plan the structure of your database carefully, moving repetitive information into separate tables. As long as you give each record in a table a unique identifier—its primary key—you can keep track of information and link it to related records in other tables through the use of foreign keys. The concept of using foreign keys can be difficult to understand at the outset, but it should become clearer by the end of this book.

You have also learned how to create MySQL user accounts with limited privileges, as well as how to define a table and import and export data using a SQL file. In the next chapter, you'll use PHP to connect to the phpsols database to display the data stored in the images table.

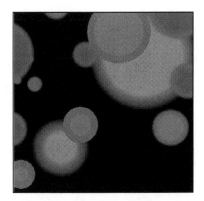

Chapter 11

Connecting to MySQL with PHP and SQL

PHP offers three different ways to connect to and interact with a MySQL database: the original MySQL extension, MySQL Improved (MySQLi), or PHP Data Objects (PDO). Which one you choose is an important decision, because they use incompatible code. You can't mix them in the same script. The original MySQL extension is no longer actively developed and is not recommended for new PHP/MySQL projects. It's not covered in this book.

The PHP documentation describes MySQLi as the preferred option recommended by MySQL for new projects. However, that doesn't mean you should discount PDO. The advantage of PDO is that it's software-neutral. In theory, at least, you can switch your website from MySQL to Microsoft SQL Server or a different database system by changing only a couple of lines of PHP code. In practice, you normally need to rewrite at least some of your SQL queries because each database vendor adds custom functions on top of standard SQL. Still, it's simpler than switching from MySQLi, which works exclusively with MySQL. Switching a MySQLi script to a different database involves rewriting all of the PHP code in addition to any changes needed to the SQL.

If you have no plans to use a database other than MySQL, I recommend that you use MySQLi. It's designed specifically to work with MySQL. Just ignore the sections on PDO. On the other hand, if database flexibility is important to you, choose PDO. Both methods are covered in the remaining chapters of this book.

Although PHP connects to the database and stores any results, the database queries need to be written in SQL. This chapter teaches you the basics of retrieving information stored in a table.

In this chapter, you'll learn the following:

- Connecting to MySQL with MySQLi and PDO
- Counting the number of records in a table
- Using SELECT queries to retrieve data and display it in a web page
- Keeping data secure with prepared statements and other techniques

Checking your remote server setup

XAMPP and MAMP support all three methods of communicating with MySQL, but you need to check the PHP configuration of your remote server to verify the degree of support it offers. Run `phpinfo()` on your remote server, scroll down the configuration page, and look for the following sections. They're listed alphabetically, so you'll need to scroll down a long way to find them.

mysql

MySQL Support	enabled
Active Persistent Links	0
Active Links	0
Client API version	5.1.41

Directive	Local Value	Master Value
mysql.allow_local_infile	On	On
mysql.allow_persistent	On	On

mysql.trace_mode

mysqli

Mysqli Support	enabled
Client API library version	5.1.41
Active Persistent Links	0
Inactive Persistent Links	0
Active Links	58
Client API header version	5.1.41
MYSQLI_SOCKET	MySQL

Directive	Local Value	Master Value
mysqli.allow_local_infile	On	On

PDO

PDO support	enabled
PDO drivers	mysql, odbc, sqlite, sqlite2

pdo_mysql

PDO Driver for MySQL	enabled
Client API version	5.1.41

All hosting companies should have the first two sections (**mysql** and **mysqli**). If you plan to use PDO, you not only need to check that PDO is enabled, but you must also make sure **mysql** is listed among the **PDO drivers**.

How PHP communicates with MySQL

Regardless of whether you use MySQLi or PDO, the process always follows this sequence:

1. Connect to MySQL using the hostname, username, password, and database name.

2. Prepare a SQL query.

3. Execute the query and save the result.

4. Extract the data from the result (usually with a loop).

Username and password are straightforward: they're the username and password of the accounts you have just created or the account given to you by your hosting company. But what about hostname? In a local testing environment it's localhost. What comes as a surprise is that MySQL often uses localhost even on a remote server. This is because in many cases the database server is located on the same server as your website. In other words, the web server that displays your pages and the MySQL server are local to each other. However, if your hosting company has installed MySQL on a separate machine, it will tell you the address to use. The important thing to realize is that the MySQL hostname is not the same as your website domain name.

Let's take a quick look at how you connect to a MySQL server with each of the methods.

Connecting with the MySQL Improved extension

MySQLi has two interfaces: procedural and object-oriented. The procedural interface is designed to ease the transition from the original MySQL functions. Since the object-oriented version is more compact, that's the version adopted here.

To connect to a MySQL server, you create a mysqli object by passing four arguments to new mysqli(): the hostname, username, password, and the name of the database. This is how you connect to the phpsols database:

```
$conn = new mysqli($hostname, $username, $password, 'phpsols');
```

This stores the connection object as $conn.

Connecting with PDO

PDO requires a slightly different approach. The most important difference is that, if you're not careful, PDO displays your database username and password onscreen when it can't connect to the database. This is because PDO throws an exception if the connection fails. So, you need to wrap the code in a try block, and catch the exception.

To create a connection to the MySQL server, you create a data object by passing the following three arguments to new PDO():

- A string specifying the database type, the hostname, and the name of the database. The string must be presented in the following format:

  `'mysql:host=hostname;dbname=databaseName'`

- The username.

305

- The user's password.

The code looks like this:

```
try {
  $conn = new PDO("mysql:host=$hostname;dbname=phpsols", $username, $password);
} catch (PDOException $e) {
  echo $e->getMessage();
}
```

Using echo to display the message generated by the exception is OK during testing, but when you deploy the script on a live website, you need to redirect the user to an error page, as described in PHP Solution 4-8.

PHP Solution 11-1: Making a reusable database connector

Connecting to a database is a routine chore that needs to be performed in every page from now on. This PHP solution creates a simple function stored in an external file that connects to the database. It's designed mainly for testing the different MySQLi and PDO scripts in the remaining chapters without the need to retype the connection details each time or to switch between different connection files.

1. Create a file called connection.inc.php in the includes folder, and insert the following code (there's a copy of the completed script in the ch11 folder):

   ```php
   <?php
   function dbConnect($usertype, $connectionType = 'mysqli') {
     $host = 'localhost';
     $db = 'phpsols';
     if ($usertype  == 'read') {
       $user = 'psread';
       $pwd = 'K1yOmi$u';
     } elseif ($usertype == 'write') {
       $user = 'pswrite';
       $pwd = 'oCh@Nom1$u';
     } else {
       exit('Unrecognized connection type');
     }
     // Connection code goes here
   }
   ```

   The function takes two arguments: the user type and the type of connection you want. The second argument defaults to mysqli. If you want to concentrate on using PDO, set the default value of the second argument to pdo.

   The first two lines inside the function store the name of the host server and database that you want to connect to.

   The if... elseif conditional statement checks the value of the first argument and switches between the psread and pswrite username and password as appropriate.

2. Replace the Connection code goes here comment with the following:

```
if ($connectionType == 'mysqli') {
  return new mysqli($host, $user, $pwd, $db) or die ('Cannot open database');
} else {
  try {
    return new PDO("mysql:host=$host;dbname=$db", $user, $pwd);
  } catch (PDOException $e) {
    echo 'Cannot connect to database';
    exit;
  }
}
```

If the second argument is set to `mysqli`, a MySQLi connection object is returned. Otherwise, the function returns a PDO connection. The rather foreboding `die()` simply stops the script from attempting to continue and displays the error message.

To create a MySQLi connection to the `phpsols` database, include `connection.inc.php`, and call the function like this for the `psread` user:

```
$conn = dbConnect('read');
```

For the `pswrite` user, call it like this:

```
$conn = dbConnect('write');
```

To create a PDO connection, add the second argument like this:

```
$conn = dbConnect('read', 'pdo');
$conn = dbConnect('write', 'pdo');
```

Finding the number of results from a query

Counting the number of results from a database query is useful in several ways. It's necessary for creating a navigation system to page through a long set of results (you'll learn how to do that in the next chapter). It's also important for user authentication (covered in Chapter 17). If you get no results from matching a username and password, you know that the login procedure should fail.

MySQLi has a convenient method of finding out the number of results returned by a query. However, PDO doesn't have a direct equivalent.

PHP Solution 11-2: Counting records in a result set (MySQLi)

This PHP solution shows how to submit a SQL query to select all the records in the `images` table, and store the result in a `MySQLi_Result` object. The object's `num_rows` property contains the number of records retrieved by the query.

1. Create a new folder called `mysql` in the `phpsols` site root, and create a new file called `mysqli.php` inside the folder. The page will eventually be used to display a table, so it should have a `DOCTYPE` declaration and an HTML skeleton.

2. Include the connection file in a PHP block above the `DOCTYPE` declaration, and create a connection to MySQL using the account that has read-only privileges like this:

   ```
   require_once('../includes/connection.inc.php');
   ```

```
// connect to MySQL
$conn = dbConnect('read');
```

3. Next, prepare the SQL query. Add this code immediately after the previous step (but before the closing PHP tag):

```
// prepare the SQL query
$sql = 'SELECT * FROM images';
```

This means "select everything from the images table." The asterisk (*) is shorthand for "all columns."

4. Now execute the query by calling the query() method on the connection object and passing the SQL query as an argument like this:

```
// submit the query and capture the result
$result = $conn->query($sql) or die(mysqli_error());
```

The result is stored in a variable, which I have imaginatively named $result. If there is a problem, the database server returns an error message, which can be retrieved using mysqli_error(). By placing this function between the parentheses of die(), the script comes to a halt if there's a problem and displays the error message.

5. Assuming there's no problem, $result now holds a MySQLi_Result object. To get the number of records found by the SQL query, assign the value to a variable like this:

```
// find out how many records were retrieved
$numRows = $result->num_rows;
```

The complete code above the DOCTYPE declaration looks like this:

```
require_once('../includes/connection.inc.php');
// connect to MySQL
$conn = dbConnect('read');
// prepare the SQL query
$sql = 'SELECT * FROM images';
// submit the query and capture the result
$result = $conn->query($sql) or die(mysqli_error());
// find out how many records were retrieved
$numRows = $result->num_rows;
```

6. You can now display the value of $numRows in the body of the page like this:

```
<p>A total of <?php echo $numRows; ?> records were found.</p>
```

7. Save mysqli.php and load it into a browser. You should see the following result:

A total of 8 records were found.

Check your code, if necessary, with `mysqli_01.php` in the `ch11` folder.

PHP Solution 11-3: Counting records in a result set (PDO)

PDO doesn't have an equivalent of the MySQLi `num_rows` property. With most databases, you need to execute a SQL query to count the number of items in the table, and then fetch the result. However, you're in luck, because the PDO `rowCount()` method fulfils a dual purpose with MySQL. Normally, the `rowCount()` method reports only the number of rows affected by inserting, updating, or deleting records; but with MySQL, it also reports the number of records found by a `SELECT` query.

1. Create a new file called `pdo.php` in the `mysql` folder. The page will eventually be used to display a table, so it should have a `DOCTYPE` declaration and an HTML skeleton.

2. Include the connection file in a PHP block above the `DOCTYPE` declaration, and create a PDO connection to MySQL using the read-only account like this:

```
require_once('../includes/connection.inc.php');
// connect to MySQL
$conn = dbConnect('read', 'pdo');
```

3. Next, prepare the SQL query:

```
// prepare the SQL query
$sql = 'SELECT * FROM images';
```

This means "select every record in the `images` table." The asterisk (*) is shorthand for "all columns."

4. Now execute the query and store the result in a variable like this:

```
// submit the query and capture the result
$result = $conn->query($sql);
$error = $conn->errorInfo();
if (isset($error[2])) die($error[2]);
```

PDO uses `errorInfo()` to build an array of error messages from the database. The third element of the array is created only if something goes wrong. I've stored the result of `$conn->errorInfo()` as `$error`, so you can tell if anything went wrong by using `isset()` to check whether `$error[2]` has been defined. If it has, `die()` brings the script to a halt and displays the error message.

5. To get the number of rows in the result set, call the `rowCount()` method on the `$result` object. The finished code in the PHP block above the `DOCTYPE` declaration looks like this:

```
require_once('../includes/connection.inc.php');
// connect to MySQL
$conn = dbConnect('read', 'pdo');
// prepare the SQL query
$sql = 'SELECT * FROM images';
// submit the query and capture the result
$result = $conn->query($sql);
$error = $conn->errorInfo();
if (isset($error[2])) die($error[2]);
// find out how many records were retrieved
$numRows = $result->rowCount();
```

6. You can now display the value of $numRows in the body of the page like this:

   ```
   <p>A total of <?php echo $numRows; ?> records were found.</p>
   ```

7. Save the page, and load it into a browser. You should see the same result as shown in step 5 of PHP Solution 11-2. Check your code, if necessary, with pdo_01.php.

In my tests, using rowCount() reported the number of items found by a SELECT query in MySQL on both Mac OS X and Windows. However, it cannot be guaranteed to work on all databases. If rowCount() doesn't work, use the following code instead:

```
// prepare the SQL query
$sql = 'SELECT COUNT(*) FROM images';
// submit the query and capture the result
$result = $conn->query($sql);
$error = $conn->errorInfo();
if (isset($error[2])) die($error[2]);
// find out how many records were retrieved
$numRows = $result->fetchColumn();
// free the database resource
$result->closeCursor();
```

This uses the SQL COUNT() function with an asterisk to count all items in the table. There's only one result, so it can be retrieved with the fetchColumn() method, which gets the first column from a database result. After storing the result in $numRows, you need to call the closeCursor() method to free the database resource for any further queries.

Displaying the results of a query

The most common way to display the results of a query is to use a loop in combination with the MySQLi or PDO method to extract the current record into a temporary array.

With MySQLi, use the fetch_assoc() method like this:

```
while ($row = $result->fetch_assoc()) {
  // do something with the current record
}
```

PDO handles it slightly differently. You can use the query() method directly inside a foreach loop to create an array for each record like this:

```
foreach ($conn->query($sql) as $row) {
  // do something with the current record
}
```

In the case of the images table, $row contains $row['image_id'], $row['filename'], and $row['caption']. Each element is named after the corresponding column in the table.

PHP Solution 11-4: Displaying the images table using MySQLi

This PHP solution shows how to loop through a MySQLi_Result object to display the results of a SELECT query. Continue using the file from PHP Solution 11-2.

1. Add the following table to the main body of mysqli.php (the PHP code that displays the result set is highlighted in bold):

```
<table>
  <tr>
    <th>image_id</th>
    <th>filename</th>
    <th>caption</th>
  </tr>
  <?php while ($row = $result->fetch_assoc()) { ?>
  <tr>
    <td><?php echo $row['image_id']; ?></td>
    <td><?php echo $row['filename']; ?></td>
    <td><?php echo $row['caption']; ?></td>
  </tr>
  <?php } ?>
</table>
```

The while loop iterates through the database result, using the fetch_assoc() method to extract each record into $row. Each element of $row is displayed in a table cell. The loop continues until fetch_assoc() comes to the end of the result set.

2. Save mysqli.php, and view it in a browser. You should see the contents of the images table displayed as shown in the following screenshot:

You can compare your code, if necessary with `mysql_02.php` in the ch11 folder.

PHP Solution 11-5: Displaying the images table using PDO

Instead of a while loop with `fetch_assoc()`, PDO uses the `query()` method in a foreach loop.

Continue working with `pdo.php`, the same file as in PHP Solution 11-3.

1. Insert the following table in the body of `pdo.php` (the PHP code that displays the result set is displayed in bold):

```
<table>
  <tr>
    <th>image_id</th>
    <th>filename</th>
    <th>caption</th>
  </tr>
  <?php foreach ($conn->query($getDetails) as $row) { ?>
  <tr>
    <td><?php echo $row['image_id']; ?></td>
    <td><?php echo $row['filename']; ?></td>
    <td><?php echo $row['caption']; ?></td>
  </tr>
  <?php } ?>
</table>
```

2. Save the page, and view it in a browser. It should look like the screenshot in PHP Solution 11-4. You can compare your code against `pdo_02.php` in the ch11 folder.

MySQL connection crib sheet

Tables 11-2 and 11-3 summarize the basic details of connection and database query for MySQLi and PDO. Some commands will be used in later chapters, but are included here for ease of reference.

Table 11-2. Connection to MySQL with the MySQL Improved object-oriented interface

Action	Usage	Comments
Connect	`$conn = new mysqli($h,$u,$p,$d);`	All arguments optional; first four always needed in practice: hostname, username, password, database name. Creates connection object.
Choose DB	`$conn->select_db('dbName');`	Use to select a different database.
Submit query	`$result = $conn->query($sql);`	Returns result object.
Count results	`$numRows = $result->num_rows;`	Returns number of rows in result object.
Release DB resources	`$result->free_result();`	Frees up connection to allow new query.
Extract record	`$row = $result->fetch_assoc();`	Extracts current row from result object as associative array.
Extract record	`$row = $result->fetch_row();`	Extracts current row from result object as indexed (numbered) array.

Table 11-3. Connection to MySQL with PDO

Action	Usage	Comments
Connect	`$conn = new PDO($DSN,$u,$p);`	In practice, requires three arguments: data source name (DSN), username, password. Must be wrapped in try/catch block.
Submit query	`$result = $conn->query($sql);`	Can also be used inside `foreach` loop to extract each record.
Count results	`$numRows = $result->rowCount()`	Should work with MySQL, but use `SELECT COUNT(*) FROM table_name` for other databases.

313

Action	Usage	Comments
Get single result	`$item = $result->fetchColumn();`	Gets first column in first record of result. To get result from other columns, use column number (from 0) as argument.
Get next record	`$row = $result->fetch();`	Gets next row from result set as associative array.
Release DB resources	`$result->closeCursor();`	Frees up connection to allow new query.
Extract records	`foreach($conn->query($sql) as $row) {`	Extracts current row from result set as associative array.

When using PDO with MySQL, the data source name (DSN) is a string that takes the following format:

`'mysql:host=hostname;dbname=databaseName'`

If you need to specify a different port from the MySQL default (3306), use the following format, substituting the actual port number:

`'mysql:host=hostname;`**`port=3307;`**`dbname=databaseName'`

Using SQL to interact with a database

As you have just seen, PHP connects to the database, sends the query, and receives the results; but the query itself needs to be written in SQL. Although SQL is a common standard, there are many dialects of SQL. Each database vendor, including MySQL, has added extensions to the standard language. These improve efficiency and functionality, but are usually incompatible with other databases. The SQL in this book works with MySQL 4.1 or later, but it won't necessarily transfer to Microsoft SQL Server, Oracle, or another database.

Writing SQL queries

SQL syntax doesn't have many rules, and all of them are quite simple.

SQL is case-insensitive

The query that retrieves all records from the `images` table looks like this:

```
SELECT * FROM images
```

The words in uppercase are SQL keywords. This is purely a convention. The following are all equally correct:

```
SELECT * FROM images
select * from images
```

```
SeLEcT * fRoM images
```

Although SQL keywords are case-insensitive, the same *doesn't* apply to database column names. The advantage of using uppercase for keywords is that it makes SQL queries easier to read. You're free to choose whichever style suits you best, but the ransom-note style of the last example is probably best avoided.

Whitespace is ignored

This allows you to spread SQL queries over several lines for increased readability. The one place where whitespace is *not* allowed is between a function name and the opening parenthesis. The following generates an error:

```
SELECT COUNT (*) FROM images   /* BAD EXAMPLE */
```

The space needs to be closed up like this:

```
SELECT COUNT(*) FROM images   /* CORRECT */
```

As you probably gathered from these examples, you can add comments to SQL queries by putting them between /* and */.

Strings must be quoted

All strings must be quoted in a SQL query. It doesn't matter whether you use single or double quotes, as long as they are in matching pairs. However, it's normally better to use MySQLi or PDO prepared statements, as explained later in this chapter.

Handling numbers

As a general rule, numbers should not be quoted, as anything in quotes is a string. However, MySQL accepts numbers enclosed in quotes and treats them as their numeric equivalent. Be careful to distinguish between a real number and any other data type made up of numbers. For instance, a date is made up of numbers but should be enclosed in quotes and stored in a date-related column type. Similarly, telephone numbers should be enclosed in quotes and stored in a text-related column type.

SQL queries normally end with a semicolon, which is an instruction to the database to execute the query. When using PHP, the semicolon must be omitted from the SQL. Consequently, standalone examples of SQL are presented throughout this book without a concluding semicolon.

Refining the data retrieved by a SELECT query

The only SQL query you have run so far retrieves all records from the images table. Much of the time, you want to be more selective.

Selecting specific columns

Using an asterisk to select all columns is a convenient shortcut, but you should normally specify only those columns you need. List the column names separated by commas after the SELECT keyword. For example, this query selects only the filename and caption fields for each record:

```
SELECT filename, caption FROM images
```

You can test this in `mysqli_03.php` and `pdo_03.php` in the `ch11` folder.

Changing the order of results

To control the sort order, add an `ORDER BY` clause with the name(s) of the column(s) in order of precedence. Separate multiple columns by commas. The following query sorts the captions from the `images` table in alphabetical order (the code is in `mysqli_04.php` and `pdo_04.php`):

```
$sql = 'SELECT * FROM images ORDER BY caption';
```

> The semicolon indicates the end of the PHP statement. It is not part of the SQL query.

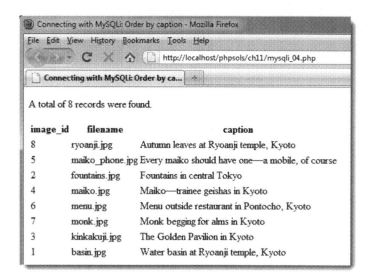

To reverse the sort order, add the `DESC` (for "descending") keyword like this:

```
$sql = 'SELECT * FROM images ORDER BY caption DESC';
```

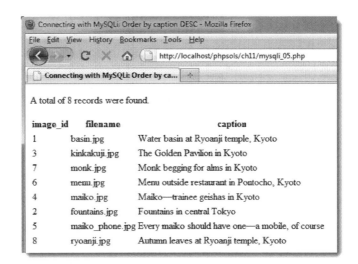

There is also an ASC (for "ascending") keyword. It's the default sort order, so is normally omitted.

However, specifying ASC increases clarity when columns in the same table are sorted in a different order. For example, if you publish multiple articles every day, you could use the following query to display titles in alphabetical order, but ordered by the date of publication with the most recent ones first:

```
SELECT * FROM articles
ORDER BY published DESC, title ASC
```

Searching for specific values

To search for specific values, add a WHERE clause to the SELECT query. The WHERE clause follows the name of the table. For example, the query in mysqli_06.php and pdo_06.php looks like this:

```
$sql = 'SELECT * FROM images
        WHERE image_id = 6';
```

Note that SQL uses a single equal sign to test for equality, unlike PHP, which uses two.

It produces the following result:

In addition to testing for equality, a WHERE clause can use comparison operators, such as greater than (>) and less than (<). Rather than go through all the options now, I'll introduce others as needed. Chapter 13 has a comprehensive roundup of the four main SQL commands: SELECT, INSERT, UPDATE, and DELETE, including a list of the main comparison operators used with WHERE.

If used in combination with ORDER BY, the WHERE clause must come first. For example (the code is in mysqli_07.php and pdo_07.php):

```
$sql = 'SELECT * FROM images
        WHERE image_id > 6
        ORDER BY caption DESC';
```

This selects the two images that have an image_id greater than 6 and sorts them by their captions in reverse order.

Searching for text with wildcard characters

In SQL, the percentage sign (%) is a wildcard character that matches anything or nothing. It's used in a WHERE clause in conjunction with the LIKE keyword.

The query in mysqli_08.php and pdo_08.php looks like this:

```
$sql = 'SELECT * FROM images
        WHERE caption LIKE "%Kyoto%"';
```

It searches for all records in the images table where the caption column contains "Kyoto," and produces the following result:

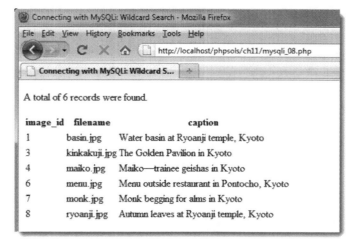

As the preceding screenshot shows, it finds six records out of the eight in the images table. All the captions end with "Kyoto," so the wildcard character at the end is matching nothing, whereas the wildcard at the beginning matches the rest of each caption.

If you omit the leading wildcard ("Kyoto%"), the query searches for captions that begin with "Kyoto." None of them does, so you get no results from the search.

The query in mysqli_09.php and pdo_09.php looks like this:

```
$sql = 'SELECT * FROM images
        WHERE caption LIKE "%maiko%"';
```

It produces the following result:

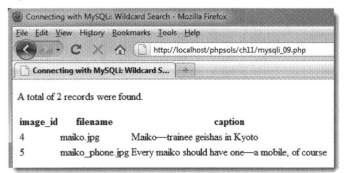

The query spells "maiko" all in lowercase, but the query also finds it with an initial capital. Wildcard searches with LIKE are case-insensitive.

To perform a case-sensitive search, you need to add the BINARY keyword like this (the code is in mysqli_10.php and pdo_10.php):

```
$sql = 'SELECT * FROM images
        WHERE caption LIKE BINARY "%maiko%"';
```

All the examples you have seen so far have been hard-coded, but most of the time, the values used in SQL queries need to come from user input. Unless you're careful, this puts you at risk from a malicious exploit know as SQL injection. The rest of this chapter explains the danger and how to avoid it.

Understanding the danger of SQL injection

SQL injection is very similar to the email header injection I warned you about in Chapter 5. An injection attack tries to insert spurious conditions into a SQL query in an attempt to expose or corrupt your data. The meaning of the following query should be easy to understand:

```
SELECT * FROM users WHERE username = 'xyz' AND pwd = 'abc'
```

It's the basic pattern for a login application. If the query finds a record where username is xyz and pwd is abc, you know that a correct combination of username and password have been submitted, so the login succeeds. All an attacker needs to do is inject an extra condition like this:

```
SELECT * FROM users WHERE username = 'xyz' AND pwd = 'abc' OR 1 = 1
```

The OR means only one of the conditions needs to be true, so the login succeeds even without a correct username and password. SQL injection relies on quotes and other control characters not being properly escaped when part of the query is derived from a variable or user input.

There are several strategies you can adopt to prevent SQL injection, depending on the situation:

- If the variable is an integer (for example, the primary key of a record), use is_numeric() and the (int) casting operator to ensure it's safe to insert in the query.

- If you are using MySQLi, pass each variable to the `real_escape_string()` method before inserting it in the query.

- The PDO equivalent of `real_escape_string()` is the `quote()` method, but it doesn't work with all databases. The PDO documentation advises against using `quote()`, strongly recommending the use of prepared statements instead.

- Use a **prepared statement**. In a prepared statement, placeholders in the SQL query represent values that come from user input. The PHP code automatically wraps strings in quotes, and escapes embedded quotes and other control characters. The syntax is different for MySQLi and PDO.

- None of the preceding strategies is suitable for column names, which must not be enclosed in quotes. To use a variable for column names, create an array of acceptable values, and check that the submitted value is in the array before inserting it into the query.

With the exception of `quote()`, let's take a look at using each of these techniques.

PHP Solution 11-6: Inserting an integer from user input into a query

This PHP solution shows how to sanitize a variable from user input to make sure it contains only an integer before inserting the value in a SQL query. The technique is the same for both MySQLi and PDO.

1. Copy either `mysqli_integer_01.php` or `pdo_integer_01.php` from the `ch11` folder to the `mysql` folder. Each file contains a SQL query that selects the `image_id` and `filename` columns from the `images` table. In the body of the page, there's a form with a drop-down menu which is populated by a loop that runs through the results of the SQL query. The MySQLi version looks like this:

```
<form action="" method="get" id="form1">
  <select name="image_id" id="image_id">
    <?php while ($row = $images->fetch_assoc()) { ?>
    <option value="<?php echo $row['image_id']; ?>"
    <?php if (isset($_GET['image_id']) && $_GET['image_id'] == ➥
      $row['image_id']) {
      echo 'selected';
    } ?>
    ><?php echo $row['filename']; ?></option>
    <?php } ?>
  </select>
  <input type="submit" name="go" id="go" value="Display">
</form>
```

The form uses the get method and assigns the `image_id` to the `value` attribute of the `<option>` tags. If `$_GET['image_id']` has the same value as `$row['image_id']`, the current `image_id` is the same as passed through the page's query string, so the `selected` attribute is added to the opening `<option>` tag. The value of `$row['filename']` is inserted between the opening and closing `<option>` tags.

The PDO version is identical apart from the fact that it runs the query directly in a `foreach` loop.

2. If you load the page into a browser, you'll see a drop-down menu that lists the files in the images folder like this:

3. Insert the following code immediately after the closing `</form>` tag. The code is the same for both MySQLi and PDO, apart from one line.

```php
<?php
if (isset($_GET['image_id'])) {
  if (!is_numeric($_GET['image_id'])) {
    $image_id = 1;
  } else {
    $image_id = (int) $_GET['image_id'];
  }
  $sql = "SELECT filename, caption FROM images
          WHERE image_id = $image_id";
  $result = $conn->query($sql);
  $row = $result->fetch_assoc();
?>
<figure><img src="../images/<?php echo $row['filename']; ?>">
  <figcaption><?php echo $row['caption']; ?></figcaption>
</figure>
<?php } ?>
```

The conditional statement checks whether image_id has been sent through the $_GET array. If it has, the next conditional statement uses the logical Not operator with is_numeric() to check whether it's not numeric. The is_numeric() function applies a strict test, accepting only numbers or numeric strings. It doesn't attempt to convert the value to a number if it begins with a digit.

If the value submitted through the query string isn't numeric, a default value is assigned to a new variable called $image_id. However, if $_GET['image_id'] is numeric, it's assigned to $image_id using the (int) casting operator. Using the casting operator is an extra precaution in case someone tries to probe your script for error messages by submitting a floating point number.

Since you know $image_id is an integer, it's safe to insert directly in the SQL query. Because it's a number, it doesn't need to be wrapped in quotes, but the string assigned to $sql needs to use double quotes to ensure the value of $image_id is inserted into the query.

The new query is submitted to MySQL by the `query()` method, and the result is stored in `$row`. Finally, `$row['filename']` and `$row['caption']` are used to display the image and its caption in the page.

4. If you are using the PDO version, locate this line:

`$row = $result->fetch_assoc();`

Change it to this:

`$row = $result->`**`fetch();`**

5. Save the page, and load it into a browser. When the page first loads, only the drop-down menu is displayed.

6. Select a filename from the drop-down menu, and click **Display**. The image of your choice should be displayed, as shown in the following screenshot:

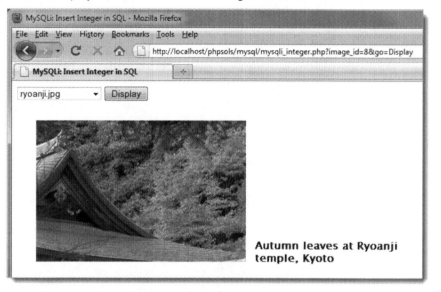

7. If you encounter problems, check your code against `mysqli_integer_02.php` or `pdo_integer_02.php` in the `ch11` folder.

8. Edit the query string in the browser, changing the value of `image_id` to a string or a string that begins with a number. You should see `basin.jpg`, which has `image_id` 1.

9. Try a floating point number between 1.0 and 8.9. The relevant image is displayed normally.

10. Try a number outside the range of 1–8. No error messages are displayed because there's nothing wrong with the query. It's simply looking for a value that doesn't exist. In this example, it doesn't matter, but you should normally check the number of rows returned by the query, using the `num_rows` property with MySQLi or the `rowCount()` method with PDO.

11. Change the code like this for MySQLi:

```php
$result = $conn->query($sql);
if ($result->num_rows) {
  $row = $result->fetch_assoc();
?>
<figure><img src="../images/<?php echo $row['filename']; ?>">
  <figcaption><?php echo $row['caption']; ?></figcaption>
</figure>
<?php } else { ?>
<p>Image not found</p>
<?php }
}?>
```

For PDO, use `$result->rowCount()` in place of `$result->num_rows`.

If no rows are returned by the query, 0 is treated by PHP as implicitly `false`, so the condition fails, and the `else` clause is executed instead.

12. Test the page again. When you select an image from the drop-down menu, it displays normally as before. But if you try entering an out-of-range value in the query string, you see the following message instead:

The amended code is in `mysqli_integer_03.php` and `pdo_integer_03.php` in the `ch11` folder.

PHP Solution 11-7: Inserting a string with real_escape_string()

This PHP solution works only with MySQLi. It shows how to insert a value from a search form into a SQL query using the `real_escape_string()` method. If you have used the original MySQL extension before, it does the same as the `mysql_real_escape_string()` function. In addition to handling single and double quotes, it also escapes other control characters, such as newlines and carriage returns. Although the functionality is the same, you must use the MySQLi version. You can't use `mysql_real_escape_string()` with MySQLi.

1. Copy `mysqli_real_escape_01.php` from the `ch11` folder, and save it in the `mysql` folder as `mysql_real_escape.php`. The file contains a search form and a table for displaying the results.

2. Add the following code in a PHP block above the `DOCTYPE` declaration:

```php
if (isset($_GET['go'])) {
  require_once('../includes/connection.inc.php');
```

```
    $conn = dbConnect('read');
    $searchterm = '%' . $conn->real_escape_string($_GET['search']) . '%';
}
```

3. This includes the connection file and establishes a MySQLi connection for the read-only user account if the form has been submitted. Then, the value of $_GET['search'] is passed to the connection object's real_escape_string() method to make it safe to incorporate into a SQL query, and the % wildcard character is concatenated to both ends before the result is assigned to $searchterm. So, if the value submitted through the search form is "hello," $searchterm becomes %hello%.

4. Add the SELECT query on the next line (before the closing curly brace):

```
$sql = "SELECT * FROM images WHERE caption LIKE '$searchterm'";
```

The whole query is wrapped in double quotes so that the value of $searchterm is incorporated. However, $searchterm contains a string, so it also needs to be wrapped in quotes. To avoid a clash, use single quotes around $searchterm.

5. Execute the query, and get the number of rows returned. The complete code in the PHP block above the DOCTYPE declaration looks like this:

```
if (isset($_GET['go'])) {
  require_once('../includes/connection.inc.php');
  $conn = dbConnect('read');
  $searchterm = '%' . $conn->real_escape_string($_GET['search']) . '%';
  $sql = "SELECT * FROM images WHERE caption LIKE '$searchterm'";
  $result = $conn->query($sql) or die($conn->error);
  $numRows = $result->num_rows;
}
```

6. Add the PHP code to the body of the page to display the results:

```
<?php if (isset($numRows)) { ?>
<p>Number of results for <b><?php echo htmlentities($_GET['search'], ↪
  ENT_COMPAT, 'utf-8'); ?></b>: <?php echo $numRows; ?></p>
<?php if ($numRows) { ?>
<table>
  <tr>
    <th scope="col">image_id</th>
    <th scope="col">filename</th>
    <th scope="col">caption</th>
  </tr>
  <?php while ($row = $result->fetch_assoc()) { ?>
  <tr>
    <td><?php echo $row['image_id']; ?></td>
    <td><?php echo $row['filename']; ?></td>
    <td><?php echo $row['caption']; ?></td>
  </tr>
  <?php } ?>
</table>
```

```php
<?php }
} ?>
```

The first conditional statement is wrapped around the paragraph and table, preventing them from being displayed if $numRows doesn't exist, which happens when the page is first loaded. If the form has been submitted, $numRows will have been set, so the search term is redisplayed using htmlentities() (see Chapter 5), and the value of $numRows reports the number of matches.

If the query returns no results, $numRows is 0, which is treated as false, so the table is not displayed. If $numRows contains anything other than 0, the table is displayed, and the while loop displays the results of the query.

7. Save the page, and load it into a browser. Enter some text in the search field, and click **Search**. The number of results is displayed, together with any captions that contain the search term, as shown in the following screenshot:

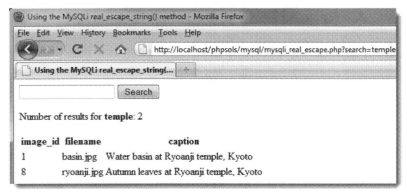

If you don't use real_escape_string() or a prepared statement, the search form still works most of the time. But if the search term includes an apostrophe or quotation marks, your page will fail to load correctly, and a SQL syntax error will be displayed like this:

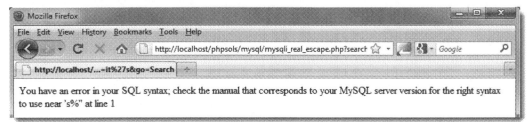

Worse, it leaves your database wide open to malicious attack.

Although `real_escape_string()` escapes quotes and other control characters in the submitted value, you still need to wrap strings in quotes in the SQL query. The `LIKE` keyword must always be followed by a string, even if the search term is limited to numbers.

Embedding variables in MySQLi prepared statements

Instead of incorporating variables directly in the SQL query, you use question marks as placeholders like this:

```
$sql = 'SELECT image_id, filename, caption FROM images WHERE caption LIKE ?';
```

Using a MySQLi prepared statement involves the following steps:

1. Initialize the statement.

2. Pass the SQL query to the statement to make sure it's valid.

3. Bind the variable(s) to the query.

4. Bind results to variables (optional).

5. Execute the statement.

6. Store the result (optional).

7. Fetch the result(s).

To initialize the prepared statement, call the stmt_init() method on the database connection, and store it in a variable like this:

```
$stmt = $conn->stmt_init();
```

You then pass the SQL query to $stmt->prepare(). This checks that you haven't used question mark placeholders in the wrong place, and that when everything is put together, the query is valid SQL. If there are any mistakes, $stmt->prepare() returns false, so you need to enclose the next steps in a conditional statement to ensure they run only if everything is still OK.

Error messages can be accessed by using $stmt->error.

Binding the parameters means replacing the question marks with the actual values held in the variables. This is what protects your database from SQL injection. You pass the variables to $stmt->bind_param() in the same order as you want them inserted into the SQL query, together with a first argument specifying the data type of each variable, again in the same order as the variables. The data type must be specified by one of the following four characters:

- b: Binary (such as an image, Word document, or PDF file)
- d: Double (floating point number)
- i: Integer (whole number)
- s: String (text)

The number of variables passed to $stmt->bind_param() must be exactly the same as the number of question mark placeholders. For example, to pass a single value as a string, use this:

```
$stmt->bind_param('s', $_GET['words']);
```

To pass two values, the SELECT query needs two question marks as placeholders, and both variables need to be bound with bind_param() like this:

```
$sql = 'SELECT * FROM products WHERE price < ? AND type = ?';
$stmt = $conn->stmt_init();
```

```
$stmt->prepare($sql);
$stmt->bind_param('ds', $_GET['price'], $_GET['type']);
```

The first argument to bind_param(), 'ds', specifies $_GET['price'] as a floating point number, and $_GET['type'] as a string.

Optionally, you can bind the results of a SELECT query to variables with the bind_result() method. This avoids the need to extract each row and access the results as $row['column_name']. To bind the results, you must name each column specifically in the SELECT query. List the variables you want to use in the same order, and pass them as arguments to bind_result(). To bind the results of the query at the beginning of this section, use this:

```
$stmt->bind_result($image_id, $filename, $caption);
```

This allows you to access the results directly as $image_id, $filename, and $caption.

Once the statement has been prepared, you call $stmt->execute(), and the result is stored in $stmt.

To access the num_rows property, you must first store the result like this:

```
$stmt->store_result();
$numRows = $stmt->num_rows;
```

Using store_result() is optional, but if you don't use it, num_rows returns 0.

To loop through the results of a SELECT query executed with a prepared statement, use the fetch() method. If you have bound the results to variables, do it like this:

```
while ($stmt->fetch()) {
  // display the bound variables for each row
}
```

If you don't bind the result to variables, use $row = $stmt->fetch(), and access each variable as $row['column_name'].

When you have finished with a result, you can free the memory by using the free_result() method. The close() method frees the memory used by the prepared statement.

PHP Solution 11-8: Using a MySQLi prepared statement in a search

This PHP solution shows how to use a MySQLi prepared statement with a SELECT query and demonstrates binding the result to named variables.

1. Copy mysql_prepared_01.php from the ch11 folder and save it in the mysql folder as mysql_prepared.php. It contains the same search form and results table as used in PHP Solution 11-7.

2. In a PHP code block above the DOCTYPE declaration, create a conditional statement to include connection.inc.php and create a MySQL read-only connection when the search form is submitted. The code looks like this:

```
if (isset($_GET['go'])) {
  require_once('../includes/connection.inc.php');
  $conn = dbConnect('read');
}
```

3. Next, add the SQL query inside the conditional statement. The query needs to name the three columns you want to retrieve from the `images` table. Use a question mark as the placeholder for the search term like this:

```
$sql = 'SELECT image_id, filename, caption FROM images
        WHERE caption LIKE ?';
```

4. Before passing the user-submitted search term to the `bind_param()` method, you need to add the wildcard characters to it and assign it to a new variable like this:

```
$searchterm = '%'. $_GET['search'] .'%';
```

5. You can now create the prepared statement. The finished code in the PHP block above the `DOCTYPE` declaration looks like this:

```
if (isset($_GET['go'])) {
  require_once('../includes/connection.inc.php');
  $conn = dbConnect('read');
  $sql = 'SELECT image_id, filename, caption FROM images
          WHERE caption LIKE ?';
  $searchterm = '%'. $_GET['search'] .'%';
  $stmt = $conn->stmt_init();
  if ($stmt->prepare($sql)) {
    $stmt->bind_param('s', $searchterm);
    $stmt->bind_result($image_id, $filename, $caption);
    $stmt->execute();
    $stmt->store_result();
    $numRows = $stmt->num_rows;
  } else {
    echo $stmt->error;
  }
}
```

This initializes the prepared statement and assigns it to `$stmt`. The SQL query is then passed to the `prepare()` method, which checks the validity of the query's syntax. If there's a problem with the syntax, the `else` block displays the error message. If the syntax is OK, the rest of the script inside the conditional statement is executed.

> The code is wrapped in a conditional statement for testing purposes only. If there's an error with your prepared statement, `echo $stmt->error;` displays a MySQL error message to help identify the problem. In a live website, you should remove the conditional statement, and call `$stmt->prepare($sql);` directly

The first line inside the conditional statement binds `$searchterm` to the `SELECT` query, replacing the question mark placeholder. The first argument tells the prepared statement to treat it as a string.

The next line binds the results of the SELECT query to $image_id, $filename, and $caption. These need to be in the same order as in the query. I have named the variables after the columns they represent, but you can use any variables you want.

Then the prepared statement is executed and the result stored. Note that the result is stored in the $stmt object. You don't assign it to a variable.

> Assigning $stmt->store_result() to a variable doesn't store the database result. It records only whether the result was successfully stored in the $stmt object.

Finally, the number of rows retrieved by the query is stored in $numRows.

6. Add the following code after the search form to display the result:

```php
<?php if (isset($numRows)) { ?>
<p>Number of results for <b><?php echo htmlentities($_GET['search'], ➥
  ENT_COMPAT, 'utf-8'); ?></b>: <?php echo $numRows; ?></p>
<?php if ($numRows) { ?>
<table>
  <tr>
    <th scope="col">image_id</th>
    <th scope="col">filename</th>
    <th scope="col">caption</th>
  </tr>
  <?php while ($stmt->fetch()) { ?>
  <tr>
    <td><?php echo $image_id; ?></td>
    <td><?php echo $filename; ?></td>
    <td><?php echo $caption; ?></td>
  </tr>
  <?php } ?>
</table>
<?php }
} ?>
```

Most of this code is the same as in PHP Solution 11-7. The difference lies in the while loop that displays the results. Instead of using the fetch_assoc() method on a result object and storing the result in $row, it simply calls the fetch() method on the prepared statement. There's no need to store the current record as $row, because the values from each column have been bound to $image_id, $filename, and $caption.

You can compare your code with mysqli_prepared_02.php in the ch11 folder.

Embedding variables in PDO prepared statements

Whereas MySQLi always uses question marks as placeholders in prepared statements, PDO offers several options. I'll describe the two most useful: question marks and named placeholders.

Question mark placeholders Instead of embedding variables in the SQL query, you replace them with question marks like this:

```
$sql = 'SELECT image_id, filename, caption FROM images WHERE caption LIKE ?';
```

This is identical to MySQLi. However, the way that you bind the values of the variables to the placeholders is completely different. It involves just two steps, as follows:

1. Prepare the statement to make sure the SQL is valid.

2. Execute the statement by passing the variables to it as an array.

Assuming you have created a PDO connection called $conn, the PHP code looks like this:

```
// prepare statement
$stmt = $conn->prepare($sql);
// execute query by passing array of variables
$stmt->execute(array($_GET['words']));
```

The first line of code prepares the statement and stores it as $stmt. The second line binds the values of the variable(s) and executes the statement all in one go. The variables must be in the same order as the placeholders. Even if there is only one placeholder, the variable must be passed to execute() as an array. The result of the query is stored in $stmt.

Named placeholders Instead of embedding variables in the SQL query, you replace them with named placeholders beginning with a colon like this:

```
$sql = 'SELECT image_id, filename, caption FROM images WHERE caption LIKE :search';
```

With named placeholders, you can either bind the values individually or pass an associative array to execute(). When binding the values individually, the PHP code looks like this:

```
$stmt = $conn->prepare($sql);
// bind the parameters and execute the statement
$stmt->bindParam(':search', $_GET['words'], PDO::PARAM_STR);
$stmt->execute();
```

You pass three arguments to $stmt->bindParam(): the name of the placeholder, the variable that you want to use as its value, and a constant specifying the data type. The main constants are as follows:

- PDO::PARAM_INT: Integer (whole number)
- PDO::PARAM_LOB: Binary (such as an image, Word document, or PDF file)
- PDO::PARAM_STR: String (text)

There isn't a constant for floating point numbers, but the third argument is optional, so you can just leave it out. Alternatively, use PDO::PARAM_STR. This wraps the value in quotes, but MySQL converts it back to a floating point number.

If you pass the variables as an associative array, you can't specify the data type. The PHP code for the same example using an associative array looks like this:

```
// prepare statement
$stmt = $conn->prepare($sql);
// execute query by passing array of variables
$stmt->execute(array(':search' => $_GET['words']));
```

In both cases, the result of the query is stored in $stmt.

Error messages can be accessed in the same way as with a PDO connection. However, instead of calling the errorInfo() method on the connection object, use it on the PDO statement like this:

```
$error = $stmt->errorInfo();
if (isset($error[2])) {
  echo $error[2];
}
```

To bind the results of a SELECT query to variables, each column needs to bound separately using the bindColumn() method before calling execute(). The bindColumn() method takes two arguments. The first argument can be either the name of the column or its number counting from 1. The number comes from its position in the SELECT query, not the order it appears in the database table. So, to bind the result from the filename column to $filename, either of the following is acceptable:

```
$stmt->bindColumn('filename', $filename);
$stmt->bindColumn(2, $filename);
```

PHP Solution 11-9: Using a PDO prepared statement in a search

This PHP solution shows how to embed the user-submitted value from a search form into a SELECT query with a PDO prepared statement. It uses the same search form as the MySQLi versions in PHP Solutions 11-7 and 11-8.

1. Copy pdo_prepared_01.php from the ch11 folder, and save it in the mysql folder as pdo_prepared.php.

2. Add the following code in a PHP block above the DOCTYPE declaration:

    ```
    if (isset($_GET['go'])) {
      require_once('../includes/connection.inc.php');
      $conn = dbConnect('read', 'pdo');
      $sql = 'SELECT image_id, filename, caption FROM images
              WHERE caption LIKE :search';
      $searchterm = '%'. $_GET['search'] .'%';
      $stmt = $conn->prepare($sql);
      $stmt->bindParam(':search', $searchterm, PDO::PARAM_STR);
      $stmt->bindColumn('image_id', $image_id);
      $stmt->bindColumn('filename', $filename);
      $stmt->bindColumn(3, $caption);
      $stmt->execute();
      $numRows = $stmt->rowCount();
    }
    ```

    When the form is submitted, this includes the connection file and creates a PDO connection to MySQL. The prepared statement uses :search as a named parameter in place of the user-submitted value. Like MySQLi prepared statements, you need to add the % wildcard characters to the search term before binding it to the prepared statement with bindParam(). The results are bound to $image_id, $filename, and $caption. The first two use the column names, but the caption column is referred to by its position in the SELECT query.

3. The code that displays the results is identical to step 6 in PHP Solution 11-8. The finished file is in `pdo_prepared_02.php` in the `ch11` folder.

PHP Solution 11-10: Changing column options through user input

This PHP solution shows how to change the name of SQL keywords in a `SELECT` query through user input. SQL keywords cannot be wrapped in quotes, so using prepared statements or the MySQLi `real_escape_string()` method won't work. Instead, you need to ensure that the user input matches an array of expected values. If no match is found, use a default value instead. The technique is identical for MySQLi and PDO.

1. Copy either `mysqli_order_01.php` or `pdo_order_01.php` from the `ch11` folder, and save it in the `mysql` folder. Both versions select all records from the `images` table and display the results in table. The pages also contain a form that allows the user to select the name of a column to sort the results in either ascending or descending order. In their initial state, the form is inactive. The pages display the details sorted by `image_id` in ascending order like this:

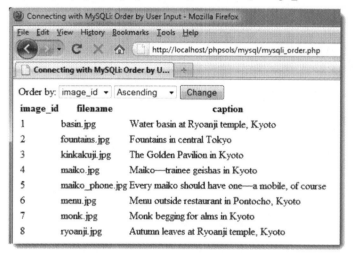

2. Amend the code in the PHP block above the `DOCTYPE` declaration like this (the following listing shows the MySQLi version, but the changes highlighted in bold type are the same for PDO):

```php
require_once('../includes/connection.inc.php');
// connect to MySQL
$conn = dbConnect('read');
// set default values
$col = 'image_id';
$dir = 'ASC';
// create arrays of permitted values
$columns = array('image_id', 'filename', 'caption');
$direction = array('ASC', 'DESC');
// if the form has been submitted, use only expected values
if (isset($_GET['column']) && in_array($_GET['column'], $columns)) {
  $col = $_GET['column'];
```

```
}
if (isset($_GET['direction']) && in_array($_GET['direction'], $direction)) {
  $dir = $_GET['direction'];
}
// prepare the SQL query using sanitized variables
$sql = "SELECT * FROM images
        ORDER BY $col $dir";
// submit the query and capture the result
$result = $conn->query($sql) or die(mysqli_error());
```

The new code defines two variables, $col and $dir, that are embedded directly in the SELECT query. Because they have been assigned default values, the query displays the results sorted by the image_id column in ascending order when the page first loads.

Two arrays, $columns and $direction, then define permitted values: the column names, and the ASC and DESC keywords. These arrays are used by the conditional statements that check the $_GET array for column and direction. The submitted values are reassigned to $col and $dir only if they match a value in the $columns and $direction arrays respectively. This prevents any attempt to inject illegal values into the SQL query.

3. Edit the <option> tags in the drop-down menus so they display the selected values for $col and $dir like this:

```
<select name="column" id="column">
  <option <?php if ($col == 'image_id') echo 'selected'; ?>>image_id</option>
  <option <?php if ($col == 'filename') echo 'selected'; ?>>filename</option>
  <option <?php if ($col == 'caption') echo 'selected'; ?>>caption</option>
</select>
<select name="direction" id="direction">
  <option value="ASC" <?php if ($dir == 'ASC') echo 'selected'; ?>> ↦
    Ascending</option>
  <option value="DESC" <?php if ($dir == 'DESC') echo 'selected'; ?>> ↦
    Descending</option>
</select>
```

4. Save the page, and test it in a browser. You can change the sort order of the display by selecting the values in the drop-down menus and clicking **Change**. However, if you try to inject an illegal value through the query string, the page uses the default values of $col and $dir to display the results sorted by image_id in ascending order.

You can check your code against mysqli_order_02.php and pdo_order_02.php in the ch11 folder.

Chapter review

PHP provides three methods of communicating with MySQL:

- **The original MySQL extension, which is no longer actively maintained**: It should not be used for new projects. If you need to maintain an existing site, you can easily recognize whether it uses the original MySQL extension, because all functions begin with `mysql_`. For help using it, consult the first edition of this book or use the online documentation at `http://docs.php.net/manual/en/book.mysql.php`.
- **The MySQL Improved (MySQLi) extension**: This is recommended for all new MySQL projects. It requires PHP 5.0 and MySQL 4.1 or higher. It's more efficient, and has the added safety of prepared statements.
- **The PHP Data Objects (PDO) abstraction layer, which is software-neutral**: You should choose this option if your projects are likely to need to be adapted to use other databases.

Although PHP communicates with the database and stores the results, queries need to be written in SQL, the standard language used to query a relational database. This chapter showed how to retrieve information stored in a database table using a `SELECT` statement, refining the search with a `WHERE` clause, and changing the sort order with `ORDER BY`. You also learned several techniques to protect queries from SQL injection, including prepared statements, which use placeholders instead of embedding variables directly in a query.

In the next chapter, you'll put this knowledge to practical use creating an online photo gallery.

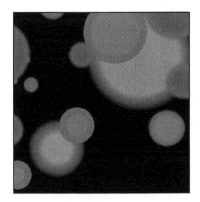

Chapter 12

Creating a Dynamic Online Gallery

The previous chapter concentrated mainly on extracting the contents of the `images` table as text. This chapter builds on those techniques to develop the mini photo gallery shown in Figure 12-1.

Figure 12-1. The mini photo gallery is driven by pulling information from a database.

The gallery also demonstrates some cool features that you'll want to incorporate into text-driven pages, too. For instance, the grid of thumbnail images on the left displays two images per row. Just by changing two numbers, you can make the grid as many columns wide and as many rows deep as you like. Clicking one of the thumbnails replaces the main image and caption. It's the same page that reloads, but exactly the same technique is used to create online catalogs that take you to another page with more details about a product. The **Next** link at the foot of the thumbnails grid shows you the next set of photographs, using exactly the same technique as you use to page through a long set of search results. This gallery isn't just a pretty face or two...

What this chapter covers:

- Why storing images in a database is a bad idea, and what you should do instead
- Planning the layout of a dynamic gallery
- Displaying a fixed number of results in a table row
- Limiting the number of records retrieved at a time
- Paging through a long set of results

Why not store images in a database?

The images table contains only filenames and captions, but not the images themselves. Even though I said in the previous chapter that you can always add new columns or tables to a database when new requirements arise, I don't intend to store the images in the database for the simple reason that it's usually more trouble than it's worth. The main problems are as follows:

- Images can't be indexed or searched without storing textual information separately.
- Images are usually large, bloating the size of tables. If there's a limit on the amount of storage in your database, you risk running out of space.
- Table fragmentation affects performance if images are deleted frequently.
- Retrieving images from a database involves passing the image to a separate script, slowing down display in a web page.

Storing images in a database is messy. It's more efficient to store images in an ordinary folder on your website and use the database for information about the images. You need just two pieces of information in the database—the filename and a caption that can also be used as alt text. Some developers store the full path to the image in the database, but I think storing only the filename gives you greater flexibility. The path to the images folder will be embedded in the HTML. You could also store the image's height and width, but it's not absolutely necessary. As you saw in Chapter 4, you can generate that information dynamically.

Planning the gallery

Unless you're good at visualizing how a page will look simply by reading its source code, I find that the best way to design a database-driven site is to start with a static page and fill it with placeholder text and images. I then create my CSS style rules to get the page looking the way I want, and finally replace each placeholder element with PHP code. Each time I replace something, I check the page in a browser to make sure everything is still holding together.

Figure 12-2 shows the static mockup I made of the gallery and points out the elements that need to be converted to dynamic code. The images are the same as those used for the random image generator in Chapter 4 and are all different sizes. I experimented by scaling the images to create the thumbnails but decided that the result looked too untidy, so I made the thumbnails a standard size (80 × 54 pixels). Also, to make life easy, I gave each thumbnail the same name as the larger version and stored them in a separate subfolder of the images folder called thumbs.

As you saw in the previous chapter, displaying the contents of the entire images table was easy. You created a single table row, with the contents of each field in a separate table cell. By looping through the result set, each record displayed on a row of its own, simulating the column structure of the database table. This time, the two-column structure of the thumbnail grid no longer matches the database structure. This means that you need to count how many thumbnails have been inserted in each row before triggering the creation of the next row.

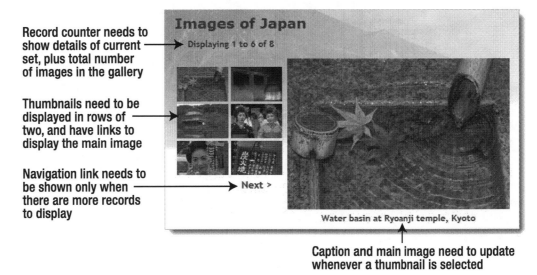

Record counter needs to show details of current set, plus total number of images in the gallery

Thumbnails need to be displayed in rows of two, and have links to display the main image

Navigation link needs to be shown only when there are more records to display

Caption and main image need to update whenever a thumbnail is selected

Figure 12-2. Working out what needs to be done to convert a static gallery to a dynamic one

Figure 12-3 shows the framework I created to hold the gallery together. The table of thumbnails and the main_image <div> are floated left and right respectively in a fixed-width wrapper <div> called gallery. I don't intend to go into the details of the CSS, but you may study that at your leisure.

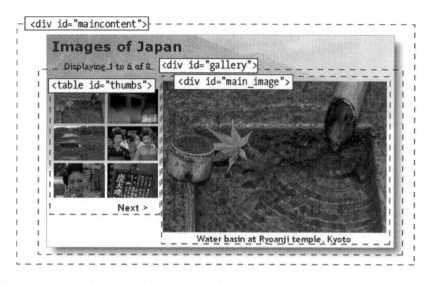

Figure 12-3. The underlying structure of the image gallery

Once I had worked out what needed to be done, I stripped out the code for thumbnails 2 to 6, and for the navigation link (which is nested in the final row of the thumbs table). The following listing shows what was left in the maincontent <div> of gallery.php, with the elements that need to be converted to PHP code highlighted in bold (you can find the code in gallery_01.php in the ch12 folder):

```
<div id="maincontent">
  <h2>Images of Japan</h2>
  <p id="picCount">Displaying 1 to 6 of 8</p>
  <div id="gallery">
    <table id="thumbs">
      <tr>
        <!-- This row needs to be repeated -->
        <td><a href="gallery.php"><img src="images/thumbs/basin.jpg" alt="" ↵
          width="80" height="54"></a></td>
      </tr>
      <!-- Navigation link needs to go here -->
    </table>
    <div id="main_image">
      <p><img src="images/basin.jpg" alt="" width="350" height="237"></p>
      <p>Water basin at Ryoanji temple, Kyoto</p>
    </div>
  </div>
</div>
```

Converting the gallery elements to PHP

Before you can display the contents of the gallery, you need to connect to the phpsols database and retrieve all the records stored in the images table. The procedure for doing so is the same as in the previous chapter, using the following simple SQL query:

```
SELECT filename, caption FROM images
```

You can then use the first record to display the first image and its associated caption and thumbnail. You don't need image_id.

PHP Solution 12-1: Displaying the first image

If you set up the Japan Journey website in Chapter 4, you can work directly with the original gallery.php. Alternatively, copy gallery_01.php from the ch12 folder, and save it in the phpsols site root as gallery.php. You also need to copy title.inc.php, menu.inc.php, and footer.inc.php to the includes folder of the phpsols site. If your editing program asks if you want to update the links in the files, choose the option not to update.

1. Load gallery.php into a browser to make sure that it displays correctly. The maincontent part of the page should look like Figure 12-4, with one thumbnail image and a larger version of the same image.

Figure 12-4. The stripped-down version of the static gallery ready for conversion

2. The gallery depends on a connection to the database, so include connection.inc.php, create a read-only connection to MySQL, and define the SQL query. Add the following code just before the closing PHP tag above the DOCTYPE declaration in gallery.php (new code is highlighted in bold):

```
include('./includes/title.inc.php');
require_once('./includes/connection.inc.php');
```

```
$conn = dbConnect('read');
$sql = 'SELECT filename, caption FROM images';
```

If you are using PDO, add 'pdo' as the second argument to dbConnect().

3. The code for submitting the query and extracting the first record from the result depends on which method of connection you are using.

For MySQLi, use this:

```
// submit the query
$result = $conn->query($sql) or die(mysqli_error());
// extract the first record as an array
$row = $result->fetch_assoc();
```

For PDO, use this:

```
// submit the query
$result = $conn->query($sql);
// get any error messages
$error = $conn->errorInfo();
if (isset($error[2])) die($error[2]);
// extract the first record as an array
$row = $result->fetch();
```

To display the first image when the page loads, you need to get the first result on its own. The code for both MySQLi and PDO submits the query, extracts the first record, and stores it in $row.

4. You now have the details of the first record image stored as $row['filename'] and $row['caption']. In addition to the filename and caption, you need the dimensions of the large version so that you can display it in the main body of the page. Add the following code immediately after the code in the preceding step:

```
// get the name and caption for the main image
$mainImage = $row['filename'];
$caption = $row['caption'];
// get the dimensions of the main image
$imageSize = getimagesize('images/'.$mainImage);
```

The getimagesize() function was described in Chapters 4 and 8.

5. You can now use this information to display the thumbnail, main image, and caption dynamically. The main image and thumbnail have the same name, but you eventually want to display all thumbnails by looping through the full result set, so the dynamic code that goes in the table cell needs to refer to the current record—in other words, $row['filename'] and $row['caption'], rather than to $mainImage and $caption. You'll see later why I've assigned the values from the first record to separate variables. Amend the code in the table like this:

```
<td><a href="gallery.php"> ➥
  <img src="images/thumbs/<?php echo $row['filename']; ?>" ➥
```

```
alt="<?php echo $row['caption']; ?>" width="80" height="54"></a></td>
```

6. Save `gallery.php`, and view it in a browser. It should look the same as Figure 12-4. The only difference is that the thumbnail and its `alt` text are dynamically generated. You can verify this by looking at the source code. The original static version had an empty `alt` attribute, but as the following screenshot shows, it now contains the caption from the first record:

```
<table id="thumbs">
  <tr>
    <!--This row needs to be repeated-->
    <td><a href="gallery.php"><img src="images/thumbs/basin.jpg" alt="Water basin at Ryoanji
temple, Kyoto" width="80" height="54"></a></td>
  </tr>
  <!-- Navigation link needs to go here -->
</table>
```

If things go wrong, make sure there's no gap between the static and dynamically generated text in the image's `src` attribute. Also check that you're using the right code for the type of connection you have created with MySQL. You can check your code against `gallery_mysqli_02.php` or `gallery_pdo_02.php` in the `ch12` folder.

7. Once you have confirmed that you're picking up the details from the database, you can convert the code for the main image. Amend it like this (new code is in bold):

```
<div id="main_image">
  <p><img src="images/<?php echo $mainImage; ?>" ➥
    alt="<?php echo $caption; ?>" <?php echo $imageSize[3]; ?>></p>
  <p><?php echo $caption; ?></p>
</div>
```

8. As explained in Chapter 8, `getimagesize()` returns an array, the fourth element of which contains a string with the width and height of an image ready for insertion into an `<img>` tag. So `$imageSize[3]` inserts the correct dimensions for the main image.

Test the page again. It should still look the same as Figure 12-4, but the images and caption are being drawn dynamically from the database. You can check your code against `gallery_mysqli_03.php`, or `gallery_pdo_03.php` in the `ch12` folder.

Building the dynamic elements

The first thing that you need to do after converting the static page is to display all the thumbnails and build dynamic links that will enable you to display the large version of any thumbnail that has been clicked. Displaying all the thumbnails is easy—just loop through them (we'll work out how to display them in rows of two later). Activating the link for each thumbnail requires a little more thought. You need a way of telling the page which large image to display.

Passing information through a query string

In the last section, you used `$mainImage` to identify the large image, so you need a way of changing its value whenever a thumbnail is clicked. The solution is to add the image's filename to a query string at the end of the URL in the link like this:

```
<a href="gallery.php?image=filename">
```

You can then check whether the $_GET array contains an element called image. If it does, change the value of $mainImage. If it doesn't, leave $mainImage as the filename from the first record in the result set.

PHP Solution 12-2: Activating the thumbnails

Continue working with the same file as in the previous section. Alternatively, copy gallery_mysqli_03.php or gallery_pdo_03.php to the phpsols site root, and save it as gallery.php

1. Locate the opening <a> tag of the link surrounding the thumbnail. It looks like this:

    ```
    <a href="gallery.php">
    ```

2. Change it like this:

    ```
    <a href="<?php echo $_SERVER['PHP_SELF']; ?>?image=<?php echo ➥
    $row['filename']; ?>">
    ```

    Be careful when typing the code. It's easy to mix up the question marks in the PHP tags with the question mark at the beginning of the query string. It's also important there are no spaces surrounding ?image=.

    $_SERVER['PHP_SELF'] is a handy predefined variable that refers to the name of the current page. You could just leave gallery.php hard-coded in the URL, but I suspect that many of you will use the download files, which have a variety of names. Using $_SERVER['PHP_SELF'] ensures that the URL is pointing to the correct page. The rest of the code builds the query string with the current filename.

3. Save the page, and load it into a browser. Hover your mouse pointer over the thumbnail, and check the URL displayed in the status bar. It should look like this:

    ```
    http://localhost/phpsols/gallery.php?image=basin.jpg
    ```

4. If nothing is shown in the status bar, click the thumbnail. The page shouldn't change, but the URL in the address bar should now include the query string. Check that there are no gaps in the URL or query string.

5. To show all the thumbnails, you need to wrap the table cell in a loop. Insert a new line after the HTML comment about repeating the row, and create the first half of a do... while loop like this (see Chapter 3 for details of the different types of loops):

    ```
    <!-- This row needs to be repeated -->
    <?php do { ?>
    ```

6. You already have the details of the first record in the result set, so the code to get subsequent records needs to go after the closing </td> tag. Create some space between the closing </td> and </tr> tags, and insert the following code. It's slightly different for each method of database connection.

    For MySQLi, use this:

    ```
    </td>
    ```

```
<?php } while ($row = $result->fetch_assoc()); ?>
</tr>
```

For PDO, use this:

```
  </td>
<?php } while ($row = $result->fetch()); ?>
</tr>
```

This fetches the next row in the result set and sends the loop back to the top. Because $row['filename'] and $row['caption'] have different values, the next thumbnail and its associated alt text are inserted into a new table cell. The query string is also updated with the new filename.

7. Save the page, and test it in a browser. You should now see all eight thumbnails in a single row across the top of the gallery, as shown in the following screenshot.

Water basin at Ryoanji temple, Kyoto

8. Hover your mouse pointer over each thumbnail, and you should see the query string display the name of the file. You can check your code against gallery_mysqli_04.php or gallery_pdo_04.php.

9. Clicking the thumbnails still doesn't do anything, so you need to create the logic that changes the main image and its associated caption. Locate this section of code in the block above the DOCTYPE declaration:

```
// get the name and caption for the main image
$mainImage = $row['filename'];
$caption = $row['caption'];
```

10. Highlight the line that defines $caption, and cut it to your clipboard. Wrap the other line in a conditional statement like this:

```
// get the name for the main image
if (isset($_GET['image'])) {
  $mainImage = $_GET['image'];
```

343

```
  } else {
    $mainImage = $row['filename'];
  }
```

The $_GET array contains values passed through a query string, so if $_GET['image'] has been set (defined), it takes the filename from the query string and stores it as $mainImage. If $_GET['image'] doesn't exist, the value is taken from the first record in the result set as before.

11. You finally need to get the caption for the main image. It's no longer going to be the same every time, so you need to move it to the loop that displays the thumbnails in the thumbs table. It goes right after the opening curly brace of the loop (around line 45). Position your cursor after the brace and insert a couple of lines, and then paste the caption definition that you cut in the previous step. You want the caption to match the main image, so if the current record's filename is the same as $mainImage, that's the one you're after. Wrap the code that you have just pasted in a conditional statement like this:

```
<?php
do {
  // set caption if thumbnail is same as main image
  if ($row['filename'] == $mainImage) {
    $caption = $row['caption']; // this is the line you pasted
  }
?>
```

12. Save the page and reload it in your browser. This time, when you click a thumbnail, the main image and caption will change. Check your code, if necessary, against gallery_mysqli_05.php, or gallery_pdo_05.php.

Passing information through a query string like this is an important aspect of working with PHP and database results. Although form information is normally passed through the $_POST array, the $_GET array is frequently used to pass details of a record that you want to display, update, or delete. It's also commonly used for searches, because the query string can easily be bookmarked. There's no danger of SQL injection in this case. If someone changes the value of the filename passed through the query string, all that happens is the image and caption fail to display.

Creating a multicolumn table

With only eight images, the single row of thumbnails across the top of the gallery doesn't look too bad. However, it's useful to be able to build a table dynamically with a loop that inserts a specific number of table cells in a row before moving to the next row. You do this by keeping count of how many cells have been inserted. When you get to the limit for the row, insert a closing tag for the current row and an opening tag for the next one. What makes it easy to implement is the modulo operator, %, which returns the remainder of a division.

This is how it works. Let's say you want two cells in each row. After the first cell is inserted, the counter is set to 1. If you divide 1 by 2 with the modulo operator (1%2), the result is 1. When the next cell is inserted, the counter is increased to 2. The result of 2%2 is 0. The next cell produces this calculation: 3%2, which results in 1; but the fourth cell produces 4%2, which is again 0. So, every time that the calculation results in 0, you know—or to be more exact, PHP knows—you're at the end of a row.

So how do you know if there are any more rows left? By putting the code that inserts the closing and opening `<tr>` tags at the top of the loop, there must always be at least one image left. However, the first time the loop runs, the remainder is also 0, so you need to prevent the tags from being inserted until at least one image has been displayed. Phew . . . let's try it.

PHP Solution 12-3: Looping horizontally and vertically

This PHP solution shows how to control a loop to display a specific number of columns in a table. The number of columns is controlled by setting a constant. Continue working with the files from the preceding section. Alternatively, use `gallery_mysqli_05.php` or `gallery_pdo_05.php`.

1. You may decide at a later stage that you want to change the number of columns in the table, so it's a good idea to create a constant at the top of the script, where it's easy to find, rather than burying the figures deep in your code. Insert the following code just before the database connection:

```
// define number of columns in table
define('COLS', 2);
```

A **constant** is similar to a variable, except that its value cannot be changed by another part of the script. You create a constant with the `define()` function, which takes two arguments: the name of the constant and its value. By convention, constants are always in uppercase. Unlike variables, they do not begin with a dollar sign.

2. You need to initialize the cell counter outside the loop and create a variable that indicates whether it's the first row. Add the following code immediately after the constant you have just defined:

```
define('COLS', 2);
// initialize variables for the horizontal looper
$pos = 0;
$firstRow = true;
```

3. The code that keeps count of the columns goes inside the PHP block at the start of the loop. Amend the code like this:

```
<?php do {
  // set caption if thumbnail is same as main image
  if ($row['filename'] == $mainImage) {
    $caption = $row['caption'];
  }
  // if remainder is 0 and not first row, close row and start new one
  if ($pos++ % COLS === 0 && !$firstRow) {
    echo '</tr><tr>';
  }
  // once loop begins, this is no longer true
  $firstRow = false;
?>
```

Because the increment operator (++) is placed after $pos, its value is divided by the number of columns before being incremented by 1. The first time the loop runs, the remainder is 0, but

345

$firstRow is true, so the conditional statement fails. However, $firstRow is reset to false. On future iterations of the loop, the conditional statement closes the current table row and starts a new one each time the remainder is 0.

4. If there are no more records, you need to check if you have an incomplete row at the bottom of the table. Add a while loop after the existing do. . . while loop. In the MySQLi version, it looks like this:

```
<?php } while ($row = $result->fetch_assoc());
while ($pos++ % COLS) {
  echo '<td> </td>';
}
?>
```

The new code is identical in the PDO version. The only difference is that the preceding line uses $result->fetch() instead of $result->fetch_assoc().

The second loop continues incrementing $pos while $pos++ % COLS produces a remainder (which is interpreted as true) and inserting an empty cell.

This second loop is not nested inside the first. It runs only after the first loop has ended.

5. Save the page and reload it in a browser. The single row of thumbnails across the top of the gallery should now be neatly lined up two by two, as shown in Figure 12-5.

Water basin at Ryoanji temple, Kyoto

Figure 12-5. The thumbnails are now in neat columns.

6. Try changing the value of COLS and reloading the page. See how easy it is to control the number of cells in each row by changing just one number. You can check your code against gallery_mysqli_06.php, or gallery_pdo_06.php.

Paging through a long set of records

The grid of eight thumbnails fits quite comfortably in the gallery, but what if you have 28 or 48? The answer is to limit the number of results displayed on each page and build a navigation system that lets you page back and forth through the results. You've seen this technique countless times when using a search engine; now you're going to learn how to build it yourself.

The task can be broken down into the following two stages:

1. Selecting a subset of records to display

2. Creating the navigation links to page through the subsets

Both stages are relatively easy to implement, although it involves applying a little conditional logic. Keep a cool head, and you'll breeze through it.

Selecting a subset of records

Limiting the number of results on a page is simple. Add the LIMIT keyword to the SQL query like this:

```
SELECT filename, caption FROM images LIMIT startPosition, maximum
```

The LIMIT keyword can be followed by one or two numbers. If you use just one number, it sets the maximum number of records to be retrieved. That's useful, but it's not suitable for a paging system. For that, you need to use two numbers: the first indicates which record to start from, and the second stipulates the maximum number of records to be retrieved. MySQL counts records from 0, so to display the first six images, you need the following SQL:

```
SELECT filename, caption FROM images LIMIT 0, 6
```

To show the next set, the SQL needs to change to this:

```
SELECT filename, caption FROM images LIMIT 6, 6
```

There are only eight records in the images table, but the second number is only a maximum, so this retrieves records 7 and 8.

To build the navigation system, you need a way of generating these numbers. The second number never changes, so let's define a constant called SHOWMAX. Generating the first number (call it $startRecord) is pretty easy, too. Start numbering the pages from 0, and multiply the second number by the current page number. So, if you call the current page $curPage, the formula looks like this:

```
$startRecord = $curPage * SHOWMAX;
```

And for the SQL, it becomes this:

```
SELECT filename, caption FROM images LIMIT $startRecord, SHOWMAX
```

If $curPage is 0, $startRecord is also 0 (0 × 6), but when $curPage increases to 1, $startRecord changes to 6 (1 × 6), and so on.

Since there are only eight records in the images table, you need a way of finding out the total number of records to prevent the navigation system from retrieving empty result sets. In the last chapter, you used the MySQLi num_rows property and rowCount() in PDO. However, that won't work this time, because you want to know the total number of records, not how many there are in the *current* result set. The answer is to use the SQL COUNT() function like this:

```
SELECT COUNT(*) FROM images
```

When used like this in combination with an asterisk, COUNT() gets the total number of records in the table. So, to build a navigation system, you need to run both SQL queries: one to find the total number of records, and the other to retrieve the required subset. MySQL is fast, so the result is almost instantaneous.

I'll deal with the navigation links later. Let's begin by limiting the number of thumbnails on the first page.

PHP Solution 12-4: Displaying a subset of records

This PHP solution shows how to select a subset of records in preparation for creating a navigation system to page through a longer set. It also demonstrates how to display the numbers of the current selection, as well as the total number of records.

Continue working with the same file as before. Alternatively, use gallery_mysqli_06.php or gallery_pdo_06.php.

1. Define SHOWMAX and the SQL query to find the total number of records in the table. Amend the code toward the top of the page like this (new code is shown in bold):

```
// initialize variables for the horizontal looper
$pos = 0;
$firstRow = true;
// set maximum number of records
define('SHOWMAX', 6);
$conn = dbConnect('read');
// prepare SQL to get total records
$getTotal = 'SELECT COUNT(*) FROM images';
```

2. You now need to run the new SQL query. The code goes immediately after the code in the preceding step but differs according to the type of MySQL connection.

For MySQLi, use this:

```
// submit query and store result as $totalPix
$total = $conn->query($getTotal);
$row = $total->fetch_row();
$totalPix = $row[0];
```

This submits the query and then uses the fetch_row() method, which gets a single row from a MySQLi_Result object as an indexed array. There's only one column in the result, so $row[0] contains the total count of records in the images table.

For PDO, use this:

```
// submit query and store result as $totalPix
$total = $conn->query($getTotal);
$totalPix = $total->fetchColumn();
$total->closeCursor();
```

This submits the query and then uses `fetchColumn()` to get a single result, which is stored in `$totalPix`. You then need to use `closeCursor()` to free the database connection for the next query.

3. Next, set the value of `$curPage`. The navigation links that you'll create later pass the value of the required page through a query string, so you need to check whether `curPage` is in the `$_GET` array. If it is, use that value. Otherwise, set the current page to 0. Insert the following code immediately after the code in the previous step:

```
// set the current page
$curPage = isset($_GET['curPage']) ? $_GET['curPage'] : 0;
```

This uses the ternary operator (see Chapter 3). If you find the ternary operator hard to understand, use the following code instead. It has exactly the same meaning.

```
if (isset($_GET['curPage'])) {
  $curPage = $_GET['curPage'];
} else {
  $curPage = 0;
}
```

4. You now have all the information that you need to calculate the start row and to build the SQL query to retrieve a subset of records. Add the following code immediately after the code in the preceding step:

```
// calculate the start row of the subset
$startRow = $curPage * SHOWMAX;
```

5. The original SQL query should now be on the next line. Amend it like this:

```
// prepare SQL to retrieve subset of image details
$sql = "SELECT filename, caption FROM images LIMIT $startRow," . SHOWMAX;
```

Notice that I've used double quotes this time, because I want PHP to process `$startRow`. Unlike variables, constants aren't processed inside double-quoted strings. So `SHOWMAX` is added to the end of the SQL query with the concatenation operator (a period). The comma inside the closing quotes is part of the SQL, separating the two arguments of the `LIMIT` clause.

Although `$curPage` comes from user input, it's safe to use it to calculate the value of `$startRow` because it's multiplied by `SHOWMAX`, which is an integer. If the value submitted through the query string is not a number, PHP automatically converts it to 0.

6. Save the page, and reload it into a browser. Instead of eight thumbnails, you should see just six, as shown in Figure 12-6.

Water basin at Ryoanji temple, Kyoto

Figure 12-6. The number of thumbnails is limited by the SHOWMAX constant.

7.   Change the value of SHOWMAX to see a different number of thumbnails.

8.   The text above the thumbnail grid doesn't update because it's still hard-coded, so let's fix that. Locate the following line of code in the main body of the page:

```
<p id="picCount">Displaying 1 to 6 of 8</p>
```

Replace it with this:

```
<p id="picCount">Displaying <?php echo $startRow+1;
if ($startRow+1 < $totalPix) {
  echo ' to ';
  if ($startRow+SHOWMAX < $totalPix) {
    echo $startRow+SHOWMAX;
  } else {
    echo $totalPix;
  }
}
echo " of $totalPix";
?></p>
```

Let's take this line by line. The value of $startRow is zero-based, so you need to add 1 to get a more user-friendly number. So, $startRow+1 displays 1 on the first page and 7 on the second page.

In the second line, $startRow+1 is compared with the total number of records. If it's less, that means the current page is displaying a range of records, so the third line displays the text "to" with a space on either side.

You then need to work out the top number of the range, so a nested if ... else conditional statement adds the value of the start row to the maximum number of records to be shown on a page. If the result is less than the total number of records, $startRow+SHOWMAX gives you the number of the last record on the page. However, if it's equal to or greater than the total, you display $totalPix instead.

Finally, you come out of both conditional statements and display "of" followed by the total number of records.

9. Save the page, and reload it in a browser. You still get only the first subset of thumbnails, but you should see the second number change dynamically whenever you alter the value of SHOWMAX. Check your code, if necessary, against gallery_mysqli_07.php, or gallery_pdo_07.php.

Navigating through subsets of records

As I mentioned in step 3 of the preceding section, the value of the required page is passed to the PHP script through a query string. When the page first loads, there is no query string, so the value of $curPage is set to 0. Although a query string is generated when you click a thumbnail to display a different image, it includes only the filename of the main image, so the original subset of thumbnails remains unchanged. To display the next subset, you need to create a link that increases the value of $curPage by 1. It follows, therefore, that to return to the previous subset, you need another link that reduces the value of $curPage by 1.

That's simple enough, but you also need to make sure that these links are displayed only when there is a valid subset to navigate to. For instance, there's no point in displaying a back link on the first page, because there isn't a previous subset. Similarly, you shouldn't display a forward link on the page that displays the last subset, because there's nothing to navigate to.

Both issues are easily solved by using conditional statements. There's one final thing that you need to take care of. You must also include the value of the current page in the query string generated when you click a thumbnail. If you fail to do so, $curPage is automatically set back to 0, and the first set of thumbnails is displayed instead of the current subset.

PHP Solution 12-5: Creating the navigation links

This PHP solution shows how to create the navigation links to page back and forth through each subset of records. Continue working with the same file as before. Alternatively, use gallery_mysqli_07.php, or gallery_pdo_07.php.

1. I have placed the navigation links in an extra row at the bottom of the thumbnail table. Insert this code between the placeholder comment and the closing </table> tag:

```
<!-- Navigation link needs to go here -->
<tr><td>
<?php
// create a back link if current page greater than 0
if ($curPage > 0) {
  echo '<a href="' . $_SERVER['PHP_SELF'] . '?curPage=' . ($curPage-1) . ↵
    '"> &lt; Prev</a>';
} else {
// otherwise leave the cell empty
  echo ' ';
  }
?>
</td>
```

```php
<?php
// pad the final row with empty cells if more than 2 columns
if (COLS-2 > 0) {
  for ($i = 0; $i < COLS-2; $i++) {
    echo '<td> </td>';
  }
}
?>
<td>
<?php
// create a forward link if more records exist
if ($startRow+SHOWMAX < $totalPix) {
  echo '<a href="' . $_SERVER['PHP_SELF'] . '?curPage=' . ($curPage+1) . ➥
    '"> Next &gt;</a>';
} else {
  // otherwise leave the cell empty
  echo ' ';
}
?>
</td></tr>
</table>
```

It looks like a lot, but the code breaks down into three sections: the first creates a back link if $curPage is greater than 0; the second pads the final table row with empty cells if there are more than two columns; and the third uses the same formula as before ($startRow+SHOWMAX < $totalPix) to determine whether to display a forward link.

Make sure you get the combination of quotes right in the links. The other point to note is that the $curPage-1 and $curPage+1 calculations are enclosed in parentheses to avoid the period after the number being misinterpreted as a decimal point. It's used here as the concatenation operator to join the various parts of the query string.

2. You now need to add the value of the current page to the query string in the link surrounding the thumbnail. Locate this section of code:

```php
<a href="<?php echo $_SERVER['PHP_SELF']; ?>?image=<?php echo ➥
  $row['filename']; ?>">
```

Change it like this:

```php
<a href="<?php echo $_SERVER['PHP_SELF']; ?>?image=<?php echo ➥
  $row['filename']; ?>&amp;curPage=<?php echo $curPage; ?>">
```

You want the same subset to be displayed when clicking a thumbnail, so you just pass the current value of $curPage through the query string.

3. Save the page, and test it. Click the **Next** link, and you should see the remaining subset of thumbnails, as shown in Figure 12-7. There are no more images to be displayed, so the **Next** link disappears, but there's a **Prev** link at the bottom left of the thumbnail grid. The record counter at the top of the gallery now reflects the range of thumbnails being displayed, and if

you click the right thumbnail, the same subset remains onscreen while displaying the appropriate large image. You're done!

Figure 12-7. The page navigation system is now complete.

You can check your code against `gallery_mysqli_08.php`, or `gallery_pdo_08.php`.

Chapter review

Wow! In a few pages, you have turned a boring list of filenames into a dynamic online gallery, complete with a page navigation system. All that's necessary is to create a thumbnail for each major image, upload both images to the appropriate folder, and add the filename and a caption to the `images` table in the database. As long as the database is kept up to date with the contents of the `images` and `thumbs` folders, you have a dynamic gallery. Not only that, you've learned how to select subsets of records, link to related information through a query string, and build a page navigation system.

The more you use PHP, the more you realize that the skill doesn't lie so much in remembering how to use lots of obscure functions but in working out the logic needed to get PHP to do what you want. It's a question of if this, do that; if something else, do something different. Once you can anticipate the likely eventualities of a situation, you can normally build the code to handle it.

So far, you've concentrated on extracting records from a simple database table. In the next chapter, I'll show you how to insert, update, and delete material.

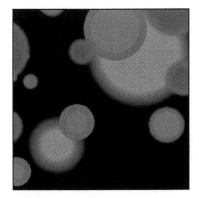

Chapter 13

Managing Content

Although you can use phpMyAdmin for a lot of database administration, you might want to set up areas where clients can log in to update some data without giving them full rein of your database. To do so, you need to build your own forms and create customized content management systems.

At the heart of every content management system lies what is sometimes called the CRUD cycle—create, read, update, and delete—which utilizes just four SQL commands: INSERT, SELECT, UPDATE, and DELETE. To demonstrate the basic SQL commands, this chapter shows you how to build a simple content management system for a table called blog.

Even if you don't want to build your own content management system, the four commands covered in this chapter are essential for just about any database-driven page, such as user login, user registration, search form, search results, and so on.

In this chapter, you'll learn how to do the following:

- Inserting new records in a database table
- Displaying a list of existing records
- Updating existing records
- Asking for confirmation before a record is deleted

Setting up a content management system

Managing the content in a database table involves four stages, which I normally assign to four separate but interlinked pages: one each for inserting, updating, and deleting records, plus a list of existing records. The list of records serves two purposes: first, to identify what's stored in the database; and more importantly, to link to the update and delete scripts by passing the record's primary key through a query string.

The blog table contains a series of titles and text articles to be displayed in the Japan Journey site, as shown in Figure 13-1. In the interests of keeping things simple, the table contains just five columns: article_id (primary key), title, article, updated, and created.

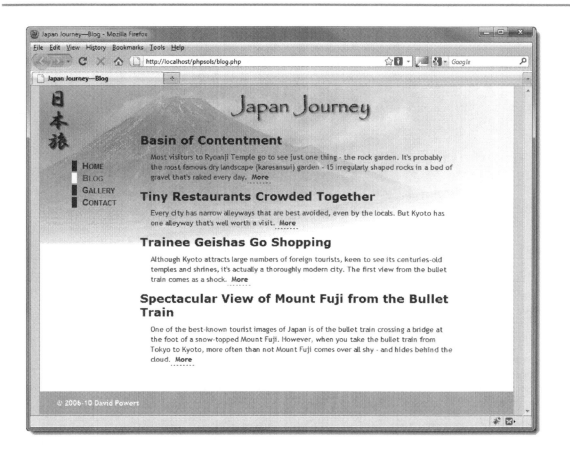

Figure 13-1. The contents of the blog table displayed in the Japan Journey website

The final two columns hold the date and time when the article was last updated and when it was originally created. Although it may seem illogical to put the updated column first, this is to take advantage of the way MySQL automatically updates the first TIMESTAMP column in a table whenever you make any changes to a record. The created column gets its value from a MySQL function called NOW(), neatly sidestepping the problem of preparing the date in the correct format for MySQL. The thorny issue of dates will be tackled in the next chapter.

Creating the blog database table

If you just want to get on with studying the content management pages, Open phpMyAdmin, select the phpsols database, and use blog.sql to import the table in the same way as in Chapter 10. The SQL file creates the table and populates it with four short articles.

If you would prefer to create everything yourself from scratch, open phpMyAdmin, select the phpsols database, and create a new table called blog with five fields (columns). Use the settings shown in the following screenshot and Table 13-1. Because there are more than three columns, phpMyAdmin displays the options horizontally. Because of the layout, the **AUTO_INCREMENT** check box is abbreviated as **A_I**.

Table 13-1. Column definitions for the blog table

Field	Type	Length/Values	Default	Attributes	Null	Index	A_I
article_id	INT			UNSIGNED	Deselected	PRIMARY	Selected
title	VARCHAR	255			Deselected		
article	TEXT				Deselected		
updated	TIMESTAMP		CURRENT_TIMESTAMP	on update CURRENT_TIMESTAMP	Deselected		
created	TIMESTAMP				Deselected		

The on update CURRENT_TIMESTAMP and CURRENT_TIMESTAMP options aren't available on older versions of phpMyAdmin and/or MySQL. This doesn't matter, because the default is for the first TIMESTAMP column in a table to update automatically whenever a record is updated. To keep track of when a record was originally created, the value in the second TIMESTAMP column is never updated.

Creating the basic insert and update form

SQL makes an important distinction between inserting and updating records by providing separate commands. INSERT is used only for creating a brand new record. Once a record has been inserted, any changes must be made with UPDATE. Since this involves working with identical fields, it is possible to use the same page for both operations. However, this makes the PHP more complex, so I prefer to create the HTML for the insert page first, save a copy as the update page, and then code them separately.

The form in the insert page needs just two input fields: for the title and the article. The contents of the remaining three columns (the primary key and the two timestamps) are handled automatically either by MySQL or by the SQL query that you will build shortly. The code for the insert form looks like this:

```
<form id="form1" method="post" action="">
  <p>
    <label for="title">Title:</label>
    <input name="title" type="text" class="widebox" id="title">
  </p>
  <p>
    <label for="article">Article:</label>
    <textarea name="article" cols="60" rows="8" class="widebox" id="article"> ↵
      </textarea>
  </p>
  <p>
    <input type="submit" name="insert" value="Insert New Entry" id="insert">
  </p>
</form>
```

The form uses the post method. You can find the full code in blog_insert_01.php in the ch13 folder. The content management forms have been given some basic styling with admin.css, which is in the styles folder. When viewed in a browser, the form looks like this:

The update form is identical except for the heading and submit button. The button looks like this (the full code is in blog_update_mysqli_01.php and blog_update_pdo_01.php):

```
<input type="submit" name="update" value="Update Entry" id="update">
```

I've given the title and article input fields the same names as the columns in the blog table. This makes it easier to keep track of variables when coding the PHP and SQL later.

> As a security measure, some developers recommend using different names from the database columns because anyone can see the names of input fields just by looking at the form's source code. Using different names makes it more difficult to break into the database. This shouldn't be a concern in a password-protected part of a site. However, you may want to consider the idea for publicly accessible forms, such as those used for user registration or login.

Inserting new records

The basic SQL for inserting new records into a table looks like this:

```
INSERT [INTO] table_name (column_names)
VALUES (values)
```

The INTO is in square brackets, which means that it's optional. It's purely there to make the SQL read a little more like human language. The column names can be in any order you like, but the values in the second set of parentheses must be in the same order as the columns they refer to.

Although the code is very similar for MySQLi and PDO, I'll deal with each one separately to avoid confusion.

> Many of the scripts in this chapter use a technique known as setting a flag. A flag is a Boolean variable that is initialized to either true or false and used to check whether something has happened. For instance, if $OK is initially set to false and reset to true only when a database query executes successfully, it can be used as the condition controlling another code block.

PHP Solution 13-1: Inserting a new record with MySQLi

This PHP solution shows how to insert a new record into the blog table using a MySQLi prepared statement. Using a prepared statement avoids problems with escaping quotes and control characters. It also protects your database against SQL injection (see Chapter 11).

1. Create a folder called admin in the phpsols site root. Copy blog_insert_01.php from the ch13 folder, and save it as blog_insert_mysqli.php in the new folder.

2. The code that inserts a new record should be run only if the form has been submitted, so it's enclosed in a conditional statement that checks for the name attribute of the submit button (insert) in the $_POST array. Put the following above the DOCTYPE declaration:

```php
<?php
if (isset($_POST['insert'])) {
    require_once('../includes/connection.inc.php');
    // initialize flag
    $OK = false;
    // create database connection
```

```
    // initialize prepared statement
    // create SQL
    // bind parameters and execute statement
    // redirect if successful or display error
}
?>
```

After including the connection function, the code sets $OK to false. This is reset to true only if there are no errors. The five comments at the end map out the remaining steps that we'll fill in below.

3. Create a connection to the database as the user with read and write privileges, initialize a prepared statement, and create the SQL with placeholders for data that will be derived from the user input like this:

```
// create database connection
$conn = dbConnect('write');
// initialize prepared statement
$stmt = $conn->stmt_init();
// create SQL
$sql = 'INSERT INTO blog (title, article, created)
        VALUES(?, ?, NOW())';
```

The values that will be derived from $_POST['title'] and $_POST['article'] are represented by question mark placeholders. The value for the created column is a MySQL function, NOW(), which generates a current timestamp. In the update query later, this column remains untouched, preserving the original date and time.

> The code is in a slightly different order from Chapter 11. The script will be developed further in Chapter 16 to run a series of SQL queries, so the prepared statement is initialized first.

4. The next stage is to replace the question marks with the values held in the variables—a process called **binding the parameters**. Insert the code the following code:

```
if ($stmt->prepare($sql)) {
  // bind parameters and execute statement
  $stmt->bind_param('ss', $_POST['title'], $_POST['article']);
  $stmt->execute();
  if ($stmt->affected_rows > 0)
    $OK = true;
  }
}
```

This is the section that protects your database from SQL injection. Pass the variables to the bind_param() method in the same order as you want them inserted into the SQL query, together with a first argument specifying the data type of each variable, again in the same order as the variables. Both are strings, so this argument is 'ss'.

Once the statement has been prepared, you call the execute() method.

The affected_rows property records how many rows were affected by an INSERT, UPDATE, or DELETE query. However, if the query triggers a MySQL error, the value of affected_rows is −1. Unlike some computing languages, PHP treats −1 as true. So, you need to check that affected_rows is greater than zero to be sure that the query succeeded. If it is greater than zero, $OK is reset to true.

5. Finally, redirect the page to a list of existing records or display any error message. Add this code after the previous step:

```
// redirect if successful or display error
if ($OK) {
    header('Location: http://localhost/phpsols/admin/blog_list_mysqli.php');
    exit;
} else {
    $error = $stmt->error;
}
}
```

6. Add the following code block in the body of the page to display the error message if the insert operation fails:

```
<h1>Insert New Blog Entry</h1>
<?php if (isset($error)) {
    echo "<p>Error: $error</p>";
} ?>
<form id="form1" method="post" action="">
```

The completed code is in blog_insert_mysqli.php in the ch13 folder.

That completes the insert page, but before testing it, create blog_list_mysqli.php, which is described in PHP Solution 13-3.

> To focus on the code that interacts with the database, the scripts in this chapter don't validate the user input. In a real-world application, you should use the techniques described in Chapter 5 to check the data submitted from the form and redisplay it if errors are detected.

PHP Solution 13-2: Inserting a new record with PDO

This PHP solution shows how to insert a new record in the blog table using a PDO prepared statement. If you haven't already done so, create a folder called admin in the phpsols site root.

1. Copy blog_insert_01.php to the admin folder and save it as blog_insert_pdo.php.

2. The code that inserts a new record should be run only if the form has been submitted, so it's enclosed in a conditional statement that checks for the name attribute of the submit button (insert) in the $_POST array. Put the following in a PHP block above the DOCTYPE declaration:

```
if (isset($_POST['insert'])) {
```

```
require_once('../includes/connection.inc.php');
// initialize flag
$OK = false;
// create database connection
// create SQL
// prepare the statement
// bind the parameters and execute the statement
// redirect if successful or display error
}
```

After including the connection function, the code sets $OK to false. This is reset to true only if there are no errors. The five comments at the end map out the remaining steps.

3. Create a PDO connection to the database as the user with read and write privileges, and build the SQL like this:

```
// create database connection
$conn = dbConnect('write', 'pdo');
// create SQL
$sql = 'INSERT INTO blog (title, article, created)
        VALUES(:title, :article, NOW())';
```

The values that will be derived from variables are represented by named placeholders consisting of the column name preceded by a colon (:title and :article). The value for the created column is a MySQL function, NOW(), which generates a current timestamp. In the update query later, this column remains untouched, preserving the original date and time.

4. The next stage is to initialize the prepared statement and bind the values from the variables to the placeholders—a process known as **binding the parameters**. Add the following code:

```
// prepare the statement
$stmt = $conn->prepare($sql);
// bind the parameters and execute the statement
$stmt->bindParam(':title', $_POST['title'], PDO::PARAM_STR);
$stmt->bindParam(':article', $_POST['article'], PDO::PARAM_STR);
// execute and get number of affected rows
$stmt->execute();
$OK = $stmt->rowCount();
```

This begins by passing the SQL query to the prepare() method of the database connection ($conn) and storing a reference to the statement as a variable ($stmt).

Next, the values in the variables are bound to the placeholders in the prepared statement, and the execute() method runs the query.

When used with an INSERT, UPDATE, or DELETE query, the PDO rowCount() method reports the number of rows affected by the query. If the record is inserted successfully, $OK is 1, which PHP treats as true. Otherwise, it's 0, which is treated as false.

5. Finally, redirect the page to a list of existing records or display any error message. Add this code after the previous step:

```
      // redirect if successful or display error
      if ($OK) {
        header('Location: http://localhost/phpsols/admin/blog_list_pdo.php');
        exit;
      } else {
        $error = $stmt->errorInfo();
        if (isset($error[2])) {
          $error = $error[2];
        }
      }
    }
    ?>
```

Since the prepared statement has been stored as $stmt, you can access an array of error messages using $stmt->errorInfo(). The most useful information is stored in the third element of the array.

6. Add a PHP code block in the body of the page to display any error message:

```
<h1>Insert New Blog Entry</h1>
<?php if (isset($error)) {
  echo "<p>Error: $error</p>";
} ?>
<form id="form1" method="post" action="">
```

The completed code is in blog_insert_pdo.php in the ch13 folder.

That completes the insert page, but before testing it, create blog_list_pdo.php, which is described next.

Linking to the update and delete pages

Before you can update or delete a record, you need to find its primary key. A practical way of doing this is to query the database and display a list of all records. You can use the results of this query to display a list of all records, complete with links to the update and delete pages. By adding the value of article_id to a query string in each link, you automatically identify the record to be updated or deleted. As Figure 13-2 shows, the URL displayed in the browser status bar (bottom left) identifies the article_id of the article **Tiny Restaurants Crowded Together** as 3.

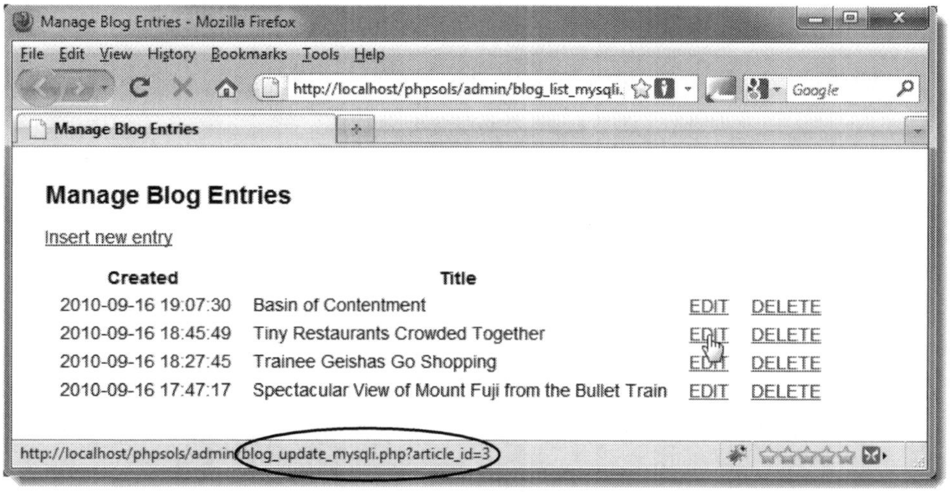

Figure 13-2. The **EDIT** and **DELETE** links contain the record's primary key in a query string.

The update page uses this to display the correct record ready for updating. The same information is conveyed in the DELETE link to the delete page.

To create a list like this, you need to start with an HTML table that contains two rows and as many columns as you want to display, plus two extra columns for the **EDIT** and **DELETE** links. The first row is used for column headings. The second row is wrapped in a PHP loop to display all the results. The table in blog_list_mysqli_01.php in the ch13 folder looks like this (the version in blog_list_pdo_01.php is the same, except that the links in the last two table cells point to the PDO versions of the update and delete pages):

```
<table>
  <tr>
    <th scope="col">Created</th>
    <th scope="col">Title</th>
    <th> </th>
    <th> </th>
  </tr>
  <tr>
    <td></td>
    <td></td>
    <td><a href="blog_update_mysqli.php">EDIT</a></td>
    <td><a href="blog_delete_mysqli.php">DELETE</a></td>
  </tr>
</table>
```

PHP Solution 13-3: Creating the links to the update and delete pages

This PHP solution shows how to create a page to manage the records in the blog table by displaying a list of all records and linking to the update and delete pages. There are only minor differences between the MySQLi and PDO versions, so these instructions describe both.

1. Copy blog_list_mysqli_01.php or blog_list_pdo_01.php to the admin folder, and save it as blog_list_mysqli.php or blog_list_pdo.php depending on which method of connection you plan to use. The different versions link to the appropriate insert, update, and delete files.

2. You need to connect to MySQL and create the SQL query. Add the following code in a PHP block above the DOCTYPE declaration:

```
require_once('../includes/connection.inc.php');
// create database connection
$conn = dbConnect('read');
$sql = 'SELECT * FROM blog ORDER BY created DESC';
```

   If you're using PDO, add 'pdo' as the second argument to the dbConnect() function.

   If you're using PDO, skip to step 4.

3. If you're using MySQLi, submit the query by adding the following line before the closing PHP tag:

```
$result = $conn->query($sql) or die(mysqli_error());
```

4. You now need to enclose the second table row in a loop and retrieve each record from the result set. The following code goes between the closing </tr> tag of the first row and the opening <tr> tag of the second row.

   For MySQLi, use this:

```
</tr>
<?php while($row = $result->fetch_assoc()) { ?>
<tr>
```

   For PDO, use this:

```
</tr>
<?php foreach ($conn->query($sql) as $row) { ?>
<tr>
```

   This is the same as in the previous chapter, so it should need no explanation.

5. Display the created and title fields for the current record in the first two cells of the second row like this:

```
<td><?php echo $row['created']; ?></td>
<td><?php echo $row['title']; ?></td>
```

6. In the next two cells, add the query string and value of the `article_id` field for the current record to both URLs like this (although the links are different, the highlighted code is the same for the PDO version):

```
<td><a href="blog_update_mysqli.php?article_id=<?php echo ➥
  $row['article_id']; ?>">EDIT</a></td>
<td><a href="blog_delete_mysqli.php?article_id=<?php echo ➥
  $row['article_id']; ?>">DELETE</a></td>
```

What you're doing here is adding `?article_id=` to the URL and then using PHP to display the value of `$row['article_id']`. It's important that you don't leave any spaces that might break the URL or the query string. A common mistake is to leave spaces around the equal sign. After the PHP has been processed, the opening `<a>` tag should look like this when viewing the page's source code in a browser (although the number will vary according to the record):

```
<a href="blog_update_mysqli.php?article_id=2">
```

7. Finally, close the loop surrounding the second table row with a curly brace like this:

```
  </tr>
  <?php } ?>
</table>
```

8. Save `blog_list_mysqli.php` or `blog_list_pdo.php`, and load the page into a browser. Assuming that you loaded the contents of `blog.sql` into the `phpsols` database earlier, you should see a list of four items, as shown in Figure 13-2. You can now test `blog_insert_mysqli.php` or `blog_insert_pdo.php`. After inserting an item, you should be returned to the appropriate version of `blog_list.php`, and the date and time of creation, together with the title of the new item, should be displayed at the top of the list. Check your code against the versions in the `ch13` folder if you encounter any problems.

> The code assumes that there will always be some records in the table. As an exercise, use the technique in PHP Solution 11-2 (MySQLi) or 11-3 (PDO) to count the number of results, and use a conditional statement to display a suitable message if no records are found. The solution is in `blog_list_norec_mysqli.php` and `blog_list_norec_pdo.php`.

Updating records

An update page needs to perform two separate processes, as follows:

1. Retrieve the selected record, and display it ready for editing

2. Update the edited record in the database

The first stage uses the primary key passed in the URL query string to select the record and display it in the update form, as shown in Figure 13-3.

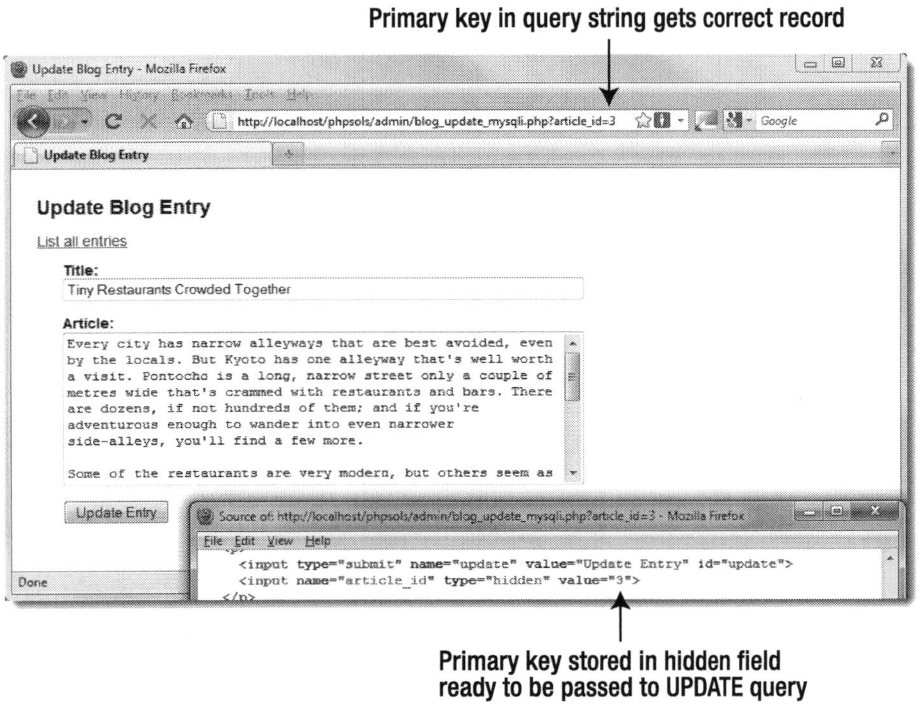

Primary key in query string gets correct record

Primary key stored in hidden field
ready to be passed to UPDATE query

Figure 13-3. The primary key keeps track of a record during the update process.

The primary key is stored in a hidden field in the update form. After you have edited the record in the update page, you submit the form and pass all the details, including the primary key, to an UPDATE command.

The basic syntax of the SQL UPDATE command looks like this:

```
UPDATE table_name SET column_name = value, column_name = value
WHERE condition
```

The condition when updating a specific record is the primary key. So, when updating article_id 3 in the blog table, the basic UPDATE query looks like this:

```
UPDATE blog SET title = value, article = value
WHERE article_id = 3
```

Although the basic principle is the same for both methods of connecting to MySQL, the code differs sufficiently to warrant separate instructions.

PHP Solution 13-4: Updating a record with MySQLi

This PHP solution shows how to load an existing record into the update form and then send the edited details to the database for updating using MySQLi. To load the record, you need to have created the management page that lists all records, as described in PHP Solution 13-3.

1. Copy `blog_update_mysqli_01.php` from the `ch13` folder, and save it in the `admin` folder as `blog_update_mysqli.php`.

2. The first stage involves retrieving the details of the record that you want to update. Put the following code in a PHP block above the DOCTYPE declaration:

```php
require_once('../includes/connection.inc.php');
// initialize flags
$OK = false;
$done = false;
// create database connection
$conn = dbConnect('write');
// initialize statement
$stmt = $conn->stmt_init();
// get details of selected record
if (isset($_GET['article_id']) && !$_POST) {
  // prepare SQL query
  $sql = 'SELECT article_id, title, article
          FROM blog WHERE article_id = ?';
  if ($stmt->prepare($sql)) {
    // bind the query parameter
    $stmt->bind_param('i', $_GET['article_id']);
    // bind the results to variables
    $stmt->bind_result($article_id, $title, $article);
    // execute the query, and fetch the result
    $OK = $stmt->execute();
    $stmt->fetch();
  }
}
// redirect if $_GET['article_id'] not defined
if (!isset($_GET['article_id'])) {
  header('Location: http://localhost/phpsols/admin/blog_list_mysqli.php');
  exit;
}
// display error message if query fails
if (isset($stmt) && !$OK && !$done) {
  $error = $stmt->error;
}
```

Although this is very similar to the code used for the insert page, the first few lines are *outside* the conditional statements. Both stages of the update process require the database connection and a prepared statement, so this avoids the need to duplicate the same code later. Two flags are initialized: $OK to check the success of retrieving the record, and $done to check whether the update succeeds.

The first conditional statement makes sure that $_GET['article_id'] exists and that the $_POST array is empty. So the code inside the braces is executed only when the query string is set, but the form hasn't been submitted.

You prepare the SELECT query in the same way as for an INSERT command, using a question mark as a placeholder for the variable. However, note that instead of using an asterisk to retrieve all columns, the query specifies three columns by name like this:

```
$sql = 'SELECT article_id, title, article
        FROM blog WHERE article_id = ?';
```

This is because a MySQLi prepared statement lets you bind the result of a SELECT query to variables, and to be able to do this, you must specify the column names and the order you want them to be in.

First, you need to initialize the prepared statement and bind $_GET['article_id'] to the query with $stmt->bind_param(). Because the value of article_id must be an integer, you pass 'i' as the first argument.

The next line binds the result to variables in the same order as the columns specified in the SELECT query.

```
$stmt->bind_result($article_id, $title, $article);
```

You can call the variables whatever you like, but it makes sense to use the same names as the columns. Binding the result like this avoids the necessity to use array names, such as $row['article_id'], later on.

Then the code executes the query and fetches the result.

The next conditional statement redirects the page to blog_list_mysqli.php if $_GET['article_id'] hasn't been defined. This prevents anyone from trying to load the update page directly in a browser.

The final conditional statement stores an error message if the prepared statement has been created, but both $OK and $done remain false. You haven't added the update script yet, but if the record is retrieved or updated successfully, one of them will be switched to true. So if both remain false, you know there was something wrong with one of the SQL queries.

3. Now that you have retrieved the contents of the record, you need to display them in the update form by using PHP to populate the value attribute of each input field. If the prepared statement succeeded, $article_id should contain the primary key of the record to be updated, because it's one of the variables you bound to the result set with the bind_result() method.

However, if there's an error, you need to display the message onscreen. But if someone alters the query string to an invalid number, $article_id will be set to 0, so there is no point in displaying the update form. Add the following conditional statements immediately before the opening <form> tag:

```
<p><a href="blog_list_mysqli.php">List all entries </a></p>
<?php if (isset($error)) {
  echo "<p class='warning'>Error: $error</p>";
}
if($article_id == 0) { ?>
```

```
<p class="warning">Invalid request: record does not exist.</p>
<?php } else { ?>
<form id="form1" name="form1" method="post" action="">
```

The first conditional statement displays any error message reported by the MySQLi prepared statement. The second wraps the update form in an else clause, so the form will be hidden if $article_id is 0.

4. Add the closing curly brace of the else clause immediately after the closing </form> tag like this:

```
</form>
<?php } ?>
</body>
```

5. If $article_id is not 0, you know that $title and $article also contain valid values and can be displayed in the update form without further testing. However, you need to pass text values to htmlentities() to avoid problems with displaying quotes. Display $title in the value attribute of the title input field like this:

```
<input name="title" type="text" class="widebox" id="title" ➥
  value="<?php echo htmlentities($title, ENT_COMPAT, 'utf-8'); ?>">
```

6. Do the same for the article text area. Because text areas don't have a value attribute, the code goes between the opening and closing <textarea> tags like this:

```
<textarea name="article" cols="60" rows="8" class="widebox" id="article"> ➥
  <?php echo htmlentities($article, ENT_COMPAT, 'utf-8'); ?></textarea>
```

Make sure there is no space between the opening and closing PHP and <textarea> tags. Otherwise, you'll get unwanted spaces in your updated record.

7. The UPDATE command needs to know the primary key of the record you want to change. You need to store the primary key in a hidden field so that it is submitted in the $_POST array with the other details. Because hidden fields are not displayed onscreen, the following code can go anywhere inside the form:

```
<input name="article_id" type="hidden" value="<?php echo $article_id; ?>">
```

8. Save the update page, and test it by loading blog_list_mysqli.php into a browser and selecting the **EDIT** link for one of the records. The contents of the record should be displayed in the form fields as shown in Figure 13-3.

The **Update Entry** button doesn't do anything yet. Just make sure that everything is displayed correctly, and confirm that the primary key is registered in the hidden field. You can check your code, if necessary, against blog_update_mysqli_02.php.

9. The name attribute of the submit button is update, so all the update processing code needs to go in a conditional statement that checks for the presence of update in the $_POST array. Place the following code highlighted in bold immediately above the code in step 1 that redirects the page:

```
      $stmt->fetch();
    }
  }
  // if form has been submitted, update record
  if (isset($_POST ['update'])) {
    // prepare update query
    $sql = 'UPDATE blog SET title = ?, article = ?
            WHERE article_id = ?';
    if ($stmt->prepare($sql)) {
      $stmt->bind_param('ssi', $_POST['title'], $_POST['article'], ➥
        $_POST['article_id']);
      $done = $stmt->execute();
    }
  }
  // redirect page on success or if $_GET['article_id']) not defined
  if ($done || !isset($_GET['article_id'])) {
```

The UPDATE query is prepared with question mark placeholders where values are to be supplied from variables. The prepared statement has already been initialized in the code outside the conditional statement, so you can pass the SQL to the prepare() method and bind the variables with $stmt->bind_param(). The first two variables are strings, and the third is an integer, so the first argument is 'ssi'.

If the UPDATE query succeeds, the execute() method returns true, resetting the value of $done. Unlike an INSERT query, using the affected_rows property has little meaning because it returns zero if the user decides to click the **Update Entry** button without making any changes, so we won't use it here. You need to add $done || to the condition in the redirect script. This ensures that the page is redirected either if the update succeeds or if someone tries to access the page directly.

10. Save blog_update_mysqli.php, and test it by loading blog_list_mysqli.php, selecting one of the **EDIT** links, and making changes to the record that is displayed. When you click **Update Entry**, you should be taken back to blog_list_mysqli.php. You can verify that your changes were made by clicking the same **EDIT** link again. Check your code, if necessary, with blog_update_mysqli_03.php.

PHP Solution 13-5: Updating a record with PDO

This PHP solution shows how to load an existing record into the update form and then send the edited details to the database for updating using PDO. To load the record, you need to have created the management page that lists all records, as described in PHP Solution 13-3.

1. Copy blog_update_pdo_01.php from the ch13 folder, and save it in the admin folder as blog_update_pdo.php.

2. The first stage involves retrieving the details of the record that you want to update. Put the following code in a PHP block above the DOCTYPE declaration:

```
require_once('../includes/connection.inc.php');
// initialize flags
```

```
$OK = false;
$done = false;
// create database connection
$conn = dbConnect('write', 'pdo');
// get details of selected record
if (isset($_GET['article_id']) && !$_POST) {
  // prepare SQL query
  $sql = 'SELECT article_id, title, article FROM blog
          WHERE article_id = ?';
  $stmt = $conn->prepare($sql);
  // bind the results
  $stmt->bindColumn(1, $article_id);
  $stmt->bindColumn(2, $title);
  $stmt->bindColumn(3, $article);
  // execute query by passing array of variables
  $OK = $stmt->execute(array($_GET['article_id']));
  $stmt->fetch();
}
// redirect if $_GET['article_id'] not defined
if (!isset($_GET['article_id'])) {
  header('Location: http://localhost/phpsols/admin/blog_list_pdo.php');
  exit;
}
// store error message if query fails
if (isset($stmt) && !$OK && !$done) {
  $error = $stmt->errorInfo();
  if (isset($error[2])) {
    $error = $error[2];
  }
}
```

Although this is very similar to the code used for the insert page, the first few lines are *outside* the first conditional statement. Both stages of the update process require the database connection, so this avoids the need to duplicate the same code later. Two flags are initialized: $OK to check the success of retrieving the record and $done to check whether the update succeeds.

The first conditional statement checks that $_GET ['article_id'] exists and that the $_POST array is empty. This makes sure that the code inside is executed only when the query string is set, but the form hasn't been submitted.

When preparing the SQL query for the insert form, you used named placeholders for the variables. This time, let's use a question mark like this:

```
$sql = 'SELECT article_id, title, article FROM blog
        WHERE article_id = ?';
```

The results are then bound to $article_id, $title, and $article with the bindColumn() method. This time, I have used numbers (counting from 1) to indicate which column to bind each variable to.

When using question marks as placeholders, you pass the variables directly as an array to $stmt->execute() like this:

```
$OK = $stmt->execute(array($_GET['article_id']));
```

Even though there is only one variable this time, it must still be presented as an array. There's only one record to fetch in the result, so the fetch() method is called immediately.

The next conditional statement redirects the page to blog_list_pdo.php if $_GET['article_id'] hasn't been defined. This prevents anyone from trying to load the update page directly in a browser.

The final conditional statement stores an error message if the prepared statement has been created, but both $OK and $done remain false. You haven't added the update script yet, but if the record is retrieved or updated successfully, one of them will be switched to true. So if both remain false, you know there was something wrong with one of the SQL queries.

3. Now that you have retrieved the contents of the record, you need to display them in the update form by using PHP to populate the value attribute of each input field. If the prepared statement succeeded, $article_id should contain the primary key of the record to be updated, because it's one of the variables you bound to the result set with the bindColumn() method.

However, if there's an error, you need to display the message onscreen. But if someone alters the query string to an invalid number, $article_id will be set to 0, so there is no point in displaying the update form. Add the following conditional statements immediately before the opening <form> tag:

```
<p><a href="blog_list_pdo.php">List all entries </a></p>
<?php if (isset($error)) {
  echo "<p class='warning'>Error: $error</p>";
}
if($article_id == 0) { ?>
  <p class="warning">Invalid request: record does not exist.</p>
<?php } else { ?>
<form id="form1" name="form1" method="post" action="">
```

The first conditional statement displays any error message reported by the PDO prepared statement. The second wraps the update form in an else clause, so the form will be hidden if $article_id is 0.

4. Add the closing curly brace of the else clause immediately after the closing </form> tag like this:

```
</form>
<?php } ?>
</body>
```

5. If $article_id is not 0, you know that $title and $article also exist and can be displayed in the update form without further testing. However, you need to pass text values to htmlentities() to avoid problems with displaying quotes. Display $title in the value attribute of the title input field like this:

```
<input name="title" type="text" class="widebox" id="title" ➥
  value="<?php echo htmlentities($title, ENT_COMPAT, 'utf-8'); ?>">
```

6. Do the same for the article text area. Because text areas don't have a value attribute, the code goes between the opening and closing <textarea> tags like this:

```
<textarea name="article" cols="60" rows="8" class="widebox" id="article"> ➥
  <?php echo htmlentities($article, ENT_COMPAT, 'utf-8'); ?></textarea>
```

Make sure there is no space between the opening and closing PHP and <textarea> tags. Otherwise, you will get unwanted spaces in your updated record.

7. The UPDATE command needs to know the primary key of the record you want to change. You need to store the primary key in a hidden field so that it is submitted in the $_POST array with the other details. Because hidden fields are not displayed onscreen, the following code can go anywhere inside the form:

```
<input name="article_id" type="hidden" value="<?php echo $article_id; ?>">
```

8. Save the update page, and test it by loading blog_list_pdo.php into a browser and selecting the **EDIT** link for one of the records. The contents of the record should be displayed in the form fields as shown in Figure 13-3.

The **Update Entry** button doesn't do anything yet. Just make sure that everything is displayed correctly, and confirm that the primary key is registered in the hidden field. You can check your code, if necessary, against blog_update_pdo_02.php.

9. The name attribute of the submit button is update, so all the update processing code needs to go in a conditional statement that checks for the presence of update in the $_POST array. Place the following code highlighted in bold immediately above the code in step 1 that redirects the page:

```
  $stmt->fetch();
}
// if form has been submitted, update record
if (isset($_POST['update'])) {
  // prepare update query
  $sql = 'UPDATE blog SET title = ?, article = ?
        WHERE article_id = ?';
  $stmt = $conn->prepare($sql);
  // execute query by passing array of variables
  $stmt->execute(array($_POST['title'], $_POST['article'], ➥
    $_POST['article_id']));
  $done = $stmt->rowCount();
}
// redirect page on success or $_GET['article_id'] not defined
```

```
if ($done || !isset($_GET['article_id'])) {
```

Again, the SQL query is prepared using question marks as placeholders for values to be derived from variables. This time, there are three placeholders, so the corresponding variables need to be passed as an array to $stmt->execute(). Needless to say, the array must be in the same order as the placeholders.

10. If the UPDATE query succeeds, the rowCount() method sets $done to 1, which is treated as true. You'll notice we have added $done || to the condition in the redirect script. This ensures that the page is redirected either if the update succeeds or if someone tries to access the page directly.

11. Save blog_update_pdo.php, and test it by loading blog_list_pdo.php, selecting one of the **EDIT** links, and making changes to the record that is displayed. When you click **Update Entry**, you should be taken back to blog_list_pdo.php. You can verify that your changes were made by clicking the same **EDIT** link again. Check your code, if necessary, with blog_update_pdo_03.php.

Deleting records

Deleting a record in a database is similar to updating one. The basic DELETE command looks like this:

```
DELETE FROM table_name WHERE condition
```

What makes the DELETE command potentially dangerous is that it is final. Once you have deleted a record, there's no going back—it's gone forever. There's no Recycle Bin or Trash to fish it out from. Even worse, the WHERE clause is optional. If you omit it, every single record in the table is irrevocably sent into cyber-oblivion. Consequently, it's a good idea to display details of the record to be deleted and ask the user to confirm or cancel the process (see Figure 13-4).

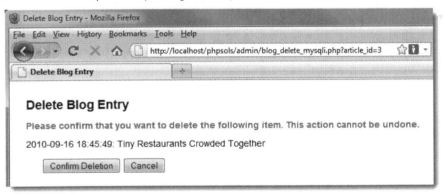

Figure 13-4. Deleting a record is irreversible, so get confirmation before going ahead.

Building and scripting the delete page is almost identical to the update page, so I won't give step-by-step instructions. However, here are the main points:

- Retrieve the details of the selected record.

- Display sufficient details, such as the title, for the user to confirm that the correct record has been selected.
- Give the **Confirm Deletion** and **Cancel** buttons different `name` attributes, and use each `name` attribute with `isset()` to control the action taken.
- Instead of wrapping the entire form in the `else` clause, use conditional statements to hide the **Confirm Deletion** button and the hidden field.

The code that performs the deletion for each method follows.

For MySQLi:

```
if (isset($_POST['delete'])) {
  $sql = 'DELETE FROM blog WHERE article_id = ?';
  if ($stmt->prepare($sql)) {
    $stmt->bind_param('i', $_POST['article_id']);
    $stmt->execute();
    if ($stmt->affected_rows > 0) {;
      $deleted = true;
    } else {
      $error = 'There was a problem deleting the record.';
    }
  }
}
```

For PDO:

```
if (isset($_POST['delete'])) {
  $sql = 'DELETE FROM blog WHERE article_id = ?';
  $stmt = $conn->prepare($sql);
  $stmt->execute(array($_POST['article_id']));
  // get number of affected rows
  $deleted = $stmt->rowCount();
  if (!$deleted) {
    $error = 'There was a problem deleting the record.';
  }
}
```

You can find the finished code in `blog_delete_mysqli.php` and `blog_delete_pdo.php` in the `ch13` folder. To test the delete script, copy the appropriate file to the `admin` folder.

Reviewing the four essential SQL commands

Now that you have seen `SELECT`, `INSERT`, `UPDATE`, and `DELETE` in action, let's review the basic syntax. This is not an exhaustive listing, but it concentrates on the most important options, including some that have not yet been covered. I have used the same typographic conventions as the MySQL online manual at `http://dev.mysql.com/doc/refman/5.1/en` (which you may also want to consult):

- Anything in uppercase is a SQL command.
- Expressions in square brackets are optional.

- Lowercase italics represent variable input.
- A vertical pipe (|) separates alternatives.

Although some expressions are optional, they must appear in the order listed. For example, in a SELECT query, WHERE, ORDER BY, and LIMIT are all optional, but LIMIT can never come before WHERE or ORDER BY.

SELECT

SELECT is used for retrieving records from one or more tables. Its basic syntax is as follows:

```
SELECT [DISTINCT] select_list
FROM table_list
[WHERE where_expression]
[ORDER BY col_name | formula] [ASC | DESC]
[LIMIT [skip_count,] show_count]
```

The DISTINCT option tells the database you want to eliminate duplicate rows from the results.

The *select_list* is a comma-separated list of columns that you want included in the result. To retrieve all columns, use an asterisk (*). If the same column name is used in more than one table, you must use unambiguous references by using the syntax *table_name.column_name*. Chapter 15 explains in detail about working with multiple tables.

The *table_list* is a comma-separated list of tables from which the results are to be drawn. All tables that you want to be included in the results *must* be listed.

The WHERE clause specifies search criteria, for example:

```
WHERE quotations.family_name = authors.family_name
WHERE article_id = 2
```

WHERE expressions can use comparison, arithmetic, logical, and pattern-matching operators. The most important ones are listed in Table 13-2.

Table 13-2. The main operators used in MySQL WHERE expressions

Comparison		Arithmetic	
<	Less than	+	Addition
<=	Less than or equal to	-	Subtraction
=	Equal to	*	Multiplication
!=	Not equal to	/	Division
<>	Not equal to	DIV	Integer division
>	Greater than	%	Modulo

Comparison		Arithmetic	
`>=`	Greater than or equal to		
`IN()`	Included in list		
`BETWEEN` *min* `AND` *max*	Between (and including two values)		

Logical		Pattern matching	
`AND`	Logical and	`LIKE`	Case-insensitive match
`&&`	Logical and	`NOT LIKE`	Case-insensitive nonmatch
`OR`	Logical or	`LIKE BINARY`	Case-sensitive match
`||`	Logical or (best avoided)	`NOT LIKE BINARY`	Case-sensitive nonmatch

Of the two operators that mean "not equal to," `<>` is standard SQL. Not all databases support `!=`.

`DIV` is the counterpart of the modulo operator. It produces the result of division as an integer with no fractional part, whereas modulo produces only the remainder.

```
5 / 2       /* result 2.5 */
5 DIV 2     /* result 2   */
5 % 2       /* result 1   */
```

I suggest you avoid using `||` because it's actually used as the string concatenation operator in standard SQL. By not using it with MySQL, you avoid confusion if you ever work with a different relational database. To join strings, MySQL uses the `CONCAT()` function (see `http://dev.mysql.com/doc/refman/5.1/en/string-functions.html#function_concat`).

`IN()` evaluates a comma-separated list of values inside the parentheses and returns `true` if one or more of the values is found. Although `BETWEEN` is normally used with numbers, it also applies to strings. For instance, `BETWEEN 'a' AND 'd'` returns true for *a, b, c,* and *d* (but not their uppercase equivalents). Both `IN()` and `BETWEEN` can be preceded by `NOT` to perform the opposite comparison.

`LIKE`, `NOT LIKE`, and the related `BINARY` operators are used for text searches in combination with the following two wildcard characters:

- `%`: matches any sequence of characters or none.
- `_` (an underscore): matches exactly one character.

So, the following WHERE clause matches Dennis, Denise, and so on, but not Aiden:

WHERE first_name LIKE 'den%'

To match Aiden, put % at the front of the search pattern. Because % matches any sequence of characters or none, '%den%' still matches Dennis and Denise. To search for a literal percentage sign or underscore, precede it with a backslash (\% or _).

> This explains why some drop-down menus in phpMyAdmin insert a backslash in names that contain an underscore. phpMyAdmin uses the value directly in a SQL query with LIKE.

Conditions are evaluated from left to right but can be grouped in parentheses if you want a particular set of conditions to be considered together.

ORDER BY specifies the sort order of the results. This can be specified as a single column, a comma-separated list of columns, or an expression such as RAND(), which randomizes the order. The default sort order is ascending (a–z, 0–9), but you can specify DESC (descending) to reverse the order.

LIMIT followed by one number stipulates the maximum number of records to return. If two numbers are given separated by a comma, the first tells the database how many rows to skip (see "Selecting a subset of records" in Chapter 12).

For more details on SELECT, see http://dev.mysql.com/doc/refman/5.1/en/select.html.

INSERT

The INSERT command is used to add new records to a database. The general syntax is as follows:

INSERT [INTO] table_name (column_names)
VALUES (values)

The word INTO is optional; it simply makes the command read a little more like human language. The column names and values are comma-delimited lists, and both must be in the same order. So, to insert the forecast for New York (blizzard), Detroit (smog), and Honolulu (sunny) into a weather database, this is how you would do it:

INSERT INTO forecast (new_york, detroit, honolulu)
VALUES ('blizzard', 'smog', 'sunny')

The reason for this rather strange syntax is to allow you to insert more than one record at a time. Each subsequent record is in a separate set of parentheses, with each set separated by a comma:

INSERT numbers (x,y)
VALUES (10,20),(20,30),(30,40),(40,50)

You'll use this multiple insert syntax in Chapter 16. Any columns omitted from an INSERT query are set to their default value. *Never set an explicit value for the primary key where the column is set to auto_increment; leave the column name out of the INSERT statement.* For more details, see http://dev.mysql.com/doc/refman/5.1/en/insert.html.

UPDATE

This command is used to change existing records. The basic syntax looks like this:

```
UPDATE table_name
SET col_name = value [, col_name = value]
[WHERE where_expression]
```

The WHERE expression tells MySQL which record or records you want to update (or perhaps in the case of the following example, dream about):

```
UPDATE sales SET q1_2011 = 25000
WHERE title = 'PHP Solutions, Second Edition'
```

For more details on UPDATE, see http://dev.mysql.com/doc/refman/5.1/en/update.html.

DELETE

DELETE can be used to delete single records, multiple records, or the entire contents of a table. The general syntax for deleting from a single table is as follows:

```
DELETE FROM table_name [WHERE where_expression]
```

Although phpMyAdmin prompts you for confirmation before deleting a record, MySQL itself takes you at your word and performs the deletion immediately. DELETE is totally unforgiving—once the data is deleted, it is gone *forever*. The following query will delete all records from a table called subscribers where the date in expiry_date has already passed:

```
DELETE FROM subscribers
WHERE expiry_date < NOW()
```

For more details, see http://dev.mysql.com/doc/refman/5.1/en/delete.html.

> Although the WHERE clause is optional in both UPDATE and DELETE, you should be aware that if you leave WHERE out, the entire table is affected. This means that a careless slip with either of these commands could result in every single record being identical—or wiped out.

Security and error messages

When developing a website with PHP and MySQL, it's essential to display error messages so that you can debug your code if anything goes wrong. However, raw error messages look unprofessional in a live website. They can also reveal clues about your database structure to potential attackers. Therefore, before deploying your scripts live on the Internet, you should go through them, removing all instances of mysqli_error() (MySQLi) or $error = $error[2] (PDO).

The simplest way to handle this is to replace the MySQL error messages with a neutral message of your own, such as "Sorry, the database is unavailable." A more professional way is to replace or die() routines with an if... else conditional statement, and to use the error control operator (@) to suppress the display of error messages. For example, you may have the following line in a current script:

```
$result = $conn->query($sql) or die(mysqli_error());
```

You can rewrite it like this:

```
$result = @ $conn->query($sql);
if (!$result) {
    // redirect to custom error page
}
```

You should also remove the conditional statements surrounding MySQLi prepared statements once you have verified that they don't generate SQL syntax errors. For example, your development code might look like this:

```
if ($stmt->prepare($sql)) {
  $stmt->bind_param('s', $searchterm);
  $stmt->bind_result($image_id, $filename, $caption);
  $stmt->execute();
  $stmt->store_result();
  $numRows = $stmt->num_rows;
} else {
  echo $stmt->error;
}
```

To deploy it on a live website, change it to this:

```
$stmt->prepare($sql);
$stmt->bind_param('s', $searchterm);
$stmt->bind_result($image_id, $filename, $caption);
$stmt->execute();
$stmt->store_result();
$numRows = $stmt->num_rows;
```

Chapter review

Content management with a database involves inserting, selecting, updating, and deleting records. Each record's primary key plays a vital role in the update and delete processes. Most of the time, generating the primary key is handled automatically by MySQL when a record is first created. Thereafter, finding a record's primary key is simply a matter of using a `SELECT` query, either by displaying a list of all records, or by searching for something you know about the record, such as a title or words in an article.

MySQLi and PDO prepared statements make database queries more secure by removing the need to ensure that quotes and control characters are properly escaped. They also speed up your application if the same query needs to be repeated during a script using different variables. Instead of validating the SQL every time, the script needs do it only once with the placeholders.

Although this chapter has concentrated on content management, the same basic techniques apply to most interaction with a database. Of course, there's a lot more to SQL—and to PHP. In the next chapter, I'll address some of the most common problems, such as displaying only the first sentence or so of a long text field and handling dates. Then, in Chapter 15 and 16, we'll explore working with more than one table in a database.

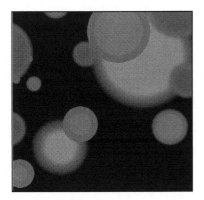

Chapter 14

Formatting Text and Dates

We have some unfinished business left over from the previous chapter. Figure 13-1 in Chapter 13 shows content from the blog table with just the first two sentences of each article displayed and a link to the rest of the article. However, I didn't show you how it was done. There are several ways to extract a shorter piece of text from the beginning of a longer one. Some are rather crude and usually leave you with a broken word at the end. In this chapter, you'll learn how to extract complete sentences.

The other piece of unfinished business is that full list of articles in blog_list_mysqli.php and blog_list_pdo.php displays the MySQL timestamp in its raw state, which isn't very elegant. You need to reformat the date to look user friendlier. Handling dates can be a major headache because MySQL and PHP use completely different methods of storing them. This chapter guides you through the minefield of storing and displaying dates in a PHP/MySQL context. You'll also learn about the powerful new date and time features introduced in PHP 5.2 and 5.3, which make complex date calculations, such as finding the second Tuesday of each month, child's play.

In this chapter, you'll learn about the following:

- Extracting the first section of a longer text item
- Using an alias in a SQL query
- Displaying text retrieved from a database as paragraphs
- Formatting dates with MySQL
- Selecting records based on temporal criteria
- Using the PHP DateTime, DateTimeZone, DateInterval, and DatePeriod classes

Displaying a text extract

There are many ways to extract the first few lines or characters from a longer piece of text. Sometimes, you need just the first 20 or 30 characters to identify an item. At other times, it's preferable to show complete sentences or paragraphs.

Extracting a fixed number of characters

You can extract a fixed number of characters from the beginning of a text item either with the PHP `substr()` function or with the `LEFT()` function in a SQL query.

Using the PHP substr() function

The `substr()` function extracts a substring from a longer string. It takes three arguments: the string you want to extract the substring from, the starting point (counted from 0), and the number of characters to extract. The following code displays the first 100 characters of `$row['article']`:

```
echo substr($row['article'], 0, 100);
```

The original string remains intact. If you omit the third argument, `substr()` extracts everything to the end of the string. This makes sense only if you choose a starting point other than 0.

Using the MySQL LEFT() function

The MySQL `LEFT()` function extracts characters from the beginning of a column. It takes two arguments: the column name and the number of characters to extract. The following retrieves `article_id`, `title`, and the first 100 characters from the `article` column of the `blog` table:

```
SELECT article_id, title, LEFT(article, 100)
FROM blog ORDER BY created DESC
```

Whenever you use a function in a SQL query like this, the column name no longer appears in the result set as `article`, but as `LEFT(article, 100)` instead. So it's a good idea to assign an alias to the affected column using the `AS` keyword. You can either reassign the column's original name as the alias or use a descriptive name as in the following example (the code is in `blog_left_mysqli.php` and `blog_left_pdo.php` in the `ch14` folder):

```
SELECT article_id, title, LEFT(article, 100) AS first100
FROM blog ORDER BY created DESC
```

If you process each record as `$row`, the extract is in `$row['first100']`. To retrieve both the first 100 characters and the full article, simply include both in the query like this:

```
SELECT article_id, title, LEFT(article, 100) AS first100, article
FROM blog ORDER BY created DESC
```

Taking a fixed number of characters produces a very crude result, as Figure 14-1 shows.

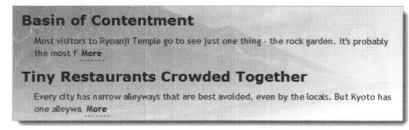

Figure 14-1. Selecting the first 100 characters from an article chops words in half.

Ending an extract on a complete word

To end an extract on a complete word, you need to find the final space and use that to determine the length of the substring. So, if you want the extract to be a maximum of 100 characters, use either of the preceding methods to start with, and store the result in $extract. Then you can use the PHP string functions strrpos() and substr() to find the last space and end the extract like this (the code is in blog_word_mysqli.php and blog_word_pdo.php):

```
$extract = $row['first100'];
// find position of last space in extract
$lastSpace = strrpos($extract, ' ');
// use $lastSpace to set length of new extract and add ...
echo substr($extract, 0, $lastSpace) . '... ';
```

This produces the more elegant result shown in Figure 14-2. It uses strrpos(), which finds the last position of a character within another string. Since you're looking for a space, the second argument is a pair of quotes with a single space between them. The result is stored in $lastSpace, which is passed as the third argument to substr(), finishing the extract on a complete word. Finally, add a string containing three dots and a space, and join the two with the concatenation operator (a period or dot).

Figure 14-2. Ending the extract on a complete word produces a more elegant result.

Extracting the first paragraph

Assuming that you have entered your text in the database using the Enter or Return key to indicate new paragraphs, this is very easy. Simply retrieve the full text, use strpos() to find the first new line character, and use substr() to extract the first section of text up to that point.

The following SQL query is used in blog_para_mysqli.php, and blog_para_pdo.php:

```
SELECT article_id, title, article
FROM blog ORDER BY created DESC
```

The following code is used to display the first paragraph of article:

```
echo substr($row['article'], 0, strpos($row['article'], PHP_EOL));
```

If that makes your head spin, then let's break it up and take a look at the third argument on its own:

```
strpos($row['article'], PHP_EOL)
```

This locates the first end of line character in $row['article'] in a cross-platform way using the PHP_EOL constant (see Chapter 7). You could rewrite the code like this:

```
$newLine = strpos($row['article'], PHP_EOL);
echo substr($row['article'], 0, $newLine);
```

Both sets of code do exactly the same thing, but PHP lets you nest a function as an argument passed to another function. As long as the nested function returns a valid result, you can frequently use shortcuts like this.

Using the PHP_EOL constant eliminates the problem of dealing with the different characters used by Linux, Mac OS X, and Windows to insert a new line.

Displaying paragraphs

Since we're on the subject of paragraphs, many beginners are confused by the fact that all the text retrieved from a database is displayed as a continuous block, with no separation between paragraphs. HTML ignores whitespace, including new lines. To get text stored in a database displayed as paragraphs, you have the following options:

- Store your text as HTML.
- Convert new lines to <br /> tags.
- Create a custom function to replace new lines with paragraph tags.

The first option involves installing an HTML editor, such as CK Editor (http://ckeditor.com/) or TinyMCE (http://tinymce.moxiecode.com/) in your content management forms. Mark up your text as you insert or update it. The HTML is stored in the database, and the text displays as intended. Installing one of these editors is beyond the scope of this book.

The simplest option is to pass your text to the nl2br() function before displaying it like this:

```
echo nl2br($row['article']);
```

Voilà!—paragraphs. Well, not really. The nl2br() function converts new line characters to <br /> tags. As a result, you get fake paragraphs. It's a quick and dirty solution, but not ideal.

> The nl2br() function inserts the slash before the closing angle bracket for compatibility with XHTML. The trailing slash is optional in HTML5, so your code remains valid even if you're not using XHTML-style markup.

To display text retrieved from a database as genuine paragraphs, wrap the database result in a pair of paragraph tags, and then use the preg_replace() function to convert consecutive new line characters to a closing </p> tag immediately followed by an opening <p> tag like this:

```
<p><?php echo preg_replace('/[\r\n]+/', '</p><p>', $row['article']); ?></p>
```

The regular expression used as the first argument matches one or more carriage returns and/or newline characters. You can't use the PHP_EOL constant here because you need to match all consecutive newline characters and replace them with a single pair of paragraph tags. Remembering the pattern for a regex can be difficult, so you can easily convert this into a custom function like this:

```
function convertToParas($text) {
  $text = trim($text);
  return '<p>' . preg_replace('/[\r\n]+/', '</p><p>', $text) . '</p>';
}
```

This trims whitespace, including newline characters from the beginning and end of the text, adds a `<p>` tag at the beginning, replaces internal sequences of newline characters with closing and opening tags, and appends a closing `</p>` tag at the end.

You can then use the function like this:

```php
<?php echo convertToParas($row['article']); ?>
```

The code for the function definition is in `utility_funcs.inc.php` in the `ch14` folder. You can see it being used in `blog_ptags_mysqli.php` and `blog_ptags_pdo.php`.

Extracting complete sentences

PHP has no concept of what constitutes a sentence. Counting periods means you ignore all sentences that end with an exclamation point or question mark. You also run the risk of breaking a sentence on a decimal point or cutting off a closing quote after a period. To overcome these problems, I have devised a PHP function called `getFirst()` that identifies the punctuation at the end of a normal sentence:

- A period, question mark, or exclamation point
- Optionally followed by a single or double quote
- Followed by one or more spaces

The `getFirst()` function takes two arguments: the text from which you want to extract the first section and the number of sentences you want to extract. The second argument is optional; if it's not supplied, the function extracts the first two sentences. The code looks like this (it's in `utility_funcs.inc.php`):

```php
function getFirst($text, $number=2) {
  // use regex to split into sentences
  $sentences = preg_split('/([.?!]["\']?\s)/', $text, $number+1, ↦
    PREG_SPLIT_DELIM_CAPTURE);
  if (count($sentences) > $number * 2) {
    $remainder = array_pop($sentences);
  } else {
    $remainder = '';
  }
  $result = array();
  $result[0] = implode('', $sentences);
  $result[1] = $remainder;
  return $result;
}
```

All you really need to know about this function is that it returns an array containing two elements: the extracted sentences and any text that's left over. You can use the second element to create a link to a page containing the full text.

If you're interested in how the function works, read on. The line highlighted in bold uses a regex to identify the end of each sentence—a period, question mark, or exclamation point, optionally followed by a double or single quotation mark and a space. This is passed as the first argument to `preg_split()`, which uses the regex to split the text into an array. The second argument is the target text. The third argument determines the maximum number of chunks to split the text into. You want one more than the number of sentences to be extracted. Normally, `preg_split()` discards the characters matched by the regex, but using `PREG_SPLIT_DELIM_CAPTURE` as the fourth argument together with a pair of capturing parentheses in the regex preserves them as separate array elements. In other words, the elements of the $sentences array consist alternately of the text of a sentence followed by the punctuation and space like this:

```
$sentences[0] = '"Hello, world';
$sentences[1] = '!" ';
```

It's impossible to know in advance how many sentences there are in the target text, so you need to find out if there's anything remaining after extracting the desired number of sentences. The conditional statement uses count() to ascertain the number of elements in the $sentences array and compares the result with $number multiplied by 2 (because the array contains two elements for each sentence). If there's more text, array_pop() removes the last element of the $sentences array and assigns it to $remainder. If there's no further text, $remainder is an empty string.

The final stage of the function uses implode() with an empty string as its first argument to stitch the extracted sentences back together and then returns a two-element array containing the extracted text and anything that's left over.

Don't worry if you found that explanation hard to follow. The code is quite advanced. It took a lot of experimentation to build the function, and I have improved it gradually over the years.

PHP Solution 14-1: Displaying the first two sentences of an article

This PHP solution shows how to display an extract from each article in the blog table using the getFirst() function described in the preceding section. If you created the Japan Journey site earlier in the book, use blog.php. Alternatively, use blog_01.php from the ch14 folder, and save it as blog.php in the phpsols site root. You also need footer.inc.php, menu.inc.php, title.inc.php, and connection.inc.php in the includes folder.

1. Copy utility_funcs.inc.php from the ch14 folder to the includes folder, and include it in the PHP code block above the DOCTYPE declaration. Also include the MySQL connection file, and create a connection to the database. This page needs read-only privileges, so use read as the argument passed to dbConnect() like this:

   ```
   require_once('./includes/connection.inc.php');
   require_once('./includes/utility_funcs.inc.php');
   // create database connection
   $conn = dbConnect('read');
   ```

2. Prepare a SQL query to retrieve all records from the blog table like this:

   ```
   $sql = 'SELECT * FROM blog ORDER BY created DESC';
   ```

3. For MySQLi, use this:

   ```
   $result = $conn->query($sql);
   ```

   There's no need to submit the query at this stage for PDO.

4. Create a loop inside the maincontent <div> to display the results.

   For MySQLi, use this:

   ```
   <div id="maincontent">
   <?php
   while ($row = $result->fetch_assoc()) {
   ```

```
?>
<h2><?php echo $row['title']; ?></h2>
  <p><?php $extract = getFirst($row['article']);
  echo $extract[0];
  if ($extract[1]) {
    echo '<a href="details.php?article_id=' . $row['article_id'] . '"> ↵
      More</a>';
  } ?></p>
<?php } ?>
</div>
```

The code is the same for PDO, except for this line:

```
while ($row = $result->fetch_assoc()) {
```

Replace it with this:

```
foreach ($conn->query($sql) as $row) {
```

The main part of the code is inside the <p> tags. The getFirst() function processes $row['article'] and stores the result in $extract. The first two sentences of article in $extract[0] are immediately displayed. If $extract[1] contains anything, it means there is more to display. So the code inside the if statement displays a link to details.php with the article's primary key in a query string.

5. Save the page, and test it in a browser. You should see the first two sentences of each article displayed as shown in Figure 14-3.

Figure 14-3. The first two sentences have been extracted cleanly from the longer text.

6. Test the function by adding a number as a second argument to getFirst() like this:

```
$extract = getFirst($row['article'], 3);
```

This displays the first three sentences. If you increase the number so that it equals or exceeds the number of sentences in an article, the **More** link won't be displayed.

You can compare your code with blog_mysqli.php and blog_pdo.php in the ch14 folder.

We'll look at details.php in Chapter 15. Before that, let's tackle the minefield presented by using dates in a dynamic website.

Let's make a date

Dates and time are so fundamental to modern life that we rarely pause to think how complex they are. There are 60 seconds to a minute and 60 minutes to an hour, but 24 hours to a day. Months range between 28 and 31 days, and a year can be either 365 or 366 days. The confusion doesn't stop there, because 7/4 means July 4 to an American or Japanese, but 7 April to a European. To add to the confusion, PHP and MySQL handle dates differently. Time to bring order to chaos . . .

How MySQL handles dates

In MySQL, dates and time are always expressed in descending order from the largest unit to the smallest: year, month, date, hour, minutes, seconds. Hours are always measured using the 24-hour clock with midnight expressed as 00:00:00. Even if this seems unfamiliar to you, it's the recommendation laid down by the International Organization for Standardization (ISO).

If you attempt to store a date in any other format than year, month, date, MySQL inserts 0000-00-00 in the database. MySQL allows considerable flexibility about the separator between the units (any punctuation symbol is OK), but there is no argument about the order—it's fixed.

I'll come back later to the way you insert dates into MySQL, because it's best to validate them and format them with PHP. First, let's take a look at some of the things you can do with dates once they're stored in MySQL. MySQL has many date and time functions, which are listed with examples at http://dev.mysql.com/doc/refman/5.1/en/date-and-time-functions.html.

One of the most useful functions is DATE_FORMAT(), which does exactly what its name suggests.

Formatting dates in a SELECT query with DATE_FORMAT()

The syntax for DATE_FORMAT() is as follows:

DATE_FORMAT(*date, format*)

Normally, *date* is the table column to be formatted, and *format* is a string composed of formatting specifiers and any other text you want to include. Table 14-1 lists the most common specifiers, all of which are case-sensitive.

Table 14-1. Frequently used MySQL date format specifiers

Period	Specifier	Description	Example
Year	%Y	Four-digit format	2006
	%y	Two-digit format	06
Month	%M	Full name	January, September
	%b	Abbreviated name, three letters	Jan, Sep
	%m	Number with leading zero	01, 09

Period	Specifier	Description	Example
	%c	Number without leading zero	1, 9
Day of month	%d	With leading zero	01, 25
	%e	Without leading zero	1, 25
	%D	With English text suffix	1st, 25th
Weekday name	%W	Full text	Monday, Thursday
	%a	Abbreviated name, three letters	Mon, Thu
Hour	%H	24-hour clock with leading zero	01, 23
	%k	24-hour clock without leading zero	1, 23
	%h	12-hour clock with leading zero	01, 11
	%l (lowercase "L")	12-hour clock without leading zero	1, 11
Minutes	%i	With leading zero	05, 25
Seconds	%S	With leading zero	08, 45
AM/PM	%p		

As explained earlier, when using a function in a SQL query, assign the result to an alias using the AS keyword. Referring to Table 14-1, you can format the date in the created column of the blog table in a common U.S. style and assign it to an alias like this:

```
DATE_FORMAT(created, '%c/%e/%Y') AS date_created
```

To format the same date in European style, reverse the first two specifiers like this:

```
DATE_FORMAT(created, '%e/%c/%Y') AS date_created
```

> *If you use the original column name as the alias, it converts the dates to strings, which frequently plays havoc with the sort order.*

PHP Solution 14-2: Formatting a MySQL date or timestamp

This PHP solution formats the dates in the blog entry management page from Chapter 13.

1. Open `blog_list_mysqli.php` or `blog_list_pdo.php` in the `admin` folder, and locate the SQL query. It looks like this:

```
$sql = 'SELECT * FROM blog ORDER BY created DESC';
```

Change it like this:

```
$sql = 'SELECT article_id, title,
        DATE_FORMAT(created, "%a, %b %D, %Y") AS date_created
        FROM blog ORDER BY created DESC';
```

I used single quotes around the whole SQL query, so the format string inside `DATE_FORMAT()` needs to be in double quotes.

Make sure there is no gap before the opening parenthesis of `DATE_FORMAT()`.

The format string begins with %a, which displays the first three letters of the weekday name. If you use the original column name as the alias, the `ORDER BY` clause sorts the dates in reverse alphabetical order: Wed, Thu, Sun, and so on. Using a different name as the alias ensures that the dates are still ordered chronologically.

2. In the first table cell in the body of the page, change `$row['created']` to `$row['date_created']` to match the alias in the SQL query.

3. Save the page, and load it into a browser. The dates should now be formatted as shown in Figure 14-4. Experiment with other specifiers to suit your preferences.

Manage Blog Entries

Insert new entry

Created	Title		
Thu, Sep 16th, 2010	Spectacular View of Mount Fuji from the Bullet Train	EDIT	DELETE
Thu, Sep 16th, 2010	Trainee Geishas Go Shopping	EDIT	DELETE
Thu, Sep 16th, 2010	Tiny Restaurants Crowded Together	EDIT	DELETE
Thu, Sep 16th, 2010	Basin of Contentment	EDIT	DELETE

Figure 14-4. The MySQL timestamps are now nicely formatted.

Updated versions of `blog_list_mysqli.php` and `blog_list_pdo.php` are in the `ch14` folder.

Adding to and subtracting from dates

When working with dates, it's often useful to add or subtract a specific time period. For instance, you may want to display items that have been added to the database within the past seven days or stop displaying articles that haven't been updated for three months. MySQL makes this easy with `DATE_ADD()` and `DATE_SUB()`. Both functions have synonyms called `ADDDATE()` and `SUBDATE()`, respectively.

The basic syntax is the same for all of them and looks like this:

```
DATE_ADD(date, INTERVAL value interval_type)
```

When using these functions, *date* can be the column containing the date you want to alter, a string containing a particular date (in YYYY-MM-DD format), or a MySQL function, such as NOW(). INTERVAL is a keyword followed by a *value* and an interval type, the most common of which are listed in Table 14-2.

Table 14-2. Most frequently used interval types with DATE_ADD() and DATE_SUB()

Interval type	Meaning	Value format
DAY	Days	Number
DAY_HOUR	Days and hours	String presented as 'DD hh'
WEEK	Weeks	Number
MONTH	Months	Number
QUARTER	Quarters	Number
YEAR	Years	Number
YEAR_MONTH	Years and months	String presented as 'YY-MM'

The interval types are constants, so don't add "S" to the end of DAY, WEEK, and so on to make them plural.

One of the most useful applications of these functions is to display only the most recent items in a table.

PHP Solution 14-3: Displaying items updated within the past week

This PHP solution shows how to limit the display of database results according to a specific time interval. Use blog.php from PHP Solution 14-1.

1. Locate the SQL query in blog.php. It looks like this:

    ```
    $sql = 'SELECT * FROM blog ORDER BY created DESC';
    ```

    Change it like this:

    ```
    $sql = 'SELECT * FROM blog
            WHERE updated > DATE_SUB(NOW(), INTERVAL 1 WEEK)
            ORDER BY created DESC';
    ```

    This tells MySQL that you want only items that have been updated in the past week.

2. Save and reload the page in your browser. Depending on when you last updated an item in the blog table, you should see nothing or a limited range of items. If necessary, change the interval type to DAY or HOUR to test that the time limit is working.

3. Open `blog_list_mysqli.php` or `blog_list_pdo.php`, select an item that isn't displayed in `blog.php`, and edit it. Reload `blog.php`. The item that you have just updated should now be displayed.

    You can compare your code with `blog_limit_mysqli.php` and `blog_limit_pdo.php` in the `ch14` folder.

Inserting dates into MySQL

MySQL's requirement for dates to be formatted as `YYYY-MM-DD` presents a headache for online forms that allow users to input dates. As you saw in Chapter 13, the current date and time can be inserted automatically by using a `TIMESTAMP` column or the MySQL `NOW()` function. It's when you need any other date that problems arise.

If you can trust users to follow a set pattern for inputting dates, such as `MM/DD/YYYY`, you can use the

`explode()` function to rearrange the date parts like this:

```
if (isset($_POST['theDate'])) {
  $date = explode('/', $_POST['theDate']);
  $mysqlFormat = "$date[2]-$date[0]-$date[1]";
}
```

This solution works, but as soon as someone deviates from the format, you end up with invalid dates in your database. It's better to ensure that dates are both valid and in the correct format.

One way of doing so is to use a date picker widget that outputs the date in the ISO format, but widgets that rely on JavaScript are useless when visitors to your website have JavaScript disabled in their browsers. Eventually, this will become less of a problem when mainstream browsers support the new types of input fields specified in HTML5. To create a date input field, set the `type` attribute to `date` like this:

`<input name="departure" **type="date"** required id="departure">`

As shown in Figure 14-5, Opera 10.62 automatically displays a date picker when you select this type of field. Browsers that don't understand the `date` type render the field as a normal text input field, so there's no need to wait for old browsers to die before you start using HTML5 form fields.

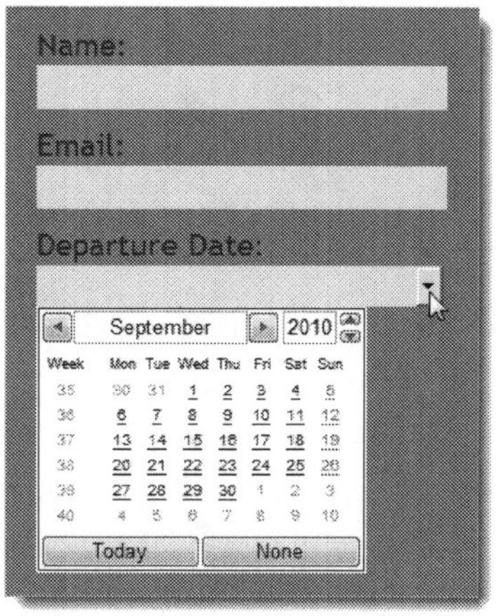

Figure 14-5. Opera 10.62 automatically displays a date picker in an HTML5 form.

Nevertheless, the most reliable method of gathering dates from an online form remains the use of separate input fields for month, day, and year.

PHP Solution 14-4: Validating and formatting dates for MySQL input

This PHP solution concentrates on checking the validity of a date and converting it to MySQL format. It's designed to be incorporated in an insert or update form of your own.

1. Create a page called date_converter.php, and insert a form containing the following code (or use date_converter_01.php in the ch14 folder):

```
<form id="form1" method="post" action="">
<p>
  <label for="select">Month:</label>
  <select name="month" id="month">
    <option value=""></option>
  </select>
  <label for="day">Date:</label>
  <input name="day" type="number" required id="day" max="31" min="1" ➥
    maxlength="2">
  <label for="year">Year:</label>
  <input name="year" type="number" required id="year" maxlength="4">
</p>
<p>
  <input type="submit" name="convert" id="convert" value="Convert">
</p>
</form>
```

This code creates a drop-down menu called month and two input fields called day and year. The drop-down menu doesn't have any values at the moment, but it will be populated by a PHP loop. The day and year fields use the HTML5 number type and required attribute. The day field also has the max and min attributes to restrict the range to between 1 and 31. Browsers that support the new HTML5 form elements display number steppers alongside the fields and restrict the type and range of input. Other browsers render them as ordinary text input fields. For the benefit of older browsers, both have maxlength attributes that limit the number of characters accepted.

2. Amend the section that builds the drop-down menu like this:

```
<select name="month" id="month">
  <?php
  $months = array('Jan','Feb','Mar','Apr','May','Jun','Jul','Aug', ➥
    'Sep','Oct','Nov','Dec');
  $thisMonth = date('n');
  for ($i = 1; $i <= 12; $i++) { ?>
    <option value="<?php echo $i; ?>"
    <?php if ($i == $thisMonth) { echo ' selected'; } ?>>
    <?php echo $months[$i-1]; ?>
    </option>
  <?php } ?>
</select>
```

This creates an array of month names and uses the date() function to find the number of the current month. A for loop then populates the menu's <option> tags. I have set the initial value of $i to 1, because I want to use it for the value of the month. If the values of $i and $thisMonth are the same, the conditional statement inserts selected into the <option> tag.

The final part of the script displays the name of the month by drawing it from the $months array. Because indexed arrays begin at 0, you need to subtract 1 from the value of $i to get the right month.

3. Save the page, and test it in a browser. In a browser that supports HTML5 form elements, it should look similar to Figure 14-6. In all browsers, the current month should be automatically displayed in the drop-down menu.

Figure 14-6. Using separate input fields for date parts helps eliminate errors.

4. If you test the input fields, in most browsers, the **Date** field should accept no more than two characters, and the **Year** field a maximum of four. Even though this reduces the possibility of mistakes, you still need to validate the input and format the date correctly.

5. The code that performs all the checks is a custom function in utilitity_funcs.inc.php. It looks like this:

```
function convertDateToMySQL($month, $day, $year) {
  $month = trim($month);
  $day = trim($day);
  $year = trim($year);
  $result[0] = false;
  if (empty($month) || empty($day) || empty($year)) {
    $result[1] = 'Please fill in all fields';
  } elseif (!is_numeric($month) || !is_numeric($day) || !is_numeric($year)) {
    $result[1] = 'Please use numbers only';
  } elseif (($month < 1 || $month > 12) || ($day < 1 || $day > 31) || ↦
    ($year < 1000 || $year > 9999)) {
    $result[1] = 'Please use numbers within the correct range';
  } elseif (!checkdate($month,$day,$year)) {
    $result[1] = 'You have used an invalid date';
  } else {
    $result[0] = true;
    $result[1] = "$year-$month-$day";
  }
```

```
    return $result;
}
```

The function takes three arguments: month, day, and year, all of which should be numbers. The first three lines of code trim any whitespace from either end of the input, and the next line initializes the first element of an array called $result. If the input fails validation, the first element of the array is false, and the second element contains an error message. If it passes validation, the first element of $result is true, and the second element contains the formatted date ready for insertion into MySQL.

The series of conditional statements checks the input values to see if they are empty or not numeric. The third test looks for numbers within acceptable ranges. The range for years is dictated by the legal range for MySQL. In the unlikely event that you need a year out of that range, you must choose a different column type to store the data.

By using a series of elseif clauses, this code stops testing as soon as it meets the first mistake. If the input has survived the first three tests, it's then subjected to the PHP function checkdate(), which is smart enough to know when it's a leap year and prevents mistakes such as September 31.

Finally, if the input has passed all these tests, it's rebuilt in the correct format for insertion into MySQL.

6. For testing purposes, add this code just below the form in the main body of the page:

```
if (isset($_POST['convert'])) {
  require_once('utility_funcs.inc.php');
  $converted = convertDateToMySQL($_POST['month'], $_POST['day'], ↪
    $_POST['year']);
  if ($converted[0]) {
    echo 'Valid date: ' . $converted[1];
  } else {
    echo 'Error: ' . $converted[1] . '<br>';
    echo 'Input was: ' . $months[$_POST['month']-1] . ' ' . $_POST['day'] ↪
      . ', ' . $_POST['year'];
  }
}
```

This checks whether the form has been submitted. If it has, it includes utility_funcs.inc.php (there's a copy in the ch14 folder) and passes the form values to the convertDateToMySQL() function, saving the result in $converted.

If the date is valid, $converted[0] is true, and the formatted date is in $converted[1]. If the date cannot be converted to MySQL format, the else clause displays the error message stored in $converted[1], together with the original input. To display the correct value for the month, 1 is subtracted from the value of $_POST['month'], and the result is used as the key for the $months array.

7. Save the page, and test it by entering a date and clicking **Convert**. If the date is valid, you should see it converted to MySQL format, as shown in Figure 14-7.

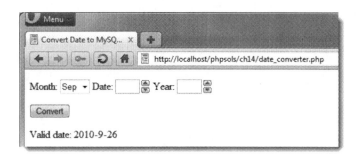

Figure 14-7. The date has been validated and formatted for MySQL.

Although the date shown at the bottom of Figure 14-7 doesn't use a leading zero for the month, it's still valid. MySQL automatically adds the leading zero when storing the date.

If you enter an invalid date, you should see an appropriate message instead (see Figure 14-8).

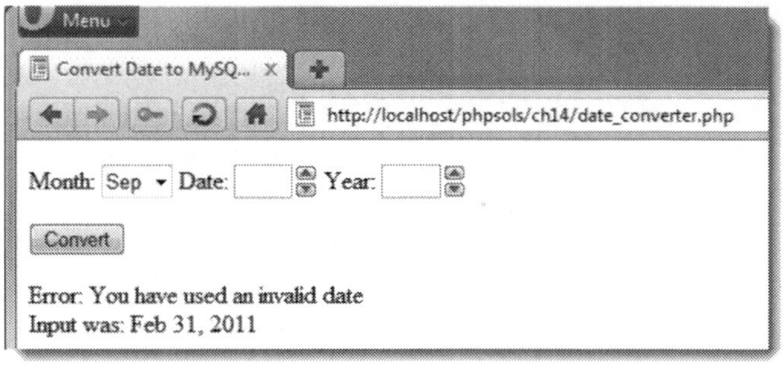

Figure 14-8. The convertDateToMySQL() function rejects invalid dates.

You can compare your code with date_converter_02.php in the ch14 folder.

When creating an insert or update form for a table that requires a date from user input, add three fields for month, day, and year in the same way as in date_converter.php. Before inserting the form input into the database, include utilitity_funcs.inc.php (or wherever you decide to store the function), and use the convertDateToMySQL() function to validate the date parts and prepare them for insertion into the database.

```
require_once('utility_funcs.inc.php');
$converted = convertDateToMySQL($_POST['month'], $_POST['day'], $_POST['year']);
if ($converted[0]) {
  $date = $converted[1];
} else {
  $errors[] = $converted[1];
}
```

If your $errors array has any elements, abandon the insert or update process, and display the errors. Otherwise, $date is safe to insert in the SQL query.

The rest of this chapter is devoted to handling dates in PHP. It's an important but complex subject. I suggest that you skim through each section to familiarize yourself with PHP's date-handling functionality and return to this section when you need to implement a particular feature.

Working with dates in PHP

The way PHP handles dates and time underwent major changes in PHP 5.2 with the introduction of the DateTime and DateTimeZone classes. Further changes were introduced in PHP 5.3 through the addition of new DateTime methods and the DateInterval and DatePeriod classes. Prior to the changes, dates and time were handled exclusively as Unix timestamps—the number of seconds since midnight UTC (Coordinated Universal Time) on January 1, 1970.

The new classes don't entirely replace the original ways of handling date and time information, but they are more flexible. PHP stores timestamps as 32-bit integers, restricting the upper limit of the range of available dates to January 2038. The new classes store date and time information internally as a 64-bit number, increasing the range from about 292 billion years in the past to the same number of years in the future. Table 14-3 summarizes the main date- and time-related classes and functions in PHP.

Table 14-3. PHP date- and time-related classes and functions.

	Name	Arguments	Description
Class			
	DateTime	Date string, DateTimeZone object	Creates a time zone-sensitive object containing date and/or time information that can be used for calculations involving dates and times.
	DateTimeZone	Time zone string	Stores time zone information for use with DateTime objects.
	DateInterval	Interval specification	Represents a fixed amount of time in years, months, hours, etc. Requires PHP 5.3 or later.
	DatePeriod	Start, interval, end/recurrence, options	Calculates recurring dates over a set period or number of recurrences. Requires PHP 5.3 or later.
Function			
	time()	None	Generates a Unix timestamp for the current date and time.
	mktime()	Hour, minute, second, month, date, year	Generates a Unix timestamp for the specified date/time.

Name	Arguments	Description
strtotime()	Date string, timestamp	Attempts to generate a Unix timestamp from an English textual description, such as "next Tuesday." The returned value is relative to the second argument if supplied.
date()	Format string, timestamp	Formats a date in English using the specifiers listed in Table 14-4. If the second argument is omitted, the current date and time are used.
strftime()	Format string, timestamp	Same as date(), but uses the language specified by the system locale.

All date and time information in PHP is stored according to the server's default time zone setting. It's common for web servers to be located in a different time zone from your target audience, so it's useful to know how to change the default.

Setting the default time zone

The server's default time zone should normally be set in the date.timezone directive in php.ini; but if your hosting company forgets to do so, or you want to use a different time zone, you need to set it yourself.

If your hosting company gives you control over your own version of php.ini, change the value of date.timezone there. That way, it's automatically set for all your scripts.

If your remote server runs Apache, you may be able to set a default time zone by putting the following in an .htaccess file in the site root:

```
php_value date.timezone 'timezone'
```

Replace timezone with the correct setting for your location. You can find a full list of valid time zones at http://docs.php.net/manual/en/timezones.php. This works only if Apache has been set up to allow .htaccess to override default settings.

If neither of those options is available to you, add the following at the beginning of any script that uses date or time functions (replacing timezone with the appropriate value):

```
ini_set('date.timezone', 'timezone');
```

Creating a DateTime object

To create a DateTime object, just use the new keyword followed by DateTime() like this:

```
$now = new DateTime();
```

This creates an object that represents the current date and time according to the web server's clock and default time zone setting.

The DateTime() constructor also takes two optional arguments: a string containing a date and/or time, and a DateTimeZone object. The date/time string for the first argument can be in any of the formats listed at http://docs.php.net/manual/en/datetime.formats.php. Unlike MySQL, which accepts only one format, PHP goes to the opposite extreme. The range of valid formats is overwhelming and potentially confusing. For example, to create a DateTime object for Christmas Day 2010, all the following formats are valid:

```
'12/25/2010'
'25-12-2010'
'25 Dec 2010'
'Dec 25 2010'
'25-XII-2010'
'25.12.2010'
'2010/12/25'
'2010-12-25'
'December 25th, 2010'
```

This is not an exhaustive list. It's just a selection of valid formats. Where the potential confusion arises is in the use of separators. For example, the forward slash is permitted in American-style (12/25/2010) and ISO (2010/12/25) dates, but not when the date is presented in European order or when the month is represented by Roman numerals. To present the date in European order, the separator must be a dot, tab, or dash.

Dates can also be specified using relative expressions, such as "next Wednesday," "tomorrow," or "last Monday." However, there's potential for confusion here, too. Some people use "next Wednesday" to mean "Wednesday next week." PHP interprets the expression literally. If today is Tuesday, "next Wednesday" means the following day.

This situation offers great flexibility—as long as you know where your date and time information is coming from, and it conforms to one of the many valid formats.

> PHP 5.3 expanded this flexibility even further by introducing a method that allows you to specify a custom format for creating a DateTime object. It's described after the next section because the same technique is used for specifying both output and input formats.

You can't use echo on its own to display the value stored in a DateTime object. In addition to echo, you need to tell PHP how to format the output using the format() method.

Formatting dates in PHP

The DateTime class's format() method uses the same format characters as the original date() function. Although this makes for continuity, the format characters are often difficult to remember and seem to have no obvious reasoning behind them. Table 14-4 lists the most useful date and time format characters.

The DateTime class and date() function display the names of weekdays and months in English only, but the strftime() function uses the language specified by the server's locale. So, if the server's locale is set to Spanish, a DateTime object and date() display **Saturday**, but strftime() displays **sábado**. In addition to the format characters used by the DateTime class and the date() function, Table 14-4 lists the equivalent characters used by strftime().

Table 14-4. The main date and time format characters

Unit	DateTime/date()	strftime()	Description	Example
Day	d	%d	Day of the month with leading zero	01 through 31
	j	%e*	Day of the month without leading zero	1 through 31
	S		English ordinal suffix for day of the month	st, nd, rd, or th
	D	%a	First three letters of day name	Sun, Tue
	l (lowercase "L")	%A	Full name of day	Sunday, Tuesday
Month	m	%m	Number of month with leading zero	01 through 12
	n		Number of month without leading zero	1 through 12
	M	%b	First three letters of month name	Jan, Jul
	F	%B	Full name of month	January, July
Year	Y	%Y	Year displayed as four digits	2006
	y	%y	Year displayed as two digits	06
Hour	g		Hour in 12-hour format without leading zero	1 through 12
	h	%I	Hour in 12-hour format with leading zero	01 through 12
	G		Hour in 24-hour format without leading zero	0 through 23
	H	%H	Hour in 24-hour format with leading zero	01 through 23
Minutes	i	%M	Minutes with leading zero if necessary	00 through 59
Seconds	s	%S	Seconds with leading zero if necessary	00 through 59
AM/PM	a	%p	Lowercase	am
AM/PM	A		Uppercase	PM

Note: %e is not supported on Windows.

You can combine these format characters with punctuation to display the current date in your web pages according to your own preferences.

To format a DateTime object, pass the format string as an argument to the format() method like this (the code is in date_format_01.php in the ch14 folder):

```php
<?php
$now = new DateTime();
$xmas2010 = new DateTime('12/25/2010');
?>
<p>It's now <?php echo $now->format('g.ia'); ?> on <?php echo ➥
  $now->format('l, F jS, Y'); ?></p>
<p>Christmas 2010 falls on a <?php echo $xmas2010->format('l'); ?></p>
```

In this example, two DateTime objects are created: one for the current date and time, and the other for December 25, 2010. Using the format characters from Table 14-4, various date parts are extracted from the two objects, producing the output shown in the following screenshot:

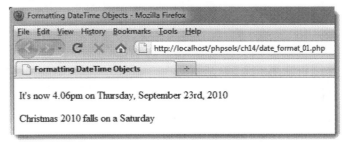

The code in date_format_02.php produces the same output using the date() and strtotime() functions like this:

```php
<?php $xmas2010 = strtotime('12/25/2010'); ?>
<p>It's now <?php echo date('g.ia'); ?> on <?php echo date('l, F jS, Y'); ?></p>
<p>Christmas 2010 falls on a <?php echo date('l', $xmas2010); ?></p>
```

The first line uses strtotime() to create a timestamp for December 25, 2010. There's no need to create a timestamp for the current date and time, because date() defaults to them when used without a second argument.

If the timestamp for Christmas Day isn't used elsewhere in the script, the first line can be omitted, and the last call to date() can be rewritten like this (the code is in date_format_03.php):

```php
echo date('l', strtotime('12/25/2010'));
```

Creating a DateTime object from a custom format

In PHP 5.3 and later, you can specify a custom input format for a DateTime object using the format characters in Table 14-4. Instead of creating the object with the new keyword, you use the createFromFormat() static method like this:

```php
$date = DateTime::createFromFormat(format_string, input_date, timezone);
```

The third argument, *timezone*, is optional. If included, it should be a DateTimeZone object.

A **static method** belongs to the whole class, rather than to a particular object. You call a static method using the class name followed by a double colon and the method name.

> *The double colon is called the **scope resolution operator**. You first used it to call the parent constructor in "Extending a class" in Chapter 8. Internally, it's called PAAMAYIM_NEKUDOTAYIM, which is Hebrew for "double colon." Why Hebrew? Because the Zend Engine that powers PHP was originally developed by Zeev Suraski and Andi Gutmans when they were students at the Technion – Israel Institute of Technology. Apart from earning points in a geek trivia quiz, knowing the meaning of PAAMAYIM_NEKUDOTAYIM could save you a lot of head scratching when you see it in a PHP error message.*

For example, you can use the createFromFormat() method to accept a date in the European format of day, month, year separated by slashes like this (the code is in date_format_04.php):

```
$xmas2010 = DateTime::createFromFormat('d/m/Y', '25/12/2010');
echo $xmas2010->format('l, jS F Y');
```

This produces the following output:

Attempting to use 25/12/2010 as the input to the DateTime constructor triggers a fatal error. If you want to use a format not supported by the DateTime constructor, you must use the createFromFormat() static method.

Although the createFromFormat() method is useful, it can be used only in circumstances where you know the date will always be in a specific format. It's also important to note that it does not work in PHP 5.2.

Choosing between date() and the DateTime class

When it comes to displaying a date, it's always a two-step process with the DateTime class. You need to instantiate the object before you can call the format() method. With the date() function, you can do it in a single pass. Since they both use the same format characters, date() wins hands down when dealing with the current date and/or time.

For simple tasks like displaying the current date, time, or year, use date(). Where the DateTime class comes into its own is when working with date-related calculations and time zones using the methods listed in Table 14-5. Note that some methods are supported only in PHP 5.3 and later.

Table 14-5. The main `DateTime` methods

Method	Arguments	Description
Since PHP 5.2		
`format()`	Format string	Formats the date/time using the format characters in Table 14-4.
`getOffset()`	None	Returns the time zone offset from UTC expressed in seconds.
`getTimezone()`	None	Returns a `DateTimeZone` object representing the `DateTime` object's time zone.
`modify()`	Relative date string	Changes the date/time using a relative expression, such as '+2 weeks'.
`setDate()`	Year, month, day	Changes the date. The arguments should be separated by commas. Months or days in excess of the permitted range are added to the resulting date. For example, using 14 as the month sets the date to February of the following year.
`setTime()`	Hours, minutes, seconds	Resets the time. Arguments are comma-separated values. Seconds are optional. Values in excess of the permitted range are added to the resulting date/time. For example, setting the hour to 26 results in 2am on the following day.
`setTimezone()`	`DateTimeZone` object	Changes the time zone.
Since PHP 5.3		
`add()`	`DateInterval` object	Increments the date/time by the set period.
`sub()`	`DateInterval` object	Deducts the set period from the date/time.
`diff()`	`DateTime` object, Boolean	Returns a `DateInterval` object representing the difference between the current `DateTime` object and the one passed as an argument. The optional second argument determines whether to convert negative values to their positive equivalent. The default is `false`.

Method	Arguments	Description
getTimestamp()	None	Returns the Unix timestamp for the date/time.
setTimestamp()	Unix timestamp	Sets the date/time according to the Unix timestamp.

As Table 14-5 explains, adding out-of-range values with setDate() and setTime() results in the excess being added to the resulting date or time. The same happens with the modify(), add(), and sub() methods.

For example, if you add one month to a DateTime object that represents January 31, 2011, the resulting value is not the last day of February, but March 3. This is because adding one month to the original date results in February 31, but February has only 28 days in a non-leap year. So, the out-of-range value is added to the month, resulting in March 3. If you subsequently subtract one month from the same DateTime object, it brings you back to February 3, not to the original starting date. The following code in date_modify.php in the ch14 folder illustrates this point:

```php
<?php
$format = 'F j, Y';
$date = new DateTime('January 31, 2011');
?>
<p>Original date: <?php echo $date->format($format); ?>.</p>
<p>Add one month: <?php
$date->modify('+1 month');
echo $date->format($format);
$date->modify('-1 month');
?>
<p>Subtract one month: <?php echo $date->format($format); ?>
```

This produces the output shown in Figure 14-9.

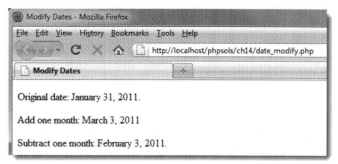

Figure 14-9. Adding and subtracting months can lead to unexpected results.

The modify() method uses ordinary text expressions to add or subtract a set period. The add(), sub(), and diff() methods added in PHP 5.3 can be used only with DateInterval objects, which are described later in this chapter.

Using the DateTimeZone class

A `DateTime` object automatically uses the web server's default time zone unless you have reset the time zone using one of the methods described earlier. However, you can set the time zone of individual `DateTime` objects through the optional second argument of the constructor or by using the `setTimezone()` method. In both cases, the argument must be a `DateTimeZone` object.

To create a `DateTimeZone` object, pass the constructor one of the supported time zones listed at `http://docs.php.net/manual/en/timezones.php` like this:

```
$UK = new DateTimeZone('Europe/London');
$USeast = new DateTimeZone('America/New_York');
$Hawaii = new DateTimeZone('Pacific/Honolulu');
```

When checking the list of supported time zones, it's important to realize that they're based on geographic regions and cities, rather than official time zones. This is because PHP automatically takes account of daylight saving time. Arizona, which doesn't use daylight saving time, is covered by `America/Phoenix`.

The organization of time zones into geographic regions produces some surprises. America doesn't mean the United States of America, but the continents of North and South America and the Caribbean. As a result, Honolulu is not listed in America, but as a Pacific time zone. Europe also means the European continent, including the British Isles but excluding other islands. So, Reykjavik and Madeira are listed as Atlantic time zones, and the Norwegian island of Longyearbyen has the exclusive privilege of being the only Arctic time zone.

The code in `timezones.php` creates `DateTimeZone` objects for London, New York, and Honolulu, and then initializes a `DateTime` object using the first one like this:

```
$now = new DateTime('now', $UK);
```

After displaying the date and time using `echo` and the `format()` method, the time zone is changed using the `setTimezone()` method like this:

```
$now->setTimezone($USeast);
```

The next time $now is displayed, it shows the date and time in New York. Finally, `setTimezone()` is used again to change the time zone to Honolulu, producing the following output:

To find the time zone of your server, you can either check `php.ini` or use the `getTimezone()` method with a `DateTime` object. The `getTimezone()` method returns a `DateTimeZone` object, not a string containing the time zone. To get the value of the time zone, you need to use the `DateTimeZone` object's `getName()` method like this (the code is in `timezone_display.php`):

```
$now = new DateTime();
$timezone = $now->getTimezone();
echo $timezone->getName();
```

The DateTimeZone class has several other methods that expose information about a time zone. For the sake of completeness, they're listed in Table 14-6, but the main use of the DateTimeZone class is to set the time zone for DateTime objects.

Table 14-6. DateTimeZone methods

Method	Arguments	Description
getLocation()	None	Returns an associative array containing the country code, latitude, longitude, and comments about the time zone. Requires PHP 5.3 or later.
getName()	None	Returns a string containing the geographic area and city of the time zone.
getOffset()	DateTime object	Calculates the offset from UTC (in seconds) of the DateTime object passed as an argument.
getTransitions()	Start, end (5.3+)	Returns a multidimensional array containing historical and future dates and times of switching to and from daylight saving time. Takes no arguments in PHP 5.2. Since PHP 5.3, accepts two timestamps as optional arguments to limit the range of results.
listAbbreviations()	None	Generates a large multidimensional array containing the UTC offsets and names of time zones supported by PHP.
listIdentifiers()	DateTimeZone constant, country code (5.3+)	Returns an array of all PHP time zone identifiers, such as Europe/London, America/New_York, and so on. Takes no arguments in PHP 5.2. Since PHP 5.3, accepts two optional arguments to limit the range of results. Use as the first argument one of the DateTimeZone constants listed at http://docs.php.net/manual/en/class.datetimezone.php. If the first argument is DateTimeZone::PER_COUNTRY, a two-letter country code can be used as the second argument.

The last two methods in Table 14-6 are static methods. Call them directly on the class using the scope resolution operator like this:

```
$abbreviations = DateTimeZone::listAbbreviations();
```

Adding and subtracting set periods with the DateInterval class

The DateInterval class was introduced in PHP 5.3 and is required to specify the period to be added or subtracted from a DateTime object using the add() and sub() methods. It's also used by the diff()

method, which returns a DateInterval object. Using the DateInterval class feels rather odd to begin with, but it's relatively simple to understand.

The DateInterval class and the associated DateTime methods do not work in PHP 5.2.

To create a DateInterval object, you need to pass to the constructor a string that specifies the length of the interval formatted according to the ISO 8601 standard. The string always begins with the letter P (for period), followed by one or more pairs of integers and letters known as **period designators**. If the interval includes hours, minutes, or seconds, the time element is preceded by the letter T. Table 14-7 lists the valid period designators.

Table 14-7. ISO 8601 period designators used by the DateInterval class

Period Designator	Meaning
Y	Years
M	Months
W	Weeks—cannot be combined with days
D	Days—cannot be combined with weeks
H	Hours
M	Minutes
S	Seconds

The following examples should clarify how to specify an interval:

```
$interval1 = new DateInterval('P2Y');          // 2 years
$interval2 = new DateInterval('P5W');          // 5 weeks
$interval3 = new DateInterval('P37D');         // 5 weeks 2 days
$interval4 = new DateInterval('PT6H20M');      // 6 hours 20 minutes
$interval5 = new DateInterval('P1Y2DT3H5M50S'); // 1 year 2 days 3 hours 5 min
                                               // 50 sec
```

Note that $interval3 needs to specify the total number of days, because weeks are automatically converted to days, so W and D cannot be combined in the same interval definition.

To use a DateInterval object with the add() or sub() method of the DateTime class, pass the object as an argument. For example, this adds 12 days to the date for Christmas Day 2010:

```
$xmas2010 = new DateTime('12/25/2010');
$interval = new DateInterval('P12D');
$xmas2010->add($interval);
```

If you don't need to reuse the interval, you can pass the DateInterval constructor directly as the argument to add() like this:

```
$xmas2010 = new DateTime('12/25/2010');
$xmas2010->add(new DateInterval('P12D'));
```

The result of this calculation is demonstrated in date_interval_01.php, which produces the following output:

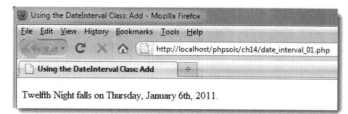

An alternative to using the period designators listed in Table 14-7 is to use the static createFromDateString() method, which takes as an argument an English relative date string in the same way as strtotime(). Using createFromDateString(), the preceding example can be rewritten like this (the code is in date_interval_02.php):

```
$xmas2010 = new DateTime('12/25/2010');
$xmas2010->add(DateInterval::createFromDateString('+12 days'));
```

This produces exactly the same result.

> *Adding and subtracting months with DateInterval has the same effect as described earlier. If the resulting date is out of range, the extra days are added. For example, adding one month to January 31 results in March 3 or 2, depending on whether it's a leap year.*

Finding the difference between two dates with the diff() method

To find the difference between two dates, create a DateTime object for both dates, and pass the second object as the argument to the first object's diff() method. The result is returned as a DateInterval object. To extract the result from the DateInterval object, you need to use the object's format() method which uses the format characters listed in Table 14-8. These are different from the format characters used by the DateTime class. Fortunately, most of them are easy to remember.

Table 14-8. Format characters used by the DateInterval format() method

Format character	Description	Examples
%Y	Years. At least two digits, with leading zero if necessary.	12, 01
%y	Years, no leading zero	12, 1
%M	Months with leading zero	02, 11

Format character	Description	Examples
%m	Months, no leading zero	2, 11
%D	Days with leading zero	03, 24
%d	Days, no leading zero	3, 24
%a *	Total number of days	15, 231
%H	Hours with leading zero	03, 23
%h	Hours, no leading zero	3, 23
%I	Minutes with leading zero	05, 59
%i	Minutes, no leading zero	5, 59
%S	Seconds with leading zero	05, 59
%s	Seconds, no leading zero	5, 59
%R	Display minus when negative, plus when positive	-, +
%r	Display minus when negative, no sign when positive	-
%%	Percentage sign	%

A bug verified in PHP 5.3.3 produces an incorrect result for the total number of days on Windows. Hopefully, this will be fixed in a subsequent release.

The following example in date_interval_03.php shows how to get the difference between the current date and the American Declaration of Independence using diff() and displaying the result with the format() method:

```php
<p><?php
$independence = new DateTime('7/4/1776');
$now = new DateTime();
$interval = $now->diff($independence);
echo $interval->format('%Y years %m months %d days'); ?>
since American independence.</p>
```

If you load date_interval_03.php into a browser, you should see something similar to the following screenshot (of course, the actual period will be different).

The format characters follow a logical pattern. Uppercase characters always produce at least two digits with a leading zero if necessary. Lowercase characters have no leading zero.

What might not be immediately obvious is that, with the exception of %a, which represents the total number of days, the format characters represent only specific parts of the overall interval. For example, if you change the format string to $interval->format('%m months'), it shows only the number of whole months that have elapsed since last July 4. It does not show the total number of months since July 4, 1776.

Calculating recurring dates with the DatePeriod class

Working out recurring dates, such as the second Tuesday of each month, is now remarkably easy thanks to the DatePeriod class. It works in conjunction with a DateInterval object and is available only in PHP 5.3 or later.

The DatePeriod constructor is unusual in that it accepts arguments in three different ways. The first way of creating a DatePeriod object is to supply the following arguments:

- A DateTime object representing the start date
- A DateInterval object representing the recurring interval
- An integer representing the number of recurrences
- The DatePeriod::EXCLUDE_START_DATE constant (optional)

The second way of creating a DatePeriod object is to replace the number of recurrences in the third argument with a DateTime object representing the end date.

The third way uses a single argument: a string formatted according to the ISO 8601 recurring time interval standard (see http://en.wikipedia.org/wiki/ISO_8601#Repeating_intervals).

Once you have created a DatePeriod object, you can display the recurring dates in a foreach loop using the DateTime format() method.

Let's take a quick look at the three ways of creating a DatePeriod object. First, using an integer to represent the number of occurrences:

The code in date_interval_04.php uses the following code to display the date of the second Tuesday of each month in 2011:

```php
$start = new DateTime('12/31/2010');
$interval = DateInterval::createFromDateString('second Tuesday of next month');
$period = new DatePeriod($start, $interval, 12, DatePeriod::EXCLUDE_START_DATE);
foreach ($period as $date) {
  echo $date->format('l, F jS, Y') . '<br>';
}
```

It produces the output shown in Figure 14-10.

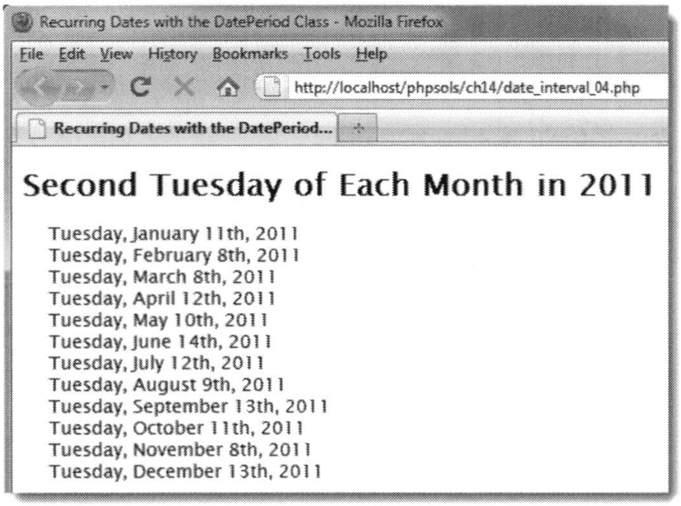

Figure 14-10. Calculating a recurring date is remarkably easy with the DatePeriod class.

The first line of PHP code sets the start date as December 31, 2010. The next line uses the DateInterval static method createFromDateString() to set the interval at the second Tuesday of next month. Both values are passed to the DatePeriod constructor, together with 12 as the number of recurrences and the DatePeriod::EXCLUDE_START_DATE constant. The constant's name is self-explanatory. Finally, a foreach loop displays the resulting dates using the DateTime format() method.

The code in date_interval_05.php has been amended to create a DatePeriod object the second way, using a DateTime object as the third argument to indicate the end date. It looks like this:

```
$start = new DateTime('12/31/2010');
$interval = DateInterval::createFromDateString('second Tuesday of next month');
$end = new DateTime('12/31/2011');
$period = new DatePeriod($start, $interval, $end, DatePeriod::EXCLUDE_START_DATE);
foreach ($period as $date) {
  echo $date->format('l, F jS, Y') . '<br>';
}
```

This produces exactly the same output as shown in Figure 14-10.

The third way of creating a DatePeriod object using the ISO 8601 recurring time interval standard is perhaps not as user,friendly, mainly because of the need to construct a string in the correct format, which looks like this:

R*n*/YYYY-MM-DDTHH:MM:SS*tz*/P*interval*

R*n* is the letter R followed by the number of recurrences; *tz* is the time zone offset from UTC (or Z for UTC, as shown in the following example); and P*interval* uses the same format as the DateInterval class.

The code in date_interval_06.php shows an example of how to use DatePeriod with an ISO 8601 recurring interval. It looks like this:

```
$period = new DatePeriod('R5/2011-02-05T00:00:00Z/P10D');
foreach ($period as $date) {
  echo $date->format('l, F j, Y') . '<br>';
}
```

The ISO recurring interval sets five recurrences from midnight UTC on February 5, 2011 at an interval of 10 days. The recurrences are subsequent to the original date, so the preceding example produces six dates, as shown in the following output.

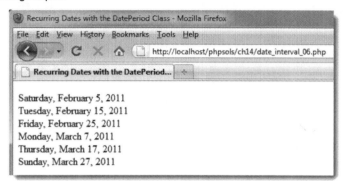

Chapter review

A large part of this chapter has been devoted to the powerful date and time features introduced in PHP 5.2 and 5.3. You don't need them every day, but they're extremely useful and represent a major improvement on the original PHP date and time functions. MySQL's date and time functions also make it easy to format dates and execute queries based on temporal criteria.

Perhaps the biggest problem with dates is deciding whether to use MySQL or PHP to handle the formatting and/or calculations. A useful feature of the PHP DateTime class is that the constructor accepts a date stored in the MySQL format, so you can use an unformatted MySQL date or timestamp to create DateTime objects. However, unless you need to perform further calculations, it's more efficient to use the MySQL DATE_FORMAT() function as part of a SELECT query.

This chapter has also provided you with three utility functions for formatting text and dates. In the next chapter, you'll learn how to store and retrieve related information in multiple database tables.

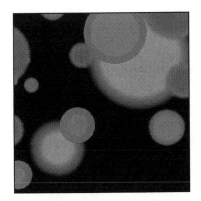

Chapter 15

Pulling Data from Multiple Tables

As I explained in Chapter 11, one of the major strengths of a relational database is the ability to link data in different tables by using the primary key from one table as a foreign key in another table. The phpsols database has two tables: images and blog. It's time to add some more and join them, so you can assign categories to blog entries and associate images with individual articles.

You don't join multiple tables physically, but through SQL. Often, you can join tables by identifying a direct relationship between primary and foreign keys. In some cases, though, the relationship is more complex and needs to go through a third table that acts as a cross reference between the other two.

In this chapter, you'll learn how to establish the relationship between tables and insert the primary key from one table as a foreign key in another table. Although it sounds difficult conceptually, it's actually quite easy—you use a database query to look up the primary key in the first table, save the result, and use it in another query to insert it in the second table.

In particular, you'll learn about the following:

- Understanding the different types of table relationships
- Using a cross-reference table for many-to-many relationships
- Altering a table's structure to add new columns or an index
- Storing a primary key as a foreign key in another table
- Linking tables with INNER JOIN and LEFT JOIN

Understanding table relationships

The simplest type of relationship is **one-to-one** (often represented as **1:1**). This type of relationship is often found in databases that contain information only certain people should see. For example, companies often store details of employees' salaries and other confidential information in a separate table from the more widely accessible staff list. Storing the primary key of each staff member's record as a foreign key in the salaries table establishes a direct relationship between the tables, allowing the accounts department to see the full range of information, while restricting others to the public information.

There's no confidential information in the `phpsols` database, but you might create a one-to-one relationship between a single photo in the `images` table with an article in the `blog` table, as illustrated by Figure 15-1.

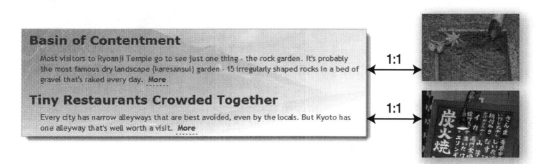

Figure 15-1. A one-to-one relationship links one record directly with another.

This is the simplest way of creating a relationship between the two tables, but it's not ideal. As more articles are added, the nature of the relationship is likely to change. The photo associated with the first article in Figure 15-1 shows maple leaves floating on the water, so it might be suitable to illustrate an article about the changing seasons or autumn hues. The crystal-clear water, bamboo water scoop, and bamboo pipe also suggest other themes that the photo could be used to illustrate. So you could easily end up with the same photo being used for several articles, or a **one-to-many (or 1:n)** relationship, as represented by Figure 15-2.

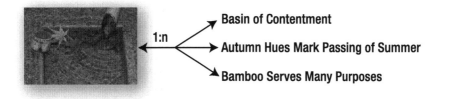

Figure 15-2. A one-to-many relationship links one record with several others.

As you have already learned, a primary key must be unique. So, in a 1:n relationship, you store the primary key from the table on the 1 side of the relationship (the primary or parent table) as a foreign key in the table on the n side (the secondary or child table). In this case, the `image_id` from the `images` table needs to be stored as a foreign key in the `blog` table. What's important to understand about a 1:n relationship is that it's also a collection of 1:1 relationships. Reading Figure 15-2 from right to left, each article has a relationship with a single image. Without this one-on-one relationship, you wouldn't be able to identify which image is associated with a particular article.

What happens if you want to associate more than one image to each article? You could create several columns in the `blog` table to hold the foreign keys, but this rapidly becomes unwieldy. You might start off with `image1`, `image2`, and `image3`, but if most articles have only one image, two columns are redundant for much of the time. And are you going add an extra column for that extra-special article that requires four images?

When faced with the need to accommodate **many-to-many (or n:m)** relationships, you need a different approach. The images and blog tables don't contain sufficient records to demonstrate n:m relationships, but you could add a categories table to tag individual articles. Most articles are likely to belong to multiple categories, and each category will be related with several articles.

The way to resolve complex relationships is through a **cross-reference table** (sometimes called a **linking table**), which establishes a series of one-to-one relationships between related records. This is a special table containing just two columns, both of which are declared a joint primary key. Figure 15-3 shows how this works. Each record in the cross-reference table stores details of the relationship between individual articles in the blog and categories tables. To find all articles that belong to the Kyoto category, you match cat_id 1 in the categories table with cat_id 1 in the cross-reference table. This identifies the records in the blog table with the article_id 2, 3, and 4 as being associated with Kyoto.

Figure 15-3. A cross-reference table resolves many-to-many relationships as 1:1.

Establishing relationships between tables through foreign keys has important implications for how you update and delete records. If you're not careful, you end up with broken links. Ensuring that dependencies aren't broken is known as maintaining **referential integrity**. We'll tackle this important subject in the next chapter. First, let's concentrate on retrieving information stored in separate tables linked through a foreign key relationship.

Linking an image to an article

To demonstrate how to work with multiple tables, let's begin with the straightforward scenarios outlined in Figures 15-1 and 15-2: relations that can be resolved as 1:1 through the storage of the primary key from one table (the parent table) as a foreign key in a second table (the child or dependent table). This involves adding an extra column in the child table to store the foreign key.

Altering the structure of an existing table

Ideally, you should design your database structure before populating it with data. However, relational databases, such as MySQL, are flexible enough to let you add, remove, or change columns in tables even when they already contain records. To associate an image with individual articles in the phpsols database, you need to add an extra column to the blog table to store image_id as a foreign key.

PHP Solution 15-1: Adding an extra column to a table

This PHP solution shows how to add an extra column to an existing table using phpMyAdmin. It assumes that you created the blog table in the phpsols database in Chapter 13.

1. Launch phpMyAdmin, select the phpsols database, and click the link for the blog table in the left-hand navigation frame.

2. Below the blog table structure in the main frame is a form that allows you to add extra columns. You want to add only one column, so the default value in the **Add field(s)** text box is fine. It's normal practice to put foreign keys immediately after the table's primary key, so select the **After** radio button, and make sure the drop-down menu is set to article_id, as shown in the following screenshot. Then click **Go**.

	Field	Type	Collation	Attributes	Null	Default	Extra
☐	article_id	int(10)		UNSIGNED	No	None	auto_increment
☐	title	varchar(255)	latin1_swedish_ci		No	None	
☐	article	text	latin1_swedish_ci		No	None	
☐	updated	timestamp		on update CURRENT_TIMESTAMP	No	CURRENT_TIMESTAMP	on update CURRENT_TIMESTAMP
☐	created	timestamp			No	0000-00-00 00:00:00	

↑ Check All / Uncheck All *With selected:* ▦ ✎ ✕ ▦ ▦ ▦ ▦

▨ Print view ▨ Relation view ▨ Propose table structure ⑦
Add 1 field(s) ○ At End of Table ○ At Beginning of Table ⊙ After article_id ▾ Go

This opens the screen for you to define column attributes. Use the following settings:

- **Field**: image_id
- **Type**: INT
- **Attributes**: UNSIGNED
- **Null**: Selected
- **Index**: INDEX

Do *not* select **AUTO_INCREMENT**. The **Null** check box has been set to selected because not all articles will necessarily be associated with an image. Click **Save**.

You will be returned to the blog table structure, which should now look like this:

Field	Type	Collation	Attributes	Null	Default	Extra
article_id	int(10)		UNSIGNED	No	None	auto_increment
image_id	int(10)		UNSIGNED	Yes	NULL	
title	varchar(255)	latin1_swedish_ci		No	None	
article	text	latin1_swedish_ci		No	None	
updated	timestamp		on update CURRENT_TIMESTAMP	No	CURRENT_TIMESTAMP	on update CURRENT_TIMESTAMP
created	timestamp			No	0000-00-00 00:00:00	

3. If you click the **Browse** tab at the top left of the screen, you will see that the value of image_id is NULL in each record. The challenge now is to insert the correct foreign keys without the need to look up the numbers manually. We'll tackle that next.

Inserting a foreign key in a table

The basic principle behind inserting a foreign key in another table is quite simple: you query the database to find the primary key of the record that you want to link to the other table. You can then use an INSERT or UPDATE query to add the foreign key to the target record.

To demonstrate the basic principle, you'll adapt the update form from Chapter 13 to add a drop-down menu that lists images already registered in the images table (see Figure 15-4).

Figure 15-4. A dynamically generated drop-down menu inserts the appropriate foreign key.

The menu is dynamically generated by a loop that displays the results of a SELECT query. Each image's primary key is stored in the value attribute of the <option> tag. When the form is submitted, the selected value is incorporated into the UPDATE query as the foreign key.

> *To focus on the structure and PHP logic, the instructions in this chapter and the next one cover only MySQLi. The only difference in the PDO version lies in the commands used to submit the SQL queries to the database and to display the results. Fully commented PDO files are in the ch15 and ch16 folders.*

PHP Solution 15-2: Adding the image foreign key

This PHP solution shows how to update records in the blog table by adding the primary key of a selected image as a foreign key. It adapts admin/blog_update_mysqli.php from Chapter 13. Use the version that you created in Chapter 13. Alternatively, copy blog_update_mysqli_03.php from the ch13 folder to the admin folder, and remove _03 from the filename.

1. The existing SELECT query that retrieves details of the article to be updated needs to be amended so that it includes the foreign key, image_id, and the result needs to be bound to a new result variable, $image_id. You then need to run a second SELECT query to get the details of the images table, but before you can do so, you need to free the database resources by applying the free_result() method on the prepared statement ($stmt). Add the following code highlighted in bold to the existing script:

```php
if (isset($_GET['article_id']) && !$_POST) {
    // prepare SQL query
    $sql = 'SELECT article_id, image_id, title, article
            FROM blog WHERE article_id = ?';
    $stmt->prepare($sql);
    // bind the query parameter
    $stmt->bind_param('i', $_GET['article_id']);
    // bind the results to variables
    $stmt->bind_result($article_id, $image_id, $title, $article);
    // execute the query, and fetch the result
    $OK = $stmt->execute();
    $stmt->fetch();
    // free the database resources for the second query
    $stmt->free_result();
}
```

Notice that the conditional statement wrapping the call to the prepare() method and subsequent code has been removed. You don't need it after verifying that the prepared statement doesn't contain any syntax errors.

2. Inside the form, you need to display the filenames stored in the images table. Since the second SELECT statement doesn't rely on external data, it's simpler to use the query() method instead of a prepared statement. Add the following code after the article text area (it's all new code, but the PHP sections are highlighted in bold for ease of reference):

```php
<p>
  <label for="image_id">Uploaded image:</label>
  <select name="image_id" id="image_id">
    <option value="">Select image</option>
    <?php
    // get the list images
    $getImages = 'SELECT image_id, filename
                    FROM images ORDER BY filename';
    $images = $conn->query($getImages);
    while ($row = $images->fetch_assoc()) {
    ?>
```

```
      <option value="<?php echo $row['image_id']; ?>"
      <?php
      if ($row['image_id'] == $image_id) {
        echo 'selected';
      }
      ?>><?php echo $row['filename']; ?></option>
    <?php } ?>
    </select>
</p>
```

The first `<option>` tag is hard-coded with the label `Select image`, and its value is set to an empty string. The remaining `<option>` tags are populated by a `while` loop that extracts each record to an array called `$row`.

A conditional statement checks whether the current `image_id` is the same as the one already stored in the `articles` table. If it is, `selected` is inserted into the `<option>` tag so that it displays the correct value in the drop-down menu.

Make sure you don't omit the third character in the following line:

`?>><?php echo $row['filename']; ?></option>`

It's the closing angle bracket of the `<option>` tag, sandwiched between two PHP tags.

3. Save the page, and load it into a browser. You should be automatically redirected to `blog_list_mysqli.php`. Select one of the **EDIT** links, and make sure that your page looks like Figure 15-4. Check the browser source code view to verify that the `value` attributes of the `<option>` tags contain the primary key of each image.

4. The final stage is to add the `image_id` to the `UPDATE` query. Because some blog entries might not be associated with an image, you need to create alternative prepared statements like this:

```
// if form has been submitted, update record
if (isset($_POST ['update'])) {
  // prepare update query
  if (!empty($_POST['image_id'])) {
    $sql = 'UPDATE blog SET image_id = ?, title = ?, article = ?
           WHERE article_id = ?';
    $stmt->prepare($sql);
    $stmt->bind_param('issi', $_POST['image_id'], $_POST['title'], ⇥
      $_POST['article'], $_POST['article_id']);
  } else {
    $sql = 'UPDATE blog SET image_id = NULL, title = ?, article = ?
           WHERE article_id = ?';
    $stmt->prepare($sql);
    $stmt->bind_param('ssi', $_POST['title'], $_POST['article'], ⇥
      $_POST['article_id']);
  }
  $stmt->execute();
  $done = $stmt->affected_rows;
}
```

If $_POST['image_id'] has a value, you add it to the SQL as the first parameter with a placeholder question mark. Since it must be an integer, you add i to the beginning of the first argument of bind_param().

However, if $_POST['image_id'] doesn't contain a value, you need to create a different prepared statement to set the value of image_id to NULL in the SQL query. Because it has an explicit value, you don't add it to bind_param().

5. Test the page again, select a filename from the drop-down menu, and click **Update Entry**. You can verify whether the foreign key has been inserted into the articles table by refreshing **Browse** in phpMyAdmin or by selecting the same article for updating. This time, the correct filename should be displayed in the drop-down menu.

6. Check your code against blog_update_mysqli_04.php in the ch15 folder, if necessary.

The PDO version is in blog_update_pdo_04.php in the ch15 folder.

Selecting records from multiple tables

There are several ways to link tables in a SELECT query, but the most common is to list the table names separated by INNER JOIN. On its own, INNER JOIN produces all possible combinations of rows (a Cartesian join). To select only related values, you need to specify the primary/foreign-key relationship. For example, to select articles and their related images from the blog and images table, you can use a WHERE clause like this:

```
SELECT title, article, filename, caption
FROM blog INNER JOIN images
WHERE blog.image_id = images.image_id
```

The title and article columns exist only in the blog table. Likewise, filename and caption exist only in the images table. They're unambiguous and don't need to be qualified. However, image_id exists in both tables, so you need to prefix each reference with the table name and a period.

For many years, it was common practice to use a comma in place of INNER JOIN like this:

```
SELECT title, article, filename, caption
FROM blog, images
WHERE blog.image_id = images.image_id
```

This is no longer recommended practice because of changes made to the way joins are handled in MySQL 5.0.12.

Using a comma to join tables can result in SQL syntax errors that can be difficult to resolve. Use INNER JOIN instead.

Instead of a WHERE clause, you can use ON like this:

```
SELECT title, article, filename, caption
FROM blog INNER JOIN images ON blog.image_id = images.image_id
```

When both columns have the same name, you can use the following syntax:

```
SELECT title, article, filename, caption
FROM blog INNER JOIN images USING (image_id)
```

This last method of matching the primary and foreign keys is my personal preference. However, if the columns you are matching have different names, you must use ON or a WHERE clause.

PHP Solution 15-3: Building the details page

This PHP solution shows how to join the blog and images tables to display a selected article with its associated photo.

1. Copy details_01.php from the ch15 folder to the phpsols site root, and rename it details.php. Do not update the links if your editing environment prompts you to do so. Make sure that footer.inc.php and menu.inc.php are in the includes folder, and load the page in a browser. It should look like Figure 15-5.

Figure 15-5. The details page contains a placeholder image and text.

2. Load blog_list_mysqli.php or blog_list_pdo.php into a browser, and update the following three articles by assigning the image filename as indicated:

    -   Basin of Contentment: basin.jpg

    -   Tiny Restaurants Crowded Together: menu.jpg

    -   Trainee Geishas Go Shopping: maiko.jpg

3. Check that the foreign keys have been registered by navigating to the blog table in phpMyAdmin and clicking the **Browse** tab. At least one article should have NULL as the value for image_id, as shown in Figure 15-6.

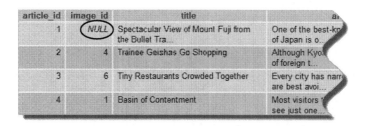

Figure 15-6. The foreign key of the article not associated with an image is set to NULL.

4. In details.php, include utility_funcs.inc.php from the previous chapter (if necessary, copy it from the ch14 folder to the includes folder). Then include the database connection file, create a read-only connection, and prepare the SQL query inside a PHP code block above the DOCTYPE declaration like this:

```
require_once('./includes/utility_funcs.inc.php');
require_once('./includes/connection.inc.php');
// connect to the database
$conn = dbConnect('read');
 // check for article_id in query string
 if (isset($_GET['article_id']) && is_numeric($_GET['article_id'])) {
   $article_id = (int) $_GET['article_id'];
 } else {
   $article_id = 0;
 }
 $sql = "SELECT title, article,
         DATE_FORMAT(updated, '%W, %M %D, %Y') AS updated, filename, caption
         FROM blog INNER JOIN images USING (image_id)
         WHERE blog.article_id = $article_id";
$result = $conn->query($sql);
$row = $result->fetch_assoc();
```

The code checks for article_id in the URL query string. If it exists and is numeric, it's assigned to $article_id using the (int) casting operator to make sure it's an integer. Otherwise, $article_id is set to 0. You could choose a default article instead, but leave it at 0 for the moment because I want to illustrate an important point.

The SELECT query retrieves the title, article, and updated columns from the blog table, and the filename and caption columns from the images table. The value of updated is formatted using the DATE_FORMAT() function and an alias as described in Chapter 14. Because only one record is being retrieved, using the original column name as the alias doesn't cause a problem with the sort order.

The tables are joined using INNER JOIN and a USING() clause that matches the values in the image_id columns in both tables. The WHERE clause selects the article identified by $article_id. Since the data type of $article_id has been checked, it's safe to use in the query. There's no need to use a prepared statement.

Note that the query is wrapped in double quotes so that the value of $article_id is interpreted. To avoid conflicts with the outer pair of quotes, single quotes are used around the format string passed as an argument to DATE_FORMAT().

5. The rest of the code displays the results of the SQL query in the main body of the page. Replace the placeholder text in the <h2> tags like this:

```
<h2><?php if ($row) {
  echo $row['title'];
} else {
  echo 'No record found';
}
?>
</h2>
```

If the SELECT query finds no results, $row will be empty, which PHP interprets as false. So this displays the title, or **No record found** if the result set is empty.

6. Replace the placeholder date like this:

```
<p><?php if ($row) { echo $row['updated']; } ?></p>
```

7. Immediately following the date paragraph is a <div> containing a placeholder image. Even if the result set isn't empty, not all articles are associated with an image, so the <div> needs to be wrapped in a conditional statement that also checks that $row['filename'] contains a value. Amend the <div> like this:

```
<?php
if ($row && !empty($row['filename'])) {
  $filename = "images/{$row['filename']}";
  $imageSize = getimagesize($filename);
?>
<div id="pictureWrapper">
<img src="<?php echo $filename; ?>" alt="<?php echo $row['caption']; ?>"
<?php echo $imageSize[3];?>>
</div>
<?php } ?>
```

This uses code that was described in Chapter 12, so I won't go into it again.

8. Finally, you need to display the article. Delete the paragraph of placeholder text, and add the following code between the closing curly brace and closing PHP tag at the end of the final code block in the previous step:

```
<?php } if ($row) { echo convertToParas($row['article']); } ?>
```

This uses the convertToParas() function in utility_funcs.inc.php to wrap the blog entry in <p> tags and replace sequences of new line characters with closing and opening tags (see "Displaying paragraphs" in Chapter 14).

9. Save the page, and load blog.php into a browser. Click the **More** link for an article that has an image assigned through a foreign key. You should see details.php with the full article and

image laid out as shown in Figure 15-7. Check your code, if necessary, with details_mysqli_01.php or details_pdo_01.php in the ch15 folder.

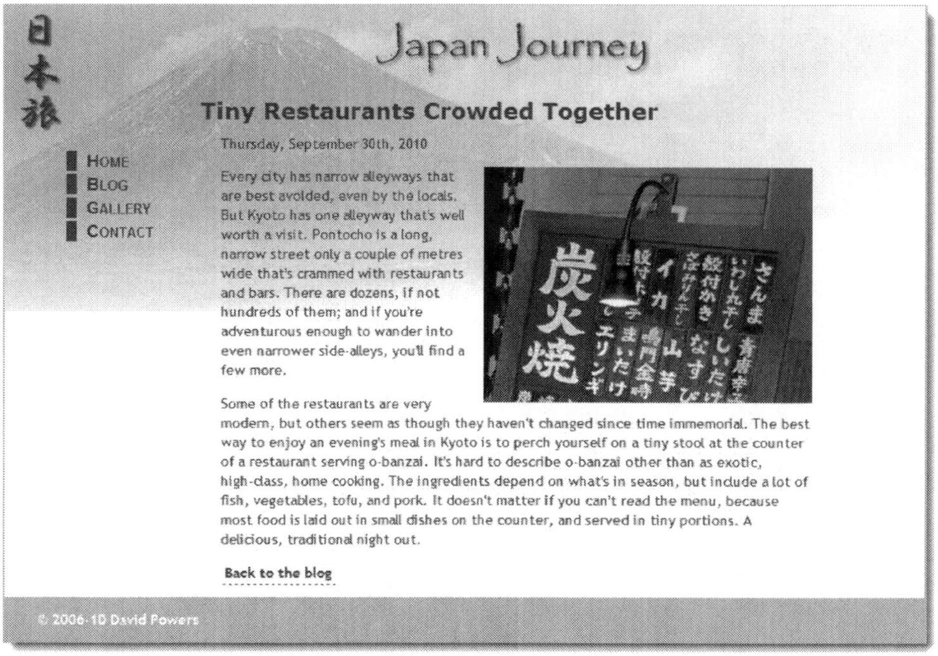

Figure 15-7. The details page pulls the article from one table and the image from another.

10. Click the link back to blog.php, and test the other items. Each article that has an image associated with it should display correctly. Click the **More** link for the article that doesn't have an image. This time you should see the result shown in Figure 15-8.

Figure 15-8. The lack of an associated image causes the SELECT query to fail.

You know that the article is in the database because the first two sentences wouldn't be displayed in `blog.php` otherwise. To understand this sudden "disappearance," see Figure 15-16. The value of `image_id` is NULL for the record that doesn't have an image associated with it. Because all the records in the `images` table have a primary key, the `USING()` clause can't find a match. The solution is to use `LEFT JOIN` instead of `INNER JOIN`, as explained in the next section.

Finding records that don't have a matching foreign key

Take the `SELECT` query from PHP Solution 15-3, and remove the condition that searches for a specific article, which leaves this:

```
SELECT title, article,
DATE_FORMAT(updated, '%W, %M %D, %Y') AS updated, filename, caption
FROM blog INNER JOIN images USING (image_id)
```

If you run this query in the **SQL** tab of phpMyAdmin, it produces the result shown in Figure 15-9.

title	article	updated	filename	caption
Trainee Geishas Go Shopping	Although Kyoto attracts large numbers of foreign t...	Thursday, September 30th, 2010	maiko.jpg	Maiko—trainee geishas in Kyoto
Tiny Restaurants Crowded Together	Every city has narrow alleyways that are best avoi...	Thursday, September 30th, 2010	menu.jpg	Menu outside restaurant in Pontocho, Kyoto
Basin of Contentment	Most visitors to Ryoanji Temple go to see just one...	Thursday, September 30th, 2010	basin.jpg	Water basin at Ryoanji temple, Kyoto

Figure 15-9. INNER JOIN finds only records that have a match in both tables.

With `INNER JOIN`, the `SELECT` query succeeds only if there is a full match. However, if you use `LEFT JOIN`, the result includes records that have a match in the left table, but not in the right one. Left and right refer to the order in which you perform the join. Rewrite the `SELECT` query like this:

```
SELECT title, article,
DATE_FORMAT(updated, '%W, %M %D, %Y') AS updated, filename, caption
FROM blog LEFT JOIN images USING (image_id)
```

When you run it in phpMyAdmin, you get all four articles as shown in Figure 15-10.

title	article	updated	filename	caption
Spectacular View of Mount Fuji from the Bullet Tra...	One of the best-known tourist images of Japan is o...	Friday, September 17th, 2010	NULL	NULL
Trainee Geishas Go Shopping	Although Kyoto attracts large numbers of foreign t...	Thursday, September 30th, 2010	maiko.jpg	Maiko—trainee geishas in Kyoto
Tiny Restaurants Crowded Together	Every city has narrow alleyways that are best avoi...	Thursday, September 30th, 2010	menu.jpg	Menu outside restaurant in Pontocho, Kyoto
Basin of Contentment	Most visitors to Ryoanji Temple go to see just one...	Thursday, September 30th, 2010	basin.jpg	Water basin at Ryoanji temple, Kyoto

Figure 15-10. LEFT JOIN includes records that don't have a match in the right table.

As you can see, the empty fields from the right table (`images`) are displayed as NULL.

If the column names are not the same in both tables, use ON like this:

```
FROM table_1 LEFT JOIN table_1 ON table_1.col_name = table_2.col_name
```

So, now you can rewrite the SQL query in details.php like this:

```
$sql = "SELECT title, article,
        DATE_FORMAT(updated, '%W, %M %D, %Y') AS updated, filename, caption
        FROM blog LEFT JOIN images USING (image_id)
        WHERE blog.article_id = $article_id";
```

If you click the **More** link to view the article that doesn't have an associated image, you should now see the article correctly displayed as shown in Figure 15-11. The other articles should still display correctly, too. The finished code is in details_mysqli_02.php, and details_pdo_02.php.

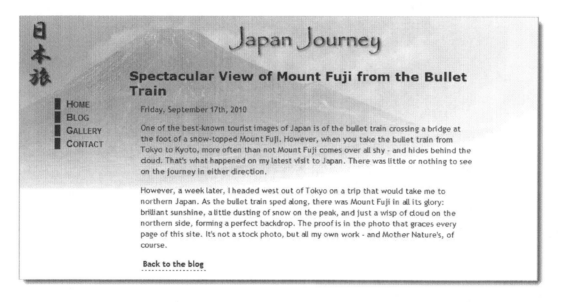

Figure 15-11. LEFT JOIN also retrieves articles that don't have a matching foreign key.

Creating an intelligent link

The link at the bottom of details.php goes straight back to blog.php. That's fine with only four items in the blog table, but once you start getting more records in a database, you need to build a navigation system as I showed you in Chapter 12. The problem with a navigation system is that you need a way to return visitors to the same point in the result set that they came from.

PHP Solution 15-4: Returning to the same point in a navigation system

This PHP solution checks whether the visitor arrived from an internal or external link. If the referring page was within the same site, the link returns the visitor to the same place. If the referring page was an external site, or if the server doesn't support the necessary superglobal variables, the script substitutes a standard link. It is shown here in the context of details.php, but it can be used on any page.

1. Locate the back link in the main body of details.php. It looks like this:

```
<p><a href="blog.php">Back to the blog</a></p>
```

2. Place your cursor immediately to the right of the first quotation mark, and insert the following code highlighted in bold:

```
<p><a href="
<?php
// check that browser supports $_SERVER variables
if (isset($_SERVER['HTTP_REFERER']) && isset($_SERVER['HTTP_HOST'])) {
  $url = parse_url($_SERVER['HTTP_REFERER']);
  // find if visitor was referred from a different domain
  if ($url['host'] == $_SERVER['HTTP_HOST']) {
    // if same domain, use referring URL
    echo $_SERVER['HTTP_REFERER'];
  }
} else {
  // otherwise, send to main page
  echo 'blog.php';
} ?>">Back to the blog</a></p>
```

$_SERVER['HTTP_REFERER'] and $_SERVER['HTTP_HOST'] are superglobal variables that contain the URL of the referring page and the current hostname. You need to check their existence with isset() because not all servers support them. Also, the browser might block the URL of the referring page.

The parse_url() function creates an array containing each part of a URL, so $url['host'] contains the hostname. If it matches $_SERVER['HTTP_HOST'], you know that the visitor was referred by an internal link, so the full URL of the internal link is inserted in the href attribute. This includes any query string, so the link sends the visitor back to the same position in a navigation system. Otherwise, an ordinary link is created to the target page.

The finished code is in details_mysqli_03.php, and details_pdo_3.php in the ch15 folder.

Chapter review

Retrieving information stored in multiple tables is relatively simple with INNER JOIN and LEFT JOIN. The key to working successfully with multiple tables lies in structuring the relationship between them so that complex relationships can always be resolved as 1:1, if necessary through a cross-reference (or linking) table. The next chapter continues the exploration of working with multiple tables, showing you how to deal with foreign key relationships when inserting, updating, and deleting records.

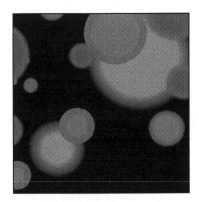

Chapter 16

Managing Multiple Database Tables

The previous chapter showed you how to use INNER JOIN and LEFT JOIN to retrieve information stored in multiple tables. You also learned how to link existing tables by adding an extra column to the child table and updating each record individually to insert a foreign key. However, most of the time, you'll want to insert data simultaneously in both tables. That presents a problem, because INSERT commands can operate on only one table at a time. You need to get around this restriction by constructing scripts that handle the INSERT operations in the correct sequence, starting with the parent table, so that you can get the new record's primary key and insert it in the child table at the same time as other details. Similar considerations also need to be taken into account when updating and deleting records. The code involved isn't difficult, but you need to keep the sequence of events clearly in mind as you build the scripts.

This chapter guides you through the process of inserting new articles in the blog table, optionally selecting a related image or uploading a new one, and assigning the article to one or more categories, all in a single operation. Then, you'll build the scripts to update and delete articles without destroying the referential integrity of related tables.

You'll also learn about foreign key constraints, which control what happens if you try to delete records that still have a foreign key relationship in another table. The widely used MyISAM storage engine doesn't currently support foreign key constraints, but they are supported by InnoDB, the default storage engine in MySQL 5.5 and later. This chapter describes how to work with both storage engines.

In particular, you'll learn about the following:

- Inserting, updating, and deleting records in related tables
- Finding the primary key of a record immediately after it has been created
- Converting a table's storage engine
- Establishing foreign key constraints between InnoDB tables

Maintaining referential integrity

With single tables, it doesn't matter how often you update a record or how many records you delete, the impact on other records is zero. Once you store the primary key of a record as a foreign key in a different table, you create a dependency that needs to be managed. For example, if you delete the second article from the blog table ("Trainee Geishas Go Shopping"), Figure 16-1 shows it linked to the Kyoto and People categories through the article2cat cross-reference table.

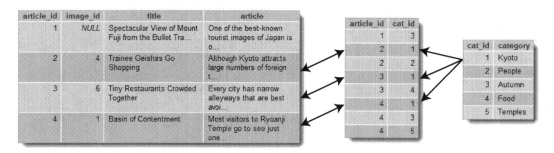

Figure 16-1. You need to manage foreign key relations to avoid orphaned records.

If you fail to delete the entries for article_id 2 in the cross-reference table, a query that looks for all articles in the Kyoto or People categories tries to match a nonexistent record in the blog table. Similarly, if you decide to delete one of the categories without also deleting matching records in the cross-reference table, a query that looks for the categories associated with an article tries to match a nonexistent category.

Before long, your database is littered with orphaned records. Fortunately, maintaining referential integrity is not difficult. SQL does it through the establishment of rules known as **foreign key constraints** that tell the database what to do when you update or delete a record that has dependent records in another table. The bad news is that the default storage engine prior to MySQL 5.5, MyISAM, doesn't support foreign key constraints. You need to use InnoDB instead.

> *Choosing between MyISAM and InnoDB isn't simply a matter of one being "better" than the other. MyISAM's strengths lie in smaller file sizes and speed. It also supports full text indexing and searching (see http://dev.mysql.com/doc/refman/5.1/en/fulltext-search.html), which InnoDB does not. Support for foreign key constraints in MyISAM tables is planned for a later version of MySQL.*

InnoDB has been an integral part of MySQL since version 4.0 was released in 2003. Unfortunately, many hosting companies disable InnoDB or offer it only on premium hosting plans. If your hosting company supports InnoDB, you can easily convert MyISAM tables and use foreign key constraints. If you don't have access to InnoDB, you need to maintain referential integrity by building the necessary rules into your PHP scripts. This chapter shows both approaches.

PHP Solution 16-1: Checking whether InnoDB is supported

This PHP solution explains how to check whether your remote server supports the InnoDB storage engine.

1. If your hosting company provides phpMyAdmin to administer your database(s), launch phpMyAdmin on your remote server, and click the **Engines** tab at the top of the screen, if it's available. This displays a list of storage engines similar to Figure 16-2.

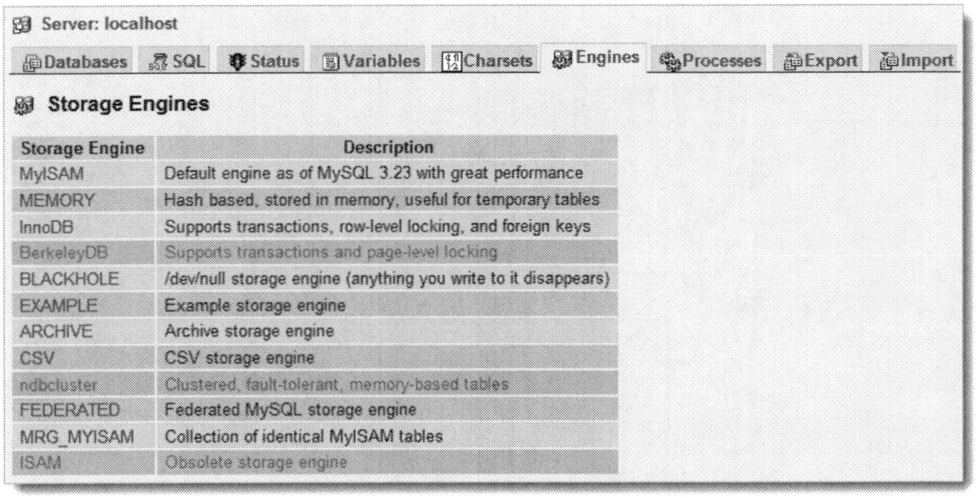

Figure 16-2. Checking storage engine support through phpMyAdmin

2. The list displays all storage engines, including those that are not supported. Unsupported or disabled storage engines are grayed out. If you're not sure of the status of InnoDB, click its name in the list.

    If InnoDB is not supported, you'll see a message telling you so. If, on the other hand, you see a list of variables similar to Figure 16-3, you're in luck—InnoDB is supported.

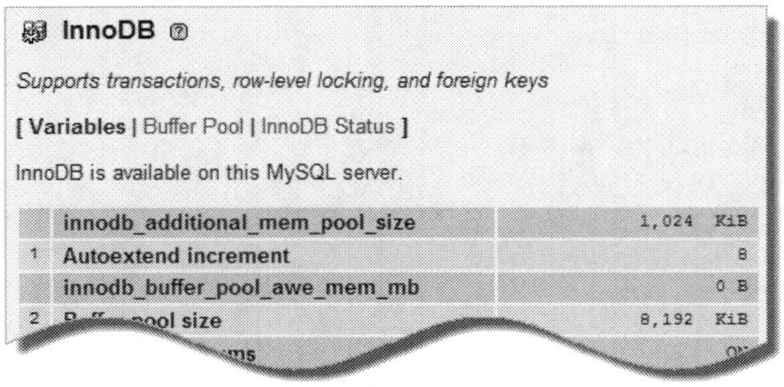

Figure 16-3. Confirmation that InnoDB is supported

3. If there's no **Engines** tab in phpMyAdmin, select any table in your database, and click the **Operations** tab at the top right of the screen. In the **Table options** section, click the down arrow to the right of the **Storage Engine** field to display the available options (see Figure 16-4). If InnoDB is listed, it's supported.

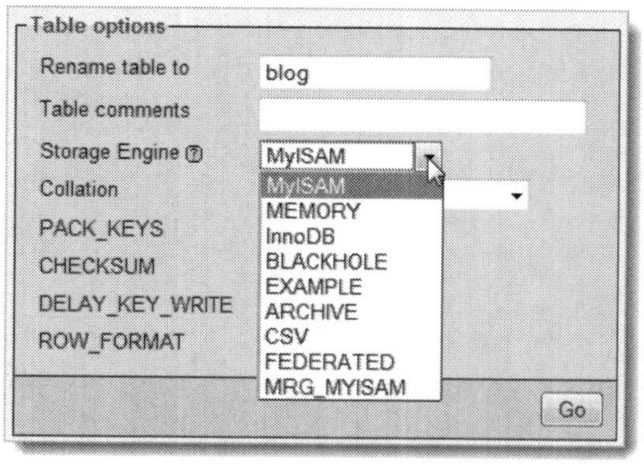

Figure 16-4. The available storage engines are listed in the Table options.

4. If neither of the preceding methods gives you the answer, open `storage_engines.php` in the `ch16` folder. Edit the first three lines to insert the hostname, username, and password for the database on your remote server.

5. Upload `storage_engines.php` to your website, and load the page into a browser. You should see a list of storage engines and level of support, as shown in Figure 16-5. In some cases, **NO** will be replaced by **DISABLED**.

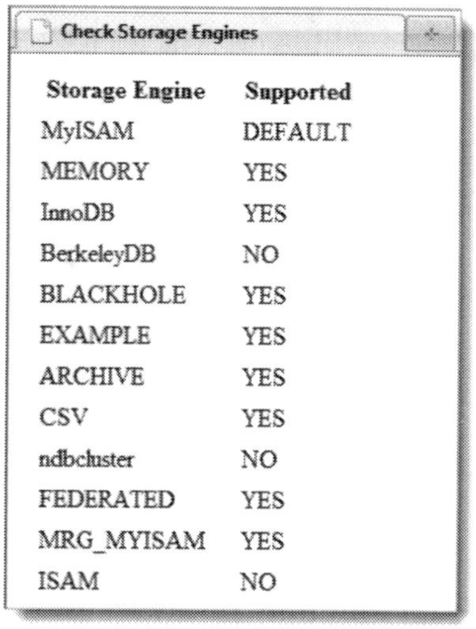

Figure 16-5. The SQL query in `storage_engines.php` reports which ones are supported.

As Figure 16-5 shows, a typical installation of MySQL supports several storage engines. What may come as a surprise is that you can use different storage engines within the same database. In fact, it's recommended that you do. Even if your remote server supports InnoDB, it's usually more efficient to use MyISAM for tables that don't have a foreign key relationship. Use InnoDB for tables that have foreign key relationships. You should also use InnoDB if you need support for transactions.

A **transaction** is a series of related SQL queries. If one part of the series fails, the transaction is terminated, and the database rolls back to its original state before the transaction. Financial databases make extensive use of transactions, which are beyond the scope of this book.

I'll explain how to convert tables to InnoDB and set up foreign key constraints later in this chapter. Before that, let's take a look at how to establish and use foreign key relationships regardless of the storage engine being used.

Inserting records into multiple tables

An INSERT query can insert data into only one table. Consequently, when working with multiple tables, you need to plan your insert scripts carefully to ensure that all the information is stored and that the correct foreign key relationships are established. PHP Solution 15-2 in the previous chapter showed how to add the correct foreign key for an image that is already registered in the database. However, when inserting a new blog entry, you need to be able to select an existing image, upload a new image, or choose to have no image at all. This means that your processing script needs to check whether an image has been selected or uploaded and execute the relevant commands accordingly. In addition, tagging a blog entry with zero or more categories increases the number of decisions the script needs to make. Figure 16-6 shows the decision chain.

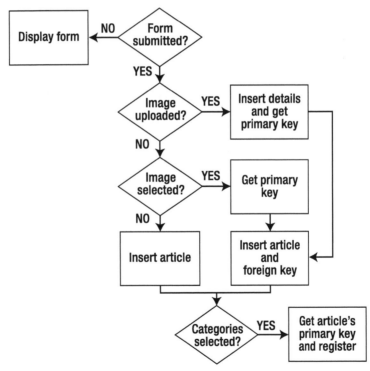

Figure 16-6. The decision chain for inserting a new blog article with an image and categories

When the page first loads, the form hasn't been submitted, so the page simply displays the insert form. Both the existing images and categories are listed in the insert form by querying the database in the same way as for the images in the update form in PHP Solution 15-2.

After the form has been submitted, the processing script goes through the following steps:

1. If an image has been uploaded, the upload is processed, the details of the image are stored in the `images` table, and the script gets the primary key of the new record.

2. If no image has been uploaded, but an existing image has been selected, the script gets its foreign key from the value submitted through the `$_POST` array.

3. In either case, the new blog article is inserted in the `blog` table along with the image's primary key as a foreign key. However, if an image has neither been uploaded nor selected from the existing ones, the article is inserted in the `blog` table without a foreign key.

4. Finally, the script checks if any categories have been selected. If they have, the script gets the new article's primary key and combines it with the primary keys of the selected categories in the `article2cat` table.

If there's a problem at any stage, the script needs to abandon the rest of the process and redisplay the user's input. The script is quite long, so I'll break it up into several sections. The first stage is to create the `article2cat` cross-reference table.

Creating a cross-reference table

When dealing with many-to-many relationships in a database, you need to build a cross-reference table like the one in Figure 16-1. What's unusual about a cross-reference table is that it consists of just two columns, which are jointly declared as the table's primary key (known as a **composite primary key**). If you look at Figure 16-7, you'll see that the `article_id` and `cat_id` columns both contain the same number several times—something that's unacceptable in a primary key, which must be unique. However, in a composite primary key, it's the combination of both values that is unique. The first two combinations, `1,3` and `2,1`, are not repeated anywhere else in the table, nor are any of the others.

article_id	cat_id
1	3
2	1
2	2
3	1
3	4
4	1
4	3
4	5

Figure 16-7. In a cross-reference table, both columns together form a composite primary key.

Setting up the categories and cross-reference tables

In the ch16 folder, you'll find categories.sql, which contains the SQL to create the categories table and the cross-reference table, article2cat, together with some sample data. The settings used to create the tables are listed in Tables 16-1 and 16-2. Both database tables have just two columns (fields).

Table 16-1. Settings for the categories table

Field	Type	Length/Values	Attributes	Null	Index	AUTO_INCREMENT
cat_id	INT		UNSIGNED	Deselected	PRIMARY	Selected
category	VARCHAR	**20**		Deselected		

Table 16-2. Settings for the article2cat cross-reference table

Field	Type	Length/Values	Attributes	Null	Index	AUTO_INCREMENT
article_id	INT		UNSIGNED	Deselected	PRIMARY	
cat_id	INT		UNSIGNED	Deselected	PRIMARY	

The important thing about the definition for a cross-reference table is that *both* columns are set as primary key, and that auto_increment is *not selected* for either column. To ensure that the table recognizes them as a composite primary key, you must declare both columns as primary key at the same time.

If, by mistake, you declare only one as the primary key, MySQL prevents you from adding the second one later. You must delete the primary key index from the single column and then reapply it to both. It's the combination of the two columns that are treated as the primary key.

Getting the filename of an uploaded image

The script makes use of the Ps2_Upload class from Chapter 6, but the class needs tweaking slightly because the filenames of uploaded files are incorporated into the $_messages property.

PHP Solution 16-2: Improving the Ps2_Upload class

This PHP solution adapts the Ps2_Upload class from Chapter 6 by creating a new protected property to store the names of successfully uploaded files, together with a public method to retrieve the array.

1. Open Upload.php in the classes/Ps2 folder. Alternatively, copy Upload_05.php from the ch06 folder, and save it in classes/Ps2 as Upload.php.

2. Add the following line to the list of properties at the top of the file:

```
protected $_filenames = array();
```

This initializes a protected property called $_filenames as an empty array.

437

3. Amend the processFile() method to add the amended filename to the $_filenames property if the file is successfully uploaded. The new code is highlighted in bold.

```
protected function processFile($filename, $error, $size, $type, ⮐
$tmp_name, $overwrite) {
$OK = $this->checkError($filename, $error);
if ($OK) {
  $sizeOK = $this->checkSize($filename, $size);
  $typeOK = $this->checkType($filename, $type);
  if ($sizeOK && $typeOK) {
    $name = $this->checkName($filename, $overwrite);
    $success = move_uploaded_file($tmp_name, $this->_destination . $name);
    if ($success) {
      // add the amended filename to the array of filenames
      $this->_filenames[] = $name;
      $message = "$filename uploaded successfully";
      if ($this->_renamed) {
        $message .= " and renamed $name";
      }
      $this->_messages[] = $message;
    } else {
      $this->_messages[] = "Could not upload $filename";
    }
  }
}
}
```

The name gets its value from the checkName() method, which replaces spaces with underscores and renames files that are the same as an existing file. It's added to the $_filenames array only if the file is successfully moved to the destination folder.

4. Add a public method to return the values stored in the $_filenames property. The code looks like this:

```
public function getFilenames() {
  return $this->_filenames;
}
```

It doesn't matter where you put this code in the class definition, but it's common practice to keep all public methods together.

5. Save Upload.php. If you need to check your code, compare it with Upload_06.php in the ch16 folder.

Adapting the insert form to deal with multiple tables

The insert form for blog articles that you created in Chapter 13 already contains the code needed to insert most of the details in the blog table. Rather than start again from scratch, it makes sense to adapt the existing page. As it stands, the page contains only a text input field for the title and a text area for the article.

You need to add a multiple-choice <select> list for categories, and a drop-down <select> menu for existing images.

To prevent a user from selecting an existing image at the same time as uploading a new one, a check box and JavaScript control the display of the relevant input fields. Selecting the check box disables the drop-down menu for existing images and displays the input fields for a new image and caption. Deselecting the check box hides and disables the file and caption fields, and reenables the drop-down menu. If JavaScript is disabled, the options for uploading a new image and captions are hidden.

PHP Solution 16-3: Adding the category and image input fields

This PHP solution begins the process of adapting the blog entry insert form from Chapter 13 by adding the input fields for categories and images.

1. In the admin folder, open the version of blog_insert_mysqli.php that you created in Chapter 13. Alternatively, copy blog_insert_mysqli.php from the ch13 folder to the admin folder.

2. The <select> elements for the categories and existing images need to query the database when the page first loads, so you need to move the connection script and database connection outside the conditional statement that checks if the form has been submitted. Locate the lines highlighted in bold:

```
if (isset($_POST['insert'])) {
  require_once('../includes/connection.inc.php');
  // initialize flag
  $OK = false;
  // create database connection
  $conn = dbConnect('write');
```

Move them outside the conditional statement like this:

```
require_once('../includes/connection.inc.php');
// create database connection
$conn = dbConnect('write');
if (isset($_POST['insert'])) {
  // initialize flag
  $OK = false;
```

3. The form in the body of the page needs to be capable of uploading a file, so you need to add the enctype attribute to the opening <form> tag like this:

```
<form id="form1" method="post" action="" enctype="multipart/form-data">
```

4. If an error occurs when trying to upload a file—for example, if it's too big or not an image—the insert operation will be halted. Amend the existing text input field and text area to redisplay the values using the same technique as in Chapter 5. The text input field looks like this:

```
<input name="title" type="text" class="widebox" id="title" ➥
  value="<?php if (isset($error)) {
  echo htmlentities($_POST['title'], ENT_COMPAT, 'utf-8');
} ?>">
```

The text area looks like this:

```
<textarea name="article" cols="60" rows="8" class="widebox" id="article"><?php
if (isset($error)) {
  echo htmlentities($_POST['article'], ENT_COMPAT, 'utf-8');
} ?></textarea>
```

Make sure there's no gap between the opening and closing PHP tags and the HTML. Otherwise, you'll add unwanted whitespace inside the text input field and text area.

5. The new form elements go between the text area and the submit button. First, add the code for the multiple-choice <select> list for categories. The code looks like this:

```
<p>
  <label for="category">Categories:</label>
  <select name="category[]" size="5" multiple id="category">
  <?php
  // get categories
  $getCats = 'SELECT cat_id, category FROM categories
              ORDER BY category';
  $categories = $conn->query($getCats);
  while ($row = $categories->fetch_assoc()) {
  ?>
  <option value="<?php echo $row['cat_id']; ?>" <?php
  if (isset($_POST['category']) && in_array($row['cat_id'], ↵
    $_POST['category'])) {
    echo 'selected';
  } ?>><?php echo $row['category']; ?></option>
  <?php } ?>
  </select>
</p>
```

To allow the selection of multiple values, the multiple attribute has been added to <select> tag, and the size attribute set to 5. The values need to be submitted as an array, so a pair of square brackets has been appended to the name attribute.

The SQL queries the categories table, and a while loop populates the <option> tags with the primary keys and category names. The conditional statement in the while loop adds selected to the <option> tag to redisplay selected values if the insert operation fails.

6. Save blog_insert_mysqli.php, and load the page into a browser. The form should now look like Figure 16-8.

Insert New Blog Entry

Title:

Article:

Categories:
Autumn
Food
Kyoto
People
Temples

Insert New Entry

Figure 16-8. The multiple-choice `<select>` list pulls the values from the `categories` table.

7. View the page's source code to verify that the primary key of each category is correctly embedded in the value attribute of each `<option>` tag. You can compare your code with `blog_insert_mysqli_01.php` in the `ch16` folder.

8. Next, create the `<select>` drop-down menu to display the images already registered in the database. Add this code immediately after the code you inserted in step 5:

```
<p>
  <label for="image_id">Uploaded image:</label>
  <select name="image_id" id="image_id">
    <option value="">Select image</option>
    <?php
    // get the list of images
    $getImages = 'SELECT image_id, filename
                  FROM images ORDER BY filename';
    $images = $conn->query($getImages);
    while ($row = $images->fetch_assoc()) {
    ?>
    <option value="<?php echo $row['image_id']; ?>"
    <?php
    if (isset($_POST['image_id']) && $row['image_id'] == $_POST['image_id']) {
      echo 'selected';
    }
    ?>><?php echo $row['filename']; ?></option>
    <?php } ?>
  </select>
</p>
```

This creates another SELECT query to get the primary key and filename of each image stored in the images table. The code should be very familiar by now, so it needs no explanation.

9. The check box, file input field, and text input field for the caption go between the code in the previous step and the submit button. The code looks like this:

```
<p id="allowUpload">
  <input type="checkbox" name="upload_new" id="upload_new">
  <label for="upload_new">Upload new image</label>
</p>
<p class="optional">
  <label for="image">Select image:</label>
  <input type="file" name="image" id="image">
</p>
<p class="optional">
  <label for="caption">Caption:</label>
  <input name="caption" type="text" class="widebox" id="caption">
</p>
```

The paragraph that contains the check box has been given the ID allowUpload, and the two other paragraphs have been assigned a class called optional. The style rules in admin.css set the display property of these three paragraphs to none.

10. Save blog_insert_mysqli.php, and load the page in a browser. The images <select> drop-down menu is displayed below the categories list, but the three form elements you inserted in step 9 are hidden. This is what will be displayed if JavaScript is disabled in the browser. Users will have the option to select categories and an existing image but not to upload a new image.

If necessary, check your code against blog_insert_mysqli_02.php in the ch16 folder.

11. Copy toggle_fields.js from the ch16 folder to the admin folder. The file contains the following JavaScript:

```
var cbox = document.getElementById('allowUpload');
cbox.style.display = 'block';
var uploadImage = document.getElementById('upload_new');
uploadImage.onclick = function () {
  var image_id = document.getElementById('image_id');
  var image = document.getElementById('image');
  var caption = document.getElementById('caption');
  var sel = uploadImage.checked;
  image_id.disabled = sel;
  image.parentNode.style.display = sel ? 'block' : 'none';
  caption.parentNode.style.display = sel ? 'block' : 'none';
  image.disabled = !sel;
  caption.disabled = !sel;
}
```

This uses the IDs of the elements inserted in step 8 to control their display. If JavaScript is enabled, the check box is automatically displayed when the page loads, but the file input field and text input field for the caption remain hidden. If the check box is checked, the drop-down menu of existing images is disabled, and the hidden elements are displayed. If the check box is subsequently unchecked, the drop-down menu is reenabled, and the file input field and caption field are hidden again.

> *JavaScript is beyond the scope of this book, but you can learn more from* Getting StartED with JavaScript *by Terry McNavage (friends of ED, 2010, ISBN: 978-1-4302-7219-9) and* DOM Scripting: Web Design with JavaScript and the Document Object Model, Second Edition *by Jeremy Keith (friends of ED, 2010, ISBN: 978-1-4302-3389-3).*

12. Link `toggle_fields.js` to `blog_insert_mysqli.php` with a `<script>` tag just before the closing `</body>` tag like this:

```
</form>
<script src="toggle_fields.js"></script>
</body>
```

Although it has been common practice for many years to put `<script>` tags for external JavaScript files in the `<head>` of a web page, more recent practice recommends adding most scripts as close to the bottom of the `<body>` as possible to speed up downloading and display. The code in `toggle_fields.js` won't work correctly if you add it to the `<head>`.

13. Save `blog_insert_mysqli.php`, and load the page in a browser. In a JavaScript-enabled browser, the check box should be displayed between the `<select>` drop-down menu and submit button. Select the check box to disable the drop-down menu and display the hidden fields, as shown in Figure 16-9.

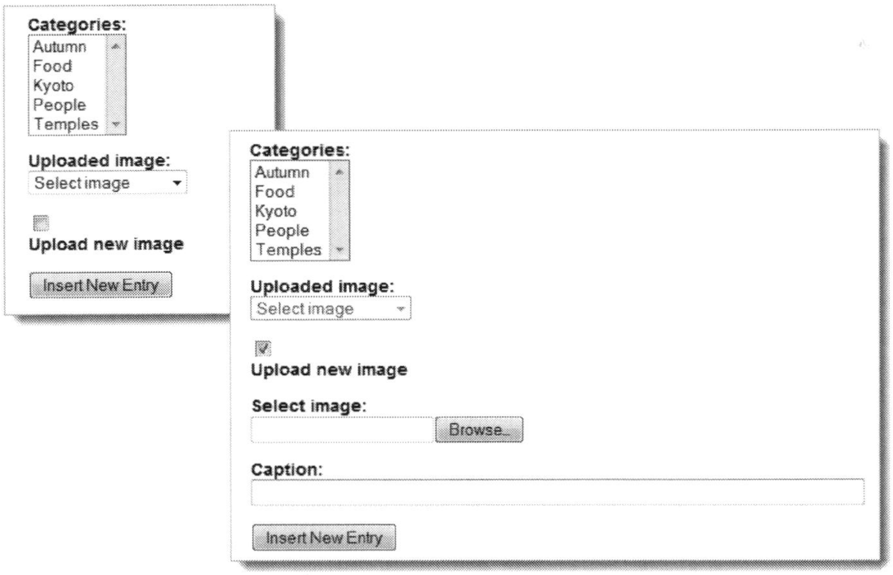

Figure 16-9. The check box controls the display of the file and caption input fields.

14. Deselect the check box. The file and caption input fields are hidden, and the drop-down menu is reenabled. You can check your code, if necessary with `blog_insert_mysqli_03.php` and `toggle_fields.js` in the ch16 folder.

If you're wondering why I used JavaScript, rather than PHP, to control the display of the file and caption input fields, it's because PHP is a server-side language. After the PHP engine has sent the output to the browser, it has no further interaction with the page unless you send another request to the web server. JavaScript, on the other hand, works in the browser, so it's able to manipulate the content of the page locally. JavaScript can also be used in conjunction with PHP to send requests to the web server in the background and can use the result to refresh part of the page without reloading it—a technique known as Ajax, which is beyond the scope of this book.

The updated insert form now has input fields for categories and images, but the processing script still handles only the text input field for the title and the text area for the blog entry.

PHP Solution 16-4: Inserting data into multiple tables

This PHP solution adapts the existing script in `blog_insert_mysqli.php` to upload a new image (if required) and insert data into the `images`, `blog`, and `article2cat` tables following the decision chain outlined in Figure 16-6. It assumes you have set up the `article2cat` cross-reference table and have completed PHP Solutions 16-2 and 16-3.

Don't attempt to rush through this section. The code is quite long, but it brings together many of the techniques you have learned previously.

1. In the conditional statement at the top of `blog_insert_mysqli.php` locate the following code highlighted in bold:

```
if (isset($_POST['insert'])) {
  // initialize flag
  $OK = false;
  // initialize prepared statement
  $stmt = $conn->stmt_init();
```

2. Immediately after the highlighted code, insert some space to add the following conditional statement to process the image, if one has been uploaded or selected.

```
// initialize prepared statement
$stmt = $conn->stmt_init();

// if a file has been uploaded, process it
if(isset($_POST['upload_new']) && $_FILES['image']['error'] == 0) {
  $imageOK = false;
  require_once('../classes/Ps2/Upload.php');
  $upload = new Ps2_Upload('../images/');
  $upload->move();
  $names = $upload->getFilenames();
  // $names will be an empty array if the upload failed
  if ($names) {
    $sql = 'INSERT INTO images (filename, caption)
            VALUES (?, ?)';
```

```
      $stmt->prepare($sql);
      $stmt->bind_param('ss', $names[0], $_POST['caption']);
      $stmt->execute();
      $imageOK = $stmt->affected_rows;
    }
    // get the image's primary key or find out what went wrong
    if ($imageOK) {
      $image_id = $stmt->insert_id;
    } else {
      $imageError = implode(' ', $upload->getMessages());
    }
  } elseif (isset($_POST['image_id']) && !empty($_POST['image_id'])) {
    // get the primary key of a previously uploaded image
    $image_id = $_POST['image_id'];
  }


// create SQL
$sql = 'INSERT INTO blog (title, article, created)
        VALUES(?, ?, NOW())';
```

This begins by checking if $_POST['upload_new'] has been set. As explained in Chapter 5, a check box is included in the $_POST array only if it has been selected. So, if the check box hasn't been selected, the condition fails, and the elseif clause at the bottom is tested instead. The elseif clause checks for the existence of $_POST['image_id']. If it exists and is not empty, an existing image has been selected from the drop-down menu, and the value is stored in $image_id.

If both tests fail, an image has neither been uploaded nor selected from the drop-down menu. The script later takes this into account when preparing the INSERT query for the blog table, allowing you to create a blog entry without an image.

However, if $_POST['upload_new'] exists, the check box has been selected, and an image has probably been uploaded. To make sure, the conditional statement also checks the value of $_FILES['image']['error']. As you learned in Chapter 6, the error code 0 indicates a successful upload. Any other error code means the upload failed or that no file was selected.

Assuming a file has been successfully uploaded from the form, the conditional statement includes the Ps2_Upload class and creates an upload object, setting the destination folder to images. It then calls the move() method to move the file to the images folder. To avoid complicating the code, I'm using the default maximum size and MIME types.

The changes you made to the Ps2_Upload class in PHP Solution 16-2 add the name of an uploaded file to the $_filenames property only if the file was moved successfully to the destination folder. The getFilenames() method retrieves the contents of the $_filenames property, and assigns the result to $names. If the file was moved successfully, its filename is stored as the first element of the $names array. So if $names contains a value, you can safely proceed with the INSERT query, which binds the values of $names[0] and $_POST['caption'] as strings to the prepared statement.

After the statement has been executed, the `affected_rows` property resets the value of `$imageOK`. If the INSERT query succeeded, `$imageOK` is 1, which is treated as `true`.

If the image details were inserted in the `images` table, the `insert_id` property retrieves the primary key of the new record and stores it in `$image_id`. The `insert_id` property must be accessed before running any other SQL queries, because it contains the primary key of the most recent query.

However, if `$imageOK` is still `false`, the `getMessages()` method of the upload object is called, and the result is stored in `$imageError`. The `getMessages()` method returns an array, so the `implode()` function is used to join the array elements as a single string. The most likely causes of failure are a file that's too big or of the wrong MIME type.

3. As long as the image upload didn't fail, the next stage in the process is to insert the blog entry into the `blog` table. The form of the INSERT query depends on whether an image is associated with the blog entry. If it is, `$image_id` exists and needs to be inserted in the `blog` table as a foreign key. Otherwise, the original query can be used.

    Amend the original query like this:

```
// don't insert blog details if the image failed to upload
if (!isset($imageError)) {
  // if $image_id has been set, insert it as a foreign key
  if (isset($image_id)) {
    $sql = 'INSERT INTO blog (image_id, title, article, created)
            VALUES(?, ?, ?, NOW())';
    $stmt->prepare($sql);
    $stmt->bind_param('iss', $image_id, $_POST['title'], $_POST['article']);
  } else {
    // create SQL
    $sql = 'INSERT INTO blog (title, article, created)
            VALUES(?, ?, NOW())';
    $stmt->prepare($sql);
    $stmt->bind_param('ss', $_POST['title'], $_POST['article']);
  }
  // execute and get number of affected rows
  $stmt->execute();
  $OK = $stmt->affected_rows;
}
```

    This whole section of code is wrapped in a conditional statement that checks whether `$imageError` exists. If it does, there's no point in inserting the new blog entry, so the entire code block is ignored.

    However, if `$imageError` doesn't exist, the nested conditional statement prepares different INSERT queries depending on whether `$image_id` exists and then executes whichever one has been prepared.

4. The next stage of the process inserts values into the `article2cat` cross-reference table. The code follows immediately after the code in the previous step and looks like this:

```php
// if the blog entry was inserted successfully, check for categories
if ($OK && isset($_POST['category'])) {
  // get the article's primary key
  $article_id = $stmt->insert_id;
  foreach ($_POST['category'] as $cat_id) {
    if (is_numeric($cat_id)) {
      $values[] = "($article_id, " . (int) $cat_id . ')';
    }
  }
  if ($values) {
    $sql = 'INSERT INTO article2cat (article_id, cat_id)
            VALUES ' . implode(',', $values);
    // execute the query and get error message if it fails
    if (!$conn->query($sql)) {
      $catError = $conn->error;
    }
  }
}
```

The value of $OK is determined by the `affected_rows` property from the query that inserted the data in the `blog` table, and the multiple-choice <select> list is included in the $_POST array only if any categories are selected. So, this code block is run only if the data was successfully inserted in the `blog` table and at least one category was selected in the form. It begins by obtaining the primary key of the insert operation from the prepared statement's `insert_id` property and assigning it to $article_id.

The form submits the category values as an array. The `foreach` loop checks each value in $_POST['category']. If the value is numeric, the following line is executed:

```php
$values[] = "($article_id, " . (int) $cat_id . ')';
```

This creates a string with the two primary keys, $article_id and $cat_id, separated by a comma and wrapped in a pair of parentheses. The `(int)` casting operator makes sure that $cat_id is an integer. The result is assigned to an array called $values. For example, if $article_id is 10 and $cat_id is 4, the resulting string assigned to the array is (10, 4).

If $values contains any elements, `implode()` converts it to a comma-separated string and appends it to the SQL query. For example, if categories 2, 4, and 5 are selected, the resulting query looks like this:

```sql
INSERT INTO article2cat (article_id, cat_id)
VALUES (10, 2),(10, 4),(10,5)
```

As explained in "Reviewing the four essential SQL commands" in Chapter 13, this is how you insert multiple rows with a single INSERT query.

Because $article_id comes from a reliable source and the data type of $cat_id has been checked, it's safe to use these variables directly in a SQL query without using a prepared statement. The query is executed with the `query()` method. If it fails, the connection object's error property is stored in $catError.

5. The final section of code handles the redirect on success and error messages. The amended code looks like this:

```
// redirect if successful or display error
if ($OK && !isset($imageError) && !isset($catError)) {
  header('Location: http://localhost/phpsols/admin/blog_list_mysqli.php');
  exit;
} else {
  $error = $stmt->error;
  if (isset($imageError)) {
    $error .= ' ' . $imageError;
  }
  if (isset($catError)) {
    $error .= ' ' . $catError;
  }
}
}
```

The condition controlling the redirect now makes sure that $imageError and $catError don't exist. If either does, the value is concatenated to the original $error, which contains any error message from the prepared statement object.

6. Save blog_insert_mysqli.php, and test it in a browser. Try uploading an image that's too big or a file of the wrong MIME type. The form should be redisplayed with an error message and the blog details preserved. Also try inserting blog entries with and without images and/or categories. You now have a versatile insert form.

   If you don't have suitable images to upload, use the images in the phpsols images folder. The Ps2_Upload class renames them to avoid overwriting the existing files.

   You can check your code against blog_insert_mysqli_04.php in the ch16 folder.

The PDO version is in blog_insert_pdo.php in the ch16 folder. PDO uses the lastInsertId() method on the connection object to get the primary key of the most recent insert operation. For example, the following line gets the primary key of the blog entry:

```
$article_id = $conn->lastInsertId();
```

Like the MySQLi insert_id property, you need to access it immediately after the INSERT query has been executed.

Updating and deleting records in multiple tables

The addition of the categories and article2cat tables means that the changes you made to blog_update_mysqli.php in PHP Solution 15-2 in the previous chapter no longer adequately cover the foreign key relationships in the phpsols database. In addition to amending the update form, you also need to create scripts to delete records without destroying the database's referential integrity.

Updating records in a cross-reference table

Each record in a cross-reference table contains only a composite primary key. Normally, primary keys should never be altered. Moreover, they must be unique. This poses a problem for updating the `article2cat` table. If you make no changes to the selected categories when updating a blog entry, the cross-reference table doesn't need to be updated. However, if the categories are changed, you need to work out which cross references to delete and which new ones to insert.

Rather than getting tied up in knots working out whether any changes have been made, a simple solution is to delete all existing cross references and insert the selected categories again. If no changes have been made, you simply insert the same ones again.

PHP Solution 16-5: Adding categories to the update form

This PHP solution amends `blog_update_mysqli.php` from PHP Solution 15-2 in the previous chapter to allow you to update the categories associated with a blog entry. To keep the structure simple, the only change that can be made to the image associated with the entry is to select a different existing image or no image at all.

1. Continue working with `blog_update_mysqli.php` from PHP Solution 15-2. Alternatively, copy `blog_update_mysqli_04.php` from the `ch16` folder, and save it in the `admin` folder as `blog_update_mysqli.php`.

2. When the page first loads, you need to run a second query to get the categories associated with the blog entry. Add the following highlighted code to conditional statement that gets details of the selected record:

```
$stmt->free_result();
// get categories associated with the article
$sql = 'SELECT cat_id FROM article2cat
        WHERE article_id = ?';
$stmt->prepare($sql);
$stmt->bind_param('i', $_GET['article_id']);
$stmt->bind_result($cat_id);
$OK = $stmt->execute();
// loop through the results to store them in an array
$selected_categories = array();
while ($stmt->fetch()) {
  $selected_categories[] = $cat_id;
}
}
```

The query selects `cat_id` from all records in the cross-reference table that match the primary key of the selected blog entry. The results are bound to `$cat_id`, and a `while` loop extracts the values into an array called `$selected_categories`.

3. In the body of the HTML page, add a multiple-choice `<select>` list between the text area and the `<select>` drop-down menu that displays the list of images. Use another SQL query to populate it like this:

449

```
<p>
  <label for="category">Categories:</label>
  <select name="category[]" size="5" multiple id="category">
  <?php
  // get categories
  $getCats = 'SELECT cat_id, category FROM categories
              ORDER BY category';
  $categories = $conn->query($getCats);
  while ($row = $categories->fetch_assoc()) {
  ?>
    <option value="<?php echo $row['cat_id']; ?>" <?php
    if (in_array($row['cat_id'], $selected_categories)) {
      echo 'selected';
    } ?>><?php echo $row['category']; ?></option>
  <?php } ?>
  </select>
</p>
```

The while loop builds each <option> tag, inserting cat_id in the value attribute and displaying the category between the opening and closing tags. If cat_id is in the $selected_categories array, selected is inserted in the <option> tag. This selects the categories already associated with the blog entry.

4. Save blog_update_mysqli.php, and select one of the **EDIT** links in blog_list_mysqli.php to make sure the multiple-choice list is populated with the categories. If you inserted a new entry in PHP Solution 16-4, the categories you associated with the item should be selected, as shown in the following screenshot.

You can check your code, if necessary, against blog_update_mysqli_05.php in the ch16 folder. The PDO version is in blog_update_pdo_05.php.

5. Next, you need to edit the section of code that updates the record when the form is submitted. The code currently looks like this:

```
// if form has been submitted, update record
if (isset($_POST ['update'])) {
  // prepare update query
  if (!empty($_POST['image_id'])) {
    $sql = 'UPDATE blog SET image_id = ?, title = ?, article = ?
            WHERE article_id = ?';
    $stmt->prepare($sql);
    $stmt->bind_param('issi', $_POST['image_id'], $_POST['title'], ➥
      $_POST['article'], $_POST['article_id']);
```

```
    } else {
      $sql = 'UPDATE blog SET image_id = NULL, title = ?, article = ?
             WHERE article_id = ?';
      $stmt->prepare($sql);
      $stmt->bind_param('ssi', $_POST['title'], $_POST['article'], ⮑
        $_POST['article_id']);
    }
    $stmt->execute();
    $done = $stmt->affected_rows;
}
```

The last two lines of this code block execute the prepared statement that updates the record in the blog table, and then assign the number of affected rows to $done. If you update a record, the affected_rows property is 1, which is treated as true. However, if you don't make any changes to the record, affected_rows is 0, which is treated as false. If you update only the categories associated with a record, without changing the record itself, $done is interpreted as false, and you won't be returned to blog_list_mysqli.php.

Delete the following line:

```
$done = $stmt->affected_rows;
```

6. Assign the return value of $stmt->execute() to $done like this:

$done = $stmt->execute();

The execute() method returns true if the prepared statement is executed successfully, even if it doesn't result in any changes to the record.

7. Immediately after the line you have just edited, insert the code to delete existing values in the cross reference table and to insert the newly selected values like this:

```
$done = $stmt->execute();

// delete existing values in the cross-reference table
$sql = 'DELETE FROM article2cat WHERE article_id = ?';
$stmt->prepare($sql);
$stmt->bind_param('i', $_POST['article_id']);
$stmt->execute();

// insert the new values in articles2cat
if (isset($_POST['category']) && is_numeric($_POST['article_id'])) {
  $article_id = (int) $_POST['article_id'];
  foreach ($_POST['category'] as $cat_id) {
    $values[] = "($article_id, " . (int) $cat_id . ')';
  }
  if ($values) {
    $sql = 'INSERT INTO article2cat (article_id, cat_id)
           VALUES ' . implode(',', $values);
    if (!$conn->query($sql)) {
      $catError = $conn->error;
```

```
        }
      }
    }
}
```

This code needs little explanation. The DELETE query removes all entries in the cross-reference table that match article_id. The remaining code inserts the values selected in the update form. It's identical to the code in step 4 of PHP Solution 16-4. The key thing to note is that it uses an INSERT query, not UPDATE. The original values have been deleted, so you're adding them anew.

8. Save blog_update_mysqli.php, and test it by updating existing records in the blog table. You can check your code, if necessary, against blog_update_mysqli_06.php in the ch16 folder. The PDO version is in blog_update_pdo_06.php.

Preserving referential integrity on deletion

In PHP Solution 16-5, there was no need to worry about referential integrity when you deleted records in the cross-reference table because the values stored in each record are foreign keys. Each record simply refers to the primary keys stored in the blog and categories tables. Referring to Figure 16-1 at the beginning of this chapter, deleting from the cross-reference table the record that combines article_id 2 with cat_id 1 simply breaks the link between the article titled "Trainee Geishas Go Shopping" and the Kyoto category. Neither the article nor the category is affected. They both remain in their respective tables.

The situation is very different if you decide to delete either the article or the category. If you delete the "Trainee Geishas Go Shopping" article from the blog table, all references to article_id 2 must also be deleted from the cross-reference table. Similarly, if you delete the Kyoto category, all references to cat_id 1 must be removed from the cross-reference table. Alternatively, you must halt the deletion if an item's primary key is stored elsewhere as a foreign key.

The best way to do this is through the establishment of foreign key restraints. To do so, you need to convert the storage engine of related tables to InnoDB.

PHP Solution 16-6: Converting tables to the InnoDB storage engine

This PHP solution shows how to use phpMyAdmin to convert the storage engine of database tables from MyISAM to InnoDB. If you plan to upload the tables to your remote server, it must also support InnoDB (see PHP Solution 16-1).

1. Select the phpsols database in phpMyAdmin, and then select the article2cat table.

2. Click the **Operations** tab at the top right of the screen.

3. In the **Table options** section, select **InnoDB** from the **Storage Engine** drop-down menu, as shown in Figure 16-10.

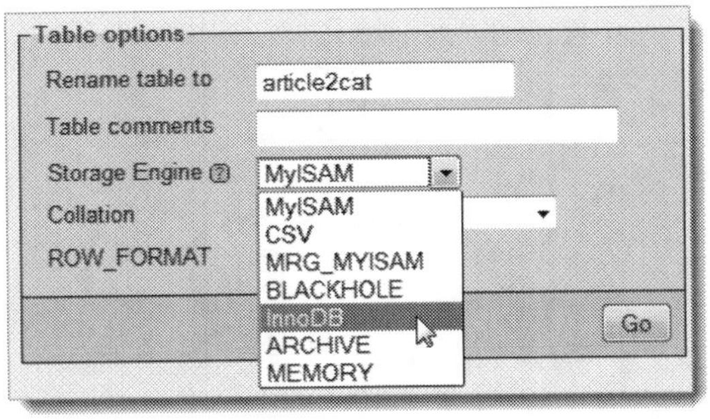

Figure 16-10. Changing a table's storage engine is very easy in phpMyAdmin.

4. Click **Go**. Changing the storage engine is as simple as that!

5. All tables related to each other through foreign key relationships need to use InnoDB. Repeat steps 1–4 with the blog, categories, and images tables.

PHP Solution 16-7: Setting up foreign key constraints

This PHP solution describes how to set up foreign key constraints between the article2cat, blog, and category tables in phpMyAdmin. The foreign key constraints must always be defined in the child table. In this this case, the child table is article2cat, because it stores the article_id and cat_id primary keys from the other tables as foreign keys.

1. Select the article2cat table in phpMyAdmin, and click the **Structure tab**.

2. Click **Relation view** (circled in Figure 16-11) at the bottom of the structure table.

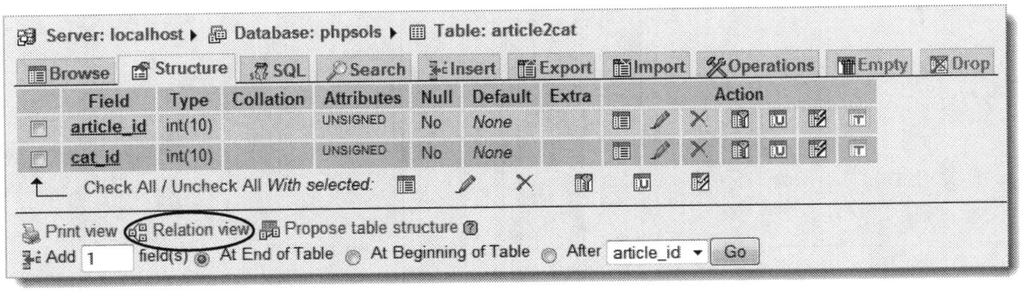

Figure 16-11. Foreign key constraints are defined in phpMyAdmin's Relation view.

3. Foreign key constraints can be set up only on columns that are indexed. The article_id and cat_id columns in article2cat are the table's composite primary key, so they're both listed in the screen that opens. If your version of phpMyAdmin has an option labeled **Internal relations**, you can ignore it. The section you're interested in is labeled **FOREIGN KEY (INNODB)**.

In the article_id row, click the down arrow to the left of **ON DELETE** to reveal the list of indexed columns in the database, and select `phpsols`.`blog`.`article_id` as shown in

Figure 16-12. This will be used to establish a formal foreign key relationship between `article_id` in the `article2cat` table and `article_id` in the `blog` table.

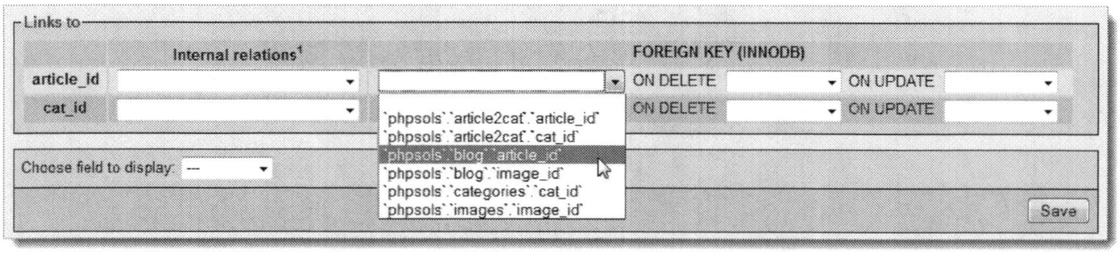

Figure 16-12. Selecting the primary key in the parent table

The **ON DELETE** drop-down menus have the following options:

- **CASCADE**: When you delete a record in the parent table, all dependent records are deleted in the child table. For example, if you delete the record with the primary key `article_id` 2 in the `blog` table, all records with `article_id` 2 in the `article2cat` table are automatically deleted.

- **SET NULL**: When you delete a record in the parent table, all dependent records in the child table have the foreign key set to NULL. The foreign key column must accept NULL values.

- **NO ACTION**: On some database systems, this allows foreign constraint checks to be delayed. MySQL performs checks immediately, so this has the same effect as **RESTRICT**.

- **RESTRICT**: This prevents the deletion of a record in the parent table if dependent records still exist in the child table.

*The same options are available for **ON UPDATE**. With the exception of **RESTRICT**, they are of limited interest, because you should change the primary key of a record only in exceptional circumstances. **ON UPDATE RESTRICT** not only stops changes being made to the primary key in the parent table; it also rejects any inserts or updates in the child table that would result in foreign key values that don't have a match in the parent table.*

In the case of a cross-reference table, **CASCADE** is the logical choice. If you decide to delete a record in the parent table, you want all cross-references to that record to be removed at the same time. However, to demonstrate the default behavior of foreign key constraints, select **RESTRICT**. Leave **ON UPDATE** blank.

4. In the `cat_id` row, select `` `phpsols`.`categories`.`cat_id` `` from the drop-down menu immediate to the left of **ON DELETE**, and set **ON DELETE** to **RESTRICT**. Click **Save**.

    If **RESTRICT** isn't available in the drop-down menu, leave the option blank

5. If you have not already done so, update at least one blog entry to associate it with a category.

6. In phpMyAdmin, select the categories table, and click the **Delete** icon next to a category that you know to be associated with a blog entry, as shown in Figure 16-13.

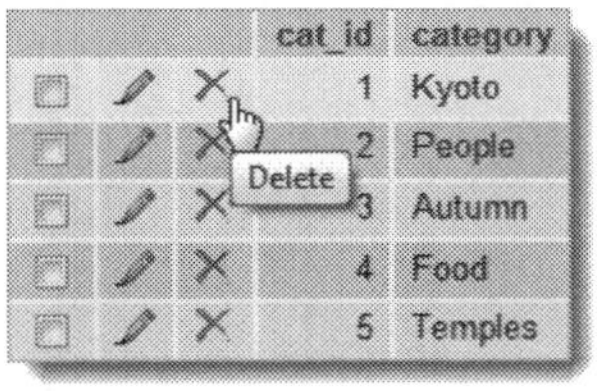

Figure 16-13. Click the large red X to delete a record in phpMyAdmin.

7. Click **OK** when phpMyAdmin asks you to confirm the deletion. If you have set up the foreign key constraints correctly, you'll see the error message shown in Figure 16-14.

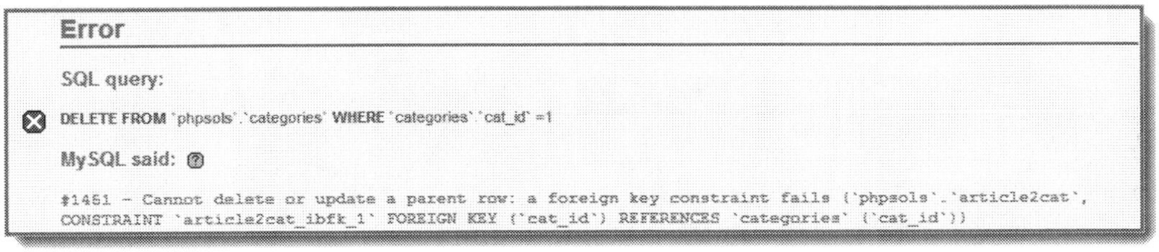

Figure 16-14. The foreign key constraint prevents the deletion if dependent records exist.

8. Select the article2cat table, and click the **Structure** tab. Then click **Relation view**. In all probability, the **ON DELETE** options will be blank. This is *not* a cause for concern, **RESTRICT** is the default for both **ON DELETE** and **ON UPDATE**. Leaving these options blank has the same effect as selecting **RESTRICT**.

9. Change both **ON DELETE** settings to **CASCADE**, and click **Save**.

10. Select a record in the blog table that you know is associated with a category, and delete it.

11. Check the article2cat table. The records associated with the record you have just deleted have also been deleted.

To continue your exploration of foreign key constraints, select the blog table, and establish a foreign key relationship with image_id in the images table. If you delete a record from the images table, the image_id foreign key in the blog table needs to be set to NULL. This is done automatically if you set the value of **ON DELETE** to **SET NULL**. Test it by deleting a record from the images table and checking the associated record(s) in the blog table.

> *If you need to convert an InnoDB table back to MyISAM, you must first remove any foreign key constraints. Select **Relation view**, set all fields to blank, and click **Save**. After removing the foreign key relationships, you can change the storage engine as described in PHP Solution 16-6. Select **MyISAM** instead of **InnoDB**.*

Creating delete scripts with foreign key constraints

Choosing the values for **ON DELETE** in InnoDB tables depends on the nature of the relationship between tables. In the case of the phpsols database, it's not only safe but desirable to set the option to **CASCADE** for both columns in the article2cat cross-reference table. If a record is deleted in either the blog or categories parent table, the related values need to be deleted in the cross-reference table.

The relationship between the images and blog tables is different. If you delete a record from the images table, you probably don't want to delete related articles in the blog table. In that case, **SET NULL** is an appropriate choice. When a record is deleted from the images table, the foreign key in related articles is set to NULL, but the articles remain intact.

On the other hand, if images are vital to the understanding of articles, select **RESTRICT**. Any attempt to delete an image that still has related articles is automatically halted.

These considerations affect how you handle deletion scripts. When the foreign key constraint is set to **CASCADE** or **SET NULL**, you don't need to do anything special. You can use a simple DELETE query and leave the rest to MySQL.

However, if the foreign key constraint is set to RESTRICT, the DELETE query will fail. To display an appropriate error message, use the errno property of a MySQLi statement object. The MySQL error code for a query that fails as a result of a foreign key constraint is 1451. After calling the execute() method, you can check for errors like this in MySQLi:

```
$stmt->execute();
if ($stmt->affected_rows > 0) {
  $deleted = true;
} else {
  $deleted = false;
  if ($stmt->errno == 1451) {
    $error = 'That record has dependent files in a child table, and cannot be ↦
      deleted.';
  } else {
    $error = 'There was a problem deleting the record.';
  }
}
```

If you are using PDO, use the errorCode() method. The code for a query that fails as a result of a foreign key constraint is HY000. After checking the number of affected rows with rowCount(), you can check the error code like this with PDO:

```
$deleted = $stmt->rowCount();
if (!$deleted) {
  if ($stmt->errorCode() == 'HY000') {
    $error = 'That record has dependent files in a child table, and cannot be ↦
      deleted.';
  } else {
    $error = 'There was a problem deleting the record.';
  }
}
```

The error codes in the PDO and MySQLi versions are different because PDO uses the codes defined by the ANSI SQL standard, whereas MySQLi uses MySQL-specific codes.

Creating delete scripts without foreign key constraints

If you can't use InnoDB tables, you need to build the same logic into your own delete scripts. To achieve the same effect as **ON DELETE CASCADE**, run two consecutive DELETE queries like this:

```
$sql = 'DELETE FROM article2cat WHERE article_id = ?';
$stmt->prepare($sql);
$stmt->bind_param('i', $_POST['article_id']);
$stmt->execute();
$sql = 'DELETE FROM blog WHERE article_id = ?';
$stmt->prepare($sql);
$stmt->bind_param('i', $_POST['article_id']);
$stmt->execute();
```

To achieve the same effect as **ON DELETE SET NULL**, run an UPDATE query combined with a DELETE query like this:

```
$sql = 'UPDATE blog SET image_id = NULL WHERE image_id = ?';
$stmt->prepare($sql);
$stmt->bind_param('i', $_POST['image_id']);
$stmt->execute();
$sql = 'DELETE FROM images WHERE image_id = ?';
$stmt->prepare($sql);
$stmt->bind_param('i', $_POST['image_id']);
$stmt->execute();
```

To achieve the same effect as **ON DELETE RESTRICT**, you need to run a SELECT query to find if there are dependent records before continuing with the DELETE query like this:

```
$sql = 'SELECT image_id FROM blog WHERE image_id = ?';
$stmt->prepare($sql);
$stmt->bind_param('i', $_POST['image_id']);
$stmt->execute();
// if num_rows is not 0, there are dependent records
if ($stmt->num_rows) {
  $error = 'That record has dependent files in a child table, and cannot be deleted.';
} else {
  $sql = 'DELETE FROM images WHERE image_id = ?';
  $stmt->prepare($sql);
  $stmt->bind_param('i', $_POST['image_id']);
  $stmt->execute();
}
```

Chapter review

Once you have learned basic SQL and the PHP commands to communicate with a database, working with single tables is very easy. Linking tables through foreign keys, however, can be quite challenging. The power of a relational database comes from its sheer flexibility. The problem is that this infinite flexibility means there is no single "right" way of doing things.

Don't let this put you off, though. Your instinct may be to stick with single tables, but down that route lies even greater complexity. The key to making it easy to work with databases is to limit your ambitions in the early stages. Build simple structures like the one in this chapter, experiment with them, and get to know how they work. Add tables and foreign key links gradually. People with a lot of experience working with databases say they frequently spend more than half the development time just thinking about the table structure. After that, the coding is the easy bit!

In the final chapter, we move back to working with a single table—addressing the important subject of user authentication with a database and how to handle encrypted passwords.

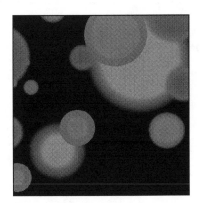

Chapter 17

Authenticating Users with a Database

Chapter 9 showed you the principles of user authentication and sessions to password protect parts of your website, but the login scripts all relied on usernames and passwords stored in text files. Keeping user details in a database is both more secure and more efficient. Instead of just storing a list of usernames and passwords, a database can store other details, such as first name, family name, email address, and so on. MySQL also gives you the option of using either one- or two-way encryption. In the first section of this chapter, we'll examine the difference between the two. Then you'll create registration and login scripts for both types of encryption.

What this chapter contains:

- Deciding how to encrypt passwords
- Using one-way encryption for user registration and login
- Using two-way encryption for user registration and login
- Decrypting passwords

Choosing an encryption method

The PHP solutions in Chapter 9 use the SHA-1 encryption algorithm. It offers a high level of security, particularly if used in conjunction with a **salt** (a random value that's added to make decryption harder). SHA-1 is a one-way encryption method: once a password has been encrypted, there's no way of converting it back to plain text. This is both an advantage and a disadvantage. It offers the user greater security because passwords encrypted this way remain secret. However, there's no way of reissuing a lost password, since not even the site administrator can decrypt it. The only solution is to issue the user a temporary new password, and ask the user to reset it.

The alternative is to use two-way encryption, which relies on a pair of functions: one to encrypt the password and another to convert it back to plain text, making it easy to reissue passwords to forgetful users. Two-way encryption uses a secret key that is passed to both functions to perform the conversion. The key is simply a string that you make up yourself. Obviously, to keep the data secure, the key needs to be sufficiently difficult to guess and should never be stored in the database. However, you need to embed the key in your registration and login scripts—either directly or through an include file—so if your scripts are ever exposed, your security is blown wide apart. MySQL offers a number of two-way encryption functions, but AES_ENCRYPT() is considered the most secure. It uses the Advanced Encryption Standard with a 128-bit key length (AES-128) approved by the U.S. government for the protection of classified material up to the SECRET level (TOP SECRET material requires AES-192 or AES-256).

Both one-way and two-way encryption have advantages and disadvantages. Many security experts recommend that passwords should be changed frequently. So, forcing a user to change a forgotten password because it can't be decrypted could be regarded as a good security measure. On the other hand, users are likely to be frustrated by the need to deal with a new password each time they forget the existing one. I'll leave it to you to decide which approach is best suited to your circumstances, and I'll concentrate solely on the technical implementation.

Using one-way encryption

In the interests of keeping things simple, I'm going to use the same basic forms as in Chapter 9, so only the username, salt, and encrypted password are stored in the database.

Creating a table to store users' details

In phpMyAdmin, create a new table called users in the phpsols database. The table needs four columns (fields) with the settings listed in Table 17-1.

Table 17-1. Settings for the users table

Field	Type	Length/Values	Attributes	Null	Index	A_I
user_id	INT		UNSIGNED	Deselected	PRIMARY	Selected
username	VARCHAR	15		Deselected	UNIQUE	
salt	INT		UNSIGNED	Deselected		
pwd	CHAR	40		Deselected		

To ensure no one can register the same username as one that's already in use, the username column is given an UNIQUE index.

In Chapter 9, the username doubled as the salt, but storing the details in a database means that you can choose something more unique and difficult to guess. Although a Unix timestamp follows a predictable pattern, it changes every second. So even if an attacker knows the day on which a user registered, there are 86,400 possible values for the salt, which would need to be combined with every attempt to guess the password. So the salt column needs to store an integer (INT).

The pwd column, which is where the encrypted password is stored, needs to be 40 characters long because the SHA-1 algorithm always produces an alphanumeric string of that length. It's a fixed length, so CHAR is used in preference to VARCHAR. The CHAR data type is more efficient when dealing with fixed-length strings.

Registering new users in the database

To register users in the database, you need to create a registration form that asks for a username and password. The processing script needs to validate the user input before inserting it in the database. MySQL returns an error if an attempt is made to insert a username that's already in use because the username column has been defined with a UNIQUE index. The script needs to detect the error and advise the user to choose a different username.

PHP Solution 17-1: Creating a user registration form

This PHP solution shows how to adapt the registration script from Chapter 9 to work with MySQL. It uses the Ps2_CheckPassword class from PHP Solution 9-6 and register_user_text.php from PHP Solution 9-7. If necessary, copy CheckPassword.php from the classes/completed folder to the classes/Ps2 folder, and use a copy of register_user_text.inc_02.php from the ch09 folder in place of register_user_text.php. You should also read the instructions in PHP Solutions 9-6 and 9-7 to understand how the original scripts work.

1. Copy register_db.php from the ch17 folder to a new folder called authenticate in the phpsols site root. The page contains the same basic user registration form as in Chapter 9 with a text input field for the username, a password field, another password field for confirmation, and a button to submit the data, as shown in the following screenshot.

2. Add the following code in a PHP block above the DOCTYPE declaration:

```
if (isset($_POST['register'])) {
    $username = trim($_POST['username']);
    $password = trim($_POST['pwd']);
    $retyped = trim($_POST['conf_pwd']);
    require_once('../includes/register_user_mysqli.inc.php');
}
```

This is very similar to the code in PHP Solution 9-7. If the form has been submitted, the user input is stripped of leading and trailing whitespace and assigned to simple variables. Then, an external file called `register_user_mysqli.inc.php` is included. If you plan to use PDO, name the include file `register_user_pdo.inc.php` instead.

3. The file that processes the user input is based on `register_user_text.inc.php`, which you created in Chapter 9. Make a copy of your original file, and save it in the `includes` folder as `register_user_mysqli.inc.php` or `register_user_pdo.inc.php`.

   Alternatively, copy `register_user_text_02.php` from the `ch09` folder to the `includes` folder, and save it as `register_user_mysqli.inc.php` or `register_user_pdo.inc.php`.

4. In the file you have just copied and renamed, locate the conditional statement that begins like this (around line 22):

```
if (!$errors) {
  // encrypt password, using username as salt
  $password = sha1($username.$password);
```

   Delete all the code inside the conditional statement (from line 23 to the line before the end). The contents of the file should now look like this:

```
require_once('../classes/Ps2/CheckPassword.php');
$usernameMinChars = 6;
$errors = array();
if (strlen($username) < $usernameMinChars) {
  $errors[] = "Username must be at least $usernameMinChars characters.";
}
if (preg_match('/\s/', $username)) {
  $errors[] = 'Username should not contain spaces.';
}
$checkPwd = new Ps2_CheckPassword($password, 10);
$checkPwd->requireMixedCase();
$checkPwd->requireNumbers(2);
$checkPwd->requireSymbols();
$passwordOK = $checkPwd->check();
if (!$passwordOK) {
  $errors = array_merge($errors, $checkPwd->getErrors());
}
if ($password != $retyped) {
  $errors[] = "Your passwords don't match.";
}
if (!$errors) {

}
```

   It doesn't matter if your script uses different values for `$usernameMinChars` and for the password strength settings.

5. The code that inserts the user's details in the database goes inside the empty conditional statement at the bottom of the script. Begin by including the database connection file and creating a connection with read and write privileges.

```
if (!$errors) {
  // include the connection file
  require_once('connection.inc.php');
  $conn = dbConnect('write');
}
```

The connection file is also in the `includes` folder, so you need only the filename.

For PDO, add `'pdo'` as the second argument to `dbConnect()`.

6. Next, use the `time()` function to get the current timestamp and assign it to `$salt`. Then concatenate the salt to the user-submitted password and encrypt them with the `sha1()` function. Amend the code like this:

```
if (!$errors) {
  // include the connection file
  require_once('connection.inc.php');
  $conn = dbConnect('write');
  // create a salt using the current timestamp
  $salt = time();
  // encrypt the password and salt
  $pwd = sha1($password . $salt);
}
```

7. The final section of the code prepares and executes the prepared statement to insert the user's details in the database. Because the `username` column has a `UNIQUE` index, the query fails if the username already exists. If that happens, the code needs to generate an error message. The code is different for MySQLi and PDO.

For MySQLi, add the code highlighted in bold:

```
if (!$errors) {
  // include the connection file
  require_once('connection.inc.php');
  $conn = dbConnect('write');
  // create a salt using the current timestamp
  $salt = time();
  // encrypt the password and salt
  $pwd = sha1($password . $salt);
  // prepare SQL statement
  $sql = 'INSERT INTO users (username, salt, pwd)
          VALUES (?, ?, ?)';
  $stmt = $conn->stmt_init();
  $stmt = $conn->prepare($sql);
  // bind parameters and insert the details into the database
  $stmt->bind_param('sis', $username, $salt, $pwd);
  $stmt->execute();
  if ($stmt->affected_rows == 1) {
    $success = "$username has been registered. You may now log in.";
  } elseif ($stmt->errno == 1062) {
    $errors[] = "$username is already in use. Please choose another ↪
```

```
        username.";
    } else {
        $errors[] = 'Sorry, there was a problem with the database.';
    }
}
```

The new code begins by binding the parameters to the prepared statement. The username and password are strings, but the salt is an integer, so the first argument to bind_param() is 'sis' (see "Embedding variables in MySQLi prepared statements" in Chapter 11) After the statement has been executed, the conditional statement checks the value of the affected_rows property. If it's 1, the details have been inserted successfully.

You need to check the value of affected_rows explicitly because it's −1 if there's an error. Unlike some programming languages, PHP treats −1 as true.

The alternative condition checks the value of the prepared statement's errno property, which contains the MySQL error code. The code for a duplicate value in a column with a UNIQUE index is 1062. If that error code is detected, an error message is added to the $errors array asking the user to choose a different username. If a different error code is generated, a generic error message is added to the $errors array instead.

The PDO version looks like this:

```
if (!$errors) {
    // include the connection file
    require_once('connection.inc.php');
    $conn = dbConnect('write', 'pdo');
    // create a salt using the current timestamp
    $salt = time();
    // encrypt the password and salt
    $pwd = sha1($password . $salt);
    // prepare SQL statement
    $sql = 'INSERT INTO users (username, salt, pwd)
            VALUES (:username, :salt, :pwd)';
    $stmt = $conn->prepare($sql);
    // bind parameters and insert the details into the database
    $stmt->bindParam(':username', $username, PDO::PARAM_STR);
    $stmt->bindParam(':salt', $salt, PDO::PARAM_INT);
    $stmt->bindParam(':pwd', $pwd, PDO::PARAM_STR);
    $stmt->execute();
    if ($stmt->rowCount() == 1) {
        $success = "$username has been registered. You may now log in.";
    } elseif ($stmt->errorCode() == 23000) {
        $errors[] = "$username is already in use. Please choose another ↵
            username.";
    } else {
        $errors[] = 'Sorry, there was a problem with the database.';
```

```
    }
}
```

The prepared statement uses named parameters, which are bound to it by the `bindParam()` method, specifying the data type as string for the `username` and `pwd` columns, and as integer for `salt`. After the statement has been executed, the conditional statement uses the `rowCount()` method to check if the record has been created.

If the prepared statement fails because the username already exists, the value generated by the `errorCode()` method is `23000`. As noted in the previous chapter, PDO uses error codes defined by the ANSI SQL standard instead of those generated by MySQL. If the error code matches, a message is added to the `$errors` array asking the user to choose a different username. Otherwise, a generic error message is used.

8. All that remains is to add the code that displays the outcome in the registration page. Add the following code just before the opening `<form>` tag in `register_db.php`:

```php
<h1>Register user</h1>
<?php
if (isset($success)) {
  echo "<p>$success</p>";
} elseif (isset($errors) && !empty($errors)) {
  echo '<ul>';
  foreach ($errors as $error) {
    echo "<li>$error</li>";
  }
  echo '</ul>';
}
?>
<form id="form1" method="post" action="">
```

9. Save `register_db.php`, and load it in a browser. Test it by entering input that you know breaks the rules. If you make multiple mistakes in the same attempt, a bulleted list of error messages should appear at the top of the form, as shown in the next screenshot.

465

10. Now fill in the registration form correctly. You should see a message telling you that an account has been created for the username you chose.

11. Try registering the same username again. This time you should get a message similar to the one shown in the following screenshot:

Register user

- davidp is already in use. Please choose another username.

Username:

Password:

Confirm password:

Register

12. Check your code, if necessary, against `register_db_mysqli.php` and `register_user_mysqli.inc.php`, or `register_db_pdo.php` and `register_user_pdo.inc.php` in the `ch17` folder.

Now that you have a username and password registered in the database, you need to create a login script. The `ch17` folder contains a set of files that replicates the setup in PHP Solution 9-9: a login page and two password protected pages.

PHP Solution 17-2: Authenticating a user's credentials with a database

This PHP solution shows how to authenticate a user's credentials stored in a database. It involves querying the database to find the username's salt and stored password and then encrypting the submitted password with the salt. If the result matches the stored password, the user is redirected to a restricted page.

1. Copy `login_db.php`, `menu_db.php`, and `secretpage_db.php` from the `ch17` folder to the `authenticate` folder. Also copy `logout_db.inc.php` and `session_timeout_db.inc.php` from the `ch17` folder to the `includes` folder.

   This sets up the same basic test platform as in Chapter 9. The only difference is that the links have been changed to redirect to the `authenticate` folder.

2. In `login_db.php` add the following code in a PHP block above the DOCTYPE declaration:

```
$error = '';
if (isset($_POST['login'])) {
  session_start();
  $username = trim($_POST['username']);
  $password = trim($_POST['pwd']);
  // location to redirect on success
  $redirect = 'http://localhost/phpsols/authenticate/menu_db.php';
  require_once('../includes/authenticate_mysqli.inc.php');
}
```

This follows a similar pattern to the code in the login form in Chapter 9. It begins by initializing `$error` as an empty string. The conditional statement initiates a session if the form has been submitted. Whitespace is trimmed from the user input fields, and the location of the page the user will be redirected to on success is stored in a variable. Finally, the authentication script, which you'll build next, is included.

If you're using PDO, use `authenticate_pdo.inc.php` as the processing script.

3. Create a new file called `authenticate_mysqli.inc.php` or `authenticate_pdo.inc.php`, and save it in the `includes` folder. The file will contain only PHP script, so strip out any HTML markup.

4. Include the database connection file, create a connection to the database with the read-only account, and use a prepared statement to fetch the user's details.

   For MySQLi use the following code:

```php
<?php
require_once('connection.inc.php');
$conn = dbConnect('read');
// get the username's details from the database
$sql = 'SELECT salt, pwd FROM users WHERE username = ?';
// initialize and prepare statement
$stmt = $conn->stmt_init();
$stmt->prepare($sql);
// bind the input parameter
$stmt->bind_param('s', $username);
// bind the result, using a new variable for the password
$stmt->bind_result($salt, $storedPwd);
$stmt->execute();
$stmt->fetch();
```

This is a fairly straightforward `SELECT` query using a MySQLi prepared statement. The username is a string, so the first argument to `bind_param()` is `'s'`. The results of the query are bound to `$salt` and `$storedPwd`. You need to use a new variable for the stored password to avoid overwriting the password submitted by the user.

After the statement has been executed, the `fetch()` method gets the result.

For PDO, use the following code instead:

```php
<?php
require_once('connection.inc.php');
$conn = dbConnect('read', 'pdo');
// get the username's details from the database
$sql = 'SELECT salt, pwd FROM users WHERE username = :username';
// prepare statement
$stmt = $conn->prepare($sql);
// bind the input parameter
$stmt->bindParam(':username', $username, PDO::PARAM_STR);
// bind the result, using a new variable for the password
```

```
$stmt->bindColumn(1, $salt);
$stmt->bindColumn(2, $storedPwd);
$stmt->execute();
$stmt->fetch();
```

This code does the same as the MySQLi version, but using PDO syntax.

5. Once you have retrieved the username's details, you need to encrypt the password entered by the user by combining it with the salt and passing them both to sha1(). You can then compare the result to the stored version of the password, which was similarly encrypted at the time of registration.

   If they match, create the session variables to indicate a successful login and the time the session began, regenerate the session ID, and redirect to the restricted page. Otherwise, store an error message in $error.

   Insert the following code after the code you entered in the preceding step. It's the same for both MySQLi and PDO.

```
// encrypt the submitted password with the salt
// and compare with stored password
if (sha1($password . $salt) == $storedPwd) {
  $_SESSION['authenticated'] = 'Jethro Tull';
  // get the time the session started
  $_SESSION['start'] = time();
  session_regenerate_id();
  header("Location: $redirect");
  exit;
} else {
  // if no match, prepare error message
  $error = 'Invalid username or password';
}
```

   As in Chapter 9, the value of $_SESSION['authenticated'] is of no real importance.

6. Save authenticate_mysqli.inc.php or authenticate_pdo.inc.php, and test login_db.php by logging in with the username and password that you registered at the end of PHP Solution 17-1. The login process should work in exactly the same way as Chapter 9. The difference is that all the details are stored more securely in a database, and each user has a unique and probably unguessable salt.

   You can check your code, if necessary, against login_mysqli.php and authenticate_mysqli.inc.php, or login_pdo.php and authenticate_pdo.inc.php in the ch17 folder. If you encounter problems, use echo to display the values of the freshly encrypted password and the stored version. The most common mistake is creating too narrow a column for the encrypted password in the database. It must be 40 characters wide.

Although storing an encrypted password in a database is more secure than using a text file, the password is sent from the user's browser to the server in plain, unencrypted text. This is adequate for most websites, but if you need a high level of security, the login and access to subsequent pages should be made through a Secure Sockets Layer (SSL) connection.

Using two-way encryption

The main differences in setting up user registration and authentication for two-way encryption are that the password needs to be stored in the database as a binary object using the BLOB data type (see "Storing binary data" in Chapter 10 for more information), and that the comparison between the encrypted passwords takes place in the SQL query, rather than in the PHP script. Although you can use a salt with the password, doing so involves querying the database twice when logging in: first to retrieve the salt and then to verify the password with the salt. To keep things simple, I'll show you how to implement two-way encryption without a salt.

Creating the table to store users' details

In phpMyAdmin, create a new table called users_2way in the phpsols database. It needs three columns (fields) with the settings listed in Table 17-2.

Table 17-2. Settings for the users_2way table

Field	Type	Length/Values	Attributes	Null	Index	A_I
user_id	INT		UNSIGNED	Deselected	PRIMARY	Selected
username	VARCHAR	15		Deselected	UNIQUE	
pwd	BLOB			Deselected		

Registering new users

The MySQL AES_ENCRYPT() function takes two arguments: the value to be encrypted and an encryption key. The encryption key can be any string of characters you choose. For the purposes of this example, I have chosen takeThisWith@PinchOfSalt, but a random series of alphanumeric characters and symbols would be more secure.

The basic registration scripts for one-way and two-way encryption are the same. The only difference lies in the section that inserts the user's data into the database.

The following scripts embed the encryption key directly in the page. If you have a private folder outside the server root, it's a good idea to define the key in an include file and store it in your private folder.

The code for MySQLi looks like this (it's in register_2way_mysqli.inc.php in the ch17 folder):

```php
if (!$errors) {
  // include the connection file
  require_once('connection.inc.php');
  $conn = dbConnect('write');
  // create a key
  $key = 'takeThisWith@PinchOfSalt';
  // prepare SQL statement
  $sql = 'INSERT INTO users_2way (username, pwd)
          VALUES (?, AES_ENCRYPT(?, ?))';
  $stmt = $conn->stmt_init();
  $stmt = $conn->prepare($sql);
  // bind parameters and insert the details into the database
  $stmt->bind_param('sss', $username, $password, $key);
  $stmt->execute();
  if ($stmt->affected_rows == 1) {
    $success = "$username has been registered. You may now log in.";
  } elseif ($stmt->errno == 1062) {
    $errors[] = "$username is already in use. Please choose another username.";
  } else {
    $errors[] = 'Sorry, there was a problem with the database.';
  }
}
```

For PDO, it looks like this (see `register_2way_pdo.inc.php` in the `ch16` folder):

```php
if (!$errors) {
  // include the connection file
  require_once('connection.inc.php');
  $conn = dbConnect('write', 'pdo');
  // create a key
  $key = 'takeThisWith@PinchOfSalt';
  // prepare SQL statement
  $sql = 'INSERT INTO users_2way (username, pwd)
          VALUES (:username, AES_ENCRYPT(:pwd, :key))';
  $stmt = $conn->prepare($sql);
  // bind parameters and insert the details into the database
  $stmt->bindParam(':username', $username, PDO::PARAM_STR);
  $stmt->bindParam(':pwd', $password, PDO::PARAM_STR);
  $stmt->bindParam(':key', $key, PDO::PARAM_STR);
  $stmt->execute();
  if ($stmt->rowCount() == 1) {
    $success = "$username has been registered. You may now log in.";
  } elseif ($stmt->errorCode() == 23000) {
    $errors[] = "$username is already in use. Please choose another username.";
  } else {
    $errors[] = 'Sorry, there was a problem with the database.';
  }
}
```

Strictly speaking, it's not necessary to use a bound parameter for $key, because it doesn't come from user input. If you embed it directly in the query, the whole query needs to be wrapped in double quotes, and $key needs to be in single quotes.

User authentication with two-way encryption

Creating a login page with two-way encryption is very simple. After connecting to the database, you incorporate the username, secret key, and unencrypted password in the WHERE clause of a SELECT query. If the query finds a match, the user is allowed into the restricted part of the site. If there's no match, the login is rejected. The code is the same as in PHP Solution 17-2, except for the following section.

For MySQLi, it looks like this (see authenticate_2way_mysqli.inc.php for the full listing—this shows only the sections that are different):

```
$conn = dbConnect('read');
// create key
$key = 'takeThisWith@PinchOfSalt';
$sql = 'SELECT username FROM users_2way
        WHERE username = ? AND pwd = AES_ENCRYPT(?, ?)';
// initialize and prepare statement
$stmt = $conn->stmt_init();
$stmt->prepare($sql);
// bind the input parameters
$stmt->bind_param('sss', $username, $password, $key);
$stmt->execute();
// store the result
$stmt->store_result();
// if a match is found, num_rows is 1, which is treated as true
if ($stmt->num_rows) {
  $_SESSION['authenticated'] = 'Jethro Tull';
```

Note that you need to store the result of the prepared statement before you can access the num_rows property. If you fail to do this, num_rows will always be 0, and the login will fail even if the username and password are correct.

The revised code for PDO looks like this (see authenticate_2way_pdo.inc.php for the full listing—this shows only the sections that are different):

```
$conn = dbConnect('read', 'pdo');
// create key
$key = 'takeThisWith@PinchOfSalt';
$sql = 'SELECT username FROM users_2way
        WHERE username = ? AND pwd = AES_ENCRYPT(?, ?)';
// prepare statement
$stmt = $conn->prepare($sql);
// bind variables when executing statement
$stmt->execute(array($username, $password, $key));
// if a match is found, rowCount() produces 1, which is treated as true
if ($stmt->rowCount()) {
  $_SESSION['authenticated'] = 'Jethro Tull';
```

Decrypting a password

Decrypting a password encrypted with two-way encryption simply involves passing the secret key as the second argument to AES_DECRYPT() in a prepared statement like this:

```
$key = 'takeThisWith@PinchOfSalt';
$sql = "SELECT AES_DECRYPT(pwd, '$key') AS pwd
        FROM users_2way
        WHERE username = ?";
```

The key must be exactly the same as the one originally used to encrypt the password. If you lose the key, the passwords remain as inaccessible as those stored using one-way encryption.

Normally, the only time you need to decrypt a password is when a user requests a password reminder. Creating the appropriate security policy for sending out such reminders depends a great deal on the type of site that you're operating. However, it goes without saying that you shouldn't display the decrypted password onscreen. You need to set up a series of security checks, such as asking for the user's date of birth or mother's maiden name, or posing a question whose answer only the user is likely to know. Even if the user gets the answer right, you should send the password by email to the user's registered address.

All the necessary knowledge should be at your fingertips if you have succeeded in getting this far in this book.

Updating user details

I haven't included any update forms for the user registration pages. It's a task that you should be able to accomplish by yourself at this stage. The most important point about updating user registration details is that you should not display the user's existing password in the update form. If you're using one-way encryption, you can't anyway.

Where next?

This book has covered a massive amount of ground. If you master all the techniques covered here, you are well on your way to becoming an intermediate PHP developer, and with a little more effort, you will enter the advanced level. If it's been a struggle, don't worry. Go over the earlier chapters again. The more you practice, the easier it becomes.

You're probably thinking, "How on earth can I remember all this?" You don't need to. Don't be ashamed to look things up. Bookmark the PHP online manual (http://docs.php.net/manual/en/), and use it regularly. It's constantly updated, and it has lots of useful examples. Type a function name into the search box at the top right of every page (as shown in the following screenshot), and it takes you straight to a full description of that function. Even if you can't remember the correct function name, it takes you to a page that suggests the most likely candidates. Most pages have practical examples showing how the function or class is used.

What makes dynamic web design easy is not an encyclopedic knowledge of PHP functions and classes but a solid grasp of how conditional statements, loops, and other structures control the flow of a script. Once you can visualize your projects in terms of "if this happens, what should happen next?" you're the master of your own game. I consult the PHP online manual many times a day. To me, it's like a dictionary. Most of the time, I just want to check that I have the arguments in the right order, but I often find that something catches my eye and opens up new horizons. I may not use that knowledge immediately, but I store it at the back of my mind for future use and go back when I need to check the details.

The MySQL online manual (`http://dev.mysql.com/doc/refman/5.1/en/index.html`) is equally useful. Make both the PHP and MySQL online manuals your friends, and your knowledge will grow by leaps and bounds.

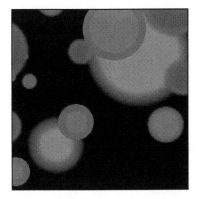

Index

You Need the Companion eBook

Your purchase of this book entitles you to buy the companion PDF-version eBook for only $10. Take the weightless companion with you anywhere.

We believe this Apress title will prove so indispensable that you'll want to carry it with you everywhere, which is why we are offering the companion eBook (in PDF format) for $10 to customers who purchase this book now. Convenient and fully searchable, the PDF version of any content-rich, page-heavy Apress book makes a valuable addition to your programming library. You can easily find and copy code—or perform examples by quickly toggling between instructions and the application. Even simultaneously tackling a donut, diet soda, and complex code becomes simplified with hands-free eBooks!

Once you purchase your book, getting the $10 companion eBook is simple:

❶ Visit **www.apress.com/promo/tendollars/**.

❷ Complete a basic registration form to receive a randomly generated question about this title.

❸ Answer the question correctly in 60 seconds, and you will receive a promotional code to redeem for the $10.00 eBook.

233 Spring Street, New York, NY 10013

Offer valid through 6/11.

Made in the USA
Lexington, KY
11 April 2011